Psychology and the Prevention of Nuclear War

PSYCHOLOGY AND THE PREVENTION OF NUCLEAR WAR
A Book of Readings

edited by
RALPH K. WHITE

NEW YORK UNIVERSITY PRESS
New York and London
1986

155.935
P95

Library of Congress Cataloging-in-Publication Data
Main entry under title:

Psychology and the prevention of nuclear war.

Bibliography: p. 569
Includes index.
1. Nuclear warfare—Psychological aspects—Addresses,
essays, lectures. 2. Nuclear warfare—Study and teach-
ing—Addresses, essays, lectures. 3. Antinuclear
movement—Addresses, essays, lectures. I. White,
Ralph K.
U263.P78 1985 155.9′35 85-15520
ISBN 0-8147-9203-0
ISBN 0-8147-9204-9 (pbk.)

Clothbound editions of New York University Press books are Smyth-sewn
and printed on permanent and durable acid-free paper.

Contents

Foreword

Some issues ought to be absolutely preemptive—to take precedence over all normal concerns whenever it appears that something useful can be done about them. Surely the prevention of nuclear war is such an issue. Informed people agree that if it occurred all-out nuclear war would be so destructive as to make other issues irrelevant. With such considerations in mind, the Council of the American Psychological Association (APA) voted in 1982 to lend its support to a bilateral nuclear freeze and generally to initiatives to reduce the likelihood of nuclear conflict. (The APA usually tends to be reluctant to take positions of social advocacy.)

In keeping with this stand, in early 1984 the Board of Social and Ethical Responsibility (BSERP) of the APA—its agency for focused concern with bringing psychology to bear on issues of human welfare—sponsored a meeting of a small number of psychologists who had been conspicuously active in research related to war, peace, and conflict resolution, to consider ways in which the potential contributions of psychology and other behavioral sciences could be mobilized (the unpeaceful metaphor inevitably intrudes!). Among several consensual proposals, the one most readily carried forward into rapid action was the preparation of a book of readings sampling what we currently think we know and understand about the prevention of nuclear war from a psychological perspective. BSERP established a committee composed of Morton Deutsch, Herbert C. Kelman, and Ralph K. White—all distinguished senior contributors to the literature—to develop a plan for such a book of readings; and Ralph White, whose *Fearful Warriors: A Psychological Profile of U.S.-Soviet Relations* is a major recent contribution, agreed to serve as editor.

On behalf of APA, BSERP wishes to facilitate and expedite the commercial publication of the book as effectively as possible.

Since the Society for the Psychological Study of Social Issues (SPSSI, a division of the APA) has a long and successful record of sponsorship of books comparable to this one, BSERP decided to invite SPSSI to undertake the direct sponsorship of the volume. In August 1984 the SPSSI Council agreed in principle to sponsor the book.

All concerned can be proud of the product, which should be widely useful to students and to broader publics. It makes readily accessible the best short selections available that represent a psychological perspective on the present situation of international conflict, on the conflict process and how it is and may be exacerbated or reduced, and on psychological and interactive processes that bear on the likelihood of war. The authors, who include political scientists, sociologists, psychiatrists, and social psychologists, constitute a stellar assembly. On behalf of BSERP, I congratulate Ralph White and his Editorial Committee.

M. BREWSTER SMITH
University of California at Santa Cruz
Chair, 1984,
Board of Social and Ethical Responsibility
American Psychological Association

Preface

On behalf of SPSSI, the Society for the Psychological Study of Social Issues, I wish to join Brewster Smith in welcoming this new volume and congratulating its originator and editor, Ralph White.

SPSSI's sponsorship of this publication continues a long history of SPSSI concern with the psychological dimensions of war and peace—a history in which Ralph White has been an active participant from its beginning. To cite a few examples: In the early 1940s, SPSSI established a Committee on the Psychology of War and Peace, chaired by Ross Stagner, of which Ralph was a member. The committee carried out and published studies on attitudes toward war prevention. It also planned to publish a book, but the project was aborted by United States entry into World War II.

Right after the war, in 1945, SPSSI published a Yearbook under the editorship of Gardner Murphy, entitled *Human Nature and Enduring Peace.** Ralph, of course, was a contributor to that volume. Starting in the 1950s, SPSSI has had a number of committees focusing on international relations and war prevention, of which Ralph was a frequent member. In 1965, SPSSI published *International Behavior: A Social-Psychological Analysis,* under my editorship, which contained an important chapter on U.S.-Soviet images by Ralph White. During the Vietnam War, Ralph again was active in various SPSSI projects. He authored an issue of the *Journal of Social Issues* on the psychological determinants of that war, which formed the basis of his subsequent book, *Nobody Wanted War.* Others of Ralph's writings, including his piece on misperceptions in the Arab-Israeli conflict, have appeared over the years in the various

* Full references to writing cited in this introductory material are given at the end of Section I.

issues of the *Journal of Social Issues* devoted to questions of war and peace.

Thus, it is highly appropriate that the present volume on *Psychology and the Prevention of Nuclear War* appear under the aegis of SPSSI and under the editorship of Ralph White, given the long-term contributions of both to the analysis of these issues.

Let me conclude with a personal comment on the focus of this volume. Nuclear war is qualitatively different from conventional war because it threatens such massive destruction that human existence on this planet may become virtually impossible. Thus, by no stretch of the imagination can nuclear war be considered an instrument of policy or a course that nations may be prepared to pursue in order to protect certain higher values. The prevention of nuclear war is, therefore, a matter of the highest priority in the interest of human survival and an issue that cuts across the usual political divisions. Yet, I would argue that, for intellectual, pragmatic, and moral reasons, the prevention of nuclear war must be seen in the broader context of war prevention in general.

Intellectually, psychological and other factors conducive to nuclear war and its prevention can only be understood within a larger, interdisciplinary framework for analyzing the global system and international relations. Such a framework can yield general theories of war and peace, for which the causation and prevention of nuclear war constitute a special case. The selections in this volume illustrate the continuities between general analyses of international conflict and analyses of nuclear war.

Pragmatically, let us keep in mind that—at least under the present circumstances—the most likely condition for the outbreak of nuclear war is through the unintentional escalation of conventional war. Thus, war prevention in general has a direct bearing on the prevention of nuclear war.

Morally, I hope that in our justifiable emphasis on ways of preventing nuclear war we will not simply be looking for ways of making the world safe for conventional warfare. The specter of nuclear destruction has brought home to us the ultimate logic of war as a means of settling international disputes. While we may differ in our view of whether war is ever justifiable—

and, if so, under what conditions—we can all agree that there must be better ways of solving problems. Psychological analysis, in particular, can contribute to the discovery of such alternatives. Having been mobilized by the threat of nuclear war, I hope we will extend our inquiry to the abolition of war in general as a social institution and as an instrument of policy.

HERBERT C. KELMAN
Harvard University
SPSSI President, 1964–65

Introduction

"The unleashed power of the atom has changed everything save our way of thinking, and thus we drift toward unparalleled catastrophe."

—Albert Einstein (1946)

This book is about our ways of thinking and about how they need to be and can be changed.

It is not about the "unparalleled catastrophe." By now many of us know much about that, and unless we can see clear, acceptable, and practical ways to prevent it, our minds recoil from the whole horrible subject. Therefore, the book is about the prevention of nuclear war and nothing else.

At least, that is its purpose. Yet its method is primarily descriptive and analytical rather than action-oriented. It explores from different perspectives the possible causes of a world war that could be at the outset, or become, nuclear, with a special focus on the often-neglected psychological aspects of those causes. It is diagnosis more than prescription. In fact, it might be described as a many-sided effort to understand the nature and roots of the "madness" of our present drift toward a great war that each side is urgently—desperately—anxious to avoid. In so doing it draws on some of the insights of psychiatry (from the psychiatrists Robert Jay Lifton, John E. Mack, Jerome D. Frank, and Erich Fromm), as well as on the three disciplines that provide the chief foundation for the book: history, political science, and social psychology.

We have designed the book to be interdisciplinary in nature. Although all the readings are in some sense psychological, its purpose is *not* to argue that "psychological" factors in the background of war are more important than historical, political, military, or other relevant factors. When all such factors are involved and dependent on each other, as they are in this case, it is artificial to separate them and talk about which are most important. As Herbert C. Kelman puts it, psychological factors "suffuse" the political picture (p. 172).

Accordingly, it is appropriate that several of the major contributions to the book have been written by persons who are neither psychiatrists nor academic psychologists. There are at least seven who can be called historians or political scientists (Marshall D. Shulman, Robert Jervis, Alexander George, Robert C. Tucker, Ole Holsti, Richard Ned Lebow, and Richard Smoke), though all of them focus here on psychological factors. In addition, the contributors include a political pollster (Daniel Yankelovich); two sociologists (Amitai Etzioni and Elise Boulding); one anthropologist-psychologist (Andrew Schmookler); three educators (Roberta Snow, Susan Alexander, and Tony Wagner); and one lawyer (Roger Fisher). Each brings to this vital and too-often-neglected psychological subject his or her special point of view and expertise.

While the chapters presented in the book were originally written mainly by and for scholars, in its present form the book is designed to be read by the general concerned public, including young people. A main hope of the contributors is that it will meet some of the emotional and intellectual needs of college students. It may add a new dimension to several kinds of courses on the college level, such as social and political psychology, international relations, and social conflict. It may also be useful on the graduate level; the references at the end of each section provide leads to further exploration and research for compositions ranging from term papers to dissertations.

A word is needed on the roles of the editor and the section editors. The initial selection of articles was ordinarily the work of the section editor, as was the initial condensation of available articles. Introductions to sections were written by the section editor when he or she so desired; otherwise they were written by the editor of this volume.

In an anthology such as this, there is always a question of where the editor should stand on the continuum from being laissez-faire to being highly active. In favor of an active role is the often-expressed complaint that an anthology lacks the integration and the punch that a single author can more readily achieve in his own work. Another frequent complaint about anthologies is unevenness of quality. When a book deals with a subject on which immediate and sustained action is as necessary as it is on issues involving the prevention of nuclear war, there is an additional reason for active editorship: without it, the relations of many thoughts and findings to action may remain obscure, so that action will not be as immediate, as sustained, or as intelligent as it could be.

Accordingly (with much help from the other members of the editorial committee, Herbert C. Kelman and Morton Deutsch), I have chosen to play a role near the active end of the scale and to include some of my own writing where gaps seemed especially evident.

In conclusion, as a way of reminding the reader of the importance of digging deeply into this subject, I will quote some of the most powerful words spoken or written in our century: the conclusion of Jonathan Schell's *The Fate of the Earth:*

> If we reject our doom, and bend our efforts toward survival—if we arouse ourselves to the peril and act to forestall it, making ourselves the allies of life—then the anesthetic fog will lift; our vision, no longer straining not to see the obvious, will sharpen; our will, finding secure ground to build on, will be restored; and we will take full and clear possession of life again. One day—and it is hard to believe that it will not be soon—we will make our choice. Either we will sink into the final coma and end it all or, as I trust and believe, we will awaken to the truth of our peril, a truth as great as life itself, and, like a person who has swallowed a lethal poison but shakes off his stupor at the last moment and vomits the poison up, we will break through the layers of our denials, put aside our faint-hearted excuses, and rise up to cleanse the earth of nuclear weapons.

The doing of it may not be as intellectually simple as Schell seems to imply, but that does not make it less urgent.

RALPH K. WHITE

Contributors

SUSAN ALEXANDER, an educator, is Associate Director of Educators for Social Responsibility, with twenty years of teaching experience on the elementary, secondary and undergraduate levels. She has a Harvard M.Ed. degree and is the author of *Why Nuclear Education: A Source Book for Educators and Parents* (1984).

ELISE BOULDING is retiring this year (1985) from the chair of the Department of Sociology, Dartmouth College. Since receiving her Ph.D. at the University of Michigan in 1969 she has written extensively on women in history (e.g., *The Underside of History: A View of Women through Time,* 1976), on aspects of the future (including imaging the future) and on cross-national and comparative studies of peace, development, and women in society.

URIE BRONFENBRENNER is Professor of Human Development and Family Studies at Cornell University. In his research on child-rearing in the Soviet Union, the United States and elsewhere (*Two Worlds of Childhood,* 1970) he has at the same time maintained close contact with many of the Soviet people. He speaks Russian fluently. In his article, "The Mirror Image in Soviet-American Relations" (1961), he introduced that term into the thinking of American social scientists.

MORTON DEUTSCH is Edward Lee Thorndike Professor of Psychology and Education at Columbia University. He is widely known for his research and theoretical writings in the areas of cooperation-competition, conflict, bargaining, distributive justice, and intergroup relations. Among others, his books include: *Interracial Housing, Preventing World War III* (with Wright and Evans), *The Resolution of Conflict: Constructive and Destructive Processes,* and *Distributive Justice: A Social Psychological Perspective* (1985).

JOHN DOBLE is a Senior Research Associate at the Public Agenda Foundation, headed by Daniel Yankelovich. A political scientist, he is the author of a number of social research studies and coauthor, with John Immerwahr and Jean Johnson, of *The Speaker and the Listener: A Public Perspective on Freedom of Expression* (1980).

AMITAI ETZIONI, a sociologist, was for many years at Columbia University. He is now University Professor at George Washington University—the first to be chosen for that honor. His great number of contributions to many aspects of social science include important contributions to peace, such as his pioneering *The Hard Way to Peace* (1962) and *Winning Without War* (1964). Both advocated gradual tension reduction and multilateral arms reductions. He has strongly favored moderate unilateral initiatives as a form of tension reduction, and has been active in the antiwar movement.

RICHARD A. FALK is Professor of Politics and Government at Princeton University. He has written widely on international affairs, including, for example, his editing of *The Vietnam War and International Law* (1968), and (with Gabriel Kolko and Robert Jay Lifton) *The Crimes of War* (1971).

SEYMOUR FESHBACH is Professor of Psychology at the University of California, Los Angeles. In addition to his groundbreaking work with Irving L. Janis on the effectiveness of fear appeals, he has focused especially on aggression. For example, he wrote *Television and Aggression* (1970), and edited *Aggression and Behavior Change: Biological and Social Processes* (1979). Most recently he has authored a text, *Personality,* and a manual for teachers, *Learning to Care.*

ROGER FISHER, an international lawyer, is Williston Professor of Law at Harvard and Director of the Harvard Negotiation Project. He was the originator of the award-winning television series *The Advocates.* In addition to his *Getting to YES: Negotiating Agreement Without Giving In* (with William Ury, 1981), his many writings include several on negotiation and conflict resolution, notably *Improving Compliance with International Law* (1981), *International Mediation: A Working Guide* (1978), and *International Conflict for Beginners* (1967), published in Britain as *Basic Negotiation Strategy.*

SUSAN T. FISKE is Associate Professor of Social Psychology in the Departments of Psychology and Social Sciences at Carnegie-Mellon University. She has a Harvard Ph.D. in social psychology. Her published articles include work on many aspects of political and social cognition; she is perhaps best known as the author, with Shelley E. Taylor, of *Social Cognition* (1984). In addition she is editor, with M. S. Clark, of *Affect and Cognition: The 17th Annual Carnegie Symposium on Cognition* (1982) and, with B. Fischhoff and M. Milburn, *Images of Nuclear War,* in the *Journal of Social Issues* (1983).

JEROME D. FRANK, with a Ph.D. in Psychology as well as an M.D. degree, has for more than 25 years been exploring relations between psychiatry and the preservation of peace. Now retired, he was Professor of Psychiatry at the Johns Hopkins Medical School from 1959 to 1974. His book *Persuasion and Healing: A Comparative Study of Psychotherapy* (1961, 1973), brought together psychology and psychiatry; and his books *Sanity and Survival* (1967), *Sanity and Survival in the Nuclear Age* (1982), brought both to bear on the question of human survival. Among many other honors, he was Chairman of the Federation of American Scientists in 1979.

ERICH FROMM, a prolific psychoanalytic writer on problems of broad human concern, and now deceased, received his Ph.D. at the University of Heidelberg in 1922. His early work, *Escape from Freedom* (1941), is a landmark in scholarly treatments of Nazism and of the proposition that human beings do not necessarily seek freedom. Among his many other books are *The Heart of Man* (1964) and *The Anatomy of Human Destructiveness* (1973).

ALEXANDER L. GEORGE is Professor of International Relations at Stanford University. His book *Woodrow Wilson and Colonel House* (1956), written with his wife, Juliette L. George, is a widely known study of the role of personality in politics. He is also the author, with Richard Smoke, of *Deterrence in American Foreign Policy,* which won the 1975 Bancroft Prize. Other books include *The Limits of Coercive Diplomacy* (with David Hall and William Simons, 1971), *Presidential Decisionmaking in Foreign Policy* (1980), *Force*

and Statecraft (with Gordon Craig, 1983), and *Managing U.S.-
Soviet Rivalry* (1983).

OLE R. HOLSTI, a political scientist, is currently the George
V. Allen Professor of International Relations at Duke University. He has also taught at Stanford, the University of
British Columbia, and the University of California (Davis).
He served as President of the International Studies Association, 1979–80. His research interests include crisis decision
making and the belief systems of foreign policy leaders. *American Leadership in World Affairs: Vietnam and the Breakdown
of Consensus* (1984) is his most recent work.

IRVING L. JANIS is Professor of Psychology at Yale University.
He has long been a contributor to research on psychological
stress and attitude change. More recently he has investigated
the area of decision making through social-psychological studies of foreign policy decisions and fiascos (reported in his
book *Groupthink*) as well as through studies of personal
decisions (Janis and Mann, *Decision Making*). He received
the American Psychological Association's Distinguished Scientific Contribution Award in 1981 and SPSSI's Kurt Lewin
Award in 1985.

ROBERT JERVIS is Professor of Political Science at Columbia
University. He works on problems of national security policy
and decision making. He is the author of *The Logic of Images
in International Relations, Perception and Misperception in
International Politics,* and, most recently, *The Illogic of American Nuclear Strategy.*

HERBERT C. KELMAN is Richard Clarke Cabot Professor of
Social Ethics at Harvard University and chair of the Middle
East Seminar at the Harvard Center for International Affairs.
A Yale Ph.D., he was a founder of the *Journal of Conflict
Resolution* in the 1950s and editor of *International Behavior:
A Social-Psychological Analysis* (1965). His peace-making role
in the Middle East became dramatically evident in his contacts
with Egyptian, Israeli and PLO leaders after Sadat's peace
initiative in 1977. He is now preparing a book on *Crimes of
Obedience.*

PAUL R. KIMMEL is the first public policy fellow at the
American Psychological Association and the Association for

the Advancement of Psychology in Washington, D.C. Representing the Society for the Psychological Study of Social Issues, he encourages psychologists to get involved in issues of public welfare. He has done much on behalf of the legislation that established the United States Institute of Peace.

RICHARD NED LEBOW, a political scientist with strong historical and psychological interests, is Director of the Peace Studies program at Cornell University. He is a Yale Ph.D. with experience also in the government. His best known work so far is *Between Peace and War: The Nature of International Crisis* (1981), and he has contributed importantly to *Psychology and Deterrence* (1984), edited by Robert Jervis, Richard Ned Lebow and Janice Stein.

ROBERT JAY LIFTON, a psychiatrist, has been Research Professor at the Yale Medical School since 1967. Among his several important works are *Thought Reform and the Psychology of Totalism: A Study of Brainwashing in China* (1961) and *Death in Life: Survivors of Hiroshima* (1969).

JOHN E. MACK, a psychiatrist, has been Professor of Psychiatry at the Harvard Medical School since 1972. In 1977 he won the Pulitzer Prize for his biography, *A Prince of Our Disorder,* the life of T. E. Lawrence. In recent years he has been studying the roots of the nuclear arms race and the impact of living in the presence of the nuclear threat.

CHARLES B. MCGUIRE, JR., received his B.A. at the University of Lowell and is now a graduate student in Psychology at the University of California, Berkeley. His research interests include the psychology of international conflict, attribution processes, and decision-making processes.

C. RONALD MEWBORN is a social psychologist and a research consultant in Northern California.

CHARLES E. OSGOOD is Research Professor Emeritus of Psychology and Communications at the University of Illinois in Urbana. His first major area of concern has been research and theory construction in the psychology of language (psycholinguistics—the semantic differential). In it he has conducted cross-cultural research in thirty societies around the world. His second major area of concern has been the *GRIT* strategy (*G*raduated and *R*eciprocated *I*nitiatives in *T*ensionreduction), a chief element in his books *An Alternative to War or Surrender* (1962), *Perspective in Foreign Policy* (1966), and *Mankind 2000??* (in progress).

DEAN G. PRUITT, a social psychologist, is Professor of Psychology at the State University of New York at Buffalo. He received his Ph.D. at Yale (1957). His main interests are conflict and bargaining. He has published a monograph, *Problem Solving in the Department of State* (1964), and two books, *Theory and Research on the Causes of War* (with Richard C. Snyder, 1969) and *Negotiation Behavior* (1981). With his students and colleagues he has also done a large amount of experimental work in these areas. He is currently (with Jeffrey Z. Rubin) completing a book on social conflict.

RONALD W. ROGERS is Professor of Psychology at the University of Alabama. He is one of the leaders in experimentation on fear appeals, and has developed a theoretical model to account for both their facilitating and their negative effects.

JEFFREY Z. RUBIN is Professor of Psychology at Tufts University. He is the author of articles and books on topics ranging from negotiation, social conflict and third party intervention to social psychology and decision making. He is the editor of *Negotiation Journal: On the Process of Dispute Settlement,* and, with Dean G. Pruitt, is now completing a book on social conflict. Probably his best known work is *Dynamics of Third Party Intervention* (1981), which he edited; it focuses on Henry Kissinger's shuttle diplomacy in the Middle East.

ANDREW B. SCHMOOKLER is an independent scholar living near Washington, D.C. His book, *The Parable of the Tribes: The Problem of Power in Social Evolution,* was awarded the Erik H. Erikson prize by the International Society of Political Psychology in 1984. He has subsequently completed another book, *Sowings and Reapings: The Cycling of Good and Evil in the Human System.* His work-in-progress is entitled *Out of Weakness: A Psychological Exploration of War and Peace.*

MARSHALL D. SHULMAN, a specialist on the USSR, is currently Adlai E. Stevenson Professor of International Relations and Director of the Institute for Advanced Study of the Soviet Union at Columbia University. He served as special adviser on Soviet affairs to Secretaries of State Cyrus Vance and Edmund Muskie. He is also a historian; among his various books is, for example, *Stalin's Foreign Policy Reappraised* (1965).

RICHARD SMOKE is a political scientist and political psychologist specializing in international security and peace. He is Professor of Political Science and Research Director of the Center for Foreign Policy Development at Brown University. In addition to *War: Controlling Escalation* (1977) he is author of *National Security and the Nuclear Dilemma,* coauthor with Alexander L. George of *Deterrence in American Foreign Policy: Theory and Practice* (1974), and author of "The Evolution of American Defense Policy" in Reichart and Sturm, eds., *American Defense Policy* (5th ed., 1982).

ROBERTA SNOW is an educator with current appointments at the Harvard Medical School and the Harvard School of Education. She has been a teacher, administrator and researcher for nearly twenty years. She is the founder of Educators for Social Responsibility (ESR) and author of a seminal peace curriculum, *Decision Making in a Nuclear Age.*

PHILIP E. TETLOCK is currently Associate Professor of Psychology at the University of California at Berkeley. He received his Ph.D. in psychology from Yale University in 1979. His research interests include social judgment and decision-making processes, impression management processes, and the study of both mass and elite political behavior (including the relation between war and insufficient "integrative complexity"). He is the author of numerous chapters and articles in professional books and journals.

ROBERT C. TUCKER, a specialist on the Soviet Union, is Professor of Government and Politics at Princeton University. After extensive experience in the USSR (he was Adlai Stevenson's interpreter when Stevenson visited the Soviet Union) he received his Ph.D. at Harvard in 1958. His many works include *Philosophy and Myth in Karl Marx* (1961), *Stalin as Revolutionary* (the first volume of a three-volume biography of Stalin, 1973), *The Soviet Political Mind* (1963, rev. ed. 1971), and *Politics as Leadership* (1981).

WILLIAM URY, consultant, writer and lecturer on negotiation and mediation, is Associate Director of the Harvard Negotiation Project. Educated in Switzerland, he has degrees from Yale and Harvard in linguistics and anthropology. He has served as a third party in disputes ranging from landlord-tenant grievances to labor-management conflict at a Kentucky coal mine.

TONY WAGNER is the Executive Director of Educators for Social Responsibility (ESR). He has taught for 14 years in public and independent schools at the elementary and high school levels. He has written a number of articles on the tools students need to deal intelligently with nuclear issues.

RALPH K. WHITE is Emeritus Professor of Social Psychology at George Washington University. A Stanford Ph.D., his professional life has been divided between government service (chiefly research in the U.S. Information Agency, with first-hand experience in Berlin, Moscow and Saigon) and academia. His writing includes *Autocracy and Democracy* (with Ronald Lippitt, 1960), *Nobody Wanted War: Misperception in Vietnam and Other Wars* (rev. ed., 1970), and *Fearful Warriors: A Psychological Profile of U.S.-Soviet Relations* (1984).

DANIEL YANKELOVICH, a public opinion specialist, has been chairman of the attitude-research firm, Yankelovich, Skelly and White, since 1959. He is now also President of the Public Agenda Foundation. A special interest of his has been the psychology of young people, exemplified by his books *The Changing Values on Campus* (1972) and *New Rules: Searching for Self-Fulfilment in a World Turned Upside Down* (1981). With Larry Kaagan he wrote "Assertive America" (*Foreign Affairs,* 1981); a comparison of it with the *Foreign Affairs* article (1984) reprinted in this volume is instructive and encouraging.

PART ONE

THE PRESENT SITUATION

INTRODUCTION

Ralph K. White

Part One differs from the others in that it does not deal directly with either the causes or the prevention of war. Rather, it discusses the psychological situation in which the world finds itself at the present time—a subject that underlies all of the later discussion of causes and prevention. For example, the psychological effects of the nuclear threat constitute much of the context of our own thinking about what can or should be done; the psychology of the American people should be a main basis for realistic judgments on what war-prevention measures the United States is now psychologically ready for, or might become ready for in the future; and the psychology of the Soviet decision makers should be a key consideration in judging what actions by the West will or will not actually promote peace.

SECTION I

Psychological Effects of
the Nuclear Threat

SECTION EDITORS: JOHN E. MACK AND
ROBERTA SNOW

INTRODUCTION

John E. Mack and Ralph K. White

The first chapter is by Dr. Robert Jay Lifton and Richard Falk. Dr. Lifton, probably more than any other psychiatrist, has studied human feelings about death from a psychiatric standpoint—including death as a result of war, especially nuclear war. His book *Death in Life: Survivors of Hiroshima* (1968; rev. ed. 1982) and his later books, *Home from the War: Vietnam Veterans—Neither Victims nor Executioners* (1973) and *The Broken Connection: On Death and the Continuity of Life* (1979), illustrate that interest.

His discussion of "psychic numbing," in the chapter reprinted here from *Indefensible Weapons: The Political and Psychological Case Against Nuclearism* (1982), written in collaboration with the political scientist Richard Falk, described what is probably the chief psychological obstacle to clear and realistic thinking about how to avoid a nuclear catastrophe. It presents a challenge to everyone to resist the inevitable temptation to avoid thinking about the entire distasteful subject. (How to avoid psychic numbing is addressed in Section XI, edited by Seymour Feshbach.)

The second chapter, by John E. Mack, M.D., and Roberta Snow, a psychiatrist and an educator, respectively, highlights comments made by young people about the threat of nuclear war. It includes a psychological analysis of these statements and poses additional areas that need further attention and research. The quotations were selected from many different research projects (see References pp. 31–33) that have been done by educators, psychiatrists, and other professionals interested in the question: "What do young people think and feel about nuclear weapons?"

Statements were chosen that might provoke discussion about how children are affected by living in a nuclear age. The authors also included quotations from Soviet young people for the purpose of raising the question of how their feelings and thoughts compare with those of American young people. In this initial research, similar feelings are reported by both Soviet and American young people.

Perhaps as increasing numbers of adults listen more carefully to children and adolescents, and reflect on their own attitudes and feelings about nuclear weapons, they will meet more fully the responsibilities they have—including educational responsibilities—as caretakers and citizens working to prevent nuclear war. (Section XII, edited by Paul Kimmel, addresses some aspects of peace education—an enterprise that is now beginning to burgeon in the United States.)

1.

On Numbing and Feeling*

ROBERT JAY LIFTON and
RICHARD A. FALK

We are always much less than we could be. We have moments of high intellect or of passionate emotion, but seem limited in our capacity to sustain optimal combinations of the two.

Diminished feeling, in one sense, begins with the structure and function of the human brain. Neurophysiologists make clear that the brain serves as much to keep out stimuli as it does to receive them. In other words, our brain is so constructed as to limit what we can eventually feel, lest it be so overwhelmed as to lose its capacity to organize or to respond at all.

For as human beings we must do considerable psychic work in connection with anything we take in. That is, we perceive nothing nakedly but must re-create anything we encounter by means of our marvelous and vulnerable cerebral cortex. If we can speak of anything as *human* nature, it is this symbolizing principle as such. Hence I speak of a "formative process," the constant creation and re-creation of images and forms that constitutes human mentation. Much of this process takes place outside of awareness, or is what we call "unconscious." But it is the existence of this formative-symbolizing tendency that makes possible the wonders of our imagination on the one

* Originally published as Chapter 10 in Robert Jay Lifton and Richard Falk, eds., *Indefensible Weapons: The Political and Psychological Case Against Nuclearism* (New York: Basic Books, 1982).

hand, and our psychological disturbances and destructive impulses on the other.

Here too psychic and physical survival require a balance between feeling and not feeling. And that balance can readily go out of kilter, causing us to feel either too much or too little. Indeed, our contemporary nuclear threat not only contributes to upsetting that balance but raises questions about just what kind of balance between feeling and numbing is desirable or possible.

In Hiroshima, people I interviewed told me how, when the bomb fell, they were aware of people dying around them in horrible ways but that, within minutes or even seconds, they simply ceased to feel. They said such things as "I simply became insensitive to human death," or referred to a "paralysis of the mind." I came to call this general process psychic numbing and, in its most acute form, psychic closing-off. For survivors it was a necessary defense mechanism, since they could not have experienced full emotions in response to such scenes and remained sane. The numbing entailed derealization of what was actually happening along such inner psychological sequences as: "If I feel nothing, then death is not taking place," or "then I cannot be threatened by the death all around me," or "then I am not responsible for you or your death."

As useful to them as it was at the time, the numbing process did not necessarily end when the immediate danger was over. It would continue over weeks, months, or even years, and become associated with apathy, withdrawal, depression, despair, or a kind of survivor half-life with highly diminished capacity for pleasure, joy, or intense feelings in general.

Observing victims, I began to wonder about the numbing that must take place in those who make, test, or anticipate the use of nuclear weapons. For potential perpetrators simply cannot afford to imagine what really happens to people at the other end of the weapon.

This was true of American scientists constructing the first atomic bombs at Los Alamos in New Mexico. Responding to the call to win the race against an evil enemy to construct a decisive weapon, then after the defeat of Germany still seeing themselves as contributing to their country's wartime military struggle and intent upon succeeding in what had been an extraordinarily dedicated collective effort and on confirming that the thing would really *work*, "they were frantically busy and extremely security conscious and . . . there was even some half-conscious closing of the mind to anything but the fact that they were trying desperately to produce a device which would end the war. . . ." (Smith, A. K., 1958) And so powerful was their scientific leadership that almost everyone else at Los Alamos "let Oppenheimer take protective custody of their emotions."

Moral questions were raised only by a few scientists from the Chicago group when they had essentially completed their work on the project. But their reflections were informed precisely by a beginning capacity to imagine and feel what might occur at the other end of the weapon. Eugene Rabinowitch, five years later, recalled how "In the summer of 1945, some of us walked the streets of Chicago vividly imagining the sky suddenly lit by a giant fireball, the steel skeletons of skyscrapers bending into grotesque shapes and their masonry raining into the streets below, until a great cloud of dust arose and settled over the crumbling city." (Rabinowitch, 1963, p. 156) And he goes on to say that "From this vision arose the weak and inadequate attempts that groups of scientists made to stop the hands of the clock before it struck the first hour of the atomic age." (Rabinowitch, 1963, p. 156).

Nuclear scientists had experienced such images long before that.

> Standing around the first nuclear fire lit under the West Stands of the athletic field of the University of Chicago in December 1942 and, two-and-a-half years later in July 1945, watching the flash of the first atomic bomb explosion at Alamogordo, the scientists had a vision of terrible clarity. They saw the cities of the world, including their own, going up in flames and falling into dust. (Rabinowitch, 1963, p. 156).

But once they embarked on making the bomb, once the numbing had set in, that kind of vision was in most cases suppressed. And subsequently, over decades, there was the psychological process of "learning to live with the bomb," which scientists came to share with political and military leaders along with the rest of us; specific forms of numbing evolved that blocked out what happened at the other end of nuclear weapons and enabled one to get on with things.

What I am calling psychic numbing includes a number of classical psychoanalytic defense mechanisms: repression, suppression, isolation, denial, undoing, reaction formation, and projection, among others. But these defense mechanisms overlap greatly around the issue of feeling and not feeling. With that issue so central to our time, we do well to devote to it a single overall category, which we can observe operating in different ways and under different conditions in virtually any individual mind.

Psychic numbing has to do with exclusion, most specifically exclusion of feeling. That exclusion can occur in two ways. There is first the blocking of images, or of feelings associated with certain images, because they are too painful or unacceptable. The second is absence of images, the lack of prior experience in relation to an event. We have difficulty imagining nuclear holocaust or responding with feeling to the idea of it happening, because we have virtually no prior images that readily connect with it. In either case—and the two patterns are likely to coexist—the formative process is affected. Indeed, just as the defense mechanisms are part of Freud's model of instinct and defense, so may we view the concept of psychic numbing as a part of the model of symbolization of life and death. When numbing occurs, the symbolizing process—the flow and re-creation of images and forms—is interrupted. And in its extreme varieties, numbing itself becomes a symbolic death: One freezes in the manner of certain animals facing danger, becomes as if dead in order to prevent actual physical or psychic death. But all too frequently the inner death of numbing has dubious value to the organism. And it may itself become a source of grave danger.

We may thus speak, very generally, of three levels of numbing: the numbing of massive death immersion; the numbing of enhancement; and the numbing of everyday life. The first, the numbing of massive death immersion, is epitomized by Hiroshima and Nagaski. The "paralysis of the mind" already mentioned involves a radical dissociation of the mind from its own earlier modes of response—from constellations of pain and pleasure, love and loss, and general capacity for fellow feeling built up over a human lifetime. We may, indeed, speak of the mind being severed from its own forms. When that happens, psychic action—mental process in general—more or less shuts down. There are in-between states in which limited forms of planning and action (flight or rescue of family members) can occur, even though feelings are largely blunted.

The numbing of enhancement is of the opposite variety. Here feeling is diminished in some spheres of the mind in order to make possible more accomplished behavior or more intense feeling in other spheres. One can point to the selective professional numbing of the surgeon, who cannot afford to feel the consequences of failure. Or to that of the painter or musician, who block out a great variety of influences in order to enhance and intensify the image or the musical phrase.

Finally, there is the problematic category of the numbing of everyday life. Here we may say that the ordinary brain function of keeping out stimuli becomes strained by the image overload characteristic of our time. Apart from nuclear weapons, the mass-media revolution creates the unique situation in which virtually any image from anywhere on the globe, and indeed from any point in our historical or cultural past, becomes available to any individual at any moment. This historically new situation contributes to a contemporary psychological style of perpetual experimentation and increasing capacity for shifts from one kind of involvement (with people, ideas, ways of living) to another. I speak of this as the Protean style, after the talented but unsteady Greek sea god who was a notorious shape-shifter and could readily change into virtually any natural, animal, or human form, but who had great difficulty holding on to a functional form of his own. . . .

More personally, I referred earlier to my discovery in Hiroshima that, seventeen years after the event, no one had studied its general human effects, but I must note here my own previous resistance to the city. Although I had first gone to Japan in 1952 (as an air force psychiatrist in response to the medical draft of that time) and had spent more than two and one-half years in Japan (about half in the military and half in connection with a study of Japanese youth), it was not until my second long stay was drawing to a close in 1962 that I first visited Hiroshima. And I did so then because I thought I should take a look at the city, having begun to be concerned about nuclear dangers through participating in the early academic peace movement at Harvard during the late 1950s. (I suspect now that a part of me anticipated the possibility of doing a psychological study there, but even then I seemed to have to complete the other, less threatening work first.) When I began to talk to various people in Hiroshima about working there, I felt encouraged by their responses and enthusiastic about proceeding. But from the first moment I began to conduct actual interviews with survivors, everything was different. Now the bomb seemed right there with us, virtually in the room. I felt myself overwhelmed and frightened by the detailed, grotesque descriptions of specific atomic bomb experiences, by the very descriptions I sought from the people I talked to. I was staying in a Japanese inn alone at the time, my wife and infant son not having yet joined me from Kyoto where we had been living. For a few days I felt anxious, and at night slept fitfully and had disturbing dreams. I began to ask myself whether I should abandon the study and leave Hiroshima.

But then, quite suddenly, my anxiety seemed to recede as I found myself listening carefully during the interviews for psychological patterns in survivors' descriptions. In other words, I had begun to carry out my professional task, with the aid of the selective professional numbing I have mentioned in connection with surgeons. Without some such numbing I would have been incapable of doing the work. And it is also true that I hardly ceased to feel the pain altogether in what I was hearing. Nonetheless, it was a form of numbing, and I go back to that experience whenever I try to sort out the never fully resolvable struggles of professionals and others around how much to feel. Since then I have frequently become aware of situations in which I used various psychological maneuvers to distance myself from precisely the nuclear weapons threat with which I have been so consistently concerned.

In response to nuclear weapons, numbing is all too easy, widespread, and "natural" for just about everyone. But in saying that, and in depicting these various forms of numbing—indeed, in exploring our mind's dilemmas around nuclear weapons—we are doing something that only human beings can do. We are reflecting on ourselves and our situation in the service of greater awareness. And in that awareness, even just its beginning, lies our hope.

2.

Psychological Effects on Children and Adolescents*

JOHN E. MACK and ROBERTA SNOW

> The grownups should take over and do something about the war threat. Us kids are too young to worry about all this.
>
> Boy, Age 10, Allentown, Pennsylvania

> An eighteen-month-old female [monkey] named Emo found that she could solve the problem by washing the potatoes in a nearby stream. She taught this trick to her mother. Her playmates also learned this new way and they taught their mothers, too. Only the adults who imitated their children learned this social improvement. Other adults kept eating the dirty sweet potatoes.
>
> Ken Keyes, Jr., *The Hundredth Monkey* (1983)

One of the effects of the nuclear arm race, even without the weapons being fired, is the impact of the threat of nuclear annihilation on the minds of young people. In the late 1970s and early 1980s, in formal studies and informal communications, many children and adolescents in the United States, the Soviet Union, and other countries expressed their personal responses to the threat of nuclear annihilation. (For American studies see especially Escalona, 1965, 1982; Schwebel, 1965, 1982; Backman, 1983; Beardslee and Mack, 1983; Coles, 1985; Goldenring and Doctor, 1985; Goodman, Mack, Beardsley, and Snow, 1983; Zeitlin, 1984; Zweigenhaft, 1983. For interview

* Written for this volume.

and questionnaire studies of children and adolescents begun in the Soviet Union in 1983 see Chivian and Goodman, 1984. See also the excellent Finnish study by Solantaus, Rimpela, and Taipale, 1984.) Although the researches to date have shown some regional and class differences, a sense of fear, powerlessness, anger, and outrage; doubt about the future; and a sense of technology rushing out of control have been common themes. Some investigators have raised questions about the impact of living with the nuclear threat on later development (Escalona, 1965; Beardslee and Mack, 1982; Schwebel, 1984). Concern has focused in particular on the relationship between the imminence of nuclear death and a live-for-now attitude, including an unwillingness to form long-term commitments; a confusion in the development of a relation to death; and difficulty in forming a stable ego ideal, which depends, in part, on a sense of continuity and confidence in a reliable future.

Public interest in the responses of young people to the nuclear threat has been out of proportion to the amount of reliable data about what the nuclear threat means to children and adolescents. It is not altogether clear why this should be the case. As adults we care about our children and do not wish to see them troubled, especially by a threat to them that is our own creation.

More important, however, may be the fact that children and adolescents, having their whole lives to live and being less emotionally defended, penetrate with their words the barriers to feeling we have erected in relation to the nuclear threat. They tell truths that apply to us all but that a great many adults have failed to acknowledge fully. Disturbing as it may be for us, children and adolescents in recent years have raised questions that we have not always wanted to raise for ourselves. In effect, we have invited them to bring to us a message we know we need to hear: that this is our problem to take hold of and control. If we are unwilling to stop the nuclear arms competition for ourselves, or to think through the problems it raises, perhaps we will be roused from our apathy to do so for the sake of our children and of the generations yet unborn.

Finally, children and adolescents by their expressed disquiet raise questions about security that have at least an indirect relation to national policy. The success of a policy designed to provide national security must be tested, at least in part, by the emotional well-being of the citizenry.

Here we have attempted only to identify some of the recurrent themes among the reactions of children and adolescents, especially in the United States, to the nuclear threat and have tried to set down communications that are representative in order to illustrate these themes. The sample of quotations probably contains a disproportionate number from professional or more intellectual families.

Recurrent Themes

PENETRATION INTO THE CONSCIOUSNESS OF YOUNG CHILDREN

The nuclear threat seems to have penetrated deeply into the consciousness of many young children as revealed in their spontaneous expressions, poetry, stories, and games. Often without the knowledge of their parents or other adults, the threat of nuclear annihilation seems to be lodged in many children's minds, unspoken but just below the surface. A five-year-old Dutch boy seeing a rabbit in the garden asked his parent, "When the bomb comes, will the rabbit die too?" A six-year-old boy wonders when he hears a plane pass overhead: "Is that the warplane?" A not quite seven-year-old girl in San Jose, California, asked her mother, "If there's a nuclear war will God make us another world because we were careless with this one?" A fifth-grader from Essex, Massachusetts, writes in a poem about the end of the world:

> The heat melts the poles.
> The world is flooded.
> All the giant bombs from under the water explode.
> Everything is turned into vapors.
> Then the earth is blown apart.

A sixth-grade boy writes a story for his teacher in which a nuclear war shatters the tranquillity of a young boy's life. In the story cosmic battles between the forces of good and evil continue for eons, and the sense of time itself is warped. When several months later his teacher asked him if he had a copy of his story "about nuclear war," he could not remember that he had written one. When she reminded him of this particular story he said, "Oh, that one," as if he did not realize that the story had dealt with nuclear war at all. A nine-year-old boy is asked as part of a class exercise to make a game. To the surprise of his parents, who know him as a warm, gentle, and unaggressive child, he responds to the assignment by converting a Monopoly game into a game called "The Cold War," in which a drawing of the globe is in the center of the board, with a jagged piece cut out of it that divides the earth into "America" and "Soviet Union."

ADDITIONAL RESPONSES OF YOUNG CHILDREN

Some young children seem confused by nuclear war and try to relate it to what is familiar to them. Some express their fears quite directly. Young children worry particularly about surviving a nuclear war without their parents.

I worry that a neighbor will drop a bomb on me.
                          Age 7, Brookline, Massachusetts
There was a nuclear war this weekend. I heard the fire engines.
                          Age 6, Chicago, Illinois
Well, El Salvador dropped a bomb on the American navy.
                          Cambridge, Massachusetts
If I did survive, even if there was enough food, I'd probably kill myself or I'd just die of sadness because all my family and all the people I love would die.
                          Girl, Age 8, Brookline, Massachusetts
I keep thinking we're all going to die from big bombs with nuclears in them and then it would be all over.
                          Age 8, Los Angeles, California

My parents, my friends and all my family would get killed and I'd just be alive and I wouldn't know what to do or anything. I'd be stuck.

Boy, Age 8, Brookline, Massashusetts

ADOLESCENT FEARS

Adolescent expressions of fear are often accompanied by a sense of powerlessness. Some teenagers seem to push the subject out of their minds. Some adolescents, particularly those in the working class, who feel especially powerless, maintain an attitude of bravado.

I've sometimes never been to sleep for days at a time because I've been so scared, but now I sleep because I convinced myself that I'd rather be asleep if a bomb was dropped.

Teenager, Akron, Ohio

I feel totally horrified and terrified of a nuclear war. At least in a regular war you have a chance to fight or not. But we'd all be vaporized whether we choose to fight or not.

Age 16, Hanscom Air Force Base,
Bedford, Massachusetts

I feel bad for kids who worry about nuclear war because I don't think it's going to happen.

Girl, Age 17, Arlington, Massachusetts

When the word is out that missiles are launched, I am having a party on top of Pratt Whitney [aircraft manufacturing company]. Bring sun tan oil.

Teenage Boy, Manchester, New Hampshire

ANGER AND OUTRAGE

Expressions of anger and outrage, especially on the part of teenagers, are usually directed at the older generation that sometimes seems to them to be playing with their futures, denying them a chance to grow up.

My view of the world has changed to one of hate and greed.

Teenager, Akron, Ohio

There are old men with their fingers on the button, and they're playing with our lives, which we haven't had yet, while they've had long full ones. It makes me mad.

Boy, Age 15, California

I feel incredibly, incredibly cheated and I feel helpless.

Girl, Age 17, Brookline, Massachusetts

. . . I nearly threw something at my TV set. Here was this guy [from the "Emergency Management"], 55 or 60 or so, and he has lived his life, but he has the nerve to say that a nuclear war in which I would probably die would be manageable.

Boy, Age 14, New York City

ATTITUDES ABOUT THE FUTURE

Some teenagers express doubt about whether they will have a chance to grow up and feel that they may be cheated out of their lives. Some say that this specifically affects their plans; for example, about whether to have children. Others seem to dismiss the idea that the threat affects their plans. Again, there is the invitation, the implicit demand, that adults do something to secure their lives and future. Some express an attitude of "live for now" because there may be no future; others speak of doing things sooner than they might otherwise, such as getting pregnant, in case there will be no opportunity for them in the future.

I don't see anyone that really cares about how we feel about the future. How are we supposed to grow up and do something important or good if we face such unsurmountable challenges.

Age 17, Madison, Wisconsin

I think some teenagers might get pregnant before a war occurs just in case it happens before we are of the right age.

Age 16, Akron, Ohio

I plan to have no children because the threat is so great. A child should not be made to suffer.

Teenager, Akron, Ohio

Yes, I always wanted to go into the medical field and become a physician, but if we did have a nuclear attack nothing could really be done, there would be no use for a physician.

Teenager, Akron, Ohio

I look forward to a healthy future and don't occupy my time with too much worry.

Age 16, Brookline, Massachusetts

POWERLESSNESS, HOPELESSNESS, AND DISILLUSIONMENT IN RELATION TO THE WORLD SITUATION

Many young people, especially adolescents, express the sense that decisions over which they have no control are being made that affect their lives. Some teenagers suggest that there is no human control and that technology is in charge.

The world is such a mess. You can't blame us for being discouraged or angry. Adults from the years gone by should be embarrassed in front of their kids.

Age 14, Atlanta, Georgia

The government is making decisions . . . that we must live by. . . . We're supposed to be free and still . . . there's nothing we can do about the arms race. We have to learn this stuff so we can figure out what to do. Why is my school so behind?

Boy, Age 17, Chicago, Illinois

The President is the one that pushes the button when . . . they see the bombs coming at us, or a computer does it or something. And I think that that's who does it—a computer, or the President. I'm not sure. I think it's a computer.

Boy, Age 15, Brookline, Massachusetts

RELATIONSHIP TO NUCLEAR WEAPONS

Some adolescents feel overwhelmed and hopeless in relation to the idea of nuclear weapons. Some try not to think about them at all. A few have expressed a fascination with what nuclear bombs do. Although generally adolescents are strongly antinuclear, some see a need to have them for the purposes of deterrence and defense.

I feel so helpless. I have no control over my life. How did nuclear war get to be imaginable?

Age 15, San Francisco, California

Truthfully I try not to think about nukes at all. I have enough to keep my life full.

Age 16, Santa Barbara, California

I viewed them as just another neat weapon. I now think of nuclear weapons as the safeguard to the U.S., and its friends and allies, and as a deterrent to war.

Teenager, Akron, Ohio

In the third grade I was fascinated how they could make a cloud like that. I am still fascinated and would like to become a nuclear engineer.

Teenager, Akron, Ohio

I first had wonder and amazement. Now I recognize the advantages of nuclear fission/fusion capabilities.

Akron, Ohio

Although it's not going to prove much . . . to bomb them, it's the only thing we can do. . . . what can we do if we don't bomb them back? Just take it and then—we would be ended. Russia would rule.

Girl, Age 15, Brookline, Massachusetts

DOUBTS ABOUT SURVIVAL AFTER A NUCLEAR WAR

The majority of adolescents doubt that they or their country could survive a nuclear war. Many have said that they would not want to. The survivalist mentality—a desire to plan for personal survival after a nuclear war—has not been encountered in the responses of teenagers to date.

If I were deep in a mineshaft in the West Virginia mountains with plenty of food, water, and radiation shields, I could probably sweat it out. My city would be destroyed. My country would survive, although in an altered state.

Teenager, Akron, Ohio

Great! You've got 15 minutes to get 20,000 people into one tiny little town—which doesn't want those people in the first place. 38 people per room. So they can all be cremated together.

Girl, Age 14, California

I really hope that if the Soviets ever do launch a first strike
that we don't strike back. I'd rather have some people survive
than none at all. They won't be communists forever.

> Boy, 11th-grader, Washington, D. C.

TEENAGERS' RESPONSES TO CIVIL DEFENSE PLANNING

There appears to have been a diminution from the late 1970s
to the early 1980s in the percentage of teenagers who believe
in the value of civil defense. An interest in the possibility of
effective protection in a nuclear war seems to be correlated with
a lack of education and information. Teenagers who are min-
imally informed about the reality of what nuclear weapons do
seem to regard civil defense planning as ridiculous.

No, the Russians aren't going to call up and say we're sending
a nuclear bomb into D. C., and we wanted to let you know
so you'll have time to evacuate.

> Teenager, Akron, Ohio

I hope civil defense works. I know it's a long shot but at least
we should have some protection. The Soviets have it.

> Age 14, Minneapolis, Minnesota

I think that any civil defense plan is ridiculous. You can't
escape the nuclear death.

> Boy, Age 18, Massachusetts

HOW ADOLESCENTS SEE THE SOVIET UNION

Adolescent attitudes toward the Soviet Union are generally
confused, superficial, and uninformed. They often express fear
of the Soviet Union and deplore what they know of Soviet
international behavior and the Soviet governmental system.
Nevertheless, many adolescents are reluctant to stereotype the
Soviet Union despite what they sense to be our government's
efforts to indoctrinate them. Some express a desire for more
information about the Soviet Union.

I stereotype them as being all evil, all ruled by one person and can't do anything else. . . . That means I don't really think they're all evil. But in my mind most of their government is evil.

> Girl, Age 15, Brookline, Massachusetts

Every time you watch a TV show and it's about war or some controversy it's always America against the Russians. . . . I don't know whose fault it is. It's probably both, you know, the two countries' fault.

> Girl, Age 16, Massachusetts

Even if the Soviets are evil what can we do about it? I think we should just stop and concentrate on our own country. Forget about the Soviets. They don't want to die either.

> Age, 14, Bar Harbor, Maine

WHAT PEOPLE CAN DO

When asked to think about what they can do about the problem, many teenagers express a sense of despair, powerlessness, and hopelessness. Once again the sense that adults are indifferent and that there is nothing they as teenagers can do about the problem is poignantly expressed. Others, although not knowing just what to do, talk about the importance of acknowledging and staying with their feelings. Some express the need for a change in consciousness and the recognition of the interdependence of the human species. Some teenagers, discouraged about the efforts of the adult generation, put their faith in their own generation. Some teenagers advocate specific actions, such as thinking actively about the nuclear threat, giving speeches, marching, and demonstrating. Those that recommend such actions seem to be more hopeful.

I feel so humbled by fear. I feel such rage, grief, sadness, terror. I always end with tears, and a hopeless feeling sunk down to the very bottom of despair. A feeling of depression, there is nothing we can do.

> Age 15, Chicago, Illinois

What good does it do to vote. Voting doesn't make any difference. The government doesn't care what you think.

> Boston, Massachusetts

What I think is going to stop the threat of war is that if everyone around the world realizes we are all a part of one large family. Not many nations can stand by themselves. We are interdependent and the issues are much larger than nuclear weapons. It's too easy to just protest. We have to find all new ways of being a world.

11th-Grader, Minneapolis, Minnesota

I think it would be someone from our generation that would change it, because older people than us, they have their fixed opinions, and we're growing up against it, more or less. I think everyone I know is growing up against it. You know, I don't hear any kids my age going, "Yeah, yeah, let's go and shoot off a few bombs." I mean, I don't really hear that many older people saying that either, but they're the ones that have them, not us, and we don't want them. So if it's changed, I think it will be someone from our generation, but it's going to take a little while.

Boy, Age 14, Brookline, Massachusetts

I think one way to get rid of nuclear bombs is to march like Martin Luther King did, you know, and make speeches and all and everything like that.

Boy, Age 10, Brookline, Massachusetts

I want to make sure I think about it, and acknowledge its presence [the nuclear threat] instead of getting upset. It's best to think of things you can do to be effective. You're always scared. It's why you act. But it does help to do something.

Girl, Age 14, California

My parents do lots for peace. I'm real glad. I'd think they were stupid if they didn't, and I would go to rallies alone or with my sister.

Girl, Age 8, California

At least little kids could make a sign saying something about their feelings about nuclear war, so others would get the message. It made me feel much better.

Girl, Age 11, California

SCHOOLS AND NUCLEAR EDUCATION

Many teenagers seem to resent the idea that they are too young to be exposed to information about nuclear matters. They feel that it is their futures that are at stake and that they have a right to know. Knowledge, some say, can give them the power to do something. In particular, knowledge can change the way they think, making them more open and powerful, though more uncertain. They seem to be particularly appreciative of courses that have enabled them to be more flexible in their thinking about the way they make decisions, whether or not the decisions are related to the nuclear issue.

> I want to learn more but where can I turn to?
>
> Age 16, Chicago, Illinois
>
> I have heard the argument that these things shouldn't be taught to children because it would destroy their childhood . . . I no longer have a childhood to destroy. . . . I've been worrying about some of our national policies for a while now, and I'm glad that the high school has begun to catch up with me.
>
> Age 14, Brookline, Massachusetts
>
> You've gotta know what is going on in the world if you want to do something about it. Once you open yourself up to these things you are never the same.
>
> Boy, Age 16, Cambridge, Massachusetts
>
> I used to be terrified [before taking a course on nuclear issues]. Now I break it down logically. I see it as a challenge to overcome this threat to our world.
>
> Age 17, Cambridge, Massachusetts
>
> I guess what I've mostly learned to do is think. Before this course, I never really thought about how I came to my decisions. My opinions were always just sort of there and it seemed as if they had always been there.
>
> Girl, Age 16, Arlington, Massachusetts
>
> Before the course [on nuclear weapons], it was just the kind of fear that you have that you don't understand. . . . Before, I just didn't understand it. It was just this huge fear, like a black hole. . . . [Now] at least, I understand a little bit about them so that . . . it's a hole with lions.
>
> Girl, Age 17, Brookline, Massachusetts

Children in the Soviet Union

The available translated expressions of Soviet children on the nuclear issue are limited to those obtained in one interview performed at two Soviet pioneer camps in the summer of 1983 by psychiatrists Eric Chivian, Jeremy Waletzky, and John Mack

(Chivian and Goodman, 1984). Permission to conduct these interviews and to administer questionnaires grew out of the trusting relationship between Soviet and American physicians in International Physicians for the Prevention of Nuclear War (IPPNW), of which Dr. Chivian was one of the founders.

The communications of these children and adolescents, ages 11–15, were remarkably similar to those of their American counterparts with respect to fear of nuclear war and doubt about the value of civil defense. The Soviet children seemed to have a more accurate idea of what would happen in the event of an actual nuclear war, possibly because they had had more extensive education on nuclear-related subjects than children in the United States. On the whole, Soviet children seemed even more doubtful than the American boys and girls about the possibility of survival after a nuclear war. Yet, there seemed to be less of a sense of powerlessness and hopelessness among Soviet boys and girls, possibly because of government-organized peace programs that give young people a sense that there is something that they are actively doing to prevent nuclear war. In addition, such programs provide a sense of unified or collective effort within the whole society.

> When I watch films or listen to the radio, I can imagine immediately how bombs will fall on my village. And sometimes at night, I cover myself with the blankets, because I'm afraid.
> Girl, Age 11, Georgievskoye, USSR

> If war starts, we might all be without parents.
> Girl, Age 11, Moscow, USSR

> Many casualties, many, many casualties. And they will principally be people who want peace, children, old people, men. Men are stronger of course than children. And many, many people will perish.
> Boy, Age 13, Moscow, USSR

> The entire earth will become a wasteland. All buildings will be destroyed, or buildings will remain, but all living things will perish—no grass, trees, no greenery.
> Boy, Age 13, Tambovskaya, USSR

> When I was little, my parents told me about it. That nuclear war is a disastrous horror and if it begins, there won't be anything left on this earth.
> Boy, Age 14, Yakutsk, USSR

It would be impossible to live. And when you come out of the bomb shelter after that kind of catastrophe, in the city there wouldn't be anything left alive. And how can that be. You'd have to start life all over again.

                              Girl, Age 13, Serov, USSR

Everyone thinks about their children. And we can help them by struggling against nuclear war—by sending letters, designing banners. These are the things that we can contribute to the struggle against nuclear war. Then they will understand that their children don't want nuclear war either.

                              Boy, Age 14, Yakutsk, USSR

Conclusions

What children and adolescents say about the threat of nuclear war tells us one of the ways that the nuclear arms race has affected the well-being of our society even without the weapons being used. There is a need for more systematic research on the impact of the threat of nuclear death on children and adolescents, especially its impact on the thoughts, feelings, and personality development of preadolescent girls and boys. We need especially to understand more about the relation between what children and adolescents experience in relation to nuclear weapons and the social context in which these psychological responses are generated. We need to know, for example, more about how the nuclear issue relates to other issues in the larger society that affect young people, such as the general feeling of powerlessness in relation to the distant and impersonal government bureaucracy. We need to know more about how this issue is handled in families and about the relationship between the attitudes of parents and other important adults in the child's life about the nuclear threat and what young people themselves think and feel. Studies are needed that are age-specific and that examine the differences that are the result of class or regional variation. We need to know about how children learn of the nuclear threat and how it relates to other, age-specific concerns in their lives.

An international study, directed by Dr. Eric Chivian with the Nuclear Psychology Program at the Cambridge Hospital and

Harvard Medical School, will include more in-depth interviews with American and Soviet young people as well as with children around the world. This research will further explore how nuclear issues affect young people and how children develop ideas about people in other countries.

The disquiet that young people express in the questions they ask about nuclear weapons and nuclear arms policies have forced us to think more deeply and to question the relationship between nuclear weapons and national security. Perhaps the most disturbing element in all this is the sense that children and teenagers have communicated of a world that is out of control and on the brink of destruction. Young people provide a forceful message to adult generations. Their voices in America, the Soviet Union, and other countries seem united in one clear respect. They ask us as adults to find new ways of conducting our relations with other nations and to gain control of nuclear technology and take responsibility for it in order to give them a fair chance of completing their lives.

References

Bachman, G. G. (1983). "American High School Seniors View the Military: 1976–82." *Armed Forces and Society* 10 : 85–104.

Beardslee, W. R., and Mack, J. E. (1982). "The Impact on Children and Adolescents of Nuclear Weapons." In *Psychosocial Aspects of Nuclear Developments.* Washington, D. C.: American Psychiatric Association.

——— (1983). "Adolescents and the Threat of Nuclear War: The Evolution of a Perspective." *Yale Journal of Biology and Medicine* 56 : 79–91.

Children's Fears of War (1984). House Hearings Before the Select Committee on Children, Youth, and Families. 98th Cong., 1st sess., Sept. 20, 1983.

Chivian, E., and Goodman, J. (1984). "What Soviet Children Are Saying About Nuclear War." International Physicians for the Prevention of Nuclear War. *Report* 2 (1) : 10–12.

Chivian, E., and Snow, R. (1983). "There's a Nuclear War Going on Inside Me." International Physicians for the Prevention of Nuclear War. (A videotape of interviews with 6–16-year-olds.)

Coles, R. (in press). "Children and the Bomb." In *The Moral Development of Children.*

Einstein, A. (1946). "The unleashed power of the atom . . ." Telegram of the Emergency Committee of Atomic Scientists, over Einstein's signature, to several hundred prominent Americans appealing for contributions. Quoted in Nathan, O., and Norden, H. (1960). *Einstein on Peace.* NY: Avenel Books, P. 376.

Escalona, S. (1965). "Children and the Threat of Nuclear War." In M. Schwebel, ed., *Behavioral Science and Human Survival.* Palo Alto, CA: Science and Behavioral Books.

——— (1982). "Growing Up with the Threat of Nuclear War: Some Indirect Effects on Personality Development." *American Journal of Orthopsychiatry* 52 : 600–607.

Goldenring, J. M., and Doctor, R. M. (1985). *Children's Fears of War,* supra. Pp. 56–66.

Goodman, L. A.; Mack, J. E.; Beardslee, W. R.; and Snow, R. M. (1983). "The Threat of Nuclear War and the Nuclear Arms Race:

Adolescent Experience and Perceptions." *Political Psychology* 4 (3) : 501–30.

Haas, S. D. (March 1984). "Class and Nuclear War: An Outline." Unpublished manuscript; and (in press) "Working Class Kids' Views of War and Peace."

Holmborg, P. O., and Bergstrom, A. (June 1984). "How Swedish Teenagers, age 13–15, Think and Feel Concerning the Nuclear Threat." Paper presented at the Fourth Congress of International Physicians for the Prevention of Nuclear War, Helsinki, Finland.

Kelman, H. G., ed. (1965). *International Behavior: A Social-Psychological Analysis.* NY: Holt, Rinehart and Winston.

Keyes, K. (1983). *The Hundredth Monkey.* Cuse Bay, OR: Vision Books.

Lifton, R. J. (1973). *Home from the War: Vietnam Veterans—Neither Victims nor Executioners.* NY: Simon and Schuster and Touchstone Books.

——— (1979). *The Broken Connection: On Death and the Continuity of Life.* NY: Touchstone Books.

——— (rev. ed., 1982). *Death in Life: Survivors of Hiroshima.* NY: Basic Books.

Mack, J. E. (April 1981). "Psychosocial Effects of the Nuclear Arms Race." *Bulletin of the Atomic Scientists.* 37 (4) : 18–23.

——— (1984). *Children's Fears of War,* supra. Pp. 47–52.

Murphy, G., ed., (1945). *Human Nature and Enduring Peace.* Boston: Houghton Mifflin.

Rabinowitch, E. (1963). "Five Years After." In Grodzins, M. and Rabinowitch, E., eds., *The Atomic Age.* NY: Basic Books.

Schwebel, M. (1965). "Nuclear Cold War: Student Opinion and Professional Responsibility. In M. Schwebel, ed., *Behavioral Science and Human Survival.* Palo Alto, CA: Science and Behavioral Books.

——— (1982). "Effects of the Nuclear War Threat on Children and Teenagers: Implications for Professionals." *American Journal of Orthopsychiatry* 52 : 608–18.

——— (April 13, 1984). "Children's Reactions to the Nuclear Threat: Trends and Implications." Paper delivered at Symposium of the New York University School of Social Work: "The Impact of the Nuclear Threat on the Mental Health of Children and Parents."

Schell, J. (1982). *The Fate of the Earth.* NY: Knopf.

Smith, A. K. (October 1958). "Behind the Decision to Use the Atomic Bomb: Chicago 1944–45." *Bulletin of the Atomic Scientists* 1 : 3–10.

Snow, C. (July 1984). "Nuclear Nightmares in Inner City Schools." *World Paper.* P. 15.

Solantaus, T.; Rimpela, M.; and Taipale, V. "The Threat of War in the Minds of 12–18-year-olds in Finland." *Lancet* 8380 (1) : 784.

Sommers, F., and Goldberg, S. (June 1984). "The Effect of the Nuclear Threat on Children: A Pilot Study." Paper presented at the Fourth Congress of International Physicians for the Prevention of Nuclear War, Helsinki, Finland.

White, R. K. (rev. ed., 1970) *Nobody Wanted War; Misperception in Vietnam and Other Wars.* NY: Doubleday/Anchor.

—— (1984). *Fearful Warriors: A Psychological Profile of U.S.-Soviet Relations.* NY: The Free Press.

Zeitlin, S. (March-April 1984). "Nuclear Secrets: What Do We Tell Mom and Dad?" *Networker.*

Zweigenhaft, R. L. (1983). "The Psychological Effects of Living in a Nuclear Age." Report of the War Planning Evaluation Committee of the Greensboro-Guilford County Emergency Management Agency.

Section II

The Psychology of the American People and the Soviet Decision Makers

SECTION EDITORS: DANIEL YANKELOVICH AND
MARSHALL D. SHULMAN

INTRODUCTION

Ralph K. White

Those who favor forms of arms control that go beyond a nuclear freeze face a formidable job of persuasion. The difficulties encountered in Congress and the White House by even a bilateral, verifiable nuclear freeze are obvious, and the American public seems accepting enough of this situation to drive many proponents of arms control to despair, despite opinion surveys that indicate the majority of the public have consistently favored a freeze.

The first chapter in this section, Chapter 3, a reprint of an article by Daniel Yankelovich and John Doble in the fall 1984 issue of *Foreign Affairs*, offers such persons a substantial measure of new hope. Although a large majority continue to favor keeping up with the Soviet Union in armed strength—that is, "not losing the arms race"—and are deeply distrustful of the USSR, in several ways they have lost much of the nationalistic self-assertiveness they showed in 1980 and are, surprisingly, even ready to take some risks for the sake of arms reduction and arms control. The article is a model of evidence-based but action-oriented writing and offers a solid base for realistic planning by those who want to influence the middle majority of the American public on issues of this sort. For instance, it shows not only that a great majority favor a no-first-use policy but also, amazingly, that a similarly large majority *believe we already have such a policy.*

Chapters 4, 5, and 6 address a similarly critical question: the psychology of the Soviet decision makers. The question of their goals and intentions surely should be a main basis for judging the broad question of whether the main emphasis of the West should be on armed deterrence or on tension reduction. If the primary goal of the Soviet leaders is aggressive, like Hitler's, a main emphasis on armed deterrence, perhaps on a scale even exceeding the present one, would make good sense. If not, the case for putting greater stress on tension-reduction would be very strong.

Chapter 4 discusses "What the Russians Really Want." It is by Marshall Shulman, a respected historian and specialist on the Soviet Union who has visited the USSR some 30 times and who was Secretary of State Cyrus Vance's right-hand man on Soviet affairs.

Chapter 5 is by Urie Bronfenbrenner, a social psychologist whose comparative studies of child-rearing in many cultures, especially the Russian and the American, are very well known. The chapter is a reprint of most of his article, "The Mirror Image in Soviet-American Relations" which was originally published in 1961 and has long since become part of the bloodstream of American social psychology. His vantage point is his combination of a psychological background with intimate first-hand knowledge of the Soviet people (not the men in the Kremlin).

Chapter 6, by Ralph K. White, is excerpted from a chapter in his recent book, *Fearful Warriors: A Psychological Profile of Soviet-American.* It focuses on the Soviet decision makers rather than the Soviet public.

3.

The Public Mood: Nuclear Weapons and the USSR*

DANIEL YANKELOVICH and JOHN DOBLE

Presidential campaigns do more than choose individuals for high office: our history shows many instances where elections have moved the country closer to a decisive resolution of long-standing issues. The 1984 presidential campaign gives the candidates a historic opportunity to build public support for reducing the risk of nuclear war. The American electorate is now psychologically prepared to take a giant step toward real arms reductions.

For several years now a great change, largely unnoted, has transformed the outlook of the American electorate toward nuclear arms. There is a dawning realization among the majority of voters that the growth in nuclear arsenals on both sides has made the old "rules of the game" dangerously obsolete. The traditional response of nations to provocations and challenges to their interest has been the threat of force and, in the event of a breakdown of relations, resort to war. However much suffering war may have created in the past, the old rules permitted winners as well as losers.

But an all-out nuclear war, at present levels of weaponry, would wipe out the distinction between winners and losers. All would be losers and the loss irredeemable. This grim truth is now vividly alive for the American electorate. Moreover, for the average voter the danger is real and immediate—far more so than among elites and experts. Americans are not clear about the policy implications of this new reality. They do not know how it should be translated into day-to-day transactions with the Soviet Union to reduce the danger. But there is an impatient awareness that the old responses are not good enough, and a sense of urgency about finding new responses.

- By an overwhelming 96 percent to 3 percent, Americans assert that "picking a fight with the Soviet Union is too dangerous in a nuclear world. . . ."
- By 89 percent to 9 percent, Americans subscribe to the view that "there can be no winner in an all-out nuclear war; both the United States and the Soviet Union would be completely destroyed."
- By 83 percent to 14 percent, Americans say that while in past wars we knew that no matter what happened some life would continue, "we cannot be certain that life on earth will continue after a nuclear war."
- And, by 68 percent to 20 percent, the majority *rejects* the concept that "if we had no alternative we could fight and win a nuclear war against the Soviet Union."

These findings are from a new national study conducted by the Public Agenda Foundation to probe attitudes toward nuclear arms. The picture of the electorate's state of mind that follows has been pieced together from a number of excellent national surveys of public attitudes conducted over the past several years by a variety of organizations. These include: Gallup, Harris, *New York Times*/CBS, *Time* Soundings (conducted by Yankelovich, Skelly, and White), ABC News/*Washington Post*, NBC News/Associated Press, *Los Angeles Times,* Research and Forecasts, and the Public Agenda study, the most recent.

The Public Agenda survey underscores what many others have discovered: Americans have come to believe that nuclear war is unwinnable, unsurvivable.

In the postwar period, United States policies toward the Soviet Union have oscillated between policies of containment (drawing lines against overt Soviet involvement), and policies of détente that depended on "managing" a carrot/stick relationship between the superpowers. Our shifts from one policy to the other have depended more on internal American politics than on Soviet actions. In the early 1970s, détente enjoyed immense popularity with the public. As the decade moved toward its close, however, differing Soviet and American interpretations of détente had begun to create tensions (for example, in Angola). The watershed event was the Soviet invasion of Afghanistan in December 1979 and the reaction of the Carter administration. This event marked the public start of the present "down phase" of disillusionment in the United States with the policies of détente, and of deeply troubled relations with the Soviets.

President Carter characterized the Afghanistan invasion as "the worst threat to world peace since World War II." The public, which had momentarily set aside its mistrust of the Soviet Union in the early and middle 1970s, now responded with renewed mistrust and frustration over our apparent impotence to counter Soviet aggression. (The frustration was aggravated, coincidentally, by this country's inability to free the hostages in Iran.) This combination of events led to a steep increase in public support for strengthening our defenses, and a mood of deep disillusionment with détente. (See Yankelovich and Kaagan, 1982, pp. 696–713.) The Public Agenda survey shows that two-thirds of the public (67 percent) endorse the view that the "Soviet Union used détente as an opportunity to build up their armed forces while lulling us into a sense of false security."

In 1980 and 1981 the backlash against détente reached a high peak of intensity. The public mood was characterized by injured national pride, unqualified support for increasing the defense budget, and a general desire to see American power become more assertive.

The public is now having second thoughts about the dangers of such an assertive posture at a time when the United States is no longer seen to maintain nuclear supremacy. The electorate is still wary, still mistrustful, and still convinced that the Soviets will seize every possible advantage they can; yet, at the same time, Americans are determined to stop what they see as a drift toward nuclear confrontation which, in the electorate's view, neither we nor the Soviets desire. The stage is being set for a new phase in our relationship with the Soviets.

For the United States, "normal relations" between the two superpowers are clearly not the "friendly relations" the American people associated with the 1970s policy of détente. At the same time, Americans are skeptical about the kind of containment policy that prevailed so often in the past. From our Vietnam experience, voters draw the lesson that we must keep uppermost in mind the limits of American power. And from the present standoff on nuclear arms they draw the lesson that we must avoid being provocative and confrontational.

Large majorities now support a relatively nonideological, pragmatic live-and-let-live attitude that potentially can provide the political support for a new approach to normalizing relations between the two superpowers.

In shaping new policy proposals it will be useful for candidates to hold clearly in view two major findings that emerge from the many studies of public attitudes toward nuclear arms. The first is that Americans have experienced a serious change of heart about the impact of nuclear weapons on our national security. The second is that voter perceptions of the Soviets are not as black and white as they once were; there are many shades of gray—nuances and subtleties that have an important bearing on policy. An inference follows from these findings: voters are psychologically prepared to consider much more dramatic and far-reaching arms control policies than existing ones, because existing policies are rooted in the old rules of the game when there was a chance of winning if war broke out.

At the very start of the nuclear age in August 1945, a Gallup poll found that the overwhelming majority of citizens approved the use of the atomic bomb on Hiroshima and Nagasaki. America was war weary, and the new weapon held the promise of ending the conflict and saving American lives. Yet, when asked in the same survey whether the United States should use poison gas against Japanese cities if it would shorten the war and save American lives, most Americans answered no. In the summer of 1945, then, in spite of the suffering the war had caused,

Americans clearly understood the ideas of deterrence and retaliation, and the need to weigh concerns other than that of
simply ending the war.

In 1954, Gallup reported that 54 percent of the public felt
that the invention of the hydrogen bomb made another world
war less likely. By 1982, however, the Gallup survey revealed
that American thinking had undergone a radical change. In that
year, responding to the same question posed a generation earlier,
nearly two in three (65 percent) now said the development of
the bomb was a bad thing.

The reasons for this change are clear-cut. Twenty-nine years
ago, Gallup had found that only 27 percent of the public agreed
that "mankind would be destroyed in an all-out atomic or
hydrogen bomb war." The Public Agenda asked those they
interviewed in 1984 if they agreed or disagreed with this statement: "There can be no winner in an all-out nuclear war; both
the U.S. and the Soviet Union would be completely destroyed."
An overwhelming 89 percent concurred. This and other responses reflect a dramatic shift in people's thinking about what
nuclear war would be like. Nuclear war is no longer seen as a
rational policy for the United States government to consider.

In part, this extraordinary change reflects Americans' revised
understanding of the relative strengths of the United States and
the Soviet Union. When the United States alone had the bomb,
most Americans had few doubts about our safety. Even after
the Soviets achieved nuclear status, and even after the advent
of the hydrogen bomb, American confidence in our nuclear
superiority gave most people a feeling of security. In 1955, for
example, when only 27 percent said an all-out nuclear war
would destroy mankind, Americans were nearly unanimous (78
percent) in believing that the United States had more nuclear
weapons than the Soviet Union. Today, only 10 percent believe
we have nuclear superiority; a majority now feels that the two
sides are roughly equal in destructive capability, and at a level
felt to be terrifying.

Concern about the issue has also increased, especially among
the young. Only 5 percent of the public say they find themselves
thinking about the possibility of nuclear war *less* than they did
five years ago. A majority—and nearly three in four young

adults between the ages of 18 and 30—say they think about the issue more often than they did five years ago. There is also majority agreement, 68 percent (rising to 78 percent among adults under 30), that if both sides keep building missiles instead of negotiating to get rid of them, it is only a matter of time before they are used. A sizable number expects that day to come soon: 38 percent of the American people, and 50 percent of those under 30, say that all-out nuclear war is likely to occur within the next ten years. This is a vision of the future that is far different from that held in the mid-1950s when most people said the development of the bomb was a good thing, deserving of a central role in our military strategy.

Americans have also arrived at an astonishingly high level of agreement that we must adapt our future policies to these "facts of life":

- That nuclear weapons are here to stay. They cannot simply be abolished, and because mankind will maintain its knowledge of how to make them, there can be no turning back to a less threatening time (85 percent).
- That both we and the Soviets now have an "overkill" capability, more destructive capability than we could ever need, and the ability to blow each other up several times over (90 percent).
- That there can be no such thing as a limited nuclear war: if either side were to use nuclear weapons, the conflict would inevitably escalate into all-out war (83 percent).
- That the United States no longer has nuclear superiority (84 percent) and that we can never hope to regain it; that the arms race can never be won, for if we did have a bigger nuclear arsenal than the Soviets, they would simply keep building until they caught up (92 percent); and that building new weapons to use as "bargaining chips" doesn't work because the Soviets would build similar weapons to match us (84 percent).

It is this fundamental sense that our own lives may be at risk that accounts for another startling change in public opinion. A consensus level of 77 percent says that by the end of the decade it should be United States policy *not* to use nuclear weapons to respond to a conventional Soviet attack. Nearly the same number (74 percent) say it should be *current* policy never to use small nuclear weapons in a battlefield situation.

Public attitudes toward the Soviet Union are highly complex. Americans believe that the Soviet Union is an aggressive nation, both militarily and ideologically, which presses every advantage, probes constantly for vulnerabilities; interprets every gesture of conciliation and friendship as weakness; fails to keep its promises; cheats on treaties; and, in general, gets the better of us in negotiations by hanging tough.

At the same time, however, there is less concern than in the past about communist subversion from within or about the political appeal of communist ideology to our closest allies. Americans hold the Russian people in high esteem, believe that America is able to live in peace with a variety of communist countries, see the Russians caught in the same plight as ourselves in seeking to avert a suicidal nuclear arms race, credit the Soviets with legitimate security concerns, and believe they are genuinely interested in negotiation. Huge majorities feel that America has been less forthcoming in working things out with the Russians than it might be and that we have to share some of the blame for the deterioration in the relationship.

This ambivalent attitude represents a change in outlook from the last presidential election in 1980 to the present one. In 1980, Americans were in an assertive anticommunist, anti-Soviet mood, ready to support cold war kinds of initiatives. But in politics, timing is all. Surveys show that Americans feel that the power imbalance that prevailed in 1980 has now been partly or wholly corrected and that more constructive negotiations are possible.

Today, the majority of Americans have reached a conclusion about communism that can best be described as pragmatic rejection. As they have in the past, Americans today firmly reject the social values of communism, and see them as opposed to all our fundamental beliefs. But there is little fear today that communist subversion threatens the United States, that communists will engage in sabotage, form a fifth column, or convert millions of Americans to their cause. Americans today are confident that communism holds little appeal in this country. They differentiate among communist countries, too, and the threat they pose to our security. For example, in the Public Agenda survey, people concur with near unanimity that "our experience with communist China proves that our mortal enemies can quickly turn into countries we can get along with" (83 percent). This sense that communism is something we can tolerate without accepting, something with which we can coexist without endorsing, represents another and perhaps fundamental shift in the public's thinking since the beginning of the nuclear age.

Admittedly, public attitudes toward dealing with the threat of communism often seem contradictory and confused. In recent years computer-based statistical methods have permitted some very subtle and powerful analyses which divide the public into like-minded subgroups. At the Public Agenda, analyst Harvey Lauer performed such an analysis on their survey findings, with some revealing and important results.

Lauer's "cluster analysis" showed that public attitudes are most sharply divided by four variables: (1) the presence or absence of ideological animosity toward the Soviet Union; (2) the inclination to see the conflict between the United States and the USSR in religious terms or pragmatic terms; (3) the tendency to minimize or to stress the threat of nuclear war; and (4) the favoring of an assertive or a conciliatory policy toward the Soviets.

The four groups that Lauer's cluster analysis reveals can be characterized as follows. One group he calls the "threat minimizers." They constitute 23 percent of the Public Agenda's national cross-section. Like virtually everyone else, they believe that nuclear war is unwinnable. But unlike most other Americans, they do not think there is any real chance that it will happen. Consequently, they are prepared to take far greater risks than the rest of the public. They are less interested in negotiation than in building up our military strength. They reject conciliatory gestures in favor of weakening the Soviet Union in every way possible. Demographically, this group is predominantly male (69 percent), older than other groups, and fairly well educated, with good incomes. Politically, they tend to be conservative and Republican.

At the opposite extreme is to be found the youngest and best educated of the four groups. Constituting 21 percent of the sample, this group believes the possibility of nuclear disaster is real and urgent; they have faith in conciliation over confrontation; they want to see the United States take the initiative in reducing our nuclear arms; and most strikingly, they are almost totally free of the ideological hostility that the majority of Americans feel toward the Soviet Union. They see the Soviet threat almost completely in military terms. Like the first group, it, too, is more male than female (56 to 44 percent), but unlike the first group it tends to be liberal rather than conservative.

What about the two middle groups where the majority of Americans are to be found? The single largest of the four groups—31 percent—is made up of Americans who are ideologically opposed to communism and the Soviets but are peaceful and nonassertive in their strategic thinking about how to deal with the Soviet threat. They see communism as an ideological threat, but they also think a lot about the possibility of nuclear war. They believe the Soviet Union takes advantage of us and cheats on our treaties with it, but they also believe that the United States has not done enough to reach serious arms control agreements with the Soviets. They urge that we reach an accommodation with the Soviets on a peaceful coexistence, "live-and-let-live" basis, and not attempt to reform or change them. Demographically, this is the most female of the four groups (60 percent); they are fairly young, of average education, and middle of the road in their political orientation.

The fourth group, representing one-quarter of the population (25 percent), tends to see the conflict between us and the Soviets in religious terms. They see the Soviet Union as an "evil empire" threatening our moral and religious values. A majority of them believe that in the event of a nuclear holocaust their faith in God would ensure their survival. Unlike all the other groups, they believe that someday the United States is going to have to fight the Russians to stop communism.

In many respects, the religious anticommunism of this group predisposes it to endorse the utmost in nuclear military strength for the United States. But, paradoxically, it is the most apprehensive about the imminent threat of a nuclear holocaust. Consequently, it sees great danger to the United States in efforts to weaken the Soviets too much, lest they respond "like cornered rats." A majority among them believe the United States has not done enough in negotiations with the Soviets, and a large minority would even opt for unilateral reductions in our nuclear stockpile.

Most of the contradictions in public responses are concentrated in this subgroup. There is, however, an emotional logic underlying their seeming inconsistency: they fear communism as an ideology and would smite it with the sword—but they fear the threat of nuclear war more than they fear communism, and therefore they are more willing than most Americans to sheathe the sword. They want the United States to be as strong militarily as possible, but they also fear the consequences of our using our military strength aggressively. Their activism derives from the fact that the likelihood of nuclear war is a living reality for them. They are concerned to do everything they can to avert catastrophe. Of all the four groups, they most yearn for strong leadership and authority to set down a policy that will allay their anxieties. They are the only one of the four groups where a majority believes that the subject of nuclear weapons is too complex for them to think about and should therefore be left "to the President and to the experts." Demographically, they are the least well educated of the four groups, disproportionately Democratic but not liberal.

A profile of ambivalent American attitudes toward the Soviet Union can be seen graphically in Table 3.1. It summarizes both the positive and negative attitudes toward the Soviet Union and toward communism as an ideology.

There is somewhat of a generation gap on attitudes toward the Soviets, with older Americans expressing more suspicion of, and hostility toward, Soviet motives and actions than younger Americans. For example, 76 percent of those over 60 agree that the Soviets lie, cheat, and steal—do anything to further the cause of communism—compared to 52 percent among those under 30. More older than younger Americans also believe that the Soviets cheat on treaties and agreements (76 percent to 49

Table 3.1
Ambivalent Attitudes Toward the Soviet Union
and Communism*

Negative Views	% Agree	% Disagree
"During the 1970s, when we were trying to improve relations, the Soviets secretly built up their military strength"†	90	6
"The Soviets are constantly testing us, probing for weaknesses, and they're quick to take advantage whenever they find any"†	82	14
"The Soviets treat our friendly gestures as weaknesses"†	73	23
"The Soviets used détente as an opportunity to build up their armed forces while lulling us into a false sense of security"‡	67	20
"If we are weak, the Soviet Union, at the right moment, will attack us or our allies in Europe and Japan"‡	65	27
"The Soviets only respond to military strength"‡	61	34
"The Soviets lie, cheat and steal—do anything to further the cause of communism"‡	61	28
"The Soviets have cheated on just about every treaty and agreement they've ever signed"‡	61	24
"In past agreements between the U.S. and the Soviet Union, the Soviets almost always got the better part of the bargain"‡	58	31
"Whenever there's trouble in the world—in the Middle East, Central America, or anywhere else—chances are the Soviets are behind it"‡	56	38

More Accepting Views		
"The Russian people are not nearly as hostile to the U.S. as their leaders are and, in fact, the Russians could be our friends if their leaders had a different attitude"†	88	6
"The U.S. has to accept some of the blame for the tension that has plagued U.S.-Soviet relations in recent years"‡	76	16
"You can't understand how the Russians behave without realizing that their homeland has been invaded many, many times. They are obsessed with their own military security"‡	75	19
"The idea that the Soviets are the cause of all the world's troubles is a dangerous oversimplification"‡	70	26

Negative Views	% Agree	% Disagree
"The U.S. often blames the Soviets for troubles in other countries that are really caused by poverty, hunger, political corruption and repression"‡	68	26
"Just 40 years ago, the Germans invaded the Soviet Union and killed millions of Russian citizens. It's perfectly understandable why they oppose our putting nuclear missiles on German soil"‡	58	35
"The Soviet leaders believe that President Reagan is trying to humiliate them, and this is not a good climate for negotiating on matters of life and death"‡	51	40
"The degree to which the Soviets cheat on arms control is overstated by Americans who oppose negotiating with them in the first place"‡	44	41

* Totals do not add to 100% because "Not Sure" responses are omitted.
† *Time*/Yankelovich, Skelly, and White, 1983.
‡ Public Agenda, 1984.

percent). On the other hand, young Americans, perhaps more skeptical of authority to begin with, believe the degree of Soviet cheating is overstated by those who oppose negotiating with them in the first place. (Fifty-nine percent of those under 30 express such a view, compared to only 32 percent among those over 60.)

Such is the nature of public ambivalence toward the Soviet Union that it dooms to failure any one-dimensional policy that appeals exclusively to one side of public attitudes. A policy of undiluted anticommunism that emphasizes only the negatives cannot hope to win solid majority support. The time is past when successful candidates can simply run against the Politburo. Similarly, a one-dimensional policy of détente—if détente is interpreted as it was in the 1970s, as "making friends" with the Russians—cannot win solid majority support either.

No amount of public opinion analysis can fashion the correct policy. What opinion polls can reveal, however, and what we propose to describe are the boundaries or constraints which the public's thinking impose on policy. To sustain a complex and difficult policy, one that may call for public sacrifice, restraint, and understanding, it is prudent to seek to win solid and lasting support from the electorate. Our analysis of opinion data suggests that to achieve such support in today's climate, such a policy would have to be conceived within the following guidelines:

1. *The United States must not adopt any policy that the majority of Americans will perceive as "losing the arms race."*

Most Americans believe that the United States cannot regain nuclear superiority, that the arms race cannot be won, and that we can never return to a time when our nuclear monopoly gave us a sense of nearly total security. People are nearly unanimous in the view that if we had a bigger nuclear arsenal than the Soviets, they would simply keep building until they caught up (92 percent). By nearly eight to one (84 percent), the public opposes the idea of building new weapons to use as "bargaining chips" to get concessions in negotiations.

But, in spite of the feeling that we can never "win" the arms race, Americans are afraid we could "lose" it. Nearly six in ten (57 percent) say we must continue to develop new and better nuclear weapons so as not to lose the arms race. A particular concern fueling this sentiment is the fear that "technological breakthroughs" could make the weapons we now have obsolete (71 percent).

2. *Americans are convinced that it is time for negotiations, not confrontations, with the Soviets.*

Following from the view that nuclear weapons can never be abolished and that the arms race cannot be won, Americans see only one way to reduce the risk of nuclear war—through negotiations. Americans overwhelmingly concur that "picking a fight" with the Soviet Union is too dangerous in a nuclear world, that we should be thinking of peaceful solutions (96 percent). Americans feel that the Soviets are as afraid of nuclear war as we are (94 percent) and that it is in our mutual interest to find ways to negotiate to reduce the risk of war.

Some people see a most ominous trend: that we and the Soviets are drifting toward catastrophe. Sixty-eight percent of Americans feel that if we and the Soviets keep building nuclear weapons instead of negotiating to get rid of them, "it's only a matter of time before they are used." This concern is especially pronounced among women (75 percent) and those under 30 (78 percent). By 50 to 22 percent, people say the United States would be safer if we spent less time and effort building up our military forces and more on negotiating with the Soviets. Again, women and the younger Americans agree even more strongly. The idea of building more dangerous nuclear weapons to get the Soviets to make concessions on arms control is rejected by a margin of 62 to 31 percent. Half the public fears that President Reagan is playing nuclear "chicken" with the Soviets (50 percent).

3. *The dominant attitude of Americans is that of "live-and-let-live" pragmatism, not an anticommunist crusade, nor a strong desire to reform the Russians.*

Americans say that peacefully coexisting with communist countries is something we do all the time (71 percent). And by a margin of 67 percent to 28 percent, people agree that we should let the communists have their system while we have ours, that "there's room in the world for both."

A solid majority also feels no strong desire to involve the United States in reforming the Soviet Union. Nearly six in ten (58 percent) agree that we've been trying to change Soviet behavior for 60 years, and that it is time we stopped trying to do so. By a margin of 59 to 19 percent, Americans also say we would be better off if we stopped treating the Soviets as enemies and tried to hammer out our differences in a live-and-let-live spirit. And, by a margin of 53 to 22 percent, Americans feel that the United States would be safer if we stopped trying to prevent the spread of communism to other countries, and learned to live with them the way we live with China and Yugoslavia.

4. *A national reconsideration of the strategic role for nuclear weapons is badly needed.*

Our present policies are almost universally misunderstood. More than eight out of ten Americans (81 percent) believe it is our *current* policy to use nuclear weapons "if and only if" our adversaries use them against us first. Almost the same massive majority believes that this is what our national policy *should* be. Only 18 percent agree that we should use nuclear weapons against a conventional Soviet attack in Europe or Japan; and more than three out of four (76 percent) agree that we should use nuclear weapons if, and only if, the Soviets use them against our allies first.

At the same time, however, the public holds many other attitudes that are actually or potentially in conflict with this majority position. Only a third of all Americans (33 percent) know that nuclear weapons are less expensive than conventional forces. At the same time, substantial majorities (66 percent) say that they would be willing to pay higher taxes for defense if we and the Soviets reduced our nuclear weapons and replaced them with nonnuclear forces.

More important than economic arguments is the concern of the majority, summarized above, that we not "lose" the arms race by falling behind the Soviets in technology or weapons. There is also great reluctance to appear "weak" in Soviet eyes, since the public is persuaded that the Soviets interpret conciliatory gestures on our part as signs of weakness.

In brief, Americans fear that the danger of nuclear war has seriously weakened our security. They also realize that the present standoff between us and the Soviets excludes the use of nuclear weapons as an option for achieving policy goals. But they have not yet thought through the strategic and policy implications of this awesome change in the rules. Their present preferences are clear: to move toward less, rather than greater reliance on, nuclear weapons.

5. *Finally, Americans are prepared—somewhat nervously— to take certain risks for peace.*

So dangerous is the present situation, and so gravely does it threaten our security, that the public feels it is time to change course and, in doing so, to take some initiatives in the cause of peace.

The idea of a bilateral and verifiable nuclear freeze has been supported by upward of 75 percent of the public for several years. But beyond a freeze, majorities also endorse other strategies containing an explicit element of risk. For example, a 61 percent majority favors the idea of declaring a *unilateral* six-month freeze on nuclear weapons development to see if the Soviets will follow suit, even if they might take advantage of it; 56 percent favor signing an arms control agreement with the Soviets, even if foolproof verification cannot be guaranteed. Finally, 55 percent favor expanding trade with the Soviets and making other cooperative gestures, even if that makes them stronger and more secure.

In sum, a fair conclusion from the variety of surveys and interviews is that the American electorate wants to reverse the present trend toward relying ever more heavily on nuclear weapons to achieve the nation's military and political objectives. The public finds the long-term risks of continuing the way we are going to be simply unacceptable.

4.

What the Russians
Really Want*

MARSHALL D. SHULMAN

Like travelers who come upon an unmarked fork in the road, we find ourselves obliged by the change in leadership in the Soviet Union to stop and think. The transition, with all the uncertainties it presents, compels us to consider where we are going in our fateful relationship with the Russians, and why, and whether we should be going in another direction.

Almost seven decades have passed since the revolution that led to the founding of the Soviet Union. For most of those years, relations between that country and our own have been animated by hostility, relieved only by brief intervals of abatement and passing hopes of some easement.

Each such interval, however, has been followed by an ever stronger expression of the conflict of power, beliefs, and purposes between the two nations. That conflict is now so deeply rooted and so intense that it evokes the destructive energies of both societies, weakening them and the fabric of the international system, threatening the possibility of catastrophe.

That hostility did not grow out of any natural antipathy between the peoples of the two countries, but with the passage of time each has come to be so persuaded of the malign intent of the other that it has become difficult to distinguish what is real and what is fancied in the perceptions each holds of the other.

In the conduct of our foreign relations, Walter Lippmann observed, we operate on the basis of "pictures in our heads." The images of the Soviet Union held most widely in this country are stereotypes, and they warp our thinking in a number of ways. They are simple caricatures of a complex society. They are static and do not take into account the changes that have taken place, particularly since the death of Stalin. They are based on prevalent assumptions that do not bear critical examination. They misrepresent the ways in which the Soviet people react to our actions and to our words. They do not distinguish between atmosphere and substance. Finally, as oversimple images informing oversimple policy, they make it difficult for us to resolve the dilemma of whether we should try to change the Soviet system or try to improve our relations with it.

After almost four decades spent studying the Soviet Union and about thirty trips there, what continues to strike me most forcefully is the sharp contrast between the complex reality of that country and the primitive perceptions of it that dominate our discussions, and the contrast between the way the world looks from Moscow and the way it appears from Washington. Even more troubling is the problem we face in bringing our values, our emotions, our apprehensions, and our judgments about the Soviet Union into some kind of reasonable balance with our relations with it.

To many Americans, including many specialists on the subject, it seems contradictory to recognize that the Soviet Union is repressive and expansionist and also to believe that we should seek to manage rationally the fundamentally competitive Soviet-American relationship. What has been absent from our thinking is the maturity to carry such apparently contradictory notions in our heads at the same time.

Good and reasonable people often come to hold fundamentally different views of the Soviet Union. There is much about that secretive society that we do not know. Into this uncertainty people tend to project either their fears or their hopes, according to their temperaments or their political prejudices or, perhaps, their experiences: a businessman who has been royally treated on his visits to the Soviet Union will have a very different picture in his mind than an émigré who may have spent years in a labor camp or years battling bureaucrats for an exit visa; a military game theorist will see the Russians as the enemy, ruthless, omnicompetent, poised to attack.

The problems presented by the Soviet Union are serious. But stereotypes do not provide us with an adequate basis for responding intelligently. My purpose here is to suggest a way of thinking about these problems, beginning with a realistic view of the Soviet Union and its behavior and ending with some guidelines for the conduct of our relations with Moscow. Not everyone, and certainly not all of those who study Soviet behavior, will agree with what I regard as realistic or with my conclusions. But I believe that the time is overdue for us to address head-on some of the questions that underlie our present thinking about that country in order to contribute to a more rational discourse, beyond the level of partisan polemics.

One: In seeking to expand its power and influence around the world, are the Soviet Union's aspirations unlimited? Does it accept practical limitations on realizing its status as a superpower? Might it even become willing to live according to the norms of the international system?

Over the last sixty-seven years, we have witnessed the ascendancy of nation-state interests over revolutionary expectations and ideology as the primary motivation of Soviet foreign policy. It became apparent to the Soviet regime in its early years—and even more so after World War II—that the proletariat of the West was showing no signs of the revolutionary potential that Lenin had ascribed to it. In response to this fact, Soviet policy was adapted to address the bourgeoisie of both the Western industrial societies and the developing world for the purpose of influencing governments to act in ways favorable to Soviet interests. Although revolutionary ideology is still part of the official rhetoric, and although it is bolstered by a bureaucratic apparatus that has a stake in it, it has been modified in such a way as to put off to the indefinite future the realization of apocalyptic goals. Peaceful coexistence, which to Lenin meant a breathing spell, has become a long-term political strategy of competition by means short of war.

While it is impossible to predict whether Soviet foreign policy will evolve in directions we would wish, it can be said that it has evolved more than is generally appreciated, largely as a result of Soviet efforts to adapt to changes in international politics, including options created by policies of the United States.

Coincident with this development—which has inclined Soviet policy toward favoring traditional balance-of-power maneuvers—has been a continuous movement away from the autarkic reliance on the Soviet economy promised by Stalin's commitment to "Socialism in One Country." In fact, the Soviet Union has become ever more deeply involved in the world economy, and the proportion of its gross national product derived from foreign trade has risen steadily.

While it does not seem likely that these trends will be reversed, it is clearly too much to say that they will necessarily lead to Soviet acceptance of the international system to the extent of being willing to act as a partner in preserving the system's stability. The Soviet Union has an interest in maintaining the status quo in Eastern Europe, but not elsewhere. A broader commitment would require a much greater departure from its residual faith that capitalist systems contain the seeds of their own destruction than any signs now indicate is likely.

Two: Are Soviet leaders, then, guided by the ideology of Marxism-Leninism?

If you were to ask them that question, their answer would be "Of course." None of them would say otherwise, and they seek sanction for every action, speech, article, or book by quoting from the storehouse of the writings of Marx, Engels, and, especially, Lenin.

Marxist-Leninist ideology, of course, is based on the prediction that capitalist systems are doomed to decay and collapse, that they will seek to stave off this outcome by imperialist aggression, but that, in the end, "socialism" as the Soviet Union defines it will prove more effective and will emerge as the universal form of social organization. In practice, Soviet theoreticians have had to take into account the fact that these predictions from the nineteenth and early twentieth centuries have not received much confirmation. The lesson has not been lost on Soviet theoreticians, who have reinterpreted some parts of the ideology while clinging to others, seeking legitimacy in hoped-for improvements in performance, or what Khrushchev called "goulash communism." In truth, there is as much variance in the Soviet interpretation of Marxism-Leninism today as there is in American Protestantism.

To say that Soviet political figures and writers claim consistency with Marxism-Leninism is not to say that their actions are derived from ideology. Certainly the historical analysis of capitalism influences the way the older Soviet political elites interpret events, but the sacred texts offer less and less guidance for making the practical decisions demanded by the complex society that the Soviet Union has become. With rare exceptions, even those youths who aspire to become members of the Soviet establishment master their catechism with cynicism (the sound of shuffling feet during lectures on "diamat"—dialectical materialism—is reminiscent of the noise during lectures for GIs on social hygiene), suggesting that when they take the levers of power into their hands, the ideas that will shape their thoughts and guide their actions will bear only the slightest resemblance to the ideas that inspired the revolution.

Three: Is the Soviet Union nevertheless inherently *expansionist?*

Some have argued that the answer to this question is yes. Should that be true, it would follow that in order to move Soviet behavior in the direction of greater restraint and responsibility it would be necessary to change the Soviet system in fundamental ways and that this should be the primary objective of American policy. Those who take this position claim that it is only by external aggrandizement that the Soviet leadership can cement its power, claim legitimacy, and validate its view of history. Some even argue that there is a parallel between the Soviet Union and Nazi Germany and that just as appeasement served to whet the Nazis' appetite, any accommodation with the Soviet Union can "only lead to disaster."

The study of Soviet behavior, however, suggests that Soviet actions are more consistently explained by reference to the pursuit of nation-state interests than by some inner compulsion related to the structure of the system. The leadership is strengthened by successes and weakened by failures, as is the case in any country, but there is no sign that Soviet adventures abroad have resulted in increased popular support. On the contrary, foreign adventures, whether in Hungary or Afghanistan, are regarded uneasily by Soviet citizens.

There is an expansive tendency in the Soviet Union's behavior, but it is impelled, not by the nature of the system, but by the sense that the country has grown into a great power. Moreover, it has been activated by opportunities that the Soviet Union itself has not created, and it has been guided by a careful calculus of risks and gains as well as by a capacity for prudence. This was illustrated most recently by the absence of an immediate Soviet reaction to the attacks on Syria during the Israeli invasion of Lebanon.

The Nazi parallel is particularly misleading. Unlike the Nazis, Soviet leaders do not seek war. No one doubts that who has seen firsthand how fresh are the memories of the destruction and loss of life in World War II, or how universal is the appreciation of the consequences of nuclear war (much more universal than is the case in the United States). Soviet leaders have accepted and accommodated themselves to the practical constraints on their expansionist tendencies. They may hope that the future will bring more favorable opportunities, but faith in their historical inevitability has become ritualistic, and is advanced on national holidays with diminishing conviction.

Four: Even if the Soviet Union is not inherently expansionist, is it possible for us to maintain peaceful relations with it so long as it seeks to maximize its power and influence?

We have to accept the fact that the Soviet-American relationship is fundamentally competitive and is likely to remain so for the foreseeable future. What we must decide is whether it is in our interest to compete at a high level of confrontation or whether it is more sensible to manage the competition at lower levels of tension. If we seek to force the pace of military competition and to maximize pressure on the Soviet Union by cutting back diplomatic contacts, trade, and all forms of co-operation, the effect will be to increase the level of conflict and the risk of war and to push both societies toward greater, and destructive, militarization.

It is sometimes said in this country that the so-called détente of the early 1970s was a failure and a deception, and that it proved that the effort to moderate relations is bound not to work, leaving us at a disadvantage. But the principal reason why détente was not successful was that neither side fulfilled the two main requirements for reducing tensions. Those requirements are the management of the nuclear competition at lower and more stable levels and the codification of the terms of political competition in the Third World. On each side there were impediments to exercising the restraint that is essential to reducing the risk of war.

On the Soviet side, the main impediments to the stabilization of the nuclear competition appeared to stem from the influence of the military bureaucracy in Soviet politics; tendencies toward overinsurance in military matters; an inclination to think in prenuclear terms; a fear of the United States advantage in advanced military technology; a fear of appearing weak and therefore vulnerable to American pressure; and a mistaken belief that a strengthened military posture would make the United States more pliant in negotiations. In the Third World, the main impediment to restraint was the Soviet Union's commitment to expand its influence wherever it could do so at acceptable costs and risks, which it rationalized as support for what it chose to call national liberation movements. The increase in Soviet logistical capabilities and conventional weapons and forces made such interventions more tempting.

On the American side, the impediments to the stabilization of the nuclear competition included a lack of rationality in defense policymaking, as a result of which decisions were dictated by parochial economic and service interests; a residual commitment to superiority rather than parity as the basis for national security; a post-Vietnam fear of appearing to be weak; and a mistaken belief that a strengthened military posture would make the Soviet Union more pliant in negotiations. Moreover, a resurgence of nationalism, a universal phenomenon throughout the industrialized world, made any form of accommodation with the Soviet Union politically difficult. The basic impediments to stabilizing the United States–Soviet competition in the Third World were America's inexperience in international affairs, its parochialism, and its ignorance of the areas involved. That led the United States to regard countries of the Third World as abstract counters in the East–West competition, driving all radical movements into the Soviet camp, and to rely primarily on military instrumentalities for dealing with them.

In addition, there have been external impediments to a regulation of the competition. This period of international politics has been characterized by an extraordinary turbulence involving dramatic transformations in the industrialized nations, postdecolonization travails in the developing ones, and anarchy in the international system. Under the best of circumstances, it would have been remarkable if Soviet-American relations had not become roiled.

Five: Has Soviet foreign policy, emboldened by what some analysts see as military supremacy, become more aggressive in the years since détente?

There is a two-part answer to the military question. Certainly the improvements in the Soviet Union's conventional capabilities, the increase in the firepower and mobility of its forces, and its greater logistical capabilities—demonstrated in the impressive airlift of matériel to Ethiopia—have made it possible to intervene where it might not have been able to a decade ago. But despite the expanded Soviet strategic nuclear arsenal, it is wrong to speak of supremacy, and there are no grounds for believing that the strategic balance influenced the Soviet decisions to act as it did in Angola, Ethiopia, or Afghanistan.

The lack of restraint shown by the Soviet Union in exacerbating local conflicts cannot be justified, but its interventions have represented a continuation of its long-standing policy of seeking to exploit opportunities, whatever their cause. The 1975 intervention in Angola, for example, was a response to the collapse of the Portuguese position in Africa. (The Soviet Union was able to respond to that collapse more effectively than was the United States, tied as we were to our Portuguese ally and restrained as we were by the post-Vietnam inhibitions against foreign interventions.) In Ethiopia, it was Chairman Mengistu Haile-Mariam's alienation from the United States and his turning to the Soviet Union for support that created the Soviet opportunity, and there, as in Angola, the messianic mission of Fidel Castro gave the Soviet Union the benefit of Cuban soldiers. (In contrast, the Soviet invasion of Afghanistan was a response, not to an opportunity, but to a perceived threat; it can best be understood as a gross political and military miscalculation, reflecting Soviet paranoia about the security of its borders.)

Of course, even though these Soviet interventions were responses to opportunities rather than manifestations of a more aggressive policy, they are still a matter for concern. But it lies within our power to reduce such opportunities by understanding better what local factors generate upheavals and conflicts, and by responding to them more appropriately ourselves.

Six: Does the Soviet Union's military buildup indicate that it has accepted the risks of nuclear war?

The great increase in its conventional forces does raise the possibility that the Soviet Union is prepared to intervene in behalf of its newly acquired global interests. And in its production and deployment of nuclear weapons like the SS-18, an intercontinental missile capable of delivering ten warheads of 500 kilotons each with great accuracy, and the SS-20, an intermediate-range missile targeted on Europe and the Far East, it has not shown reasonable restraint and has aroused concerns in the West that have had the effect of reducing its own security. (In this respect, neither Soviet nor American defense policies have been marked by much rationality or foresight.) But it strains any plausible scenario to see Soviet strategic forces as capable of anything other than preventing a military attack or political intimidation.

Monetary measures of the Soviet Union's military effort have sometimes been used to show that its programs are alarmingly larger than ours, but these are not a reliable basis for comparison. The statistics cited in such comparisons are questionable: they depend on estimates of what it would cost us to produce Soviet weapons using American labor costs, and also on calculations of dollar-ruble equivalencies; they do not take into account the actual Soviet production costs; and even if it is argued that the percentage of the Soviet gross national product devoted to military programs is twice that of the United States, it must be borne in mind that the Soviet GNP is half our own. Moreover, the CIA has recently revised downward its estimates of Soviet military expenditures; those estimates now suggest that after annual increases of about 4 percent a year beginning in the early 1960s, the rate of increase began to level off in the mid-1970s, once the Soviet Union reached parity with the United States.

Judgments about parity are, of course, inexact, seeking as they do to compare quite different force structures (the Soviet Union has three-quarters of its strategic force in land-based intercontinental missiles, compared with only one-third of ours; the rest is in bombers and submarines). The Soviet Union fears that America's superior industrial technology may give us an edge in the future, and it continues to develop new weapons, duplicating our innovations when it can and compensating for others simply by doing more of what it can do. By any measure, however, it is apparent that, given the destructiveness of nuclear weapons, neither side has or can hope to have a usable military superiority over the other. But neither country has had the self-confidence to regard a secure retaliatory force as sufficient.

It has been said that Soviet military writings imply that Soviet leaders believe they can fight and win a nuclear war, but that argument reflects a superficial reading of the literature. Soviet military doctrine has evolved considerably since the time of Stalin, when nuclear weapons were discussed in pre-nuclear age terms, and the authoritative statements of Yuri Andropov, Konstantin Chernenko, Minister of Defense Dmitri Ustinov, and Chief of the General Staff Nikolai Ogarkov have shown unequivocal awareness that nuclear war would be a danger to the security of their country.

Seven: Does it follow, then, that the Soviet Union is prepared to engage seriously in arms control negotiations?

Arms control negotiations about nuclear weapons seemed a radical idea to the Russians when they were first proposed in the Baruch plan in 1946. In the early years of the Strategic Arms Limitation Treaty negotiations, which began in November 1969, the Russians were obviously reluctant to consider entrusting their security to such arrangements—perhaps because they didn't feel strong enough, or their military was resistant, or they did not trust us any more than we trusted them. Most of the SALT proposals were advanced by the American negotiators, and many of the Soviet proposals (for nonaggression agreements, a ban on first use of nuclear weapons, and international conferences to discuss disarmament) had an agitprop character. Although the Soviet Union accepted the American proposal for strategic arms limitation talks, it did not appear to have accepted the fundamental SALT concepts: parity, mutual deterrence, and strategic stability.

But the situation has changed in two respects. We have changed. Despite our formal acceptance of deterrence as a guiding principle, we have moved toward developing war-fighting capabilities. Our defense plans are now based on the requirement that we be able to prevail in a prolonged nuclear conflict. In this respect, both the declaratory and the actual policies of the two countries have moved closer.

The Soviet Union has also changed: it became more than a passive partner in the negotiations. In the SALT II talks, it offered considerably more major concessions than did the United States; it was also prepared to agree that no new land-based intercontinental missiles be allowed, had we been willing to agree to what had originally been an American proposal. The Russians were stubborn bargainers, but they manifested a serious interest in limiting the nuclear competition.

Eight: What does this say about the belief that the United States must develop "positions of strength" in order to make the Soviet Union negotiate in good faith or accept our deterrent as credible?

To the Soviet Union, it appears that a military balance now exists and that American efforts to secure "positions of strength" mask attempts to achieve superiority. The Soviet reaction will be contrary to what is expected. Instead of feeling pressured to make concessions at the negotiating table, the Soviet Union will match every new American program with one of its own (as it has done in the past; for example, when we introduced multiple-warhead systems). It is for this reason that the search for such "positions of strength" will lead to an upward spiral in the nuclear military competition, involving weapons that are less stable (the MX missile and the proposed space-based defense system) and less verifiable (cruise missiles) than those now in existence, with the consequence that it will be increasingly difficult to achieve any agreement.

Nine: Is the Soviet system capable of change?

It is here that we come to a question that is absolutely fundamental to the way we think about the Soviet Union, and it is here that our stereotypes are most strikingly out of date. Since the Revolution, the Soviet Union has evolved from a predominantly peasant society to one that is largely urban and industrializing. Although the process of industrialization has moved forward unevenly, and although large parts of the country do not seem to have changed in the past 100 years, the spread of education and the growth of cadres of specialists have made for a much more complex society, in which controls have been increasingly internalized and "privatization" stubbornly protects pockets of autonomy from intrusion by the central authorities. Leaving the intellectuals aside, for most people the system works, since they compare their living standards not with those of other countries but with their own in the past.

The engine of change is the emergence of new generations, with new expectations and experiences, and a vast generational shift is already in progress. Although it is not yet reflected in the composition of the top party leadership, it is to be seen at lower levels of the party, in the military, and in the various bureaucracies. The younger elite are well educated and competent. Not liberals in a Western sense, their thinking is nevertheless far more sophisticated than that of high-level party members, which has been characterized by parochial fundamentalism. They are free of the formative influences of the Revolution and the Stalinist terror and are relatively knowl-

edgeable about the outside world and prepared to learn from it.

The prevailing Western images of the Soviet elite, based on monolithic totalitarian models, tend to stereotype Soviet officialdom, leading some observers to conclude that the system is brittle and cannot change without risk of collapse. This obscures the spectrum of views to be found even within the party establishment, which encompasses not only those who are careerists and bureaucrats supreme but also those who might be called "within-system critics," those who, within the bounds of loyalty to the system, possess and sometimes express unorthodox views about modernization. Because the changes they favor may provoke resistance, in the short run their activities may reinforce or even increase the authority of the political police. Whether in the long run such changes will moderate the repressiveness of the Soviet system may depend in part on the international climate.

In the end, one must wonder if the system will be able to cope with its enormous problems. That is a question no one can answer, not even the Soviet leadership. The decline in the country's growth rates is symptomatic of the contradiction between the rigidities of its political structure and the requirements of advanced industrialization. No one was more severe in cataloguing the deficiencies of the Soviet system than Yuri Andropov. The new leadership is also aware of the problems it faces. But it must deal with a profoundly conservative society, changing but resistant to change, fearful, above all, of the effects of reform on the party's control.

How these contending forces will resolve their differences is the most intriguing question of all, and the answer, when it becomes clear, will affect our thinking about our future relations with the Soviet Union.

There are, of course, other questions that we might wish to ask, but the issues we have already touched on point toward something that should be taken into account far more than has been the case: the factor of change. If instead of viewing the Soviet Union as a static system we view it as one in the midst of a historical transformation, then the starting point for thinking through our own policies should be to ask ourselves how they are likely to affect the processes of change in the Soviet system, Soviet conduct in the world, and opportunities for peaceful relations between the two countries.

Our capacity to influence the nature of change in the Soviet Union is limited. At the very least, however, we should exercise care lest our actions and words impair the prospects for changes we would like to see. It should be clear from past experience that if we are perceived to be bellicose, or if we declare our intent to undermine the Soviet order, we strengthen the backward elements in the Soviet political system.

It follows that our long-term policy should have an evolutionary purpose: it should be designed to encourage future generations of Soviet leaders to see that acting with restraint and enlarging the area of genuine cooperation between the United States and the Soviet Union serve their own self-interest. The main objective of our policy should therefore be to respond to the Soviet challenge in ways that will protect our security, our interests, and our values, rather than to try to force changes in the Soviet Union or to bring about changes in its foreign policy indirectly by seeking to undermine the Soviet system.

This does not mean that we are not interested in what happens inside the Soviet Union, nor that we should put aside our humanitarian concern about its repressive practices. None of us can remain unmoved by the cruelty with which the Soviet police apparatus deals with dissidents or with those who wish to emigrate. But we should have learned from our recent experience that it is counterproductive for our government to make the human rights issue an instrument in a political offensive aganist the Soviet Union and to engage the prestige of the Soviet leadership by frontal, public ultimatums, as it did with the Jackson-Vanik amendment and in the tragic cases of Andrei Sakharov and Anatoly Shcharansky. We should also remember that although decreased international tension may in the short run inspire campaigns of ideological vigilance designed to control the spread of bourgeois ideas within the Soviet Union, increased levels of international tension reduce the restraints on the Soviet police apparatus and encourage greater pressures for retrogressive movement toward neo-Stalinism.

Perhaps the best that can be hoped for in our relations with the Soviet Union, in the aftermath of the transition to the Chernenko leadership, is a Cold Truce, an improvement in the climate of confrontation that is now patently leading toward greater military competition and a greater risk of misperception and miscalculation in responses to local crises. Beyond the immediate period, we should recognize that the only sensible alternative to a relationship based on confrontation is one that seeks a modus vivendi, in order to manage the competition between us at a less destructive level of tension.

The most important aspect of such a policy is the military competition. Clearly, a military balance is required, but what kind, and at what level? If our political leaders and the public really accept the proposition that our security is better safeguarded by a stable nuclear balance than by unregulated competition, it follows that we should accept stability, parity, and mutual deterrence. We pay lip service to these concepts but have not been guided by them in practice. Their genuine acceptance would make possible serious negotiations that would take into account legitimate Soviet security concerns, as well as our own. Neither in the negotiations on strategic systems nor in those on theater nuclear weapons in Europe are the positions of the two sides so far apart that they cannot be bridged. That is also true of the negotiations on treaties for a comprehensive test ban and on the use of chemical weapons, among others. Meanwhile, it does not make sense for us to introduce systems that are destabilizing, systems that will make us more trigger sensitive. There also must be a balance in conventional weapons. There, too, our long-term objective should be to seek a balance at a moderate level through negotiations, on the basis of the same kind of mutual deterrence that should guide our nuclear weapons policy.

In the political competition between the United States and the Soviet Union, containment by military force is clearly an inadequate response. There may be occasions when we will need sufficient forces on the ground to prevent Soviet intervention, but this is only a negative capability. More important, we must learn to respond to the causes of the strains and instabilities that create opportunities for exploitation by the Soviet Union.

For example, we have allowed our relations with our allies among the industrialized nations to become strained by economic tensions and by their growing lack of confidence in the sobriety and wisdom of our leadership. Yet it ought to be the very heart of our policy to maintain the closest possible ties with them. In the Third World, we must show greater awareness of the sources of instability than we have so far. If we are prepared to deal with the causes of revolutionary change, to address the issues of health, food, literacy, and equity with more understanding, we will be able to respond to these problems before all hope of peaceful resolution is lost and the only solution becomes military arbitration between equally unsavory extremes.

In our relations with the Soviet Union we should rely on incentives as well as on constraints. This means that we must sustain a reasonable level of trade and exchanges and encourage limited measures of cooperation. Holding out the prospect of widening ties as the Soviet Union shows its readiness to act responsibly is a token of our hope that the relationship can move to a less dangerous stage. This, indeed, is the link to our longer-term policy. We cannot assume that Soviet behavior will evolve in this way, but we can let future generations of Soviet leaders know that if they do move in this direction we are prepared to accept this more productive relationship.

At the center of our thinking should always be the concern that the protection of our security and our values depends not only on the sensible management of relations with the Soviet Union but on the condition of the international system itself, on those fragile restraints on the behavior of nations that have been created so slowly and painfully over the years. It must be strengthened against the anarchy and chaos that now threaten it. To do this we must seek, not to preserve the status quo, but to codify processes of nonviolent change. We must work toward placing constraints on the use of force to produce or to prevent change, and we must be willing, ourselves, to live within these constraints.

One more thing needs to be said. Essential to a modus vivendi are diplomatic communications with the Soviet Union, firm but not bellicose, conducted with civility and common sense—recently so uncommon in American politics.

5.

The Mirror Image in Soviet-American Relations*

URIE BRONFENBRENNER

I should explain by way of introduction that I was in the Soviet Union during the summer of 1960, about a month after the U-2 incident. The primary purpose of my trip was to become acquainted with scientific developments in my field, which is social psychology. But in addition to visiting laboratories at universities and institutes, I wanted also to become acquainted with *living* social psychology—the Soviet people themselves. It was my good fortune to be able to speak Russian. I was traveling with a tourist visa on a new plan which permitted me to go about alone without a guide. Accordingly, after spending the first two or three days of my visit in a particular city at scientific centers, I would devote the remaining days to walking about the town and striking up conversations with people in public conveyances, parks, stores, restaurants, or just on the street. Since foreigners are a curiosity, and I was obviously a foreigner (though, I quickly learned, not obviously an American), people were eager to talk. But I also went out of my way to strike up conversations with people who weren't taking the initiative— with fellow passengers who were remaining silent, with strollers in the park, with children and old people. Or I would enter a restaurant deciding in advance to sit at the third table on the

* Excerpted from "The Mirror-Image in Soviet-American Relations: A Social Psychologist's Report," *Journal of Social Issues* 16, no. 3, pp. 45–56.

left with whoever should turn out to be there. (In Soviet restaurants it is not uncommon to share a table with strangers.)

These conversations convinced me that the great majority of Russians feel a genuine pride in the accomplishments of their system and a conviction that communism is the way of the future not only for themselves but for the rest of the world as well. For several reasons my Soviet journey was a deeply disturbing experience. But what frightened me was not so much the facts of Soviet reality as the discrepancy between the real and the perceived. At first I was troubled only by the strange irrationality of the Soviet view of the world—especially their gross distortion of American society and American foreign policy as I knew them to be. But then, gradually, there came an even more disquieting awareness—an awareness which I resisted and still resist. Slowly and painfully, it forced itself upon me that *the Russian's distorted picture of us was curiously similar to our view of them—a mirror image.* But of course our image was real. Or could it be that our views too were distorted and irrational—a mirror image in a twisted glass?

It was—and is—a frightening prospect. For if such reciprocal distortion exists, it is a psychological phenomenon without parallel in the gravity of its consequences. For this reason, the possibility deserves serious consideration.

The Mirror Image Magnified

Let us then briefly examine the common features in the American and Soviet view of each other's societies. For the Russian's image I drew mainly, not on official government pronouncements, but on what was said to me by Soviet citizens in the course of our conversations. Five major themes stand out.

1. THEY ARE THE AGGRESSORS

The American view: Russia is the warmonger bent on imposing its system on the rest of the world. Witness Czechoslovakia,

Berlin, Hungary, and now Cuba and the Congo. The Soviet Union consistently blocks Western proposals for disarmament by refusing necessary inspection controls.

The Soviet view: America is the warmonger bent on imposing its power on the rest of the world and on the Soviet Union itself. Witness American intervention in 1918; Western encirclement after World War II with American troops and bases on every border of the USSR (West Germany, Norway, Turkey, Korea, Japan); intransigence over proposals to make Berlin a free city; intervention in Korea, Taiwan, Lebanon, Guatemala, Cuba. America has repeatedly rejected Soviet disarmament proposals while demanding the right to inspect within Soviet territory—finally attempting to take the right by force through deep penetration of Soviet airspace.

2. THEIR GOVERNMENT EXPLOITS AND DELUDES THE PEOPLE

The American view: Convinced communists, who form but a small proportion of Russia's population, control the government and exploit the society and its resources in their own interest. To justify their power and expansionist policies they have to perpetuate a war atmosphere and a fear of Western aggression. Russian elections are a travesty, since only one party appears on the ballot. The Russian people are kept from knowing the truth through a controlled radio and press, and conformity is insured through stringent economic and political sanctions against deviant individuals or groups.

The Soviet view: A capitalistic-militaristic clique controls the American government, the nation's economic resources, and its media of communication. The group exploits the society and its resources. It is in their economic and political interest to maintain a war atmosphere and engage in militaristic expansion. Voting in America is a farce, since candidates for both parties are selected by the same powerful interests leaving nothing to choose between. The American people are kept from knowing the truth through a controlled radio and press and through economic and political sanctions against liberal elements.

3. The Mass of Their People are not Really Sympathetic to the Regime

The American view: In spite of the propaganda, the Soviet people are not really behind their government. Their praise of the government and the party is largely perfunctory, a necessary concession for getting along. They do not trust their own sources of information and have learned to read between the lines. Most of them would prefer to live under our system of government if they only could.

The Soviet view: Unlike their government, the bulk of the American people want peace. Thus, the majority disapproved of American aggression in Korea, the support of Chiang Kai-shek, and above all, of the sending of U-2. But of course they could do nothing, since their welfare is completely under the control of the ruling financier-militaristic clique. If the American people were allowed to become acquainted with communism as it exists in the USSR, they would unquestionably choose it as their form of government. ("You Americans are such a nice people; it is a pity you have such a terrible government.")

4. They Cannot be Trusted

The American view: The Soviets do not keep promises and they do not mean what they say. Thus, while they claim to have discontinued all nuclear testing, they are probably carrying out secret underground explosions in order to gain an advantage over us. Their talk of peace is but a propaganda maneuver. Everything they do is to be viewed with suspicion, since it is all part of a single coordinated scheme to further aggressive communist aims.

The Soviet view: The Americans do not keep promises and they do not mean what they say. Thus, they insist on inspection only so that they can look at Soviet defenses; they have no real intention of disarming. Everything the Americans do is to be viewed with suspicion (e.g., they take advantage of Soviet hospitality by sending in spies as tourists).

5. THEIR POLICY VERGES ON MADNESS

The American view: Soviet demands on such crucial problems as disarmament, Berlin, and unification are completely unrealistic. Disarmament without adequate inspection is meaningless; a "free Berlin" would be equivalent to a Soviet Berlin; and a united Germany without free elections is an impossibility. In pursuit of their irresponsible policies the Soviets do not hesitate to run the risk of war itself. Thus, it is only due to the restraint and coordinated action of the Western alliance that Soviet provocations over Berlin did not precipitate World War III.

The Soviet view: The American position on such crucial problems as disarmament, East Germany, and China is completely unrealistic. They demand to know our secrets before they disarm; in Germany they insist on a policy which risks the resurgence of a fascist Reich; and as for China, they try to act as if it did not exist while at the same time supporting an aggressive puppet regime just off the Chinese mainland. And, in pursuit of their irresponsible policies, the Americans do not hesitate to run the risk of war itself. Were it not for Soviet prudence and restraint, the sending of a U-2 deep into Russian territory could easily have precipitated World War III.

It is easy to recognize the gross distortions in the Soviet views summarized above. But is our own outlook completely realistic? Are we correct, for example, in thinking that the mass of the Soviet people would really prefer our way of life and are unenthusiastic about their own? Certainly the tone and tenor of my conversations with Soviet citizens hardly support this belief.

But, you may ask, why is it that other Western observers do not report the enthusiasm and commitment which I encountered?

I asked this very question of newspapermen and embassy officials in Moscow. Their answers were revealing. Thus one reporter replied somewhat dryly, "Sure, I know, but when a communist acts like a communist, it isn't news. If I want to be sure that it will be printed back home, I have to write about what's wrong with the system, not its successes." Others voiced an opinion expressed most clearly by representatives at our embassy. When I reported to them the gist of my Soviet conversations, they were grateful but skeptical: "Professor, you underestimate the effect of the police state. When these people talk to a stranger, especially an American, they *have* to say the right thing."

The argument is persuasive, and comforting to hear. But perhaps these very features should arouse our critical judgment. Indeed, it is instructive to view this argument against the background of its predecessor voiced by the newspaperman. To put it bluntly, what he was saying was that he could be sure of getting published only the material that the *American people wanted to hear*. But notice that the second argument also fulfills this objective, and it does so in a much more satisfactory and sophisticated way. The realization that "Soviet citizens *have* to say the right thing" enables the Western observer not only to discount most of what he hears but even to interpret it as evidence in direct support of the West's accepted picture of the Soviet Union as a police state.

It should be clear that I am in no sense here suggesting that Western reporters and embassy officials deliberately misrepresent what they know to be the facts. Rather, I am calling attention to the operation, in a specific and critical context, of a phenomenon well known to psychologists—the tendency to assimilate new perceptions to old, and unconsciously to distort what one sees in such a way as to minimize a clash with previous expectations. In recent years, a number of leading social psychologists, notably Heider (1958), Festinger (1957), and Osgood (1960), have emphasized that this "strain toward consistency" is especially powerful in the sphere of social relations—that is, in our perceptions of the motives, attitudes, and actions of other persons or groups. Specifically, we strive to keep our views of other human beings compatible with each other. In the face of complex social reality, such consistency is typically accomplished by obliterating distinctions and organizing the world in terms of artificially simplified frames of reference. One of the simplest of these, and hence one of the most inviting, is the dichotomy of good and bad. Hence we often perceive others, be they individuals, groups, or even whole societies, as simply "good" or "bad." Once this fateful decision is made, the rest is easy, for the "good" person or group can have only desirable social characteristics and the "bad" can have only reprehensible traits. And once such evaluative stability of social perception is established, it is extremely difficult to alter. Contradictory stimuli arouse only anxiety and resistance. When confronted with a desirable characteristic of something already known to be "bad," the observer will either just not "see" it, or will reorganize his perception of it so that it can be perceived as "bad." Finally, this tendency to regress to simple categories of perception is especially strong under conditions of emotional stress and external threat. Witness our readiness in times of war to exalt the virtues of our own side and to see the enemy as thoroughly evil.

Still one other social-psychological phenomenon has direct relevance for the present discussion. I refer to a process demonstrated most dramatically and comprehensively in the experiments of Solomon Asch (1956), and known thereby as the "Asch phenomenon." In these experiments, the subject finds himself in a group of six or eight of his peers, all of whom are asked to make comparative judgments of certain stimuli presented to them; for example, identifying the longer of two lines. At first the task seems simple enough; the subject hears others make their judgments and then makes his own. In the beginning he is usually in agreement, but then gradually he notices that more and more often his judgments differ from those of the rest of the group. Actually, the experiment is rigged. All the other group members have been instructed to give false responses on a predetermined schedule. In any event, the effect on our subject is dramatic. At first he is puzzled, then upset. Soon he begins to have serious doubts about his own judgment, and in an appreciable number of cases, he begins to "see" the stimuli as they are described by his fellows.

What I am suggesting, of course, is that the Asch phenomenon operates even more forcefully outside the laboratory where the game of social perception is being played for keeps. *Specifically, I am proposing that the mechanisms here described contribute substantially to producing and maintaining serious distortions in the reciprocal images of the Soviet Union and the United States.*

My suggestion springs from more than abstract theoretical inference. I call attention to the possible operation of the Asch phenomenon in the Soviet-American context for a very concrete reason: I had the distressing experience of being its victim. While in the Soviet Union I deliberately sought to minimize association with other westerners and to spend as much time as I could with Soviet citizens. This was not easy to do. It was no pleasant experience to hear one's own country severely criticized and to be constantly outdebated in the bargain. I looked forward to the next chance meeting with a fellow westerner so that I could get much-needed moral support and enjoy an evening's invective at the expense of Intourist and the "worker's paradise." But though I occasionally yielded to temptation, for the most part I kept true to my resolve and spent many hours in a completely Soviet environment. It was difficult but interesting. I liked many of the people I met. Some of them apparently liked me. Though mistaken, they were obviously sincere. They wanted me to agree with them. The days went on, and strange things began to happen. I remember picking up a Soviet newspaper which featured an account of American activities in the Near East. "Oh, what are they doing now!" I asked myself, and stopped short; for I had thought in terms of "they," and it was my own country. Or I would become aware that I had been nodding to the points being made by my Soviet companion where before I had always taken issue. In short, when all around me saw the world in one way, I too found myself wanting to believe and belong.

And once I crossed the Soviet border on my way home, the process began to reverse itself. The more I talked with fellow westerners, especially fellow Americans, the more I began to doubt the validity of my original impressions. "What would you expect them to say to an American?" my friends would ask. "How do you know that the person talking to you was not a trained agitator?" "Did you ever catch sight of them following you?" I never did. Perhaps I was naive. But then, recently I reread a letter written to a friend during the last week of my stay. "I feel it is important," it begins, "to try to write to you in detail while I am still in it, for just as I could never have conceived of what I am now experiencing, so, I suspect,

it will seem unreal and intangible once I am back in the West."
The rest of the letter, and others like it, contain the record of
the experiences reported in this account.

In sum, I take my stand on the view that there *is* a mirror
image in Soviet and American perceptions of each other and
that this image represents serious distortions by *both* parties of
realities on either side.

The Mirror Image Projected

And if so, what then? Do not distortions have adaptive
functions? Especially in war is it not psychologically necessary
to see the enemy as thoroughly evil and to enhance one's self-
image? And are we not engaged in a war, albeit a cold war,
with the Soviet Union?

But is not our hope to bring an end to the cold war and,
above all, to avoid the holocaust of a hot one? And herein lies
the terrible danger of the distorted mirror image, for *it is
characteristic of such images that they are self-confirming;* that
is, each party, often against its own wishes, is increasingly driven
to behave in a manner which fulfills the expectations of the
other. As revealed in social-psychological studies, the mechanism
is a simple one: if A expects B to be friendly and acts accordingly,
B responds with friendly advances; these in turn evoke additional
positive actions from A, and thus a benign circle is set in
motion. Conversely, where A's anticipations of B are unfavorable, it is the vicious circle which develops at an accelerating
pace. And as tensions rise, perceptions become more primitive
and still further removed from reality. Seen from this perspective,
the primary danger of the Soviet-American mirror image is that
it impels each nation to act in a manner which confirms and
enhances the fear of the other to the point that even deliberate
efforts to reverse the process are reinterpreted as evidences of
confirmation.

Manifestations of this mechanism in Soviet-American relations are not difficult to find. A case in point is our policy of
restricting the travel of Soviet nationals in the United States by
designating as "closed areas" localities that correspond as closely

as possible to those initially selected by Soviet authorities as "off limits" to Americans in the USSR. As was brought home to me in conversations with Soviet scientists who had visited the United States, one of the effects of this policy is to neutralize substantially any favorable impressions the visitor might otherwise get of American freedoms.

To take another example in a more consequential area: in a recent issue of *Atlantic Monthly* (August 1960), Dr. Hans Bethe, an American physicist who participated in negotiations at the Geneva Conference on nuclear testing, reports that our tendency to expect trickery from the Soviets led us into spending considerable time and energy to discover scientific loopholes in their proposals which could have permitted them to continue nuclear tests undetected. As a result, our scientists did succeed in finding a theoretical basis for questioning the effectiveness of the Soviet plan. It seems that if the Soviets could dig a hole big enough, they could detonate underground explosions without being detected. Says Dr. Bethe:

> I had the doubtful honor of presenting the theory of the big hole to the Russians in Geneva in November 1959. I felt deeply embarrassed in so doing, because it implied that we considered the Russians capable of cheating on a massive scale. I think they would have been quite justified if they had considered this an insult and walked out of the negotiations in disgust.
>
> The Russians seemed stunned by the theory of the big hole. In private, they took Americans to task for having spent the last year inventing methods to cheat on a nuclear test cessation agreement. Officially, they spent considerable effort in trying to disprove the theory of the big hole. This is not the reaction of a country that is bent on cheating.

But the most frightful potential consequence of the mirror image lies in the possibility that it may confirm itself out of existence. For if it is possible for either side to interpret concessions as signs of treachery, it should not be difficult to recognize an off-course satellite as a missile on its way. After all, we, or they, would be expecting it.

But it is only in the final catastrophe that the mirror image is impartial in its effects. Short of doomsday, we have even more to lose from the accelerating vicious circle than do the Soviets. Internally, the communist system can justify itself to the Soviet people far more easily in the face of external threat than in times of peace. And in the international arena, the more the United States becomes committed to massive retaliation and preventive intervention abroad, the more difficult it becomes for uncommitted or even friendly nations to perceive a real difference in the foreign policies of East and West.

Breaking the Mirror Image

How can we avoid such awesome consequences? One step seems clearly indicated: we must do everything we can to break down the psychological barrier that prevents both us and the Russians from seeing each other and ourselves as we really are. If we can succeed in dispelling the Soviet Union's bogeyman picture of America, we stand to gain, for to the same degree that militant communism thrives in a context of external threat, it is weakened as this threat is reduced. And as the raison d'être for sacrifice, surveillance, and submission disappears there arises opportunity for the expression of such potential for liberalization as may still exist in Russian society.

6.

Empathizing with the Soviet Government*

RALPH K. WHITE

For anyone caught in a conflict, a resolution of that conflict begins with an attempt to understand how the conflict looks from the other fellow's point of view. In our case the "other fellows" who matter most are the men who govern the USSR, and our first task must be an attempt to empathize realistically with them.

Two words in that statement, "empathize" and "govern," call for definition and some discussion.

A sharp distinction is made here between empathy and sympathy. Although the two words are often used almost interchangeably, "empathy" will be defined as a realistic *understanding* of the thoughts and feelings of others, while "sympathy" will be defined in accordance with its Greek derivation, as *feeling with* others—being happy because they are or unhappy because they are—which often implies doing what one can to help them. Empathy is cognitive, in the language of psychology; sympathy is affective.

While the two processes often occur together and are often related as cause and effect, each facilitating the other, the distinction between them is important, and it is especially important

* Excerpted from *Fearful Warriors: A Psychological Profile of U. S.-Soviet Relations* (New York: The Free Press, 1984). Reprinted with permission of The Free Press, a Division of Macmillan, Inc. Copyright © 1984 by The Free Press. A somewhat modified form of an article published under the title "Empathizing with the Rulers of the USSR" in *Political Psychology* 4 no. 1 (1983).

when the "others" are an opposing group in an acute conflict situation. It is extremely difficult if not impossible to "feel with" such an opponent, chiefly because its hostility to one's own group is so genuine and often so genuinely dangerous. A plea for warmhearted sympathy with the men in the Kremlin would be psychologically naive. We could not achieve it even if we tried, and there is no need to try. A plea for realistic empathy with them, though, is not naive. It is vital. If we do not clearly recognize their hostility to us, we will not be tough in the ways we should be tough, and if we do not clearly recognize the ways in which they are human beings like us, with thoughts and feelings resembling ours, we will not be reasonable and cooperative in the ways we must be in order to survive.

The word "govern" also calls for discussion. Governing in the Soviet Union is not the same as in the United States. It is far closer to total control. As most of us see the Soviet system (with good reason), it is as inefficient economically as it is undemocratic politically. It is still essentially totalitarian, as it was in the days of Stalin's one-man rule and his mammoth Gulag Archipelago, though without his special kind of sadism, and now oligarchic rather than autocratic. Those who govern are still grimly determined to cling to the essentials of their own power both in the USSR and in the outlying but adjacent areas (Eastern Europe, Afghanistan, Mongolia) that they now control. In this respect the term "mirror image," made familiar by Urie Bronfenbrenner (1961; cf. White, 1965; Frank, 1982, pp. 115–36), breaks down. There are significant psychological differences between them and our own elected leaders, along with many similarities, and in our effort to see their humanity there is no need to lean over backward and ignore those differences. The real similarities, though, need to be understood too.

In any case, those who govern—not the general Soviet public— make the decisions on which war and peace may depend. If we want realistic ways to prevent war, they are the ones it is most urgent to understand.

Their Underlying Insecurity

The first and perhaps the most important thesis is that the Soviet decision makers are driven mainly by a deeply ingrained sense of insecurity in their foreign policies and defense policies. Their aggressive behavior, when they are aggressive, is more defensive than offensive in its underlying motivation. So is the steady military buildup that has been going on at least since 1963. Therefore, if we want peace, their insecurity—not a grim determination to conquer the world—is the most important obstacle that the West needs to understand and try to overcome.

The most accurate word here is insecure, not frightened. The Soviet decision makers are not shaking in their shoes. For one thing they are tough individuals, with more than a touch of machismo. (We Americans have more than a touch of it too.) For another, they have been impressed and reassured by the fact that the West has not attacked them since 1945, or used against them the immense nuclear superiority that it had for many years. And, in the third place, the armies and the weapons that they now possess have given the Soviets confidence in their ability to deter or, if necessary, to hold their own against any future aggressor.

Nevertheless, many kinds of evidence suggest that they have an underlying sense of anxiety which these sources of reassurance enable them to push into the back of their minds but which would quickly leap into the front of their minds if the sources of reassurance were not there. They feel an emotional *need* for the reassurance that their strength and that their control of contiguous territory give them.

One kind of evidence of this anxiety is the testimony of respected Western students of Soviet affairs, including many who have intimate firsthand knowledge of the USSR.

George Kennan, perhaps the best known of all Western experts on the USSR, says that he sees in the Kremlin "a group of troubled men . . . prisoners of certain ingrained peculiarities of the Russian statesmanship of past ages—the congenital sense of insecurity, the lack of inner self-confidence . . ." (1982, p. 153).

Robert C. Tucker, author of *The Soviet Political Mind:* "From the standpoint of the latter-day Stalinists . . . to imagine that it is possible to come to terms with the other side strategically, if only on the question of steps to survival, is to misunderstand the changeless nature of the enemy" (1971, p. 251).

Adam Ulam, author of *The Rivals:* "It was not until 1947 that the Soviets became convinced through a most amazing misunderstanding that the United States had an elaborate plan to undermine the Soviet empire" (1971, p. 99).

Robert Kaiser, in *Russia: The People and the Power:* "A siege mentality has infected the leaders of Soviet society since its birth in 1917" (1976, p. 500).

Craig Whitney, the *New York Times* bureau chief in Moscow in 1980, speaks of a general "sense of isolation and insecurity. . . . They have basic misperceptions about the West, and at times of crisis they tend to listen to fears and ideologies, not facts" (1980, pp. 91, 30).

Strobe Talbott, the editor and translator of *Khrushchev Remembers* and *Time's* diplomatic correspondent in Moscow, writing with his colleague Bruce Nelan: "What the United States sees—and seeks—as 'containment' of Soviet power, the Kremlin sees and fears as 'encirclement' by its enemies. That fear has driven Soviet foreign policy since 1917" (1980, p. 18).

Another body of evidence is provided by Russian history. For more than 1,000 years it has been largely a history of foreign invasions. In the midst of a vast plain, with no natural barriers to protect it such as we in America have had, Russia in Europe has repeatedly fallen prey to invaders. The Germans in the days of Alexander Nevsky; the Tartar conquest, which began in 1237 and effectively cut Russia off from European civilization for more than two centuries (Pares, 1947, pp. 7, 54–102); the Turks; the Poles (ibid., pp. 141, 165); the Swedes (ibid., pp. 189–97); the French under Napoleon; the British and French in the Crimea; the Germans in World War I, for Russia a disaster; and the Germans again, with results still more disastrous, in World War II (Halle, 1967, p. 14). Besides, although most Americans have forgotten it or never knew it, the United States and its allies had troops in Russia in 1918–20.

It has not by any means been wholly one-sided. Russia joined in the partitioning of Poland, and in the East occupied the relatively empty wastes of Siberia, comparable to our American West. It has also expanded elsewhere (the Caucasus, Central Asia), especially in the nineteenth century, when all the Great Powers were engaged in colonial competition and Britain's expansion far exceeded Russia's (Karpovich, 1951). Recently, of course, there has been the occupation of the Baltic states (again) and Eastern Europe, though there is a strong case for interpreting the occupation of Eastern Europe as primarily defensive in motivation after the extreme trauma of Hitler's invasion of the USSR. Nothing said here should be interpreted as indicating that either czarist Russia or communist Russia has been less aggressive or expansionist than most of the other Great Powers. On the other hand, the evidence has not shown either one to be more so. And, when Russia has expanded, it has probably always had defensive as well as purely power-oriented reasons for doing so. That is, in addition to their expectable human relishing of power and prestige for their own sake, the Russians have always had in the back of their minds the thought that in controlling borderlands they were establishing buffers between themselves and potentially aggressive enemies.

In any case, there is every reason to think that *their* conception of their past is overwhelmingly in terms of long-suffering, stubborn, and in the long run successful self-defense. From Tolstoy's description of the battle of Borodino against Napoleon's Grand Army to present-day novels and films of the defense of Stalingrad against Hitler's legions their memories cling, not to glorious conquests (of which there have been very few), but to the central theme of defending Mother Russia against foreign invaders. Like many other peoples, and perhaps more than most, the Russians have a strong tendency to focus selectively on the episodes in their history that cast no doubt on either their virtue or their virility. The homeland, the motherland, the *rodina,* is precious and must be defended. Ordinary Russians will look at you in amazement if you suggest that their role in a war could be anything but self-defense.

There is much other evidence in support of the thesis that Soviet motivation is basically more defensive than offensive. It includes for instance the evidence that in overall military strength the Soviet Union (with only about 6 percent of the world's population and not much more than half of America's GNP, leaving aside Western Europe's) is by no means clearly superior to the combination of its various present and potential enemies, including most of Western Europe, China, and perhaps Japan, as well as the United States; the old ideology of world revolution has faded in Soviet minds; the United States, like the USSR, has since 1950 done a number of things, mainly defensive in purpose, that could look offensive to its chief opponent; and, in accord with their own black-and-white picture (the reverse of ours), the Soviet rulers and public have tended to put the worst possible interpretation on our ambiguous actions.

There are three questions, though, that cannot be postponed, because, quite legitimately, they are uppermost in American minds today. They are: What about Afghanistan? What about the Soviet arms buildup since 1963, which to us seems far greater than the Soviet Union needs for self-defense? And what about the shooting down of the Korean airliner in 1983? Can "empathy" square any of these with the hypothesis of defensive motivation?

It can.

Afghanistan

The essential question about Afghanistan is not whether the armed intervention by the Soviet Union should be called aggression. It should. (The definition of aggression proposed here is the use or threat of force, in territory not clearly one's own, without clear evidence that a majority of the emotionally involved people in that territory want such intervention. By that definition the Soviet action was clearly an act of aggression.) The psychologically interesting question is whether the motivation behind the action, from the Soviet government's own point of view, was mainly defensive—as defensive as, for example, the motivation of the United States in Vietnam. (For a detailed discussion of America's motivation in Vietnam, see White [1970, pp. 182–237]. For a high-level Soviet view of the

USSR's motivation in Afghanistan, see Arbatov [1982, pp. 177–78]. The judgment of American observers appears later in this chapter.)

That is not a far-fetched comparison, and in our task of empathizing realistically with the Soviet rulers it may be useful, since we ourselves went through the Vietnam experience, believing—at least most of us did, at least at the beginning—that our own motives were strictly defensive.

There are a number of interesting similarities, the chief one being that in each case a superpower intervened by force in support of an unpopular government threatened by a formidable popular revolt. Another is that the superpower had helped to install the unpopular government in the first place. Americans had something to do with establishing Diem in Saigon in 1954 and much to do with keeping him in power after that; the Soviet Union, we have much reason to suspect, had much to do with the "April Revolution" in Kabul in April 1978, when, apparently, a small minority group consisting mainly of urban Marxist intellectuals and left-wing army officers seized power. (It may well be that Soviet support for that coup was more blameworthy, in the sense of being less readily explained by defensive motives, and also more of a blunder, than any of the later Soviet actions that flowed from it.) From that point on there was in each case a sense of commitment—and an investment of national pride, prestige, and credibility hinging on the outcome—that carried the intervening nation on and on in spite of mounting regrets that the whole affair had ever been started.

Another similarity, psychologically fundamental, is that in both cases the world situation was seen by the intervening power, rightly or wrongly, as threatening enough to justify drastic action.

During the years 1962–65, when the United States in Vietnam was becoming more and more involved and committed, most of the interested American public, and especially America's leaders, saw an advancing communist movement threatening the entire free world. We saw it using new "Chinese" techniques of subversion and guerrilla warfare that the West was only beginning to understand and learn how to combat effectively.

The four-year Soviet threat to Berlin, 1958–62, and the Cuban missile crisis of 1962, were freshly remembered events, and the idea of a domino process, resembling the spread of a fire, an epidemic, or a spreading cancer, was widely accepted. Ngo Dinh Diem appeared to be not exactly a democratic leader, but a firm ruler, valiantly trying to hold back the communist tide and deserving America's help in doing so.

What we did not remember, or think much about, was the Vietnamese people. Feeling that they did not really matter much when compared with the worldwide communist menace, most of us contented ourselves with the proposition (not really based on evidence) that the Vietnamese peasants "couldn't care less" about which side won, as long as peace came soon; then we forgot about that last provision and prolonged the war for several years, in opposition to what we ourselves thought the Vietnamese people wanted. And, chiefly because we were not really thinking about the Vietnamese people, we lost the war.

Something similar can be reasonably inferred about the psychology of the Soviets in their thinking about the world context of Afghanistan. After high hopes of détente and lasting peace during the Nixon Administration, they saw four years go by, 1975–79, during which, mysteriously (from their point of view), American actions deflated those hopes. Their own armament, which in their eyes probably was simply catching up with America's and NATO's hitherto always overweening strategic strength, was continuing at a steady pace of about a 3 percent annual increase. But (naturally rationalizing all their own dubious actions during the same period) they saw (as they apparently interpreted it) America giving up mutually beneficial trade opportunities in order to interfere with their internal affairs by way of the Jackson-Vanik amendment on behalf of Jews who wanted to emigrate; they saw America, after fine initial cooperation between Vance and Gromyko, totally excluding them from the peacemaking process in the Middle East, which was far from America but just next to their own border; they saw America sidling up to their archenemy, China; they saw President Carter stepping up America's arms program to a figure much higher than an annual increase of 3 percent, though probably in their eyes they were just beginning to be equal to the United States in strategic strength; they saw SALT II, on which they had sweated blood with their American counterparts, dying in Congress; they saw the dread prospect of Pershing II missiles and cruise missiles. All *before* Afghanistan.

And all exaggerated and one-sided, of course. We from our perspective may judge that all of it was grossly exaggerated threat perception, to a point that might almost be called paranoid. It was nevertheless more or less natural and expectable, given both what America did and the inevitably distorted perception of those things by Soviet decision makers. Nor would it be surprising if, against this background, most of the men in the Kremlin decided that détente was dead, that President Carter had finally succumbed to the baleful influence of the military-industrial complex (called by them the capitalist and militarist "ruling circles in America"), and that they must fall back upon their own military strength in order to be safe, plus, of course, keeping friendly nations on their borders.

It was in this anxiety-filled psychological context that the Afghan situation went from bad to worse. Hafizullah Amin, a strong-willed but impractical, ultraleft dictator, was making the situation steadily worse, prematurely (as seasoned Moscow authorities saw it) pushing such things as land reform and rights for women, and needlessly provoking the fiercely independent Afghan nationalists and the Islamic fundamentalists. He refused to listen to what Moscow thought was its sane, prudent advice. It was natural for the politburo to begin to see images of the future in which Afghanistan would fall into anarchy, break up into its ethnic parts, and the vultures of capitalism and feudalism—Pakistan, the CIA, and China—would be right on hand to pick up the pieces. Something *had* to be done. Amin had to be done away with, and Babrak Karmal, the leader of the saner faction, the Parcham faction, within the coalition that had engineered the April Revolution in 1978, who after all had as much right to lead as Amin had, could be brought back from exile. He could lead the reform movement toward moderation, which would restore order and keep a friendly nation, rather than a disintegrated and then hostile nation, on the southern border of the USSR, next to its Moslem republics.

There is a real parallel, here, to the situation in Vietnam in 1965, just before America began to send in its own troops on a large scale. Washington at that time saw the Viet Cong riding high, the shaky military government of Diem's successors in danger of imminent collapse, and if it did collapse the probability of a domino process extending at least to Laos and Cambodia and possibly much further (*Pentagon Papers,* 1971, pp. xix, 106). Less realistically, there was in Washington selective inattention to the disconcerting evidence, already available, that most of the really emotionally involved people in South Vietnam hated the Saigon government and saw the Viet Cong either as good or as the lesser evil (White, 1970, pp. 37–103).

Similarly, in 1979, just before the Kremlin began to use its troops in Afghanistan, there was a realistic Soviet perception that the Islamic, antiforeign, antiatheist rebellion was riding high; that the shaky leftist government of Amin in Kabul was in danger of imminent collapse; and that if or when it did collapse the influence of the USSR would suffer throughout the Middle East, conceivably including the neighboring Islamic parts of the USSR itself. That would seriously hurt Soviet pride if not Soviet security. Less realistically, there was probably selective inattention to available evidence that the opposition to land reform and to "socialism" was not confined to reactionary mullahs and infiltrators from Pakistan, supposedly paid by the CIA, but might include most of the emotionally involved people in the country itself.

There are other interesting psychological similarities. Like the politburo, the decision makers in Washington in 1963 were sorely tempted to replace an incompetent leader (Diem in their case, Amin in the Soviet case) whose incompetence and unmanageability seemed likely to lead to humiliating defeat. Perhaps we did have a hand in the death of Diem; perhaps not. The Soviets quite probably did have a hand in the death of Amin, with a particularly repulsive pretext that "the government" in Kabul, which presumably meant Amin and not the Parcham faction opposed to him, had asked for Soviet armed intervention. Like the men in the Kremlin, the men in Washington, including President Johnson, covered their intervention with the dubious claim that they were protecting an allied nation from a danger originating mainly outside its borders. Like them, the men in Washington covered an antidemocratic action with a bit of semantic legerdemain: Johnson announced that "South Vietnam" had asked for American help—not Ky or Thieu or the Saigon government, but "South Vietnam" had done it—a blurring of the important distinction between the government and the people. Similarly, the men in Moscow said that "Afghanistan" had asked for Soviet help—not Babrak Karmal, not the Parcham faction within the group that had engineered the April Revolution, or even the Kabul government, but "Afghanistan," with a similar blurring of the important distinction between government and people.

Naturally, since no two historical events are ever identical, there were differences as well as similarities, and some of the differences were important. Perhaps, but only perhaps, the chemical and biological weapons apparently now being used by the Soviet forces are more despicable than anything used by the United States or its allies in Vietnam. (We used napalm and Agent Orange, and our allies used widely attested torture.) More important, but not in our favor, is the fact that Afghanistan is on the border of the USSR, while Vietnam is about as far from the United States as it could possibly be. Psychologically that is very important to the Russians, with their special sensitivity to the danger of having hostile rather than friendly or neutral nations on their borders. Also important, and not necessarily in our favor, is the fact that the Kabul government was and is (in spite of its new moderation) leftist, while the Saigon government was rightist, much influenced by landowers who were opposing, not promulgating, drastic land reform. On that basis, Soviet observers could believe that the Babrak Karmal government is on the side of "the people" (though in fact most of "the people" reject it), while we in Vietnam were on the side of the exploiters of the people. That would be a gross distortion of our reasons for being there, but perhaps our turning our minds away from the fact that our allies in Vietnam were not on the side of the people was an equal distortion.

More fundamental than any of these other similarities and differences, however, is the psychological fact that in both cases the primary underlying motive appears to have been, in a sense, defensive. It is true that, by at least one definition of aggression, both were unequivocally acts of aggression. Probably, too, on a less conscious level, both were motivated in part by the normal nationalistic desire to expand, or retain, national power and prestige for their own sake—an unlovely motive that is unfortunately not confined to the two superpowers. Nevertheless, in both cases the primary underlying motive seems to have been defensive in the sense that the psychological context of the intervention, in the eyes of the intervenors, was one of superpower competition for influence within the Third World—a competition in which national security was believed by each side to be basically, ultimately in danger because of the power and villainy of the superpower opponent—and there was perception, realistic or not, of an imminent, substantial loss of power and influence if intervention did not occur (Petrov, 1980, 30–34).

The practical consequences of America's present focus on the indubitable fact of Soviet aggression in Afghanistan, rather than on its mainly defensive motivation, are important. The belief of many Americans that the whole Middle East is in imminent danger of further Soviet expansionism is largely based on our interpretation of Soviet motivation in Afghanistan. Our present insistence on hurting our own economy in order to be at least equal to the Russians in the economy-breaking nuclear arms race has been much influenced by it. Therefore, it is appropriate to end this discussion with some examples of interpretation of the Soviet intervention by Americans who speak with special authority, either as knowledgeable observers who were in Moscow in the early stages of the intervention or as highly respected students of the psychology of the Soviet rulers. What were they saying, shortly after the initial armed intervention occurred? (Some have already been quoted on the more general question of Soviet insecurity.)

Craig Whitney, the *New York Times* bureau chief in Moscow, was speaking about a general "sense of isolation and insecurity that helped push them into Afghanistan" (1980, p. 91).

Strobe Talbott, *Time* correspondent, writing with his colleague Bruce Nelan, was saying: "they have moved into Afghanistan primarily because the Moslem insurgency there threatened to turn a friendly neighbor into an unfriendly one. . . . The Afghan rebellion is doubly dangerous because it has Chinese backing. . . . One reason why détente has all but failed is that the Soviets believe the Carter Administration is rushing headlong into an alliance with China. That raises the old specter of encirclement" (1980, p. 18).

Jerry Hough, a specialist on the Soviet government, on the basis of conversations he had between December 17, 1979, and January 12, 1980, with Soviet foreign affairs specialists in Moscow, was saying: "the usual answer given by Soviet scholars was that Afghanistan had long been in the Soviet sphere of influence and that a collapse of a Communist regime on the Soviet border could not be tolerated, especially when it would be replaced by a fundamentalist Islamic regime that might arouse fellow Moslems in the Central Asian republics of the Soviet Union" (1980, p. 202).

George Kennan was saying: "In the official American interpretation of what occurred in Afghanistan, no serious account appears to have been taken of such specific factors as geographical proximity, ethnic affinity of peoples on both sides of the border, and political instability in what is, after all, a border country of the Soviet Union. Now specific factors of that nature, all suggesting defensive rather than offensive impulses, may not be all there was to Soviet motivation, nor would they have sufficed to justify the action, but they were related to it" (1980, p. 7).

The theme of geographical proximity came up repeatedly. Whitney wrote: "The other day a Russian arms control official asked: "If Mexico, on your southern border, were suddenly in danger of being taken over by Communist infiltrators from Cuba, wouldn't you react? Of course you would, and we would understand' " (1980, p. 32). For further evidence, see Guroff and Grant (1981).

The main point of this whole discussion is not to mitigate the responsibility of the men in the Kremlin for their aggression in Afghanistan. It *was* aggression, as well as a major blunder. The main point is rather to raise a question about their reasons for doing it. That question has great relevance to any predictions about their future behavior. Considering their various motives, is there any good reason to infer that, like Hitler in 1938–39, they have embarked on a far-reaching career of conquest?

As a step toward realistic empathy, let us ask the same question of ourselves. Considering the defensive motives behind our intervention in Vietnam, is there any good reason to think that, like Hitler, *we* were then embarking on a far-reaching career of conquest? The question answers itself. We were not. Therefore, the similar action of the Soviet decision makers does not prove that they were. Their primary motive was fear, comparable to ours in Vietnam.

The Soviet Arms Buildup

As in the case of the Soviet aggression in Afghanistan, there is no question here as to the reality of the fact that is to be interpreted. The steady, strong Soviet buildup of nuclear arms since the Cuban missile crisis of 1962 is a fact that the West has to face and somehow cope with. How we should cope, though, depends primarily on why they have done it. Does it, as a great many in the West believe, indicate a new determination, or underline an old determination, to dominate the world by force of arms? Or is it mainly based on the Soviet decision makers' underlying sense of insecurity—an enormously exaggerated sense of insecurity, from our point of view, but perhaps quite genuine? Does it resemble Hitler's buildup in the 1930s, which was almost certainly a conscious preparation for a war of conquest? Or our own nuclear buildup since 1945, the motives of which, we have every reason to believe, have been essentially defensive?

Only a broad, general answer will be attempted here. It is this: the bulk of the evidence indicates that the underlying Soviet motives are primarily, though by no means entirely, defensive. Fear, not cold-blooded aggression, is the primary reason for the Soviet arms buildup, as it is of ours.

References

Arbatov, G. (1982). "A Soviet Commentary." In A. M. Cox, *Russian Roulette: The Superpower Game.* NY: Times Books, Pp. 173–95.

Asch, S. E. (1956). "Studies of Independence and Conformity: I. A Minority of One Against a Unanimous Majority." *Psychological Monographs* 70 (9).

Bronfenbrenner, U. (1961). "The Mirror-image in Soviet-American Relations." *Journal of Social Issues* 17 (3) : 45–56.

Festinger, L. (1957). *A Theory of Cognitive Dissonance.* Evanston, IL: Row, Peterson.

Frank, J. (rev. ed., 1982). *Sanity and Survival in the Nuclear Age: Psychological Aspects of War and Peace.* NY: Vintage Books.

Guroff G., and Grant, S. (Oct. 25, 1981). "Soviet Elites; World View and Perceptions of the U. S." (Washington, D.C.: USIA study summarized by M. Marder in *Washington Post*, p. A6.)

Halle, L. J. (1967). *The Cold War as History.* NY: Harper Colophon.

Heider, F. (1958). *The Psychology of Interpersonal Relations.* NY: Wiley.

Hough, J. (March 1, 1980). "Why the Russians Invaded." *The Nation.* Pp. 225–32.

Kaiser, R. G. (1976). *Russia: The People and the Power.* NY: Pocket Books.

——— (1981). "U. S.-Soviet Relations: Goodbye to Détente." *Foreign Affairs.* Special issue, "America and the World, 1980" 59 (3) : 500–26.

Karpovich, M. (June 4, 11, 1951). "Russian Imperialism or Communist Aggression?" *New Leader.* Reprinted in R. A. Goldwin, ed., *Readings in Russian Foreign Policy.* NY: Oxford University Press, 1959, Pp. 657–66.

Kennan, G. F. (April, 1980). "Imprudent Response to the Afghanistan Crisis?" *Bulletin of the Atomic Scientists,* Pp. 7–9. Reprinted from *New York Times Magazine,* February 1, 1980.

——— (1982). *The Nuclear Delusion: Soviet-American Relations in the Nuclear Age.* NY: Pantheon.

Lyons, E. (1954). *Our Secret Allies.* NY: Duell, Sloan and Pearce.

Osgood, C. (1960). *Graduated Reciprocation in Tension-Reduction.* Urbana: University of Illinois, Institute of Communications Research.

Pares, B. (5th ed., 1947). *A History of Russia.* NY: Knopf.

Pentagon Papers. (1975, Bantam edition). Sheehan et al., eds. NY: Times Books, Pp. xix, 106.

Petrov, V. (1980). "New Dimensions of Soviet Foreign Policy." In F. D. Margiotta, ed., *Evolving Strategic Realities: Implications for U. S. Policymakers.* Washington, D.C.: National Defense University Press. Pp. 16–38.

Talbott, S. and Nelan B. (Feb. 4, 1980). "The View from Red Square." *Time.* P. 18.

Tucker, R. C. (rev. ed., 1971). *The Soviet Political Mind.* NY: Praeger.

Ulam, A. B. (1971). *The Rivals: America and Russia Since World War II.* NY: Viking.

White, R. K. (1965). "Soviet Perceptions of the U.S. and the U.S.S.R." In H. C. Kelman, ed., *International Behavior.* NY: Holt, Rinehart and Winston.

——— (rev. ed., 1970). *Nobody Wanted War: Misperception in Vietnam and Other Wars.* NY: Doubleday/Anchor.

Whitney, C. (April 20, 1980). "The View from the Kremlin." *New York Times Magazine.* Pp. 30–91.

Yankelovich, D., and Kaagan, L. (1982). "Assertive America." *Foreign Affairs.* Special issue, "America and the World, 1980." 59 (3) : 696–713.

PART TWO

MAJOR ALTERNATIVES

INTRODUCTION

Ralph K. White

The decision theorists tell us that rational decision making includes at least two key elements: paying adequate attention to (1) most (not just some) of the alternatives that might prove practical and effective in a given situation (2) many (not just a few) of the consequences that might result if they are chosen. Within whatever time constraints exist—and given a reasonably realistic set of basic assumptions—that is what rational behavior means in this context.

That applies to decision making about how to prevent nuclear war in general, as well as to the innumerable specific decisions that must be made as situations change. Part II is composed of attempts to be rational in that sense.

SECTION III

The Deterrence Model and the Spiral Model

SECTION EDITOR: ROBERT JERVIS

INTRODUCTION

Robert Jervis

Everyone agrees that the United States and the Soviet Union are involved in a costly and dangerous pattern of hostile interactions. But there is strong disagreement about both the sources of the hostility and the likely effects of alternative policies that are designed to deal with it. Similarly, most people who have looked at previous cases of conflict agree that two patterns of interactions that led to avoidable wars can be determined. Best known to many is the pattern of the 1930s. In retrospect, it seems clear that Adolf Hitler was out to dominate Europe. At the time, however, most statesmen believed that his goals were limited and that a policy of conciliation would be effective. The term "appeasement," which now has the pejorative meaning of making concessions to an implacable adversary, then was used in the favorable sense of trying to make a situation more peaceful.

The other pattern is less familiar to most citizens—and to most statesmen—but is central to the concerns of many of the authors in this volume. This is the pattern in which national differences are in fact reconcilable but decision makers on one or both sides doubt whether they are. The statesmen believe they are in a situation like that of the 1930s. They think that conciliation, rather than being reciprocated, would only embolden the adversary. Firmness and military superiority are believed to be required to show the other side that it cannot expand. But if the other side in fact desires mainly security, the result will be an undesired and unnecessary spiral of tensions and hostility, perhaps leading to war. Just as the first model is based on the experience of the 1930s, this model is based on one reading of the origins of World War I.

We all want to avoid war and preserve freedom; we all realize that these objectives can be endangered both by Hitlers and by spirals of unnecessary conflict that are generated by self-defensive motives. But some crucial disagreements and problems remain. Perhaps the greatest disagreement is whether a World War I or a World War II model is closer to our present situation. This, in turn, is tightly linked to the question of what Soviet (and perhaps American) intentions are. Are the Soviets driven largely by a sense of insecurity that is only fed by American belligerence and arms increases? Or are they relentlesly seeking opportunities for expansion that can be contained only by firm American diplomacy and military superiority? If the Soviet motives are a mixture of fear and desire for expansion, how do we design a policy that also has an appropriate mix? If we cannot be sure what the Soviets intentions are, how do we develop a policy that will at least avoid a disaster no matter what goals they seek?

The two models of conflict—the parallel policy prescriptions, and ways of dealing with unnecessary conflict—are explored in the chapters of Section III. It would be nice to promise complete answers to the questions posed here, but we can at least point out the issues and present what knowledge we have. It seems clear that statesmen often fail to recognize the possibility that others' hostility is to be explained, not by their evil designs, but by their fears. To understand the perceptual and interaction processes that are involved, to increase our ability to judge the states we are dealing with, and to be able to take actions that cannot be seen as provocative but that also will not lead aggressors to think that they can expand are enormous challenges.

The first chapter in this section, Chapter 7, is a discussion by me, in the broadest terms, of the nature and consequences of the two major alternative courses of action and the assumptions underlying them. The second, Chapter 8, by Morton Deutsch, focuses somewhat more specifically on one of them, tension reduction, and on the spiral model that underlies it.

7.

Deterrence, the Spiral Model, and Intentions of the Adversary*

ROBERT JERVIS

Two Views of International Relations and the Cold War

Differing perceptions of the other state's intentions often underlie policy debates. In the frequent cases when the participants do not realize that they differ on this crucial point, the dispute is apt to be both vituperative and unproductive. This has been the case with much of the debate in the United States over deterrence theories and policies. Although the arguments have been couched in terms of clashing general theories of international relations, most of the dispute can be accounted for in terms of disagreements about Soviet intentions. An examination of this debate will reveal the central significance of perceptions of intentions for most decision making and will shed light on the causes and consequences of several common misperceptions. (For an excellent treatment of the contrasting beliefs of "hard" and "soft" liners that in several respects parallels the discussion here—without, however, stressing the importance of differing perceptions of the adversary—see Glenn Snyder and Paul Diesing [1977, *Conflict Among Nations* chap. 4].)

DETERRENCE

For our purposes we need not be concerned with the many subtleties and complexities of deterrence theory, but only with the central argument that great dangers arise if an aggressor believes that the status quo powers are weak in capability or resolve. This belief will lead the former to test its opponents, usually starting with a small and apparently unimportant issue. If the status quo powers retreat, they will not only lose the specific value at stake but, more important in the long run, will encourage the aggressor to press harder. Even if the defenders later recognize their plight and are willing to pay a higher price to prevent further retreats, they will find it increasingly difficult to convince the aggressor of their new-found resolve. The choice will then be between continuing to retreat and thereby sacrificing basic values or fighting.

To avoid this disastrous situation, the state must display the ability and willingness to wage war. It may not be able to ignore minor conflicts or to judge disputes on their merits. Issues of little intrinsic value become highly significant as indices of resolve.

This does not mean that the state should never change its position. At times superior power must be recognized. Legitimate grievances can be identified and rectified, although care must be taken to ensure that the other side understands the basis on which the state is acting. In other cases, fair trades can be arranged. And at times concessions will have to be made to entice the other to agree. But while carrots as well as sticks are to be employed, the other's friendship cannot be won by gratuitous concessions. As Eyre Crowe put it in his famous memorandum: "there is one road which . . . will most certainly not lead to any permanent improvement of relations with any Power, least of all Germany, and which must therefore be abandoned: that is the road paved with grateful British concessions—concessions made without any conviction either of their justice or of their being set off by equivalent counter-services," (Crowe, 1907).

In this view, the world is tightly interconnected. What happens in one interaction influences other outcomes as each state scrutinizes the others' behavior for indications of interests, strengths, and weaknesses. As the German foreign minister said during the Moroccan crisis of 1905, "If we let others trample on our feet in Morocco without a protest, we are encouraging a repetition of the act elsewhere." As we will discuss below, this view often rests on the belief that the other side's aims are unlimited.

In a less extreme version, the other side is seen as without a plan but opportunistically hoping to move where there is least resistance. Lord Palmerston urged firmness in dealing with the United States over a minor dispute: "A quarrel with the United States is . . . undesirable . . . [but] in dealing with Vulgar minded Bullies, and such unfortunately the people of the United States are, nothing is gained by submission to Insult & wrong; on the contrary the submission to an Outrage only encourages the commission of another and a greater one—such People are always trying how far they can venture to go; and they generally pull up when they find they can go no further without encountering resistance of a formidable Character" (quoted in Bourne, 1967, p. 182).

The Spiral Model

The critics of deterrence theory provide what seems at first to be a contrasting general theory of international influence. The roots of what can be called the spiral model reach to the anarchic setting of international relations. The underlying problem lies neither in limitations on rationality imposed by human psychology nor in a flaw in human nature but in a correct appreciation of the consequences of living in a Hobbesian state of nature. In such a world without a sovereign, each state is protected only by its own strength. Furthermore, statesmen realize that, even if others currently harbor no aggressive designs, there is nothing to gurantee that they will not later develop them.

The lack of a sovereign in international politics permits wars to occur and makes security expensive. More far-reaching complications are created by the fact that most means of self-protection simultaneously menace others. Rousseau made the basic point well:

It is quite true that it would be much better for all men to remain always at peace. But so long as there is no security for this, everyone, having no guarantee that he can avoid war, is anxious to begin it at the moment which suits his own interest and so forestall a neighbour, who would not fail to forestall the attack in his turn at any moment favourable to himself, so that many wars, even offensive wars, are rather in the nature of unjust precautions for the protection of the assailant's own possessions than a device for seizing those of others. However salutary it may be in theory to obey the dictates of public spirit, it is certain that, politically and even morally, those dictates are liable to prove fatal to the man who persists in observing them with all the world when no one thinks of observing them towards him. (trans. Vaughan, 1917, pp. 78–79)

In extreme cases, states that seek security may believe that the best, if not the only, route to that goal is to attack and expand. Thus the tsars believed that "that which stops growing begins to rot" (Ulam, 1968, p. 5), the Japanese decision makers before World War II concluded that the alternative to increasing their dominance in Asia was to sacrifice their "very existence" (Butow, 1961, p. 203), and some scholars have argued that German expansionism before World War I was rooted in a desire to cope with the insecurity produced by being surrounded by powerful neighbors (Epstein, 1972, p. 290). After World War I, France held a somewhat milder version of this belief. Although she knew that the war had left her the strongest state on the Continent, she felt that she had to increase her power still further to provide protection against Germany, whose recovery from wartime destruction might someday lead her to try to reverse the verdict of 1918. This view is especially likely to develop if the state believes that others have also concluded that both the desire for protection and the desire for increased values point to the same policy of expansionism.

Even in less extreme situations, arms procured to defend can usually be used to attack. Economic and political preparedness designed to hold what one has is apt to create the potential for taking territory from others. What one state regards as insurance, the adversary will see as encirclement. This is especially true of the great powers. Any state that has interests throughout the world cannot avoid possessing the power to menace others. For example, as Admiral Mahan noted before World War I, if Britain was to have a navy sufficient to safeguard her trading routes, she inevitably would also have the ability to cut Germany off from the sea (Brodie, 1973, p. 345). Thus, even in the absence of any specific conflicts of interest between Britain and Germany, the former's security required that the latter be denied a significant aspect of great power status.

When states seek the ability to defend themselves, they get too much and too little—too much because they gain the ability to carry out aggression; too little because others, being menaced, will increase their own arms and so reduce the first state's security. Unless the requirements for offense and defense differ in kind or amount, a status quo power will desire a military posture that resembles that of an aggressor. For this reason others cannot infer from its military forces and preparations whether the state is aggressive. States therefore tend to assume the worst. The other's intentions must be considered to be coextensive with his capabilities. What he can do to harm the state, he will do (or will do if he gets the chance). So to be safe, the state should buy as many weapons as it can afford.

But since both sides obey the same imperatives, attempts to increase one's security by standing firm and accumulating more arms will be self-defeating. Earlier we quoted Palmerston's belief that, when dealing with "Vulgar minded Bullies" like the Americans, "the submission to an Outrage only encourages the commission of another and a greater one." In a dispute a few years earlier, James Polk expressed the same sentiment, arguing that "if Congress faultered [sic] or hesitated in their course, John Bull would immediately become arrogant and more grasping in his demands; & that such had been the history of the Brittish [sic] Nation in all their contests with other Powers for the last two hundred years" (quoted by McCoy, 1960). These symmetrical beliefs produce incompatible policies with results that are in neither side's interest.

These unintended and undesired consequences of actions meant to be defensive constitute the "security dilemma" that Herbert Butterfield sees as that "absolute predicament" that "lies in the very geometry of human conflict. . . . [H]ere is the basic pattern for all narratives of human conflict, whatever other patterns may be superimposed upon it later" (1951, pp. 19–20). From this perspective, the central theme of international relations is not evil but tragedy. States often share a common interest, but the structure of the situation prevents them from bringing about the mutually desired situation. This view contrasts with the school of realism represented by Hans Morgenthau and Reinhold Niebuhr, which sees the drive for power as a product of man's instinctive will to dominate others. As John Herz puts it, "It is a mistake to draw from the universal phenomenon of competition for power the conclusion that there is actually such a thing as an innate 'power instinct.' Basically it is the mere instinct of self-preservation which, in the vicious circle [of the security dilemma], leads to competition for ever more power" (Herz, 1959, p. 4).

If much of deterrence theory can be seen in terms of the game of Chicken, the spiral theorists are more impressed with the relevance of the Prisoner's Dilemma. Although they realize that the current situation is not exactly like the Prisoner's Dilemma because of the unacceptable costs of war, they believe that the central characteristic of current world politics is that, if each state pursues its narrow self-interest with a narrow conception of rationality, all states will be worse off than they would be if they cooperated. Not only would cooperation lead to a higher level of total benefits—and this is of no concern to a self-interested actor—but it would lead to each individual actor's being better off than he would be if the relations were more conflictful. States are then seen as interdependent in a different way than is stressed by the theorists of deterrence; either they cooperate with each other, in which case they all make significant gains, or they enter into a conflict and all suffer losses. A second point highlighted by the Prisoner's Dilemma is that cooperative arrangements are not likely to be reached through coercion. Threats and an adversary posture are likely to lead to counteractions with the ultimate result that both sides will be worse off than they were before. As we will discuss below, states must employ and develop ingenuity, trust, and institutions if they are to develop their common interests without undue risks to their security.

Psychological Dynamics

The argument sketched so far rests on the implications of anarchy, not on the limitations on rationality imposed by the way people reach decisions in a complex world.

Although we noted earlier that it is usually hard to draw inferences about a state's intentions from its military posture, decision makers in fact often draw such inferences when they are unwarranted. They frequently assume, partly for reasons to be discussed shortly, that the arms of others indicate aggressive intentions. So an increase in the other's military forces makes the state doubly insecure—first, because the other has an increased capability to do harm, and, second, because this behavior is taken to show that the other is not only a potential threat but is actively contemplating hostile actions.

But the state does not apply this reasoning to its own behavior. A peaceful state knows that it will use its arms only to protect itself, not to harm others. It further assumes that others are fully aware of this. As John Foster Dulles put it: "Khrushchev does not need to be convinced of our good intentions. He knows we are not aggressors and do not threaten the security of the Soviet Union." Herbert Butterfield catches the way these beliefs drive the spiral of arms and hostility:

> It is the peculiar characteristic of the . . . Hobbesian fear . . . that you yourself may vividly feel the terrible fear that you have of the other party, but you cannot enter into the other man's counter-fear, or even understand why he should be particularly nervous. For you know that you yourself mean him no harm, and that you want nothing from him save guarantees for your own safety; and it is never possible for you to realize or remember properly that since he cannot see the inside of your mind, he can never have the same assurance of your intentions that you have. As this operates on both sides the Chinese puzzle is complete in all its interlockings and neither party can see the nature of the predicament he is in, for each only imagines that the other party is being hostile and unreasonable (1951, pp. 19–20).

Because statesmen believe that others will interpret their behavior as they intend it and will share their view of their own state's policy, they are led astray in two reinforcing ways. First, their understanding of the impact of their own state's policy is often inadequate—that is, differs from the views of disinterested observers—and, second, they fail to realize that other states' perceptions are also skewed. Although actors are aware of the difficulty of making their threats and warnings credible, they rarely believe that others will misinterpret behavior that is meant to be more compatible with the other's interests. Because we cannot easily establish an objective analysis of the state's policy, these two effects are difficult to disentangle. But for many purposes this does not matter because both pressures push in the same direction and increase the differences between the way the state views its behavior and the perceptions of others.

The degree to which a state can fail to see that its own policy is harming others is illustrated by the note that the British foreign secretary sent to the Soviet government in March 1918 trying to persuade it to welcome a Japanese army that would fight the Germans: "The British Government have clearly and constantly repeated that they have no wish to take any part in Russia's domestic affairs, but that the prosecution of the war is the only point with which they are concerned." When reading Bruce Lockhart's reply that the Bolsheviks did not accept this view, Balfour noted in the margin of the dispatch: "I have constantly impressed on Mr. Lockhart that it is *not* our desire to interfere in Russian affairs. He appears to be very unsuccessful in conveying this view to the Bolshevik Government," (quoted in Wheeler-Bennett, 1971, pp. 295–96). The start of World War I witnessed a manifestation of the same phenomenon when the tsar ordered mobilization of the Baltic fleet without any consideration of the threat this would pose even to a Germany that wanted to remain at peace (Holsti, 1972, p. 132).

Similarly, when at the start of the Korean War Truman and his advisers decided to "neutralize" Formosa, they had little idea that by doing so they were depriving Communist China of a central national value. And later in the war the United States failed to realize the degree to which its advance to the Yalu objectively menaced Chinese security. Looking back on this incident, Dean Acheson argued that "no possible shred of evidence could have existed in the minds of the Chinese Communist authorities about the [peaceful] intentions of the forces of the United Nations" (Spanier, 1965, p. 97). That China probably overestimated the danger should not obscure the American failure to realize that conquering North Korea would have given it a greater ability to threaten China. Because American leaders thought they would never utilize this resource, they failed to understand that their actions in fact decreased China's ability to protect herself. Four years later, President Eisenhower similarly failed to see the extent to which American signals of readiness to "unleash" Chiang Kai-shek were arousing Communist Chinese insecurity (George and Smoke, 1974, p. 279).

With a disinterested perspective and access to documents from both sides, historians have seen a number of cases that fit the spiral model. Sometimes contemporary third parties also detect them. In 1904 President Roosevelt noted that the kaiser "sincerely believes that the English are planning to attack him and smash his fleet, and perhaps join with France in a war to the death against him. As a matter of fact, the English harbour no such intentions, but are themselves in a condition of panic terror lest the kaiser secretly intend to form an alliance against them with France or Russia, or both, to destroy their fleet and blot out the British Empire from the map! It is as funny a case as I have ever seen of mutual distrust and fear bringing two peoples to the verge of war" (quoted in Mowat, 1925, p. 296). The humor was lost on the powers concerned. Each side's claim that it was peaceful and afraid of the other only deepened the dilemma. Since each knew that there were no grounds for the other's supposed anxiety and believed that the other had enough of a grasp on reality to see this, each sought a darker meaning for the assertion. Thus, the British foreign secretary wrote to his ambassador in Berlin: "They cannot seriously believe that we are meditating a coup against them. Are they perchance meditating one against us and are they seeking to justify it in advance?" (quoted in Anderson, 1966, p. 115). Similarly, a few years earlier when Salisbury heard that the kaiser thought that he was the kaiser's enemy, he wrote: "So groundless is the charge that I cannot help fearing that it indicates a consciousness on the part of His Majesty that he cherishes some design which is bound to make me his enemy—and that he looks forward

116

Major Alternatives

to the satisfaction of saying . . . 'I told you so' " (quoted in Grenville, 1964, p. 277).

The explication of these psychological dynamics adds to our understanding of international conflict, but incurs a cost. The benefit is in seeing how the basic security dilemma becomes overlaid by reinforcing misunderstandings as each side comes to believe that not only is the other a potential menace, as it must be in a setting of anarchy, but that the other's behavior has shown that it is an active enemy. The inability to recognize that one's own actions could be seen as menacing and the concomitant belief that the other's hostility can only be explained by its aggressiveness help explain how conflicts can easily expand beyond that which an analysis of the objective situation would indicate is necessary. But the cost of these insights is the slighting of the role of the system in inducing conflict and a tendency to assume that the desire for security, rather than expansion, is the prime goal of most states. As we will discuss at greater length below, spiral theorists, like earlier students of prejudice, stereotypes, and intergroup relations, have given a psychological explanation for perceptions of threat without adequate discussion of whether these perceptions are warranted (e.g., Burton, 1970; Doob, 1970). . . .

This distinction between psychological and reality factors can be very useful, and we shall employ it in much of this chapter. But it takes attention away from the vital kind of system-induced incompatibility that cannot be easily classified as either real or illusory. If both sides primarily desire security, then the two images of the future do not clash, and any incompatibility must, according to one reading of the definition, be illusory. But the heart of the security dilemma argument is that an increase in one state's security can make others less secure, not because of misperception or imagined hostility, but because of the anarchic context of international relations.

Under some circumstances, several states can simultaneously increase their security. But often this is not the case. For a variety of reasons, nations' security requirements can clash. While an understanding of the security dilemma and psychological dynamics will dampen some arms-hostility spirals, it will not change the fact that some policies aimed at security will threaten others. To call the incompatibility that results from such policies "illusory" is to misunderstand the nature of the problem and to encourage the illusion that if the states only saw themselves and others more objectively they could attain their common interest.

SELF-DEFEATING POWER

When we compare deterrence and spiral theories, what is most striking is that they give opposite answers to the central question of the effect of negative sanctions. Deterrence theory, while elaborating a sophisticated logic of bargaining that often runs counter to common sense, generally endorses the conventional view that power must be met by power. The only way to contain aggression and cope with hostility is to build up and intelligently manipulate sanctions, threats, and force. The greater the aggressor's relative strength, the more valuable the concessions that will have to be made to him. Even Neville Chamberlain recognized this. In defending the Munic agreement, he told the cabinet: "I hope . . . that my colleagues will not think that I am making any attempts to disguise the fact that, if we now possessed a superior force to Germany, we should probably be considering these proposals in a very different spirit. But we must look facts in the face," (Parkinson, 1971, p. 41). In the current context this sentiment was expressed by Senator Henry Jackson when he argued that the increases in Soviet nuclear force would lead to political outcomes unfavorable to the United States:

> You see, this is what really disturbs me. The Russians have taken enormous risks when they have been in a totally inferior position; they took Czechoslovakia when they didn't even have a nuclear bomb; they tried to move into Cuba with missiles when they were at a 7 to 1 strategic disadvantage, I think it was, 5 or 7 to 1, but it is way up there, was it not, in October of 1962? Look at the risks they took. I wonder what kind of risk they are going to take in the mid-1970's and late 1970's and the 1980's when they have a situation that is totally reversed with this enormous power and a more confident Soviet Union,

in my judgment, that will be a more dangerous Soviet Union? (Senate Committee on Armed Services, 92d Cong., 2nd sess., p. 273).

The spiral model, in contrast to deterrence, argues that it is often not to the state's advantage to seek a wide margin of superiority over its adversary. In situations that resemble the Prisoner's Dilemma rather than Chicken, coercion is not likely to produce the desired results. There are two general reasons for this. First, an increase in the adversary's military strength may lead, not to greater assertiveness, but to a more conciliatory stance. The explanation for this is the other side of the dynamics that drive the security dilemma. If the adversary is mainly seeking security, increased arms may give it the confidence to be reasonable. Thus, some students of Soviet behavior take the opposite position to the one of Senator Jackson quoted earlier in this section: they argue that the USSR is more tractable when it has enough strength to feel secure (Bloomfield, Clemens, and Griffiths, 1966). A similar argument was made in 1894 when the German ambassador to France told the French minister of war that the Franco-Russian alliance will make it "very difficult to you to remain quiet." The French leader replied that the Germans did not understand the roots of French policy:

> What makes us sensitive and touchy as you say, is mainly the idea that we are thought to be weak and that insufficient account is taken of us. The stronger we shall be the less distrustful we shall be. Rest assured that our relations with you will become easier when we shall feel on a footing of equality. So long as we were facing the Triple Alliance our pride was constantly on the alert. We shall now be much less easily impressed. As you can see, our understanding with Russia is a token of peace (Albrecht-Carrié, 1970, pp. 254–55).

The second branch of this position is the argument that threats and negative sanctions, far from leading to the beneficial results predicted by deterrence theory, are often self-defeating as a costly and unstable cycle is set in motion. Short-run victories are possible, but will prove Pyrrhic if they convince the other that the victorious state is a threat that must be met by force.

Thus, if the spiral theory is correct, it is so partly because the actors do not understand it or follow its prescriptions. By acting according to a crude version of deterrence theory, states bring about results predicted and explained by the spiral theory. The former then provides an understanding of the world as seen by decision makers and thus an explanation for their specific actions, but the latter provides an explanation for the dynamics of their interaction. Acting on the premises of deterrence theory creates a self-denying prophecy, and if statesmen understood the validity of the spiral theory they could behave in ways that would similarly undermine its validity. Thus, it is interesting to note that people who understand the nature of the Prisoner's Dilemma play the game more cooperatively than do those who do not (Kanouse and Wiest, 1967, pp. 206–13).

PRESCRIPTIONS

The ideal solution for a status quo power would be to escape from the state of nature. But escape is impossible. The security dilemma cannot be abolished; it can only be ameliorated. The first step must be the realization, by at least one side but preferably by both, that they are, or at least may be, caught in a dilemma that neither desires.

On the basis of this understanding, one side must take an initiative that increases the other side's security. Reciprocation is invited and is likely to be forthcoming because the initiative not only reduces the state's capability to harm the other but also provides evidence of its friendly intentions (Osgood, 1962, pp. 85–134; Etzioni, 1962, pp. 83–110, 141–72). For these measures to be most effective, the state should place them in the proper setting; that is, they should not be isolated gestures but must be a part of a general strategy to convince the other side that the first state respects the legitimate interests of the other. Indeed the initiatives may not be effective unless the state first clearly explains that it feels that much of the incompatibility is illusory and thus provides the other with an alternative to the conflict framework in which specific moves can be seen (Osgood, 1962, pp. 6–9).

The central argument is that properly executed concessions lead the other side to reciprocate rather than, as in the deterrence model, leading it to expect further retreats from the first state. The first state does not, and does not appear to, retreat under pressure. Indeed "concedes" is not the best term for what the first state does. It makes a move to break the arms-hostility cycle. The end result is not that the state has given something up, or even that it has proposed a trade, but that a step is taken toward a mutually beneficial relationship. The states must learn to approach issues from a problem-solving perspective rather than from a competitive one. Instead of seeking to gain an advantage over each other, both sides should work together to further and develop their common goals.

Implicit in these prescriptions is the belief that, once each side loses its unwarranted fear of the other, some level of arms can be maintained that provides both sides with a reasonable measure of security. Here the spiral theorists' stress on understanding the position of the other side makes them more optimistic than the earlier proponents of the security dilemma. First, the latter's concentration on the degree to which the dilemma is inherent in the anarchic nature of the international system leads them to doubt that an understanding of the situation is sufficient for a solution. Even if the state does not fear immediate attack, it will still have to design policies that will provide safety if this trust is misplaced or if peaceful rivals later develop aggressive intentions. So even if both sides believe that the other desires only protection, they may find that there is no policy and level of arms that is mutually satisfactory. Second, those who stress the impact of the security dilemma usually are keenly aware that states often seek expansion as well as security and that conciliation, no matter how skillfully undertaken, will sometimes lead to greater demands.

Universal Generalizations?

In summary, both the spiral and the deterrence theorists are deeply concerned with the danger of misunderstandings and the consequent importance of states' making their intentions clear.

But the deterrers worry that aggressors will underestimate the resolve of the defenders, while the spiral theorists believe that each side will overestimate the hostility of the other. Policies that flow from deterrence theory (e.g., development of potent and flexible armed forces, a willingness to fight for issues of low intrinsic value, avoidance of any appearances of weakness) are just those that, according to the spiral model, are most apt to heighten tensions and create illusory incompatibility. And the behavior advocated by the spiral theorists (attempts to reassure the other side of one's nonaggressiveness, the avoidance of provocations, the undertaking of unilateral initiatives) would, according to deterrence theory, be likely to lead an aggressor to doubt the state's willingness to resist.

Spiral and deterrence theories thus contradict each other at every point. They seem to be totally different conceptions of international relations claiming to be unconditionally applicable. If this were true, it would be important to gather evidence that would disconfirm at least one of them. A look at the basic question of the effects of the application of negative sanctions makes it clear that neither theory is confirmed all the time. There are lots of cases in which arms have been increased, aggressors deterred, significant gains made, without setting off spirals. And there are also many instances in which the use of power and force has not only failed or even left the state worse off than it was originally (both of these outcomes can be explained by deterrence theory) but has led to mutual insecurity and misunderstandings that harmed both sides.

Deterrence and World War II; Spiral Model and World War I

The sketch of one of the main versions of the origins of World War I that we have given not only fits the spiral model very well; it is this case that has provided much of the inspiration for the model. Lewis Richardson, the originator of quantitative peace research, applied his equations to this era, and later scholars have used both the Anglo-German interaction and the frantic maneuvering of the last weeks of peace to drive home their arguments. The deterrence theorists, on the other hand, often hark back to, and derive much of their analysis from, the failure of appeasement in the 1930s. Given the histories of these two conflicts, it is not surprising that deterrence theories have little to say about World War I and that the spiral theorists rarely discuss the 1930s.

Although both sets of theorists fail to discuss the conditions under which their theories will not apply, and so imply that they are universal, what they say on the infrequent occasions when they discuss the war that does not fit their model shows that they actually do not apply their model to all cases. When the deterrence theorists discuss World War I, they do not concentrate on how either side could have made their threats more credible. Instead, they talk about the mobilization races in terms that are consistent with the spiral theory (Kahn, 1969, pp. 357–72). Indeed one of the major policy contributions of the deterrence theorists was to stress that mutual first-strike capability, by creating a "reciprocal fear of surprise attack," is highly destabilizing (Schelling, 1963, pp. 207–29).

Deterrence theorists thus understand the workings of spiral dynamics and see them operating in some conflicts; they merely deny that the cold war fits this model. Similarly, spiral theorists do not claim that deterrence is never possible or necessary. Even Neville Chamberlain argued that "we must not by showing weakness encourage Mussolini to be more intransigent," and noted that "it would be a tragic blunder to mistake our love of peace, and our faculty for compromise, for weakness." He finally realized that "it is perfectly evident . . . that force is the only argument Germany understands" (Feiling, 1970, pp. 272, 292, 341). Were the spiral theorists to argue that their model always applies, they would have to claim that events of the 1930s fit their analysis of the cold war—"the arms race is a tension-inducing system," "both sides are caught in the same blind alley of trying to achieve 'peace through military strength,' " and "mutual insecurity rather than the struggle for power has become the major source of international tensions. [The quotations are from pages 8, 49 and 142 of the psychologist Charles Osgood's *An Alternative to War or Surrender,* 1962, from which Chapter 11 of this volume is excerpted.] Churchill would have to be, to use the term Osgood applies to those who seek security through arms, a "Neanderthal," and Chamberlain, to use the words of the psychoanalyst Erich Fromm, a "sane" thinker. In fact, there are only occasional hints of this universalistic position, as when Singer argues that the Anglo-German negotiations for arms limitations in the mid-1930s "to some extent . . . resulted in a temporary reduction of mutually perceived threat and consequently of international tensions" (Singer, 1958, p. 101).

WHEN WILL FORCE AND THREATS WORK? THE DECISION MAKER'S CHOICE

If neither theory covers all cases, if force is sometimes effective and sometimes self-defeating, we are faced with two questions. First, what explains the differences between the spiral and deterrence theorists? What are they arguing about? Second, more important but much harder to answer, what are the conditions under which one model rather than the other is appropriate? When will force work and when will it create a spiral of hostility? When will concessions lead to reciprocations, and when will they lead the other side to expect further retreats?

To return to the cases of World Wars I and II, the British had to predict the effects of firmness and conciliation. Would a commitment to outdo the Germans in the building of Dreadnoughts curb the naval race? Could the conflict be ameliorated by meeting German grievances? Similar questions arose in the last days of peace. Asquith, the prime minister, and Grey, the foreign secretary, considered sending an ultimatum but decided that to do so would only antagonize Germany and destroy the possibility of a peaceful settlement (Jenkins, 1964, p. 326). Similarly, in March 1938 Foreign Minister Halifax told the cabinet that moves to protect Czechoslovakia would lead to unintended consequences: "The more closely we associate ourselves with France and Russia, the more we produce on German minds the impression that we are plotting to encircle Germany" (Hazlehurst, 1971, p. 84). At the time of the Nuremberg rally six months later, two leading foreign office officials wanted to send Germany a stiff warning "to prevent Hitler committing himself irretrievably." But the view prevailed that such a measure would infuriate, not deter, Hitler and reduce the chances of British mediation in the conflict (Colvin, 1971, pp. 109, 148). In March 1939 the permanent undersecretary of the foreign office, Alexander Cadogan, summed up his disagreement with the ambassador in Berlin, Nevile Henderson, when he wrote the latter: "you express the wish that we could rearm a little more quietly, as you say that the noise we make about it leads Germans to believe that we want after all to attack them. . . . What seems to me to be a far greater danger is that they might believe they could attack and smash us. . . . For that reason, I had always hoped that, when the time came . . . we should advertise our strength as much as possible" (Dilks, 1972, pp. 155–56).

WHEN WILL FORCE AND THREATS WORK? HYPOTHESES

Unfortunately, no well-structured or verified theory exists that tells us when force and threats work. Several fairly obvious propositions can be advanced, however, and one simple but important conclusion drawn. Threats are more apt to work and the deterrence model is more apt to apply when: (1) the other side sees the costs of standing firm as very high. More specifically, this will be the case when: (1a) the other side is relatively weak or vulnerable; (1b) the other places an especially high subjective value on preserving the lives and property of its citizens; (1c) the other is highly risk-averse; and (1d) the other has a short-run perspective. (2) The other side believes that the state making the threats sees its costs of standing firm as low. The specifics of this proposition are the reverse of those we have just given. (3) The other side sees the costs of retreating as relatively low. More specifically, this will be the case when: (3a) the other's central values are not involved in the issue at stake; (3b) the issue does not involve principles that apply to other important cases; (3c) the other can retreat without breaking important commitments; (3d) the goals of the side making the threat are seen as limited; (3e) the other believes that the demands derive from the state's desire for security and thinks that the state may see the other as a menace; (3f) neither the goals sought nor the means employed violate common standards of proper relations between juridically equal actors; and, related to the last proposition, (3g) the actor making the threat refrains from humiliating the other, inflicting gratuitous punishment, raising demands that lack any legitimacy, or asking for something that is of significantly greater value to the other than it is to him. All these kinds of behavior limit the costs of retreating to the other side by decreasing the other's fear that a retreat will be followed by further demands. They involve avoiding those traits that observers associate with extreme ambitions and taking care to observe lines of salience that differentiate present demands from many others that could be raised in the future.

To turn from the question of whether an actor will back down in the face of a threat to the question of the effects of retreats, concessions are more apt to encourage new demands, as the deterrence theory holds, when: (4) a retreat takes the state past a salient point; (5) the adversaries do not have a common conception of fair play and reciprocation; (6) the concession is made in a way that indicates that the state would sacrifice a great deal in order to avoid a war; and (7) the state retreats even though the costs of doing so are very high (i.e., the conditions specified in proposition 3 are not met).

We should note one thread that runs through these hypotheses. A major determinant of the effect of threats is the intention of the other side. When faced with an aggressor, threats and force are necessary. Concessions may serve important tactical needs, but they will not meet the underlying sources of dissatisfaction. When concessions are made under pressure or when the aggressor thinks that the status quo power is under no illusions about the nature of the conflict between them, the concessions are likely to quicken the pace of future demands. (We should briefly note the other side of this coin: when a state believes that the other has responded to conciliation by claiming that the state retreated only because of the other's superior force and by raising new demands, it will be likely to infer that the other is an aggressor who must be dealt with firmly.)

If this conclusion is correct, then the argument between the spiral and deterrence theorists is not over a general model of

international relations, but over which model applies to the cold
war and, as a main determinant of the answer to this question,
what Soviet intentions are. This is why Rapoport asks: "Why
is the power game being played at all? Is the game worth the
candle?" (quoted in de Reuck and Knight, eds., p. 293).

Perceptions of Intention and Analyses of What Is at Stake

Differences in perceptions of Soviet intentions also explain
why spiral and deterrence theorists have such different attitudes
toward the handling of minor issues. The former see them as
opportunities for reducing tensions. The outcomes are less important than the learning that can take place. Each side can
show that it is no menace and respects the other's legitimate
interests. This view was presented by Neville Chamberlain when
he briefed his advisers after returning from Godesberg: "Herr
Hitler had said that if we got this question [of the Sudetenland]
out of the way without conflict, it would be a turning point in
Anglo-German relations. That, to the Prime Minister, was the
big thing of the present issue" (quoted in Colvin, 1971, p. 162).

Deterrence theorists agree that the way the conflict is handled
is usually more important than the intrinsic value of what is
at stake. But they fear positive feedback of a different kind. As
Schelling has explained, "what is in dispute [in the game of
Chicken] is usually not the issue of the moment, but everyone's
expectations about how a participant will behave in the future"
(Schelling, 1966, p. 118). Khrushchev agrees: "Think what would
have happened if we had sat down to negotiate [in the Paris
Summit Conference of 1960] without having received an apology
from the United States. . . . The aggressors would have wanted
to bend us. But if we had bent our back, they would immediately
have thrown a saddle on us, and then they would have sat
themselves on top of us and begun to drive on us" (quoted in
Leites, 1963, pp. 11–12).

When one state sees another as extremely hostile, it is apt to
find most compromises on specific issues unattractive. Since the
other's demands are considered illegitimate, having to give in

even slightly will be seen as unreasonable. And since the other will be expected to accept the compromise only as a temporary solution, at best a little breathing space will have been gained. At worst, the state will have lost a clear and tenable position by sacrificing a defensible principle and placing itself in an unstable middle ground from which it can be more easily forced back. If the other is aggressive, what is at stake is not an issue of little intrinsic importance, but each side's image of the other's values, strength, and resolve. Firmness can help set relations right; retreats incur a high, long-run cost because they lead the adversary to expect further retreats. Thus in 1885 a British cabinet minister argued for a strong response to Russian expansion in Afghanistan: "It is now not a mere question about a few miles more or less of Afghan territory but of our whole relations with Russia in Asia" (Lowe, 1967, p. 88). In the Agadir crisis the anti-German faction in Britain argued "the point that it is not merely Morocco which is at stake. Germany is playing for the highest stakes. If her demands are acceded to . . . , it will mean definitely the subjection of France. . . . The details of the terms are not so very important now. . . . Concession means not loss of interest or loss of prestige. It means defeat with all its inevitable consequences" (Hazlehurst, 1971, p. 62). In July 1914 Eyre Crowe made the same kind of argument: "France and Russia consider that these charges are the pretext and the bigger cause of the Triple Alliance versus the Triple Entente is definitely engaged. . . . [T]his struggle . . . is not for the possession of Serbia, but . . . [is] between Germany aiming at political dictatorship in Europe and the Powers who desire to retain individual freedom" (quoted in Steiner, 1969, p. 156).

The belief that the other side is highly aggressive and the resulting analysis of the issues at stake will also lead the state to refrain from reciprocating if the other modifies its demands. Thus, those Finns who favored standing firm in the negotiations with Russia in 1939 were not swayed when the Soviets eased their position. If Russia were out to dominate Finland, true compromise was impossible (Jakobson, 1961, pp. 133–39).

Suggestions

Instead of incorrectly believing that he is calling for a dominant strategy, the policy advocate should try to reach the more
modest goal of developing policies that have high payoffs if the
assumptions about the adversary that underlie them are correct,
yet have tolerable costs if these premises are wrong. One way
to do this would be to procure the kinds and numbers of
weapons that are useful for deterrence without simultaneously
being as effective for aggression. Such a posture would break
out of the security dilemma. Given the logic of nuclear weapons,
this would mean avoiding systems that are useful only for a
counterforce first strike (e.g., large, soft missiles) and paying
extra for weapons that are especially effective for retaliation
(e.g., relatively invulnerable Polaris-type submarines). There are
three major problems, however. First, it is hard to tell what
inferences the adversary would draw from various military postures. What would appear threatening to one state's decision
makers may not be so to another's. Second, a state that is
pledged to protect a third area that it cannot defend with
conventional forces will need to rely for deterrence on the threat
to launch a nuclear strike in response to a conventional attack.
To the extent that the state cannot convince the adversary that
it values the third area as much as it values its own homeland,
it will need something more than a second-strike capability.
Third, and most important, nuclear weapons do not have to
be used all at once. One side could threaten to destroy one or
more of the other's cities if the other did not do as it demanded.
While there are reasons why, if both sides are close to equal
in general resolve, threats of this kind are more apt to be
credible if they are deterrent (demanding that the other not do
something) rather than compellent (demanding that it take
positive action) (Schelling, 1966, pp. 69–91), the military hard-
ware required cannot be classified as either defensive or threatening.

A second suggestion is that because the effect of initiatives
and threats depends to a large extent on the other's intentions
and its perceptions of the first state, people who are debating
policy should not only realize what they are arguing about but

should also ask themselves what possible behavior on the part of the adversary would they take as evidence against the interpretation that they hold. This is especially true of those who see the other as aggressive because it is easy to see almost any evidence as consistent with this image. This means that it is often very hard for the other to show that it has only limited ambitions, especially if it fears that the first side is aggressive. The more such an adversary adheres to the familiar view that the state is apt to interpret friendly overtures as weakness, the more hesitant it will be to take unambiguous actions and the more sensitive the state should be to evidence of the adversary's willingness to support the status quo. Decision makers would certainly have cause to worry if the only actions that would convince them that the adversary is not aggressive are measures they believe to be too risky for their own state to undertake (e.g., drastic arms cut, abolition of spheres of influence, or even unilateral initiatives). Similarly, those who feel that the adversary is not aggressive should consider what behavior would distinguish an aggressive, but cagey, state from a peaceful one caught in the security dilemma.

These suggestions show that the well-known arguments for the importance of empathizing with one's adversary in order to predict how he will react are insufficient. One must try to empathize with a variety of possible outlooks, any one of which could be a true representation of the adversary. It is not enough to calculate how the other will respond to your action if your image of him is correct. You must also try to estimate how the other will respond if he has intentions and perceptions that are different from those that you think he probably has. (In doing so you must also keep in mind that he is likely to think that you do understand him and so will view your policy as though it were designed to deal with his own policy as he, rather than you, sees it.)

If it is true that perceptions of the other's intentions are a crucial element of policymaking and that such perceptions are often incorrect, we need to explore how states perceive others and why and where they often go wrong. Military analysts talk of the "fog of battle"—the severe limits on the ability of each side to tell what the other's army (and often what its own army) is doing. But more important is the "fog of foreign policy-making." It is terribly hard to tell what others are up to, to infer their predispositions, and to predict how they will behave. Because of the importance and difficulty of these tasks, decision makers do and must employ shortcuts to rationality, often without being aware of the way they are doing so. But these shortcuts often produce important kinds of systematic errors, many of which increase conflict.

8.

The Malignant (Spiral) Process of Hostile Interaction*

MORTON DEUTSCH

Characteristics of the Malignant Social Process

A number of key elements contribute to the development and perpetuation of a malignant process. They include (1) an anarchic social situation, (2) a win-lose or competitive orientation, (3) inner conflicts (within each of the parties) that express themselves through external conflict, (4) cognitive rigidity, (5) misjudgments and misperceptions, (6) unwitting commitments, (7) self-fulfilling prophecies, (8) vicious escalating spirals, and (9) a gamesmanship orientation which turns the conflict away from issues of what in real life is being won or lost to an abstract conflict over images of power.

Although this discussion centers on the superpowers, my description of the malignant process can, I believe, be applied to the Arab-Israeli conflict and many other protracted, destructive conflicts.

THE ANARCHIC SOCIAL SITUATION

There is a kind of situation which does not allow the possibility of "rational" behavior so long as the conditions for social order

* Reprinted, with some condensation, from "The Prevention of World War III: A Psychological Perspective" (the writer's presidential address to the International Society of Political Psychology), in *Political Psychology 4*, no. 1 (1983).

or mutual trust do not exist. I believe the current security dilemmas facing the superpowers partially result from their being in such a situation.

A characteristic symptom of such "nonrational situations" is that an attempt on the part of an individual or nation to increase its own welfare or security without regard to the security or welfare of others is self-defeating.

Comprehension of the nature of the situation we are in suggests that *mutual security* rather than national security should be our objective. The basic military axiom for both the East and the West should be that only those *military actions that increase the military security of both sides should be taken; military actions that give military superiority to one side or the other should be avoided.* The military forces of both sides should be viewed as having the common primary aim of preventing either side from starting a deliberate or accidental war.

The key point we must recognize is that, if military inferiority is dangerous, so is military "superiority"; it is dangerous for either side to feel *tempted* or *frightened* into military action. Neither the United States nor the USSR should want its weapons *or* those of the other side to be vulnerable to a first strike. Similarly, neither side should want the other side to be in a situation where its command, control, and communication systems have become so ineffective that the decision to use nuclear weapons will be in the hands of individual uncontrolled units.

COMPETITIVE ORIENTATION

A malignant social process usually begins with a conflict that leads the parties to perceive their differences as the kind that create a situation in which one side will win and the other lose. There will be a tendency, then, for perpetuation and escalation of the conflict. These are some of the characteristics of a competitive conflict process (Deutsch, 1973):

1. The poor communication enhances the possibility of error and misinformation of the sort likely to reinforce preexisting orientations and expectations. Thus, the ability of one party to

notice and respond to shifts away from a win-lose orientation by the other party becomes impaired.

2. The conflict stimulates the view that the solution can be imposed only by one side or the other through superior force, deception, or cleverness. The enhancement of one's own and the minimization of the other's power become objectives. The attempt by each party to create or maintain a power difference favorable to its own side tends to expand the scope of the conflict from a focus on the immediate issue to a conflict over the power to impose one's preference upon the other.

3. The competitive conflict leads to a suspicious, hostile attitude that increases sensitivity to differences and threats while minimizing awareness of similarities. This, in turn, makes the usually accepted norms of conduct and morality less applicable.

I have written extensively (Deutsch, 1973, 1980, 1982) about the diverse conditions leading people to define a situation with a mixture of cooperative and competitive features as a win-lose or competitive situation rather than as a cooperative one. Much of this can be summarized by what I have termed Deutsch's crude law of social relations: the characteristic processes and effects elicited by any given type of social relation tend also to induce that type of social relation (if introduced into the social relation before its character has been strongly determined).

In terms of competition, my crude hypothesis would indicate that competition induces and is induced by use of tactics of coercion, threat, or deception; attempts to enhance the power differences between oneself and the other; poor communication; minimization of awareness of similarities in values and increased sensitivity to opposed interests; suspicious and hostile attitudes; the importance, rigidity, and size of the issues in conflict; and so on.

In contrast, cooperation induces and is induced by perceived similarity in beliefs and attitudes, readiness to be helpful, openness in communication, trusting and friendly attitudes, sensitivity to common interests and deemphasis of opposed interests, orientation toward enhancing mutual power rather than power differences, and so on.

INNER CONFLICTS

Although competition is a necessary condition for malignant conflict, it is not a sufficient one. Malignant conflict persists because internal needs require the competitive process between the conflicting parties.

There are many kinds of internal needs for which a hostile external relationship can be an outlet:

- It may provide an acceptable excuse for internal problems; the problems can be held out as caused by the adversary or by the need to defend against the adversary.
- It may provide a distraction so internal problems appear less salient.
- It can provide an opportunity to express pent-up hostility arising from internal conflict through combat with the external adversary.
- It may enable one to project disapproved aspects of oneself (which are not consciously recognized) onto the adversary and to attack them through attack on the adversary.
- It may permit important parts of one's self—including attitudes, skills, and defenses developed during conflictual relations in one's formative stages—to be expressed and valued because the relations with the present adversary resemble earlier conflictual relations; and so on.

When an external conflict serves internal needs, it may be difficult to give it up until other means of satisfying these needs are developed. There is little doubt that the conflict between the superpowers has served important internal functions for the ruling establishments in the United States and the Soviet Union.

It seems clear that an external enemy or "devil" has served many useful functions for those in power in both the Soviet Union and the United States. However, there is growing recognition by important elements within each superpower that the increasing dangers and costs of the arms race may begin to dwarf the gains from having a superpower as an external devil.

COGNITIVE RIGIDITY

Malignant conflict is fostered by cognitive rigidity which leads to becoming set in positions because of inability to envisage alternatives. An oversimplified black-and-white view of issues in a dispute contributes to the rigidity. So does the high level of tension that may be generated by an intense conflict. The excessive tension leads to a constriction of thought, impairing capability for conceiving of new alternatives and options. To the extent that parties in a conflict rigidly set themselves in their initial positions, they are unable to explore the range of potentially available solutions, among which might be one which satisfies the interests of both sides. In contrast, cognitive openness and flexibility facilitate a creative search for alternatives that may be mutually satisfying, with the initial, opposed positions evaporating as new, concordant options emerge.

Although the views of knowledgeable American scholars on the Soviet Union may be sophisticated and the same may also be true for Soviet scholars who specialize in American studies, there is little reason to think that this is true of the policymakers of the superpowers. They appear to have developed conceptions of the other power which reflect ideological indoctrinations they were exposed to in their earlier years. They have not traveled to the other superpower, nor have they had informal contacts with counterparts in the other nation. In short, they have had little opportunity to learn that the other does not neatly fit the rigid stereotypes developed in their younger years. This is an important defect in the experience of the leaders of the superpowers and should be remedied through systematic attempts to cultivate such experiences.

MISJUDGMENTS AND MISPERCEPTIONS

Impoverished communication, hostile attitudes, and oversensitivity to differences—typical effects of competition—lead to distorted views that may intensify and perpetuate conflict; other distortions commonly occur in the course of interaction. Elsewhere (Deutsch, 1962, 1965b), I have described some of the common sources of misperception in interactional situations. Many of these misperceptions function to transform a conflict into a competitive struggle—even if the conflict did not emerge from a competitive relationship.

Since most people are more strongly motivated to hold a positive view of themselves than to hold such a view of others, a bias toward perceiving one's own behavior as being the more benevolent and legitimate is not surprising. This is a simple restatement of a well-demonstrated psychological truth, namely, that the evaluation of an act is affected by the evaluation of its source—and the source is part of the context of behavior. Research has shown, for example, that American students are likely to rate more favorably an action of the United States directed toward the Soviet Union than the same action directed by the Soviet Union toward the United States. We are likely to view American espionage activities in the Soviet Union as more benevolent than similar activities by Soviet agents in the United States.

If each side in a conflict tends to perceive its own motives and behavior as the more benevolent and legitimate, it is evident that the conflict will intensify. If A perceives its actions as a benevolent, legitimate way of interfering with actions that B has no right to engage in, A will be surprised by the intensity of B's hostile response and will have to escalate its counteraction to negate B's response. But how else is B likely to act if it perceives its own actions as well motivated? And how unlikely is it not to respond to A's escalation with counterescalation if it is capable of doing so?

There are, of course, other types of processes leading to misperceptions and misjudgments (see Jervis, 1976, for an excellent discussion). In addition to distortions arising from pressures for self-consistency and dissonance reduction (which are discussed below), intensification of conflict may induce stress and tension beyond a moderate optimal level, and this over-activation, in turn, may lead to an impairment of perceptual and cognitive processes in several ways. It may reduce the range of perceived alternatives; it may reduce the time perspective in such a way as to cause a focus on the immediate rather than the overall consequences of the perceived alternatives; it may polarize thought so that percepts will tend to take on a simplistic black or white, for or against, good or evil cast; it may lead to stereotyped responses; it may increase the susceptibility to fear- or hope-inciting rumors; it may increase defensiveness; it may increase the pressures for social conformity.

In effect, excessive tension reduces the intellectual resources available for discovering new ways of coping with a problem or new ideas for resolving a conflict. Intensification of conflict is the likely result, as simplistic thinking and polarization of thought push the participants to view their alternatives as being limited to victory or defeat.

There are three basic ways to reduce the misjudgments and misperceptions that typically occur during the course of conflict. They are not mutually exclusive, and if possible all should be used.

One method entails making explicit the assumptions and evidence which underlie one's perceptions and judgments. Then, one would examine how likely these were to have been influenced by any of the common sources of misperception and misjudgment and how reliable and valid they would be considered by an objective outsider—for example, as in a court of law.

A second method entails bringing in outsiders to see whether their judgments and perceptions of the situation are in agreement or disagreement with one's own. They may have different vantage points, different sources of information, and more objectivity, which would enable them to recognize errors of judgment and misperceptions developing from enmeshment in the conflict. The outsiders should have the independence to ensure that they are free to form their own views and the stature to be able to communicate them so that they will be heard.

Finally, there are agreements that can be made with one's adversary to reduce the chances of malignant misjudgment and misperception during conflict. Such agreements could promote continuing informal contacts among international affairs and military specialists on both sides. They could provide for regular feedback of each side's interpretations of the other's communications. They could enable each side to present its viewpoints on television and in the mass media of the other side on a regular basis. They could provide for "role-reversal" enactments, where each side is required to state the position of the other side to the other side's complete satisfaction before either side advocates its own position (Rapoport, 1960).

UNWITTING COMMITMENTS

In a malignant social process, the parties not only become overcommitted to rigid positions but also become committed, unwittingly, to the beliefs, defenses, and investments involved in carrying out their conflictual activities. The conflict, then, is maintained and perpetuated by the commitments and investments given rise to by the malignant conflict process itself. Consider, for example, the belief by leaders of the American government that the Soviet Union would destroy us militarily if it could. This leads to actions such as intensifying military buildup which, in turn, produce an increased psychological commitment to the belief.

Parties to a conflict frequently get committed to perpetuating the conflict by the investments they have made in conducting the conflict. Thus, for example, in explaining his opposition to an American proposal shortly before Pearl Harbor, Prime Minister Tojo said that the demand that Japan withdraw its troops from China was unacceptable (as quoted in Jervis, 1976, p. 398).

> We sent a large force of one million men [to China] and it has cost us well over 100,000 dead and wounded, [the grief of] their bereaved families, hardships for four years, and a national expenditure of several tens of billions of yen. We must by all means get satisfactory results from this.

Similarly, there is considerable evidence to suggest that those who have acquired power, profit, prestige, jobs, knowledge, or skills during the course of conflict may feel threatened by the diminution or ending of conflict. Both the Soviet and United States military-industrial complex have developed vested interests in the cold war: it justifies large military budgets, gives them positions of power and prestige, and makes their skills and knowledge useful. They have good reason to be apprehensive about an "outbreak of peace," which would make them obsolete, deprive them of power and status, and make them lose financially. Under such conditions, it is quite natural to accentuate those perspectives and aspects of reality that justify the continuation of an arms race.

These understandable fears have to be dealt with constructively, or else they may produce defensive adherence to the views that justify a war. I suggest that we must carefully plan to anticipate the psychological difficulties in the transition to a peaceful world; otherwise the resistance to such a transition may be overwhelming.

As a basic strategy to overcome some of these difficulties, I would recommend that we consider a policy of overcompensating those who otherwise might be adversely affected by the change. We want to alter the nature of their psychological investment from one in military pursuits to one in peaceful pursuits.

SELF-FULFILLING PROPHECIES

Merton, in his classic *The Self-fulfilling Prophecy* (1957), has pointed out that distortions are often perpetuated because they may evoke new behavior that makes the originally *false* conception come true. The specious validity of the self-fulfilling prophecy perpetuates a reign of error. The prophet will cite the actual course of events as proof that he was right from the very beginning.

The dynamics of the self-fulfilling prophecy help to explain individual pathology—for example, the anxious student who, afraid he might fail, worries so much that he cannot study, with the consequence that he does fail. It also contributes to our understanding of social pathology—for example, how prejudice and discrimination against blacks keeps them in a position that seems to justify the prejudice and discrimination.

So, too, in international relations. If the policymakers of East and West believe that war is likely and either side attempts to increase its military security vis-à-vis the other, the other side's response will justify the initial move. The dynamics of an arms race has the inherent quality of folie à deux, wherein the self-fulfilling prophecies mutually reinforce one another. As a result, both sides are right to think that the other is provocative, dangerous, and malevolent. Each side, however, is blind to how its own policies and behavior have contributed to the development of the other's hostility. If each superpower could recognize its own part in maintaining the malignant relations, it could lead to a reduction of mutual recrimination and an increase in mutual problem solving.

Vicious Escalating Spirals

In recent years, a number of social psychologists have concerned themselves with understanding the conditions under which people become entrapped in a self-perpetuating cycle of escalating commitment (Teger, 1980; Rubin, 1981; Levi, 1981).

Decision makers sometimes face the problem of deciding whether to persist in a failing, costly course of action; they must choose between, on the one hand, changing their course of action so as to cut their losses and, on the other hand, continuing to invest in the hope of reaching their goal.

Ariel Levi (1981) has developed a model of the factors affecting decision making when such a dilemma has to be faced. The model implies that the tendency to escalate commitments after failure should be greatest when the decision maker (1) evaluates his or her losses thus far as very negative; (2) considers that further losses will not make his or her position much worse than the losses already suffered; and (3) believes that the previous failures do not reduce the chances of success of an increased commitment of resources.

From Levi's model, it can be predicted that decision makers who see themselves as highly accountable to others for their decisions are likely to be cautious before losses have occurred but increasingly ready to take risks as losses increase. Also, since gains or losses are evaluated from a reference point, the greater the losses are perceived to be from this reference point, the greater will be the decision maker's tendency to escalate his or her commitment. In addition, if the decision maker attributes the previous losses to changeable factors, escalation of commitments is likely.

Levi's model is based, in part, upon Kahneman and Tversky's (1979) Prospect Theory, which seeks to explain why decision makers systematically violate the basic tenets of rational, economic decision making. One of their basic assumptions is that people undervalue outcomes that are merely probable in comparison with outcomes that are obtainable with certainty. This "certainty effect" means that a gambler facing the prospect of a sure loss of a smaller amount if he or she stops now and an uncertain loss of a larger amount if he or she continues to gamble is apt to choose to take the risk of increasing his or her losses.

We are progressively tightening the noose around our necks out of the increasing fears that each side is creating by its development of nuclear weapons that have a first-strike capability. The notion that each side must be prepared to "launch on warning" is the culmination of the escalating, competitive "game of strategy" being played by the superpowers in which each side has initiated moves to improve its strategic position without adequate recognition of how the other would be forced to respond and without positive concern for what would happen to the strategic position of the other.

GAMESMANSHIP

What is so psychologically seductive about nuclear weapons and hypothetical nuclear war scenarios that strategists and decision makers in both superpowers are drawn to them like moths to a flame? There are so many dimensions of power— economic, political, cultural, scientific, sports, educational, and so on—in which the struggle between the superpowers could be played out. What is the special fascination to playing the international power game with nuclear weapons?

I speculate that two key psychological features make the nuclear game a supergame: it has a tremendous emotional kick for those with strong power drives, and it is a very tidy, abstract game.

For those with strong power drives, being in a position of nuclear superiority can be seen as a sure way to dominate and control others, while being in a position of nuclear inferiority can be seen as a sure way to be dominated and humiliated by others. In the eyes of those driven by power, nuclear weapons are the purest and most concentrated form of power that exists. As Barnet (1972) has pointed out, the national security managers and our governing class are educated and selected in a way that ensures that many will have strong power drives and a conception of human life that leads them to believe that, unless one controls and dominates, one will be controlled and dominated.

In order to be a competent participant in nuclear war games, one must be "steel-like" and unflinching in resolve not to allow the other side to prevail no matter how catastrophic the consequences. Maccoby (1976) has suggested that the "gamesman" differs from the "jungle fighter." The latter's lust for power is passionate and open, and the domination he seeks is personal and concrete. In contrast, the gamesman's power drive is more depersonalized. His game of power is played coolly, analytically, and with emotional detachment. As Maccoby (1976, p. 100) has indicated:

> he is energized to compete not because he wants to build an empire, not for riches, but rather for fame, glory, the exhilaration of running his team and of gaining victories. His main goal is to be known as a winner, and his deepest fear is to be labeled a loser.

Maccoby (1976, pp. 108–9) further describes gamesmen in these terms:

> imaginative gamesmen tend to create a new reality, less limiting than normal, everyday reality. Like many adolescents, they seem to crave a more romantic, fast-paced, semifantasy life, and this need puts them in danger of losing touch with reality and of unconsciously lying. The most successful gamesmen keep this need under control and are able to distinguish between the game and reality, but even so, in boring meetings they

sometimes imagine that they are really somewhere else—at a briefing for an air-bombing mission, or in a hideout where the detested manager who is speaking is really a Mafia chieftain whom the gamesman will someday rub out. . . . At their worst moments gamesmen are unrealistic, manipulative, and compulsive workaholics. Their hyped-up activity hides doubt about who they are and where they are going. Their ability to escape allows them to avoid unpleasant realities. When they let down, they are faced with feelings that make them feel powerless. The most compulsive players must be "turned on," energized by competitive pressures. Deprived of challenge at work, they are bored and slightly depressed. Life is meaningless outside the game, and they tend to sit around watching TV or drinking too much. But once the game is on, once they feel they are in the Super Bowl or one-on-one against another star, they come to life, think hard, and are cool.

The abstract character of nuclear war scenarios appeals to the talented, imaginative gamesmen, who are the leading strategic analysts in the national security establishments of the United States and the USSR. The game is exciting and competitive, calling for the use of inventive thought, cool, analytic ability, and emotional toughness. It has little of the messiness of war games involving real soldiers, battlefield commanders, rain, mud, and pestilence. It is basically an abstract, impersonal, computerized game, involving nuclear weapons with strategists on each side trying to outsmart the other.

This alluring, involving, imaginative game is played in an abstracted, unreal world in which the real costs of playing (extravagant damage being done to the economic systems of the superpowers and the world) and the real horrors of nuclear war are not faced. There is a continuing need to make these costs and horrors "psychologically real" to the people and decision makers of the superpowers as well as a continuing necessity to challenge the dubious "hard facts" underlying the "psychological realities" of the strategic gamesmen on both sides.

Let me summarize my presentation so far. I believe the United States and the Soviet Union are entrapped in a malignant social process giving rise to a web of interactions and defensive maneuvers, which, instead of improving their situations, make them both feel less secure, more vulnerable, more burdened, and a threat to one another and to the world at large. This malignant social process is fostered and maintained by anachronistic competition for world leadership; security dilemmas created for both superpowers by competitive orientations and the lack of a strong world community; cognitive rigidities arising from archaic, over-simplified, black-and-white, mutually antagonistic ideologies; misperceptions, unwitting commitments, self-fulfilling prophecies, and vicious escalating spirals which typically arise during the course of competitive conflict; gamesmanship orientations to security dilemmas which turn a conflict from what in real life is being won or lost to an abstract conflict over images of power in which nuclear missiles become the pawns for enacting the game of power; and by internal problems and conflicts within each of the superpowers that can be managed more easily because of external conflicts.

Reducing the Danger

What can be done to reverse this malignant social process and how can we begin to reduce the dangers resulting from the military gamesmanship and security dilemmas of the super-powers? Let me turn to the latter question first.

I shall outline a number of proposals, none original. They are based upon what I consider to be common sense rather than on specialized knowledge of military affairs or international relations, although I have informed myself as best I could in these areas. These matters are too important to be left to consideration only by specialists.

1. "The truly revolutionary nature of nuclear weapons as instruments of war" (Keeny and Panofsky, 1981/82, p. 287) suggests that the United States and the USSR should quickly come to an agreement banning the first use of nuclear weapons and should, as part of this accord, jointly agree to punitive actions to deter any other nation's first use of nuclear weapons. Such an agreement between the superpowers should be presented to the United Nations for discussion and ratification.

2. Immediately following the signing of a "no-first-use" agreement, representatives from NATO and the Soviet bloc should meet continuously to seek verifiable agreements which would (a) eliminate all short-range and intermediate-range nuclear missiles including all missiles in Western Europe and all missiles in the Soviet bloc that could not reach the United States; (b) reduce conventional armaments in the Soviet bloc and NATO bloc, particularly those weapons that have little value for defense, and reduce the possibility of surprise attack; (c) create a demilitarized zone in Central Europe which would separate the military forces of the Soviet bloc and NATO by a militarily significant amount of space.

3. The United States and the USSR should each unilaterally and through agreement seek to increase the stability of nuclear deterrence by removing those nuclear weapons from their arsenals that are vulnerable to a first strike; by renouncing use of "launch on warning"; and by a verifiable freeze on further deployment, research, development, and testing of nuclear weapons. After the "freeze," a verifiable reduction to about 300 strategic weapons on each side should take place.

4. Since the Middle East is so volatile, the United States should seek to become independent of oil supplied from the Middle East as rapidly as possible. The development of alternative sources of energy—shale oil, coal, solar power, geothermal, and so forth—should be fostered by governmental policy. The United States should not be in the position of having to intervene militarily in the Middle East in order to preserve a supply of energy for itself or its allies.

At the same time, the United States would initiate a "graduated reciprocation in tension reduction" (GRIT) process (Osgood, 1962). We would state our determination to end the nuclear arms race and would announce an across-the-board unilateral reduction of, for example, 10 percent of our existing nuclear weapons, inviting the USSR and other nations to verify that so many nuclear weapons in each category were being destroyed. We would request the USSR to reciprocate in a similar fashion.

I believe our superfluity of nuclear weapons is such that we could afford to make several rounds of unilateral cuts, even if the Soviets did not initially reciprocate, without losing our capacity to retaliate against any nuclear attack so that destruction of the Soviet society would still be assured. Such repeated unilateral initiations, if sincere in intent and execution, would place the Soviet Union under the strongest pressure to reciprocate. We could replace the arms race with a peace race.

Undoing the Malignant Social Process

Although some of the dangers of living in a MAD nuclear world can be controlled by arms control and disarmament agreements, the reality is that we cannot put the genie back into the bottle; the possibility of making hydrogen bombs, nuclear missiles, and other weapons of mass destruction will continue to exist—*forever*. This is why we must seek to remove the malignancy from relations between the superpowers and develop sufficiently cooperative relations among all major powers to make a major war unlikely.

How do we undo the malignant social process in which the superpowers are enmeshed? The first step is to heighten everyone's consciousness of how crazy the process is and to make people aware of both its very real dangers and its enormous economic costs. The people of the United States, the Soviet Union, and the rest of the world should be encouraged to recognize the craziness of the process and to denounce it as unacceptably dangerous and costly to humanity. It is difficult to induce a therapeutic change in a pathological process until the pathology is recognized as such and seen to be unacceptably harmful.

The second step is to focus on the underlying dynamics which foster and maintain the pathology. In my earlier description of the key features of a malignant social process, I sketched out the dynamics in general terms. Here, I want to highlight two features which are central to the pathological relations between the superpowers: the security dilemma and their competitive orientations.

The security dilemma stems from the development of nuclear weapons which have made the world a more uncertain, dangerous, and anxious place and have revolutionized the nature of war. They have outmoded the concepts of "military victory," "military supremacy," and "nuclear superiority" as pertinent to the relations between the superpowers and made the anachronistic pursuit of such goals endangering to self as well as to others.

As for competition orientation, it is evident that the superpowers have such an orientation toward their conflicts, and this makes it difficult for them to handle their security dilemma cooperatively and constructively. But, must their conflicts for power and prestige be conducted as "cutthroat" affairs or can "fair rules for competition" be developed? Is it possible to develop a cooperative framework to support adherence to fair rules?

Fair Rules for Competition

A contest is considered to be fair if the conditions and rules are such that no contestant is systematically advantaged or disadvantaged in relation to other contestants. All have equal rights and opportunities, and all are in the same category—that is, more or less matched in characteristics relevant to the contest's outcome.

We have lived through several close calls. It is time to rely on more than nerve and luck to avert disaster. I suggest that we take the initiative to propose fair rules in the competition for the unaligned countries. As Amitai Etzioni (1962) has pointed out, a set of rules would include such principles as the following:

1. No nonaligned country would be allowed to have military ties with other countries, particularly not with any major power.

2. No foreign troops, bases, or arms would be permitted to remain in or to enter the nonaligned country. Foreign arms would be prohibited to rebels and governments of nonaligned countries alike.

3. United Nations observer forces consisting largely of personnel from nonaligned countries and equipped with the necessary scientific equipment and facilities (flashlights, infrared instruments, helicopters, aerial photographs, lie detectors, etc.)

to check the borders, ports, airfields, roads, railroads, and the like would be deployed at the request of any of the major powers or by the secretary general of the United Nations. Costs would be allocated so as to reduce the incentive to create repeated false alarms.

4. A United Nations research and development staff would be established to keep informed about the development of new observational techniques and equipment.

5. Violations of the arms embargo—once certified as such by an appropriate UN tribunal—would set in motion a cease-and-desist order aimed at the sender of arms or troops and a disarm order aimed at the receiver. Obedience to these orders would be checked by the UN observer force. Lack of compliance would result in sanctions appropriate to the nature of the violation—for example, trade and communications embargo, blockade, sending of armed forces into the nonaligned country.

Suppose such rules could be established: What effects might be expected? Clearly, the revolutionary ferment in Asia, Africa, and Latin America would not disappear, nor would communist governments be unlikely to take power in some countries. These rules would not have prevented Castro from overthrowing Batista in Cuba. However, I suggest that the critical issue is not whether local communists or their sympathizers can achieve power in a given country without external military aid but rather whether, after achieving power, they retain it because of foreign military aid and whether they become a base for military aid to communists in other countries.

I assume that the major technical problems center about the need to reduce the likelihood that the rules can be violated to give any side an insuperable advantage. Without going into this issue in detail, I think it can be seen that any given violation is not likely to have catastrophic consequences for the military security of the superpowers. And even if an underdeveloped country is subverted or taken over as a result of violations, this is hardly likely to be catastrophic. Moreover, violations are hardly likely to be undetected, but are more apt to become evident before they substantially threaten security.

Developing a Cooperative Framework

Acceptance of fair rules for competition means an abandonment of cutthroat rivalry. It implies a change in one's conception of the adversary, from an enemy to a fellow contestant. Then, the conflict changes character. The rules, which limit forms of conflict, bind the contestants together in terms of common interest. However, common interest in the rules is not, by itself, likely to prevail against the debilitating effects of inevitable misunderstandings and disputes associated with any rule system. The tie between the contestants must be strengthened by enhancing their community or cooperative interests.

How can this be done? The key to development of cooperation can be stated very simply. It is *the provision of repeated and varied opportunities for mutually beneficial interactions.* In relation to the Soviet Union, we have done some of this, but obviously not enough.

Many equate appeasement with cooperation. They seem to feel that the only credible stance toward someone who might have hostile intentions is a self-righteous, belligerent counter-hostility. There is, of course, an alternative stance: one of firmness and friendliness. It *is* possible to communicate both a firm, unwavering resolve not to allow oneself to be abused, intimidated, or made defenseless *and* a willingness to get along peacefully and to cooperate for mutual benefit. In other words, willingness to cooperate does not imply willingness to be abused.

"Firmness" in contrast to "belligerence" is not provocative and, thus, while aborting development of vicious spirals, it does not abort development of cooperation. It is, of course, difficult to resist the temptation to respond with belligerence to the belligerent provocations of some communist nations. It requires a good deal of self-confidence to feel no need to demonstrate that one is "man enough" to be tough or that one is not "chicken." It is just this kind of firm, nonbelligerent, self-confident, friendly attitude that appears to be most effective in reforming aggressive delinquents and that our research (Deutsch, 1973) suggests is most effective in inducing cooperation.

Can we adopt such an attitude? Our defensiveness is rather high, suggesting that we do not feel confident of ourselves. Our defensiveness comes from two sources. First, we have too high a level of aspiration. Throughout most of our history, we have been in the uniquely fortunate position of having had pretty much our own way in foreign affairs. Initially, this was due to our powerful isolated position in the Americas. Since World War II we have been, moreover, the leading world power. We face a loss of status. It seems evident that we cannot remain in our former unique position. We can no longer be isolated from the physical danger of a major war; nor can we remain the only powerful nation. We have to adjust our aspirations to changing realities or suffer constant frustration.

The second root of our national defensiveness is lack of confidence in our ability to maintain ourselves as a thriving, attractive society that can cope effectively with its own internal problems. The fact is that we have not been coping well with economic growth, unemployment, civil rights, the education of our children, the rebuilding of our cities, the care of our aged.

Conflict is more likely to take the form of lively controversy rather than deadly quarrel when the disputants respect themselves as well as each other. The process of reforming another, of inducing an opponent to adhere to fair rules of competition, often requires self-reform. The achievement of a sincere peace will require a sincere, sustained effort by both sides.

References

Albrecht-Carrié, R. (1970). *Britain and France.* Garden City, NY: Doubleday. Pp. 254–55.

Anderson, E. (1966). *The First Moroccan Crisis, 1904–1906.* Hamden, CT: Archon Books. P. 115.

Barnet, R. J. (1972). *Roots of War.* NY: Atheneum.

Bloomfield, L.; Clemens, W., Jr.; and Griffiths, F. (1966). *Khrushchev and the Arms Race.* Cambridge: MIT Press.

Bourne, K. (1967). *Britain and the Balance of Power in North America, 1815–1908.* Berkeley: University of California Press. P. 182.

Brodie, B. (1973). *War and Politics.* NY: Macmillan. P. 345.

Burton, J. (1970). *Controlled Communication.* NY: The Free Press.

Butow, R. (1961). *Tojo and the Coming of the War.* Princeton: Princeton University Press.

Butterfield, H. (1951). *History and Human Relations.* London: Collins. Pp. 19–20.

Colvin, I. G. (1971). *The Chamberlain Cabinet.* NY: Taplinger.

Crowe, E. (January 1, 1907). "Memorandum on the Present State of British Relations with France and Germany." In Gooch and Temperley, eds., *British Documents.* Vol. 3 : 419 and 428.

Deane, J. (1947). *The Strange Alliance.* NY: Viking.

DeReuck, A. Y. and Knight, J., eds. (1966). *Conflict in Society.* Boston: Little, Brown.

Deutsch, M. (1962). "A Psychological Basis for Peace." In Q. Wright, W. N. Evan, and M. Deutsch, eds., *Preventing World War III: Some Proposals.* NY: Simon and Schuster.

——— (1965). "Conflicts: Productive and Destructive." *Journal of Social Issues* 25 : 7–41.

——— (1965). "A Psychological Approach to International Conflict." In G. Sperrazzo, ed., *Psychology and International Relations.* Washington, D. C.: Georgetown University Press.

——— (1973). *The Resolution of Conflict: Constructive and Destructive Processes.* New Haven: Yale University Press.

——— (1980). "Fifty Years of Conflict." In L. Festinger, ed., *Restrospections on Social Psychology.* NY: Oxford University Press.

—— (1982). "Conflict Resolution: Theory and Practice." *Political Psychology, 4* no. 1.

Dilks, D., ed. (1972). *The Diaries of Sir Alexander Cadogan.* NY: Putnam.

Doob, L., ed. (1970). *Resolving Conflict in Africa.* New Haven: Yale University Press.

Epstein, K. (1972). "Gerhard Ritter and the First World War." In H. W. Koch, ed., *The Origins of the First World War.* London: Macmillan.

Etzioni, A. (1962). *The Hard Way to Peace.* NY: Collier Books.

Feiling, K. (1970). *The Life of Neville Chamberlain.* London: Macmillan.

Fromm, E. (1961). *May Man Prevail?* Garden City, NY: Doubleday.

George, A., and Smoke, R. (1974). *Deterrence in American Foreign Policy.* NY: Columbia University Press.

Gooch, G. P. and Temperley, H. (1927). *British Documents on the Origins of the World War.* London.

Grenville, J. A. S. (1964). *Lord Salisbury and Foreign Policy.* London: Athlone. P. 277.

Hazlehurst, C. (1971). *Politicians at War.* New York: Alfred A. Knopf. Pp. 62, 84.

Herz, J. (1959). *Political Realism and Political Idealism.* Chicago: University of Chicago Press.

Holsti, O. (1972). *Crisis Escalation War.* Montreal: McGill-Queen's University Press.

Jakobson, M. (1961). *The Diplomacy of the Winter War.* Cambridge: Harvard University Press. Pp. 133–39.

Jenkins, R. (1964). *Asquith.* London: Collins.

Jervis, R. (1976). *Perception and Misperception in International Politics.* Princeton: Princeton University Press.

Kahn, H. (2d ed., 1969). *On Thermonuclear War.* NY: The Free Press. Pp. 357–72.

Kahneman, D., and Tversky, A. (1979). "Prospect Theory: An Analysis of Decision Under Risk." *Econometrika* 47 : 263–92.

Kanouse, D., and Wiest, W. (June 1967). "Some Factors Affecting Choice in the Prisoner's Dilemma." *Journal of Conflict Resolution* 11 : 206–13.

Keeny, S. M., Jr., and Panofsky, S. K. H. (1981–82). "Mad versus Nuts." *Foreign Affairs* 60 : 287–304.

Leites, N. (1963). "The Kremlin's Horizon." Santa Monica: The RAND Corporation.

Levi, A. (August 1981). "Escalating Commitment and Risk Taking in Dynamic Decision Behavior." Paper presented at the 89th Annual Convention of the American Psychological Association, Los Angeles.

Lowe, C. J. (1967). *The Reluctant Imperialists.* NY: Macmillan.

Maccoby, M. (1976). *The Gamesman.* NY: Simon and Schuster.

McCoy, C. (1960). *Polk and the Presidency.* Austin: University of Texas Press. P. 91.

Merton, R. K. (rev. ed., 1957). "The Self-Fulfilling Prophecy." In *Social Theory and Social Structure.* Glencoe, IL: Free Press.

Mowat, R. B. (1925). *The Diplomatic Relations of Great Britain and the United States.* London: Edward Arnold. P. 296.

Osgood, C. E. (1962). *An Alternative to War or Surrender.* Urbana: University of Illinois Press. Pp. 85–134.

Parkinson, R. (1971). *Peace for Our Time.* London: Rupert Hart-Davis. P. 41.

Rapoport, A. (1960). *Fights, Games, and Debates.* Ann Arbor: University of Michigan Press.

Rubin, J. Z. (1981). "Psychological Traps." *Psychology Today* 15 : 52–63.

Schell, J. (1982). *The Fate of the Earth.* NY: Knopf.

Schelling, T. C. (1963). *The Strategy of Conflict.* NY: Oxford University Press.

———— (1966). *Arms and Influence.* New Haven: Yale University Press.

Senate Committee on Armed Services. *Hearings on the Military Implications of the Treaty on the Limitations of Anti-Ballistic Missile Systems and the Interim Agreement on Limitation of Strategic Offensive Arms.* 92d Cong., 2d sess. P. 273.

Singer, J. D. (March 1958). "Threat-Perception and the Armament-Tension Dilemma." *Journal of Conflict Resolution* 2 : 101.

Snyder, G., and Diesing, P. (1977). *Conflict Among Nations.* Princeton: Princeton University Press. Chap. 4.

Spanier, J. (1965). *The Truman-MacArthur Controversy and the Korean War.* NY: Norton. P. 97.

Sperrazo, G. (1965). *Psychology and International Relations.* Washington, D. C.: Georgetown University Press.

Steiner, Z. (1969). *The Foreign Office and Foreign Policy 1898–1914.* Cambridge: Cambridge University Press.

Teger, A. I. (1980). *Too Much Invested to Quit.* NY: Pergamon Press.

Ulam, A. (1968). *Expansion and Coexistence.* NY: Praeger. P. 5.
Vaughan, D., trans. (1917). *A Lasting Peace Through the Federation of Europe.* London: Constable.
Wheeler-Bennett, J. (1971). *Brest-Litovsk.* NY: Norton. Pp. 295–96.

SECTION IV

Nonviolent Paths
to Security

SECTION EDITOR: RALPH K. WHITE

INTRODUCTION

Ralph K. White

In Section III two main strategies of war prevention were outlined: a strategy of armed deterrence, based on a model of an offensively motivated opponent resembling Hitler, and a strategy of tension reduction based on a model of a primarily defensively motivated opponent not very different in this respect from ourselves. In this section, Section IV, various possible forms of a tension-reduction strategy will be elaborated, with an emphasis on its psychological aspects. Deterrence will be considered in more detail in Section VIII.

This does not mean, however, that the two major strategies are inherently incompatible, or that those who want the primary emphasis to be given to tension reduction are necessarily opposed to armed deterrence. In fact, three of the four contributors to this section—Morton Deutsch, Charles E. Osgood, and Amitai Etzioni—explicitly favor some combination of the two strategies, including some forms and amounts of armed deterrence.

In Chapter 9 Deutsch's highly creative attempt to put international conflict into a laboratory test tube, so to speak, brings out the futility, in his laboratory situation, of a "turn-the-other-cheek strategy." It leads, he says, only to being exploited by the opponent. His results also favor a purely defensive type of deterrence. In Chapter 11 Charles Osgood advocates a carefully planned strategy of Graduated and Reciprocated Initiatives in Tension Reduction (GRIT). As part of the plan he favors keeping at all times both an adequate second-strike nuclear capability and adequate conventional forces. In Chapter 12 Amitai Etzioni describes President Kennedy's use, after the Cuban missile crisis, of a series of very moderate unilateral initiatives in the direction of tension reduction—a strategy resembling Osgood's GRIT, though there is no good reason to think Kennedy knew about either Etzioni's or Osgood's writing. The significant and very encouraging fact is that it "worked." Each American step was followed by an appropriate Soviet reciprocation. Etzioni points out, though, the moderate and mainly symbolic nature of the steps on both sides. No significant reductions of American armed forces were attempted.

Chapter 10, by Herbert C. Kelman, differs from the others in that the research for it has been primarily on the small group rather than on the national level, and questions of armed deterrence do not enter into it. Kelman describes here in some detail the theory and practice of his form of "conflict-resolution workshop," chiefly in the context of Arab-Israeli contacts, in a group atmosphere that puts a premium not on winning debating points but on achieving genuine understanding of the other side.

Naturally, these four chapters do not and cannot exhaust the possibilities of what can be done to stop and perhaps reverse a vicious circle of hostile interaction before it results in large-scale violence. Nor are those possibilities exhausted in later parts of the book. This is perhaps the best place to mention some of them, very briefly, that will not be covered elsewhere and can only be mentioned here.

Among them are some that are frequently dismissed as "unthinkable." They are not unthinkable. They deserve to be thought about.

With a few notes on possible reading, here is a list of alternatives that harder-line people often reject without real thinking:

- The Gandhi type of nonviolent, organized resistance (Sharp, 1984).
- Eventual world federation (Reves, 1945; Cousins, 1945; Einstein, 1945, pp. 347–51).
- An immediate total elimination of all the West's land-based nuclear weapons in Western Europe, including tactical battlefield weapons (see Lt. Gen. Collins, 1976, pp. 356–65), even if the USSR does not agree to eliminate its SS-20s— while retaining adequate conventional forces and sea-based nuclear weapons.

- Deployment of enough nuclear weapons for deterrent purposes but with an unannounced, absolute determination not to "press the button" even if the Soviet Union were to strike first (with less than all-out force).
- Elimination, in stages, of Soviet and American troops in Europe—mutual and balanced force reductions (Cox, 1982, 224–25).
- A military nonintervention pact banning the use of combat forces in the Third World by either superpower (Cox, 1982, pp. 149–64).
- A nearly total policy of not intervening in the Third World with military force even if the Soviet Union does. Let them take the blame, worldwide.
- Elimination of the nonintelligence, action functions of the CIA, such as assassination and arming rebels.

Here are some alternatives that softer-line people often reject without real thinking:

- Achievement of decisive Western superiority to the USSR in conventional forces (along with drastic unilateral nuclear reductions and tension reduction in many other ways)—if and when events make such an achievement possible (White, 1984, pp. 67–74).
- Genuine federation of the advanced democratic countries, leaving the Soviet Union out if it does not want to join. (Remember Clarence Streit's "Union Now"?)
- Reinstatement of conscription (along with drastic unilateral nuclear reductions and tension reduction in many other ways) if circumstances seem to require it.

And here are some that active members of the peace movement are almost automatically in favor of but that many of them would do well to study much more carefully, even if only to defend them adequately in public talks and private conversations:

- A no-first-use policy, implemented in action (no deployment of first-strike weapons or of tactical, battlefield nuclear weapons) as well as in words (Bundy, Kennan, McNamara, and Smith, 1982; Collins, 1976).

- The Gayler plan for simultaneous, public destruction of nuclear weapons, with "an equal number of explosive nuclear devices" destroyed on each side but with each side free to choose "the devices it wishes to turn in, whether missile warheads, bombs, or artillery shells. . . . Self-interest will make each side turn in its more vulnerable weapons. This is good" (1982).
- The Midgetman idea: elimination or drastic reduction of MIRVs (Kissinger, 1983), unilaterally if necessary.
- The build-down idea (Frye, 1983–1984), with consistent substitution of second-strike for first-strike weapons, including drastic reduction of MIRVs.
- Banning antisatellite (ASAT) devices.
- As part of a no-first-use policy, a public declaration that even battlefield nuclear weapons will not be used against a merely conventional attack (McNamara, 1983; Collins, 1976). (Whether they should be deployed is a separate question.)
- Candid opposition to the present undiscriminating taboo on the word "unilateral" when applied to *partial* and graduated measures such as Osgood's "GRIT" (Chapter 11, below). They sound quite different when a word like "initiative" is used instead or in addition. Etzioni's term "unilateral initiatives" (Chapter 12, below) is appropriate and deserves wide use. (See also Adelman, 1984–1985).
- *Great* emphasis on the need to avoid acute crises when they are avoidable (see Sections IX and X below), on avoiding a hair-trigger, launch-on-warning policy, on avoiding weapons that make such a policy rational, and on avoiding such a buildup of tension that either side might, in an acute crisis, mistakenly perceive imminent danger and take measures that would precipitate nuclear preemption by the other. The present readiness of each side to do this "if necessary" is now well established (Daniel Ford, 1985).
- An international mediation service (Azar and Burton, eds., 1985). On the nature of acceptable and effective mediation, see especially Kelman's Chapter 10 and Rubin's Chapter 30 in this book.
- Active employment and official encouragement of the right kind of unofficial, "track two" diplomacy, a term stressed especially by Joseph Montville (Davidson and Montville, 1981–1982; Landau, 1984; Rogers and Ryback, 1984;

Saunders, 1984). It too can be regarded as a promising form of mediation.

- Total rejection of the "Star War" concept. In addition to its fantastic cost and probable technical impracticality, three psychological considerations count against it: serious impairment of the arms control process, significant impairment of the Western alliance, and a major exacerbation of the entire "malignant process of hostile interaction." (John Newhouse, *The New Yorker,* July 22, 1985, 37–54).

9.

Strategies of Inducing Cooperation*

MORTON DEUTSCH

The effectiveness of several different strategies was investigated in a two-person laboratory game that permits players to act altruistically, cooperatively, individualistically, or aggressively toward one another. One of the players in each game was always an accomplice of the experimenter; he followed a predetermined strategy in response to the true subject's behavior in the game. The true subject, of course, did not know that he was playing with an experimenter's accomplice.

One strategy, termed "turn the other cheek," had the accomplice respond to attacks or threats by exhibiting altruistic behavior (doing something that rewarded the other) and by showing cooperative behavior otherwise. The "nonpunitive deterrent" strategy had the accomplice react self-protectively rather than with counterthreats or counterattacks when the subject threatened or attacked; otherwise, he reciprocated the subject's behaviors. The "punitive deterrent" strategy had the accomplice respond threateningly to any noncooperative acts of the subject and also had him counterattack when attacked; he responded cooperatively to any cooperative behavior from the subject.

The three basic strategies were selected in an attempt to represent, even if only crudely, three widely held positions

* Adapted from Morton Deutsch, *The Resolution of Conflict: Constructive and Destructive Processes* (New Haven: Yale University Press, 1973). See the original work for a fuller description of the experimental procedures and results.

regarding how to elicit cooperation. The turn-the-other-cheek strategy seeks to elicit cooperation by appealing to the social conscience and goodwill of the subject; such an approach has characterized many religious groups and the advocates of non-violence. The punitive deterrent strategy attempts to elicit co-operation by use of the carrot and the stick—that is, by rewarding cooperation and punishing noncooperation; it appeals to the economic motives of the subject by increasing the costs of noncooperative behavior. In so doing, it does not distinguish between the psychological effects of reward and those of pun-ishment. The implication is that rewards and punishments exist on a psychologically unidimensional continuum. Such an ap-proach often characterizes viewpoints that have been described as rationalistic, utilitarian, authoritarian, tough-minded, disci-plinarian, and militaristic; these viewpoints are, of course, not necessarily similar in other respects. The nonpunitive strategy places its emphasis on rewarding cooperation and on neutralizing or nonrewarding aggressive behavior; it appeals to the self-interests of the subject through positive rather than negative incentives and thus attempts to avoid the misunderstanding and hostility that may result from the subject's experience of pun-ishment. This type of strategy is often popular among progressive educators, psychotherapists, liberals, the "tender-minded," and the like.

We assumed that the subjects who were individualistically oriented (they were told "to earn as much money as you can for yourself regardless of how much the other earns") would tend to exploit the accomplice if he employed the turn-the-other-cheek strategy. Thus, it could be anticipated that the subjects' game outcomes in this condition would be relatively high, whereas those of the accomplices would be relatively low, with the discrepancy between their outcomes being quite large. In addition, the subjects, being individualistically oriented, could be expected to have difficulty in understanding why anyone would use such a strategy, and they might think that its use was stupid or bizarre. In contrast, we expected the nonpunitive strategy to elicit cooperation from the subjects and, hence, to result in relatively high outcomes for both the accomplices and the subjects. The punitive deterrent strategy, in comparison with the nonpunitive one, was expected to be relatively ineffective in eliciting cooperation, and it was anticipated that the game outcomes for both the subjects and the accomplices would be relatively low. It was expected that the punitive strategy would produce the most competitive behaviors (defensive and aggressive) of any of the strategies.

Several different experiments were conducted (see Deutsch, 1973, for details). The first, which will be described in some detail here, compared the effectiveness of five different strategies in a relatively noncompetitive situation. The strategies compared were: turn the other cheek, nonpunitive deterrence, punitive deterrence, and in addition (not discussed here): reformed sinner–turn the other cheek, and reformed sinner–nonpunitive.

Subjects

The subjects in this experiment consisted of a fairly diverse group of thirty-eight men and sixty-seven women, ranging in age from early twenties to late forties, who were randomly assigned to the various experimental conditions. The subject pool consisted of nonstudents as well as students.

Experimental Situation and Instructions

Recorded instructions for the game were played to the subjects over a tape recorder. A transcript of the instructions follows. (The material in brackets of the following was not included in those original instructions; it is included here to make the rationale of the procedure clear to the reader.)

> There are two of you who are going to play a game in which you can either win money or lose money. I want you to earn as much money as you can regardless of how much the other earns. This money is real and you will keep whatever you earn. This game consists of a series of trials; you each have a pegboard in front of you. This board is divided into two areas: a resource area and an allocation area. Your task on each of these trials will be to select one peg from the resource area and place it

in the allocation area. At the end of each trial, you will be told what the other has chosen for that trial and how much money you have each won or lost on that trial. [The subject does not know, until he has made his selection, what the other will do or has done on the same trial. He makes his decision in the light of what the other has done on previous trials. There is no direct communication between the subject and the accomplice.]

Now let me tell you something about these pegs; there are five different kinds of pegs: black, white, blue, red, and green. In addition, there are two specially shaped markers—orange and beige—and they each have pins on the top of them.

Whenever you choose a black peg it will earn money for you [6¢] regardless of what the other player chooses [though less than the 9¢ that each would earn if both cooperated by choosing a blue peg].

Whenever you choose a white peg it will earn money [7¢] for the other player but not for you. [This of course seems strange—and did seem strange to the subjects—in a game in which the basic instruction was to "earn as much money as you can." The white pegs were included chiefly so that the accomplice might use them in carrying out the "turn-the-other-cheek" strategy, and so that the subject himself might use them on occasion if he wanted to show unequivocal goodwill, or perhaps placate the other's anger if he thought the other was angry.]

Blue pegs are worth a large amount of money [i.e., relatively large—9¢] if you both choose them on the same trial, but they are only worth a small amount of money [1¢] if they are not matched on the same trial. [This is the cooperative choice, which in the long run was unquestionably the best for each player to make, most of the time, even from the standpoint of pure economic self-interest.]

Red pegs can only be used to attack the other and take away his money [i.e., taking away 6¢ and adding the same amount to what the subject himself gets. It will be noticed that the immediate effect of choosing a red peg, which meant both subtracting 6¢ from the opponent's earnings and adding 6¢ to one's own, was to gain a *relative* advantage of 12¢, but that in terms of adding to one's own earnings, which after all was the announced purpose of the game, it contributed less than the 9¢ that could be gained by cooperation. Pure economic self-interest was on the side of blue rather than red pegs.

But presumably attacking the other with red pegs gave more sense of relative superiority, in the short run, and also a venting of anger, giving the satisfaction of "punishing" the other for something he has just done. It expresses the punitive type of deterrence.]

[As the outcome showed, the great disadvantage of punitive deterrence as compared with the nonpunitive strategy was that in it the red pegs were much more often used on *both* sides. Red pegs—when first selected and held in reserve—had some resemblance to arms piled up in an arms race, and their later use had some resemblance to the use of arms in a war.]

Green pegs can only be used to defend your money from the opponents' attacks. [When a subject selected a green peg, it added nothing immediately to his own earnings but enabled him later to "neutralize" the other's attack, if the other attacked by using a red peg. It represented the nonpunitive strategy in that it took away from the other exactly the 6¢ that his use of a red peg, against no defense, would have netted him—no more and no less.] Red pegs and green pegs are worth nothing unless they are used in an attack.

Orange markers indicate that you wish to attack the other player. [That is, they indicate that you intend to do so on the next trial. It is understood that a red peg will not be used without a previous threat, which alerts the other to use a green peg on the next trial if he has one. The orange marker, therefore, performs a function similar to that of an ultimatum or a declaration of war in an international crisis.]

Beige markers indicate that you have disarmed—that is, you have destroyed all the red attack pegs that you have accumulated up to that trial.

Experimental Design

Although there were five experimental conditions (i.e., strategies) in the first of four experiments, only the three main ones will be described here, and only in the context of the first experiment. The results of the other experiments were essentially the same. The three main strategies were:

1. *Turn the other cheek.* The experimenter's accomplice chose blue on the first trial, white on the second trial, and blue on

the third trial. (In other words, he was "nice" in that he was cooperative [blue peg] on the first and third trials and supercooperative [white peg] on the second.) He did so no matter what the actual subject chose. Thereafter, he chose blue (cooperation), except that he chose white if the subject had chosen red or orange on the preceding trial. (That is, he returned good for evil.)

2. *Nonpunitive* (or nonpunitive deterrent). The accomplice chose blue on the first three trials. Thereafter, he matched what the subject chose on the preceding trial. (This resembles Rapoport's TIT-FOR-TAT, used with great effectiveness in the computerized tournament organized by Axelrod. He did so with the following exceptions: if the subject chose red or orange (attack), the accomplice chose green (defense); if the subject chose green (defense), the accomplice chose blue (cooperation). (In effect, the accomplice was teaching the subject that he could gain nothing by attacking and that he could gain the profits of cooperation, thereafter, if he simply defended himself when attacked.)

3. *Deterrent* (or punitive deterrent). The accomplice chose blue on the first trial, and whenever the subject chose blue, white or beige. To a choice of black (noncooperative self-interest), green (noncooperative defense), or red (attack), he responded with red; if the subject chose orange (threat of attack), he counterattacked with orange on the next trial. (In effect, he was trying to teach the subject that he would suffer if he did anything except cooperate—but the subject usually responded with anger and with counterattacks to this attempt to dominate his behavior.)

Results of the First Experiment

The accomplice's outcome. Figure 9.1 gives the answer to the question of which strategy benefited the accomplice most. Evidently, the nonpunitive strategy was considerably more rewarding than either the turn-the-other-cheek or the punitive deterrence strategy. Although the outcomes for the accomplice who employed the punitive deterrent strategy were, on the average, worse than those for the turn-the-other-cheek strategist, the outcomes for the former improved over the last several trial blocks but worsened for the latter.

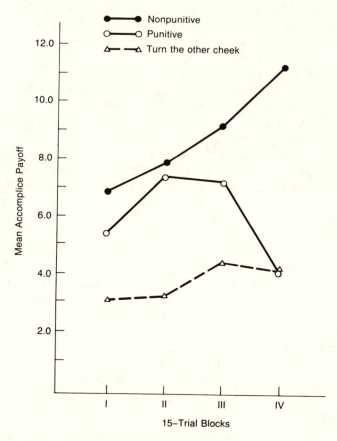

Figure 9.1
Mean payoffs of accomplices (in cents, divided by 10 by 15-trial blocks

   Postexperimental questionnaires showed that the subjects perceived the accomplices in the nonpunitive condition as the most cooperative, most stable, and most fair; they were also perceived as being relatively kind, generous, and peaceful. The punitive strategists were rated as the most uncooperative, least kind, and most selfish of the accomplices; they were also considered to be relatively unstable.

Overall Summary of the Experiments

The results of the four experiments are very consistent, and they can be summarized as follows:

(1) The "nonpunitive" strategy was most effective in eliciting cooperative behavior from the subjects and, overall, resulted in the highest joint outcomes as well as the highest outcomes for the accomplice. The effectiveness of this strategy varied least from situation to situation. In none of the experiments were any of the other strategies more effective than the nonpunitive one in eliciting cooperation and reducing aggression from the subjects. Only under the extremely competitive conditions of the fourth experiment was this strategy no more effective than the punitive deterrent one, and even then, when the accomplice had equal power with the subject, he elicited less competitive behavior when he employed a nonpunitive rather than a punitive strategy.

(2) The effectiveness of the turn-the-other-cheek strategy was very much influenced by the competitiveness of the situation; the more competitive the incentives of the subjects, the more massively they exploited the accomplice who employed this strategy.

(3) The punitive deterrent strategy elicited more aggressive and self-protective, as well as less cooperative, behavior from the subjects than did the other strategies. The punitive deterrent accomplice was rated as the most uncooperative, least kind, and most selfish of the accomplices; he was also considered to be relatively unstable.

Implications

It is sometimes assumed that the best way to deter the Soviet Union from initiating aggressive actions and to encourage them to engage in cooperative actions is to threaten them with a severe punitive retaliation if they behave aggressively or non-cooperatively. Our experiments suggest that this may be a dangerous strategy; it may discourage rather than encourage cooperative behavior and provoke rather than deter aggressive action. The Soviet Union is apt to experience a threatening, punitive stance from the United States as being aggressive rather than deterrent in intent. When deterrence is combined with punitive threat, the punitive threat in the message is more likely to be perceived than the deterrence.

In contrast, a nonpunitive deterrent strategy that emphasizes protecting oneself rather than punitive retaliation in response to aggression is much less likely to provoke aggression and much more apt to elicit cooperation. The clear implication is that the United States and the Soviet Union, as well as other nations, should be engaged in a buildup of self-protective defensive weapons while they should drastically reduce the weapons that could be used for attacks (whether labeled "defensive" or not). Military research and development as well as strategic and tactical thinking on both sides should be reoriented toward developing the capability to protect oneself and one's allies rather than toward being able to prevail over the other.

The ability of each of the superpowers to change from a threatening to a self-protective orientation would be greatly enhanced if the superpowers could come to the following sorts of agreements: (1) not to be the first to use nuclear weapons; (2) to put a verifiable freeze on further deployment, research, development, and testing of nuclear weapons; (3) to reduce conventional arms in the Soviet and NATO blocs, particularly those weapons that have little value for defense; (4) to create a demilitarized zone in Central Europe that would separate the military forces of the opposing blocs by a militarily significant amount of space and reduce the likelihood of a successful surprise attack; (5) to reduce drastically the nuclear weapons of both sides so that the combined total is below the threshold of a possible nuclear attack; and (6) to develop procedures for continuing consultation between the military leaders of both sides to develop procedures to reduce the likelihood of war due to accident, mischief, misunderstanding, or craziness.

10.

An Interactional Approach to Conflict Resolution*

HERBERT C. KELMAN

Substantial reductions in armaments would contribute significantly to the goal of avoiding nuclear war. They would decrease the likelihood and danger of nuclear accidents and create an atmosphere more conducive to defusing crises before they lead to peace-threatening actions and to avoiding escalation once such actions have occurred. But it is at least equally important to develop and institutionalize mechanisms of crisis management and conflict resolution. Such mechanisms would allow adversaries to engage in communication that sets off a deescalatory dynamic and a search for mutually satisfactory solutions. The work reported here represents an effort in that direction.

In this work, my colleagues and I have not focused directly on the United States–Soviet conflict but on regional conflicts that have obvious repercussions on the relations between the superpowers. Apart from some work on the Cyprus conflict, my major efforts in recent years have concentrated on the Middle East conflict. This work relates to the goal of avoiding nuclear war in at least two respects. First, given the high degree of superpower involvement in all the globe's trouble spots, regional conflicts present the danger of escalating United States-Soviet confrontation that might touch off an unintentional military exchange—an exchange that might start with conventional weap-

* Taken, with minor modifications, from an article that originally appeared in *International Interactions* 6, 1979, no. 2 (1979): 99–122.

ons and move on to nuclear ones. The danger that the super-powers might inadvertently, through a succession of small commitments, be drawn into a regional war is probably greater in the Middle East than in any other area of the world. Second, the orientation and techniques that we have been developing can be applied, with appropriate adaptations, to efforts to manage and resolve the United States–Soviet conflict.

Our approach to conflict resolution starts with a focus on the way in which *interactions* between the parties—at different levels—create the conditions for conflict and help to feed, escalate, and perpetuate it. Conflict resolution, in this view, requires the introduction of interactions that are capable of reversing these processes.

Social-Psychological Analysis

The emphasis on interaction processes in the evolution and resolution of conflict suggests the potential relevance of a social-psychological analysis. Social psychology, in addition to taking social interaction as its central focus, bridges the individual level and the social system level of analysis (Kelman, 1965). Thus, social-psychological analysis suggests an approach to conflict resolution in which changes in individual attitudes and images, produced through direct interaction between the conflicting parties, serve as a vehicle for, and an accompaniment of, changes at the policy level. Such an analysis, however, cannot be seen as a substitute for or an alternative to political analysis. Psychological factors suffuse and interact with political factors, and the two must be integrated in a comprehensive theory of international conflict and its resolution.

Psychological conditions cannot be divorced from objective conditions that underlie the conflict. International conflicts typically evolve out of real conflicts of interest and ideological differences that cannot be attributed simply to misperception and distrust. Psychological factors, however, contribute to escalation and perpetuation of conflict by creating barriers to both the occurrence and the perception of change. The dynamics of a conflict relationship create conceptual and structural commitments to the conflict. They make it difficult for the parties to change their policies even when the objective conditions have changed and new policies might be more congruent with their perceived national interests. Often, the political leadership and various interest groups in each society are tightly bound into the conflict: their thinking is dominated by the assumption that the conflict is inevitable; their raison d'être often depends on the continuation of the conflict. Moreover, the dynamics of conflict make it difficult to perceive changes that have already occurred in the behavior of the adversary, or to conceive of the possibility of change under changing circumstances. Change tends to be dismissed or assimilated to rigidly held negative images of the adversary. These perceptual tendencies are reinforced by a fear of underestimating the hostile intentions of the adversary and of thus being caught off guard. Failure to perceive change in the other further reduces each party's inclination to change its own behavior. Thus, barriers to the perception of change produce barriers to the occurrence of change.

Overcoming these psychological barriers does not in itself resolve a conflict. I go on the assumption that the settlement of an international conflict must ultimately take place at the political level, through political processes. But, to the extent that such psychological barriers can be overcome, new possibilities may be created for negotiations on the basis of objective conditions and of the current interests of the parties. As long as these barriers persist, the parties are locked into rigid assumptions and postures rooted in past history.

Even though, as I have argued, social-psychological analysis cannot be separated from, or placed in opposition to, political analysis, it typically does represent a different set of assumptions and emphases. I have become increasingly aware of some of the biases that distinguish a social-psychological approach—or, at least, the particular social-psychological approach pursued by my colleagues and myself—from more traditional approaches to international conflict that emphasize balance of power and military strategy. Some of the main biases of our approach can be summarized as follows:

(1) It views international conflict not only as a conflict between nation-states but also as a conflict between societies. Thus,

while acknowledging the significance of the strategic, military, and diplomatic dimensions, it also considers the psychological, cultural, social-structural, and economic dimensions as central to the analysis of the conflict.

(2) It sees the goal of negotiations as not merely to conclude a politically acceptable agreement but to achieve a state of peace. Thus, it always asks whether particular arrangements that have been worked out between the parties or by third parties advance or impede the kinds of attitudinal and structural changes within the conflicting societies and within the region that spell the conditions for a stable peace. It evaluates diplomatic agreements in terms of their contribution to a larger process of psychological and social change consistent with long-run peace.

(3) It tends to be suspicious about imposed agreements, sponsored by the great powers. It generally favors a process that allows agreements to emerge from the parties themselves, representing commitments to a new relationship within each of the societies involved.

(4) It tends to assign a significant role to public opinion, while recognizing that basic foreign policy decisions are made by political elites and that public opinion itself is shaped by these elites to a considerable degree. It sees public opinion as expressing general moods within the society, which serve as important resources or constraints to decision makers.

(5) It favors "best-case" analyses, in contrast to the "worst-case" analyses that traditional analysts often prefer. In contrast to traditional analyses, it starts with a broader view of national interests, an assumption that changes can and do take place, and a concern with recognizing and utilizing opportunities for change in the direction of peace. Whereas a worst-case analysis is designed to protect us from the danger of inadequate defense against all possible threats, a best-case analysis is designed to protect us from the danger of inadequate response to new opportunities. Each kind of analysis contributes to creating its own self-fulfilling prophecies. A best-case analysis is sometimes misread as an indication of optimism. It can be understood more properly as a form of "strategic" or "possibilistic" optimism: by focusing on positive outcomes that are possible (even if not highly probable under existing circumstances), it may

help to create self-fulfilling prophecies in a positive direction. Thus, optimism serves as a strategy designed to bring about the peace-promoting conditions that it envisages.

These general assumptions have governed the work on the Middle East conflict in which I have been engaged over the last few years, in collaboration with a number of colleagues. (I am especially indebted to Stephen P. Cohen, who played a central role in the development of this program and in the elaboration of the theory of practice that underlies it [see Kelman and Cohen, 1976; Cohen et al., 1977; Kelman and Cohen, 1979]. I am also grateful for the support and stimulation provided by Samir N. Anabtawi, Edward E. Azar, and A. Hussain Tuma. As members, along with Stephen Cohen and myself, of an ethnically mixed [Arab and Jewish American] team, they were active and essential participants in the early work of the program.) Our work can best be described as an action research program, which combines and integrates efforts at conflict resolution in the Middle East with unique opportunities to observe and learn about the dynamics of the Middle East conflict and of international conflict in general. Our action is designed to contribute to conflict resolution by creating opportunities for communication between influential Arabs and Israelis, under the auspices of our group of social scientists. My colleagues and I perform, in essence, the role of a special, unofficial third party in conflict resolution. Our status as social scientists is the primary source of our potential contribution, as well as of our legitimacy as a third party.

The starting point and in many ways the prototype for our work has been the "problem-solving workshop in conflict resolution." Our conception of problem-solving workshops flows directly from the work of John Burton (1969) and his associates on controlled communication. Our approach represents an elaboration of Burton's model with certain modifications. For example, substantively, we tend to place special emphasis on what my colleague, Stephen Cohen, has called "the negotiation of identity"; and, procedurally, we place greater emphasis on the analysis of group process and "here-and-now" interactions. In the emphasis on group process, we have also been influenced by the work of Doob and his associates (Doob, 1970; Doob and Foltz, 1973; Doob, 1974). (See Kelman [1972] for a description and comparison of the Burton and Doob models.) The problem-solving workshops on the Middle East conflict that we have organized have mainly involved Israeli and Palestinian participants (see Cohen et al., 1977; Kelman, 1978), although we have also worked with other groupings of Arabs and Israelis.

The purpose of a problem-solving workshop is to bring together representatives of conflicting parties in a relatively isolated setting—preferably an academic context—where they can engage, free from diplomatic protocol and publicity, in face-to-face communication in the presence and under the guidance of social scientists knowledgeable about group process and conflict theory. In general, ideal participants for such interactions are individuals who are highly influential within their respective communities but are not themselves in policymaking positions. The participants come in their private capacities, rather than as designated representatives. To maximize the impact of the workshop on the policy process, however, it is usually best that they participate with the knowledge and tacit consent of relevant official agencies. Although communications are strictly unofficial, workshops are explicitly designed to facilitate, supplement, and feed into official actions or negotiations. They are not just scholarly conferences or opportunities for personal encounters across the conflict lines but are meant to provide relevant inputs into national and international political and social processes. They are not governed by norms of politeness and efforts to avoid confrontation; rather, they are designed to focus on central issues in the conflict. And, even though the participants are invited as individuals, the composition of the teams and the structure of the situation encourage the members of each party to function as a group with some degree of collective responsibility.

Discussions are relatively unstructured but are guided by the social scientists in their third-party role. Setting, agenda, ground rules, procedures, and third-party interventions are designed to counteract the accusatory, legalistic, and conflict-expressive atmosphere that usually characterizes interaction between conflicting parties, and to promote, instead, a task-oriented, analytical approach. The assumption is that the atmosphere created by the workshop has a potential for producing changes in perceptions and attitudes, and for generating new ideas and creative solutions that can then be fed into the decision-making process.

From a theoretical point of view, the problem-solving workshop represents a systematic effort to utilize social-psychological principles in achieving a specific set of effects—both within the communication situation itself and within the larger conflict system. Social-psychological principles enter into the formulation of the structure, the process, and the content of the problem-solving workshop. The *structure* is based on analysis of the place of the workshop within the larger social system in which the conflict takes place. The *process* is designed to create the conditions conducive to establishing and maintaining certain patterns of social interaction and to utilize the ongoing interactions themselves as raw materials for gaining greater understanding of the dynamics of the conflict. The *content* focuses to a considerable degree on social-psychological analyses of collective experiences and processes, such as mutual perceptions and images, national self-images and national identity, sources and forms of nationalist ideology, interaction processes conducive to the escalation of conflict, and structural changes conducive to its perpetuation.

In the remainder of this chapter, I shall examine problem-solving workshops—and conflict resolution more generally—from the theoretical perspective of social interaction. From this perspective, as I said earlier, conflict resolution requires creating situations in which productive interaction between conflicting parties becomes possible, and which are conducive to individual-level changes that can be translated into changes at the level of national policies and political structures. What are the theoretical and procedural implications of this interactional view of conflict resolution? And what are the kinds of new learning that are made possible in situations conducive to productive interaction and to personal attitude change? I shall explore these questions with reference to our experiences with problem-solving workshops, particularly in relation to the Israeli-Palestinian conflict.

The Workshop as a Unique Context for Social Interaction

A central characteristic of social interaction, under "normal" conditions, is that its participants try to take into account, not only each other's behavior, but also each other's purposes, perceptions, and intentions, and the structural constraints within which these are formed. As interaction proceeds over time, each participant becomes aware of changes in the other's situation, ideas, and actions—and, indeed, of the possibilities of influencing these through his or her own actions.

These normal processes and consequences of social interaction are impaired by the special dynamics that mark interaction between conflicting parties. Often the parties in conflict do not interact at all—as has been true, to a large extent, in the history of the Arab-Israeli conflict. When they do interact, it is precisely in the kind of context in which they are unable to learn anything new about the other party or about themselves. The norms that govern interaction between representatives of conflicting parties require each to express their own grievances and to proclaim their own rights as firmly and militantly as possible. If the adversary describes atrocities in which hundreds were killed, they must counter with atrocities in which thousands were killed. If the adversary cites historical claims that go back 100 years, they must counter with claims that go back 1,000 years. Each party comes prepared (often literally) with historical and legal documents that are brought out at appropriate moments to demonstrate their allegations or claims.

The representatives of conflicting parties engaged in such interactions are judged by their constituencies—and indeed judge themselves—by how well they have been able to advance and defend their positions and how strong a case they have presented. They focus only on what they themselves have to say, not on what the other has to say. There is little attempt, as in more usual interaction situations, to gain an understanding of the other's perspective—except perhaps in the crudest strategic terms. Nor are they particularly interested in influencing the adversary; their communications are directed to their own constituencies and to third parties, rather than to the representatives of the other party. Thus, even when there is interaction between conflicting parties, it is typically of such a nature as to reinforce existing images and to strengthen each party's commitment to its original position.

The purpose of problem-solving workshops is to create a situation in which genuine social interaction between conflicting parties becomes possible and in which there is thus an opportunity for new learning. Participants are encouraged to attend to the other party, to try to grasp the other's perspective, and to examine their own impact on the other. They thus focus on the conflict analytically: they try to analyze, with each other's help, how each perceives itself and its antagonist. This kind of analytical approach is designed to promote a collaborative problem-solving process, which is intended to go beyond intellectual exchange between the parties to a confrontation of each other's fundamental identity concerns. The assumption is that creative possibilities for conflict resolution can emerge once the parties treat the conflict as a shared dilemma requiring some common effort for its solution.

There is no substitute for direct interaction in producing these new insights and ideas for conflict resolution. Certain kinds of solutions can emerge only from the mutual confrontation of assumptions, concerns, and identities in the course of face-to-face communication. In other words, the parties need each other if creative new ideas are to evolve—ideas for solution that are responsive to each party's fundamental needs and anxieties.

The Contributions of the Third Party

These kinds of emergent ideas are, by definition, products of social interaction between the parties themselves and cannot be supplied by a third party. In this respect, our approach contrasts with certain other forms of mediation, in which the third party plays an active role in proposing or imposing ideas for solution. The third party does, however, play an essential role in our approach in bringing the conflicting parties together and in creating a situation in which they will engage in constructive interaction. In our view, the primary role of the third party is to *facilitate* communication by providing the appropriate context, norms, and interventions.

One of the most important contributions of the third party is in creating an appropriate normative context for interaction. As was pointed out in the preceding section, interaction among conflicting parties is governed by a set of strict norms and expectations that circumscribe the role of representative of a party in conflict. To facilitate constructive interaction, one needs a context that can counteract these norms with an appropriate set of alternative norms. One of the innovative features of Burton's (1969) model is the insight that the academic context is especially suited to provide such an alternative set of norms. Participants come to a workshop with the understanding that they will be working with a group of academics in the analysis of conflict. They come into the academics' setting, which is governed by its own set of norms, encouraging and indeed requiring an analytic approach. Having committed themselves to an academic framework, the participants feel both obligated and free to abide by its norms. They can listen and speak in ways that would be impossible if they were functioning under the strict constraints of their conflict roles.

Third-party interventions are designed to establish and maintain these norms and to keep the discussions moving along productive channels. Interventions may take the form of: (1) theoretical inputs, which help participants distance themselves from their own conflict, provide them conceptual tools for analysis of their conflict, and offer them relevant illustrations from previous research; (2) content observations, which suggest interpretations and implications of what is being said and point to convergences and divergences between the parties, to blind spots, to possible signals, and to issues for clarification; or (3) process observations at the intergroup level, which suggest possible ways in which interactions between the parties "here and now" may reflect the dynamics of the conflict between their communities.

The potential usefulness of process observations can be illustrated with two events that took place during our very first workshop on the Israeli-Palestinian conflict, which was held late in 1971 (see Cohen et al., 1977). There were many points during the workshop when the Palestinians attacked the Israelis, and attributed imperialism, expansionism, and other negative traits to Israel. The Israelis responded firmly but they seemed to accept such attacks as a legitimate part of the process. There was only one point during the entire proceedings when the Israelis threatened to walk out—and this was when one of the Palestinians, quite innocently it seems, told a classic anti-Semitic joke. The Palestinians were quite surprised by the intensity of the Israeli reaction. The second event was one in which the Israelis were caught by surprise. They were giving the Palestinians what they considered to be "friendly" advice on how to organize their political movement more effectively. The Palestinians responded with an outburst of anger. Clearly the Palestinians saw the Israeli advice giving as an act of arrogance and condescension, which underscored their own sense of powerlessness.

These two incidents illustrate in concrete, "here-and-now" fashion central elements of the national identities of the two parties. They touch areas of special sensitivity for each group by surfacing negative elements of their identities that are of central concern to them. These negative identity elements represent sources of profound humiliation and fear for the groups, reminding them of their current or historical powerlessness and vulnerability. In the case of the Israelis, the reaction to the anti-Semitic joke illustrated the centrality of the Jewish historical experience of persecution and exclusion in Israeli national identity. In the case of the Palestinians, the reaction to Israeli advice giving illustrated their intense frustration over being unable to control their own fates and their view of Israel as the central symbol and current source of this frustration.

The intense reactions to these events and the fact that, in each case, these reactions were unanticipated by the other party, make them excellent raw material for third-party intervention. Each party can concretely see the intensity of the other's reactions and the genuine and spontaneous nature of that reaction. Moreover, they can see that it was their own actions that produced this response, without intention on their part to be provocative or even awareness that they were touching on sensitive areas. The third party can use such incidents, which are part of the participants' shared immediate experience, as a springboard for exploring some of the issues and concerns that define the conflict between their societies. Through such exploration, they can gain some insight into the preoccupations of the other side, and the way these are affected by the actions of their own side. That these preoccupations, which surfaced so dramatically in the course of our 1971 workshop, play an important role in the relations between the conflicting societies, was illustrated in the Egyptian-Israeli negotiations in 1978. Incidents that contributed most visibly to the souring of the relationship between the two parties were Egyptian actions that Israelis saw as anti-Semitic (such as references in the Egyptian press to Begin or to Israel as "Shylock") and Israeli actions that Egyptians saw as arrogant (such as statements to the effect that Israel does not "need" Egypt's recognition). Thus, interventions that focus on such incidents in the course of a workshop may lead to discussion and analysis of issues that form a significant part of the dynamics of the conflict between the two societies.

It is important that such interventions be pitched at the intergroup level, rather than the interpersonal level. Analysis of "here-and-now" interactions is not concerned with the personal characteristics of the participants or with their personal relations to each other but only with what these interactions can tell us about the relationship between their national groups. Experiences within the workshop do provide an especially effective springboard for helping parties gain greater insight into their own and their adversary's concerns and sensitivities because of the immediacy and the emotional strength of the experience. Analysis of intense reactions as they happen is instructive both for those who experience the reaction in themselves and those who observe it in the other. What is particularly instructive for the observers is the opportunity to see directly the impact that they have had upon the other.

To provide the context, norms, and interventions that can facilitate constructive interaction, the third party clearly needs to possess certain special characteristics. In our work, our status as academics, social scientists, and students of international conflict provides an important basis for our credibility and legitimacy in the eyes of the parties. There is the presumption that we have the necessary skill, knowledge, and objectivity to perform the third-party function—a presumption that is, of course, continually being put to the test. In addition, it is generally assumed that a third party needs to be neutral; our own experience suggests a qualification of that assumption. Since the initiators of the program described here were two Jewish social scientists, it was difficult for us to present ourselves as totally neutral in the Middle East conflict. Instead, we developed a team that was ethnically balanced. Perhaps we are making a virtue out of necessity, but on the basis of both theory and experience, we are now persuaded that a team marked by "engagement" in the conflict (as long as its composition is balanced) has many advantages over one marked by "neutrality" in the sense of disinterestedness. In profound conflicts, neutrality of this sort may be interpreted as a superior attitude and may in fact create resentment against the third party and reduce its credibility. By contrast, a team that, collectively, approaches the conflict with a sense of urgency and a variety of perspectives, conveys greater sensitivity to nuances of the parties, greater alertness to the cultural and psychological dimensions of the conflict, and greater sympathy for the emotional and symbolic issues at stake. This kind of engagement, of course, must be clearly distinguished from partisanship. The team cannot be seen as systematically biased toward either side. Nor is it desirable for the team to be committed to any particular solution, although it must be committed to the search for solutions that are peaceful and just.

Dialectics of Problem-Solving Workshops

Social interaction in the context of a workshop takes place among individuals. The procedures are directed at the individual participants' affective and cognitive processes, yet the ultimate aim of the intervention is to produce changes at the level of social systems. The unique claim of the approach is precisely that it is capable of promoting system-level changes by producing changes in individuals—that is, changes in *policy* by way of changes in individual *perceptions* and *attitudes*. This strategy creates certain contradictory requirements. The specific requirements for maximizing impact on the individuals are different from those for maximizing impact on the system, and they may in fact conflict with each other.

Thus, the theoretical task of identifying the requirements of an effective workshop represents, to a large extent, a dialectical process. We need to develop an intervention model that is cognizant of the potential contradictions between different requirements and that seeks to establish a balance between them. I shall examine several elements of a workshop, each of which is marked by certain contradictory requirements that the intervenor must take into account and attempt to balance against one another. (The following discussion of the dialectics of workshops is taken, in abbreviated form, from Kelman and Cohen [1979].)

Goals. A major source of potential contradictions, with implications for many other elements of the workshop, are the requirements for *change* and those for *transfer.* Workshops are designed to achieve two goals: (1) to give participants the freedom, opportunity, and motivation to move away from the rigid reiteration of official positions and from efforts to justify their own side and score points against the adversary, and, instead, to absorb new information, explore new ideas, revise their perceptions, reassess their attitudes, and engage in a process of creative problem solving; and (2) to increase the likelihood that the new information and ideas, the changed perceptions and attitudes, and the innovative proposals for solutions generated by the discussion will be fed into the policy process. The conditions most conducive to the achievement of the first goal, the production of change, may in fact hamper the achievement of the second goal, the transfer of changes to the policy process. Such contradictions affect, for example, the selection of participants and the choice of the setting in which the workshop is held. Decisions on these and other dimensions that may seem ideally suited to maximize the first goal may do so at the expense of the second goal. Thus, in planning a workshop, it is essential to keep in mind at all times the delicate balance between conditions for change and conditions for transfer. It is particularly important, in this connection, to see the workshop in relation to the larger conflict and to other ongoing or possible efforts at resolution, rather than as a self-contained exercise.

Participants. What kinds of participants are most appropriate depends, of course, on the nature, purpose, and timing of a particular workshop. In general, however, the most suitable participants in my view are individuals who are *unofficial* but politically *influential.* There is a certain contradiction here, in that officials themselves would have the most immediate influence and be in the best position to transfer new ideas to the policy process. Unofficial participants, on the other hand, are less constrained by public postures, more free to take an analytical role, more open to new information and insights, and more available for change in their perceptions and attitudes. Thus, the criterion of openness to change favors unofficial participants, but the criterion of maximization of transfer underscores the importance of political influence. A good balance is provided by participants who—though not decision makers themselves—are able to reflect "representative" points of view, to serve as conduits for ideas that the leadership would like to explore, and to feed their new learning and insights into the policy process. They should, thus, be influential within their respective societies, speak for (and to) some significant constituencies, and have access to the political leaders. Scholars of the conflict, business leaders, leading intellectuals, journalists, government advisers, and parliamentarians are examples of the types of groups that might represent the proper balance between the contradictory requirements for participation.

Setting. The workshop setting must combine the partially contradictory characteristics of *novelty* and *realism.* A novel context is essential to override the norms that generally govern interactions between conflicting parties and to introduce norms that favor analytic communication, in which each side is able to consider the perspective of the other side and to engage in collaborative problem solving. Only in such a setting can new ideas emerge and new learning take place. In our design, the academic setting provides the context which both frees and obligates the participants to adhere to an alternative set of norms. New thinking is also facilitated by insulating the workshop from outside distractions and pressures—by developing a "cultural island" (Walton, 1970). But if the new ideas and learning are to be maintained outside the workshop and to find their way into the policy process, then the novelty and insulation of the setting must be balanced by realism. It would not be helpful to create an illusory atmosphere of friendship and camaraderie in which participants are encouraged to forget that they represent communities engaged in a bitter conflict. Such an atmosphere may hamper the reality testing of new ideas and produce proposals that are unacceptable in the "real world" to which the participants will be returning.

Interaction focus. The requirement of realism suggests that workshop participants must, to a certain extent, function as members of a national team rather than as totally independent individuals. This consideration raises the issue of balancing the *interpersonal* and the *intersocietal* levels as the foci for interaction within a workshop. On the one hand, the process itself is of necessity interpersonal: individuals learn from interaction with other individuals. On the other hand, the object of the exercise is to learn about and produce changes in intersocietal relations. Insofar as participants function as individuals, rather than team members, the opportunities for certain kinds of learning are enhanced: members of each party can deviate more readily from official positions and communicate variations in point of view within their group, thus making available a wider range of ideas for discussion and a more differentiated picture of the parties. Insofar as participants function as national teams, however, they provide a more realistic picture of the collective processes involved in the perpetuation and possible resolution of the conflict. By the same token, ideas around which the members of the national team are able to achieve a certain degree of consensus are more likely to survive beyond the workshop and enter into the policy process.

Tone. In setting the tone for the discussions, the third party encourages the participants to combine an attitude of profound *seriousness* with a certain degree of *playfulness.* Since workshops are conceived as inputs to policy formation and negotiation, it is important that the participants view the discussions as a very serious opportunity to gain information and develop ideas that may help to shape the thinking and action of their political leadership and be directly relevant to the course of future events. The workshop should ideally be seen as more than an intellectual exercise of merely academic interest. At the same time, one of the special advantages of the academic context is that it offers the parties an opportunity to communicate with minimum commitment and risk. This has a bearing, not only on their willingness to participate (at a time when official discussions would represent unacceptable commitments and risks), but also on the type of communication they are prepared to engage in. They can discuss issues and entertain ideas they would have to avoid if they were speaking "for the record." The workshop thus encourages participants to be playful, not in the sense of engaging in discussions whose substance and manner lack seriousness, but in the sense of expressing novel ideas and exploring hypothetical scenarios without the usual inhibitions of immediate public accountability. In short, participants should ideally bring to the discussions an attitude of serious commitment to the issues without feeling irrevocably committed to every word they utter.

Interventions. Third-party interventions must combine the *intellectual* and the *emotional* dimensions. On the one hand, they consist of intellectual inputs that may suggest theoretical formulations, conceptual tools, or research findings potentially useful for understanding and analysis of the conflict. On the other hand, they call attention (always in a tentative way) to the emotional and symbolic meanings of what is being conveyed through both the content and the process of interaction. The intellectual and the emotional emphases are in some sense contradictory, but it is precisely the balanced integration of the two that lies at the heart of the interactional approach to conflict resolution, both in the procedures it uses and in the substantive issues on which it dwells. Procedurally, it is a form of intervention designed to enhance the parties' understanding of the conflict—and hence of the possibilities of conflict resolution—through a process of interaction that gives them access to the adversary's perspective, in its emotional and symbolic richness. Substantively, it treats conflict and conflict resolution as social processes that can best be understood through analysis of the internal structures, the identity concerns, and the symbolic meaning systems of each society and the ways in which they interact with each other.

Learning from Social Interaction

Throughout this article, I have argued that there are certain kinds of new learning that are made possible by social interaction. Problem-solving workshops are designed to facilitate interaction between conflicting parties in ways that are conducive to such new learning. In this concluding section, I shall illustrate the kinds of learning that may emerge from a successful workshop. The illustrations are derived from recent workshops with Israeli and Palestinian participants.

The perspective of the other party. Interactions in the context of a workshop enable each party to acquire some insight into the perspective of the other. They can gain a better understanding of the psychological environment and internal structure of the adversary's society. Thus, they become better able to take into account, not only each other's actions, but also each other's purposes, perceptions, intentions, and structural constraints—and particularly each other's fundamental concerns.

In the Arab-Israeli conflict—especially in the conflict between Palestinians and Israelis—these fundamental concerns center around national survival and the right to national existence. The core element of the Israeli-Palestinian conflict is the mutual denial of the other's national identity. Participants in a workshop can gain a better understanding of how the other party defines them, as well as how it defines itself. They can learn what acceptance means to the other—that is, what Israelis mean when they speak of being accepted by the Arabs, and what Palestinians mean when they speak of acceptance by Israel. They can learn why it is so difficult for the other to accord them acceptance— why each side perceives the fulfillment of the other's identity as equivalent to the destruction of its own identity. They can see how each party sees acceptance of the other, on the kinds of terms that would be meaningful to the other, as its trump card, which it dares not play unless it has full assurance that its own conditions will be met. They can learn about the other's genuine fears for security and survival and the perspective that gives rise to these fears. It is through these kinds of insights that they can begin to formulate some of the steps that need to be taken, individually and jointly, if progress toward mutual acceptance is to be achieved.

Insight into each other's perspective can, of course, be acquired in a variety of ways, but there is no substitute for the concreteness and emotional immediacy of insights gained through direct interaction in a context that encourages analysis. In a workshop setting, each party can observe and analyze how its own actions affect the adversary, and how the adversary's actions affect it. They can observe and analyze the other's response to the concerns that they have expressed. And they can discuss each other's deeply felt concerns in a context in which both sets of concerns are simultaneously on the table.

The occurrence and the possibility of change. A second type of learning that interaction in a workshop context can produce is the development of greater awareness of changes that have taken place in the adversary, of the possibilities for change under changing circumstances, and of ways of promoting such change in the other through one's own actions. Such learning is particularly important because the dynamics of conflict create a strong tendency to dismiss change—and the possibility of change—on the part of the adversary, which then makes change less likely by way of self-fulfilling prophecy.

There are four kinds of impacts related to the perception of change that we have observed, at least to some degree, in the context of Israeli-Palestinian interactions: learning that there is someone to talk to and something to talk about; learning to distinguish between dreams and operational programs; learning that mutual concessions may create a new situation, setting a process of change into motion; and learning about the occurrence or possibility of structural changes in the leadership of the other side.

(1) Israelis and Palestinians have generally assumed that there is no one to talk to on the other side and nothing to talk about. In our Israeli-Palestinian workshops, participants on both sides became persuaded that there may be someone to talk to and something to talk about. This may be a limited conclusion, but

it is a highly significant one. It reflects the development of a more differentiated view of the other party and the recognition that some change has occurred.

Typically, parties in conflict are very slow in noticing change in the adversary's posture. They look at change in the other from their own perspective and evaluate it in terms of how close it comes to their own preferred position. Even sizable change will be seen as insignificant if the adversary's position remains far removed from their own preference. The opposite effect tends to occur when parties look at changes in their own posture. Here, even a small change may be seen as a major concession. They evaluate their own change in terms of the distance they moved from their original starting point. Frequently, what seems like a small change to outsiders may reflect a great deal of internal struggle. For those who were involved in the struggle—within themselves and within their group—the change looms large, even though the adversary may barely notice it. The picture is complicated by the fact that those who have gone through the change, with the compromises and sacrifices that it may have entailed, assume that it is obvious to others, including the adversary. They usually consider it unnecessary to persuade the adversary that they have indeed made a change; in fact, they often try to minimize the magnitude of the change (for the benefit of their own constituencies), assuming all the time that the adversary knows very well what is happening. Thus, in a workshop setting, awareness of change may be enhanced in two ways: each party may discover that there have indeed been some meaningful changes on the other side; and each party may discover that its own changes are not at all apparent to the other and may therefore make the effort to demonstrate their reality.

(2) Through interaction in a workshop context, participants may come to recognize the possibility of changes in the adversary's operational programs without accompanying changes in dreams and the proclamation of such dreams. Israelis tend to take seriously the Palestinian demand for a united Palestine; they regard it as an operational program even though many Palestinians describe it as a dream. Similarly, Palestinians regard the Zionist vision of the ingathering of the exiles as an oper-

ational program, even though most Israelis do not realistically expect it or plan for it. It is, of course, possible for dreams to be turned into operational programs. It is also possible, however, for a group to continue proclaiming certain dreams that are central to its ideology, while abandoning any serious effort to put them into operation. Through interaction, conflicting parties may learn to distinguish between those dreams of the adversary that are meant to be operationalized and those that are meant to be merely proclaimed.

This kind of distinction is closely linked to the way ideological changes typically come about. The process rarely takes the form of abandoning one set of beliefs and replacing it with an alternative set. Rather, the tendency is for new (and sometimes contradictory) beliefs and principles to develop alongside the old ones. The old beliefs are not explicitly rejected—indeed, they are often ritualistically proclaimed—but they become increasingly nonoperational. Adversaries, however, continue to assume that the original beliefs remain in full force, particularly since they have little opportunity to observe the other society at firsthand or to engage in face-to-face communication with members of it. They derive most of their information from written documents, which are typically the last strongholds of fading beliefs. Insofar as direct communication enables parties to make subtler distinctions between different levels of beliefs, it may help them find an accommodation. In workshops, we have seen representatives of opposing parties help each other in making such distinctions.

(3) There is a tendency for conflicting parties to underestimate, not only the extent to which changes have occurred, but also the prospects for change. There is a general assumption that the adversary's actions in the future will replicate those in the past, regardless of new events. Thus, the parties often fail to consider that actions on their own parts may create a new situation, leading to changes in the other's behavior. In short, they give little credence to the dynamics of a changing situation.

In the context of a workshop, participants can learn about ways in which mutual concessions may create a new situation, setting a process of change into motion. They can try to spell out specific scenarios for the likely consequences of different actions. They might ask, for example, how the PLO would react if Israel were to accept it as a negotiating partner or were to acknowledge the principle of Palestinian self-determination. Conversely, they might ask how Israel would react if the PLO were to agree to cooperate with a plan for Palestinian autonomy or were to declare its willingness to coexist with Israel. The main effect of such interactions is to sensitize the participants to the dynamics of change. They may help them to at least recognize the possibility that new events—and particularly new actions on their own parts—may alter the situation and may thus make the consequences less mortally dangerous than they fear.

(4) Conflicting parties tend to assume that the leadership on the other side is static—that it has not changed and is unlikely to change. In the context of a workshop, participants can describe the structure of their own leadership and thus help the other party make differentiations within that structure. They can demonstrate in detail the kinds of transformations that have taken place within the leadership, and they can present specific scenarios of further transformations or of the development of alternative leadership groups under changing circumstances. The important contribution here would be to clarify to the other side that the political process in their own society is less monolithic and more dynamic than it might appear to outsiders, particularly to adversaries.

These and other kinds of learning become possible because, in the course of a successful workshop, participants develop sufficient trust and sufficient motivation to help each other work through the complexities of their respective political situations, with all of the internal differences and developments over time that they reflect.

The significance of gestures and symbolic acts. In most conflicts—and this is certainly true in the Israeli-Palestinian conflict—symbolic gestures are of enormous significance. This was clearly demonstrated by the reactions to Sadat's visit to Jerusalem—both the positive reactions among Israelis and the negative reactions among Palestinians and many other Arabs. Each party brings to the conflict a fundamental concern about its national identity and an awareness that this identity is problematic (at least for others). Thus, any gesture from the adversary that indicates acceptance of you as a people can have a profound impact. More generally, any act that implies basic human acceptance of the other is likely to provide a needed degree of reassurance and to evoke a favorable reaction. For example, Sadat's round of handshakes when he stepped off the plane in Israel produced a powerful response in the Israeli public, who saw the earlier refusal of Arab officials to shake the hands of their Israeli counterparts as excluding them from the human family. Similarly, a clear statement from the Israeli government, acknowledging the suffering of the Palestinian people and the injustice that they have experienced, would probably have a major impact on Palestinians and on the Arab world in general.

Once we recognize the significance of such symbolic gestures, it becomes apparent that there are meaningful things that each side can give to the other. Each has at its disposal acts that can reassure the other, raise its hope, enhance its self-respect. Moreover, these things can often be given at minimal cost to the giver—at least in strategic terms. Typically, however, the parties are not even aware of the fact that they have something meaningful (other than surrender) that they can give to the other. In a conflict relationship, the parties generally do not ask themselves the question of what they can give to the other or do for the other.

This, then, is another kind of learning that can emerge out of interactions in the context of a problem-solving workshop. In this setting, participants can begin to ask what they can give to each other and to identify gestures from the other that they would find meaningful. In doing so, they would essentially be exploring ways in which they can influence one another without resorting to violence. This is precisely what genuine social interaction is designed to make possible: by taking each other's perspective, the participants learn how they can influence one another in subtle, constructive ways that are conducive to a mutually satisfactory outcome.

11.

Graduated and Reciprocated Initiatives in Tension Reduction: GRIT*

CHARLES E. OSGOOD

I believe there is a way out of the dilemma of being either Red or Dead. It is not merely drifting along doing what comes naturally until fate decides the issue for us. It is not trying to erect stabilized deterrence on the shifting sands of human fallibility and hoping that it will somehow last forever. It is neither getting it all over with in an angry burst of hellfire nor passively hoping for the best from an aggressive opponent as we lay down our arms. It is not merely keeping up the effort to reach negotiated agreements with the enemy, although such efforts should be continued. The way out, I think, lies in an approach quite novel for competing sovereign states: taking the initiative, not by creating threats and tensions, but by reducing and controlling them.

In this chapter I want you to join me in exploring the possibilities that may lie in unilateral initiative of a particular kind. The technical term for this policy is *Graduated Reciprocation in Tension Reduction* (later revised to "Graduated and Reciprocated Initiatives in Tension Reduction"). This mouthfilling phrase was the title of a paper of mine in which I first elaborated the nature of this approach to international relations.

* Excerpts from *An Alternative to War or Surrender* (Urbana: University of Illinois Press, 1962). Reprinted by permission of the publisher, © 1962 by the University of Illinois Press.

It says exactly what I want to say, as you will see, but I soon discovered that no one could correctly remember it. I also discovered—while doodling and making notes at a conference one day—that the initials of this technical term spell GRIT. This was a happy, if entirely unintentional, discovery. GRIT is not only something everyone can remember; it also suggests the kind of national determination that will be required if we are to escape from being either Red or Dead.

The Arms Race in Reverse

John and Ivan stand facing each other near the middle, but on opposite sides, of a long, rigid, neatly balanced seesaw. This seesaw is balanced on a point that juts out over a bottomless abyss. As either of these two husky men takes a step outward on his side away from the center, the other must quickly compensate with an equal step outward on his side, or the balance will be destroyed. The farther out they move, the greater the unbalancing effect of each unilateral step, and the more agile and quick to react both John and Ivan must be to keep the precarious equilibrium.

To make the situation even worse, both of these men realize full well that this teetering board must have some limit to its tensile strength; sooner or later, if they keep moving out against each other, it is bound to crack, dropping them both down to destruction. So both John and Ivan are frightened. Yet neither is willing to admit his own fear because his opponent might take advantage of him.

How are these two men to escape from this dangerous situation—a situation in which the fate of each is bound up with that of the other? One reasonable solution immediately presents itself. Let both of them agree to walk slowly and carefully back toward the center of the teetering board in unison. To reach such an agreement they must trust each other. But the whole trouble is that these two husky men do *not* trust each other; each believes the other to be irrational enough to destroy them both unless he himself preserves the balance.

But now let us suppose that, during a quiet period in their strife, it occurs to one of these men that perhaps the other is really just as frightened as he himself is. If this were so, he would also welcome some way of escaping from this intolerable situation. So this man decides to gamble a little on his new insight. Loudly he calls out, "I am taking a small step *toward* you when I count to ten!" The other man, rather than risk having the precious balance upset, also takes a small, tentative step forward at the count of ten. Whereupon the first announces another larger step forward, and they both take it as the count is made. Thus John and Ivan gradually work their ways back to safety by a series of self-initiated, but reciprocated, steps— very much as they had originally moved out against each other.

This little parable contains the essential idea of GRIT. It is simply this—that the tensions/arms race spiral may offer the model for its own reversal. As a type of international behavior, just what is an arms race? *An arms race is a kind of graduated and reciprocated, unilaterally initiated, internation action.* Is it unilaterally initiated? A nation developing a new weapon, increasing its stockpile of nuclear warheads, or setting up a new military base certainly does not wait for any prior agreement with the opponent. Is it reciprocal? Each increase in military power by one side provides the threat stimulus for the other to try to catch up and get ahead. Is it graduated? Necessarily— first by the irregular and somewhat unpredictable nature of technological breakthroughs and second by the oscillating nature of the threat stimulus itself.

But an arms race is obviously a *tension-increasing* system; it is a spiral of terror. By reversing one of the characteristics of an arms race, we may be able to transform it into a spiral of trust. This would be a graduated and reciprocated, unilaterally initiated, internation system that was *tension-decreasing* in nature. This is entirely conceivable, you may say, but the real question is this: Is it *feasible* under present conditions of national sovereignty, of mutual fear and distrust? I will try to show that, with anything like the dedication and energy now being thrown into the arms race, GRIT would be feasible. This does not mean that it would be easy. There is no magically simple formula for peace.

Before plunging into the details of this plan, we should get an overview of its nature and purpose. GRIT must be sharply distinguished from the kind of abrupt and complete disarmament sponsored by many pacifist groups. To the contrary, what

I am proposing is a flexible, self-regulating procedure in which the participants carefully monitor their own initiatives on the basis of their own evaluation of the reciprocating actions taken by the other side. It is broader than disarmament, or even disengagement as this is usually conceived, since it would include programs of graded initiatives of a tension-reducing nature in areas of science and secrecy, of economic, social, and cultural exchanges, of Communist China and the United Nations, of controls and inspections, of diplomatic adjustments, and so forth—as well as actual military and disarmament steps.

It could be viewed as a "peace offensive." In a way, it is an application of the Golden Rule on an international scale—but a Golden Rule with built-in safeguards. It is perhaps best viewed as a kind of international (rather than interpersonal) communicating and learning situation, where the communication is more by deeds than by words and where what is learned—hopefully and gradually—is increased mutual understanding and trust.

What are the aims of GRIT? One is *to reduce and control international tension levels.* The intimate relation we have found between tension and both irrationality in human decision making and instability of the military environment puts a high premium on devising and applying techniques of tension control. Another aim is *to create gradually an atmosphere of mutual trust within which negotiations on critical political and military issues will have a better chance of succeeding.* Significant agreements are almost impossible when mutual fears and suspicions are running high. Yet another aim of GRIT is *to enable this country to take the initiative in foreign policy.* We have been passively defending the status quo too long, and nuclear weaponry has further frozen initiative along traditional lines; there is much to be done in the real war with communism, and it is high time we were about it. A final aim I will mention is *to launch a new kind of international behavior that is appropriate to the nuclear age.* Traditional forms of international relations have been outmoded by our technology, and our sociopolitical machinery must catch up if we are to survive.

However, being unconventional in nature—and worse, being conciliatory—GRIT is open to suspicion abroad and resistance at home, particularly under the conditions of the cold war mentality. Therefore, it needs to be spelled out in detail and critically evaluated. We need to demonstrate that it is possible for a nation to take the initiative in reducing tensions, and yet operate within reasonable limits of national dignity and security.

Maintaining National Security

Maintaining security means more than avoiding military defeats, more than protecting and keeping what belongs to us, and even more than preventing nuclear suicide. It also means strengthening the institutions that keep us free at home and supporting the freedoms of others to choose the institutions under which they will live. The notion of "national security" thus includes two of the prime criteria of policy we established in an earlier chapter: biological survival and preserving our way of life. The unilateral initiatives that give substance to Graduated Reciprocation in Tension Reduction must be shown to satisfy reasonable requirements of national security, while at the same time risking enough of it in small bits to induce reciprocation from opponents and thereby reduce world tensions. Impossible, you say? We shall see.

(a) *Unilateral initiatives must not reduce our capacity to inflict unacceptable nuclear retaliation on an opponent should we be attacked.*

I would be the first to agree that nuclear deterrence does not provide any real security in the long run, and GRIT is designed to create conditions under which nuclear weapons could eventually be eliminated. But, on the other hand, both the United States and the Soviet Union are moving as rapidly as they can toward what strategists call "stabilized deterrence," a situation in which both sides have highly invulnerable second-strike (retaliatory) nuclear capabilities. These may consist of "hardened" land bases, mobile, nuclear-powered submarines armed with Polaris-type missiles, or even some fantastic weapons systems not dreamed of as yet. Given present levels of tension, it is not likely that these ultimate weapons will be given up. This is an unpleasant fact about life in the dawn of the nuclear age, and we must deal with it if our policy is to meet the criterion of feasibility.

Nuclear retaliatory capacity can serve rational foreign policy (1) *if it is viewed not only as a deterrent but also as a security base from which to take limited risks in the direction of reducing tensions.* This is a very important point. The capacity to carry certain and completely unacceptable nuclear destruction to an opponent obviously is a means of deterring him from launching an attack—as long as he behaves rationally. But except for first-strike possibilities, this has been the *only* function given this capacity by military and political strategists. The same capacity can also function as a base for security. Since the enemy knows that we can literally wipe him off the face of the map if he attacks or otherwise tries to take advantage of us (and we know the same about his capacity), both sides are able to take limited risks, secure in the knowledge that the opponent will be cautious. This applies to limited risk in tension-induction (as has been going on in Berlin), but it also applies to limited risk in tension-reduction—and only the latter offers long-run security.

Nuclear retaliatory capacity can serve rational foreign policy (2) *if the retaliatory or second-strike nature of the capacity is made explicit.* Now, it is true that militarily it is difficult to distinguish cleanly between first- and second-strike weapons. The missiles on a Polaris submarine could be used for a surprise attack as well as for retaliation. On the other hand, it is also true that technological and political, as well as psychological, steps can be taken to emphasize the second-strike possibility and deemphasize the first-strike possibility. Technologically, anything that makes missile sites less vulnerable to attack emphasizes second-strike use, because we are better able to delay and weigh decisions without seriously weakening our retaliatory capacity. Hence the urge to preempt becomes less. Politically, we can accept a moral prohibition against the first use of nuclear weapons. Some elements of the military establishment resist such political inhibition, on the ground that it reduces their freedom of choice in responding to aggression, but reducing freedom of choice by the military is a necessary ingredient of arms control and tension control. Psychologically, we can cease and desist from "rocket rattling" as a tactic in the cold war. This tactic does not increase the credibility of our *retaliatory* capacity, since the enemy knows full well we will use it if attacked.

Nuclear retaliatory capacity can serve rational foreign policy (3) *if the minimum capacity required for effective deterrence is maintained and the arms race discontinued.* What is the distinction between an "arms race mentality" and a "deterrence philosophy"? The arms race mentality takes it for granted that we must keep ahead of the opponent in total military power in order to be secure; it assumes that if some new weapon can be devised, then the enemy (who is always seeking the advantage) will develop it, and therefore so must we; it also assumes that the credibility of our deterrence increases directly with the sheer power and number of our weapons. The essence of a deterrence philosophy is that there is some maximum degree of destruction that the opponent can rationally tolerate (and if he is irrational, he is not going to be deterred anyhow); therefore, there must be some limited capacity for nuclear retaliation which will be sufficient to deter him.

The approach to disarmament implicit in GRIT is to give up nuclear deterrents last. This is a somewhat novel approach and quite the opposite of most disarmament proposals, which ask for nuclear disarmament first and popguns last. The usual approach has emotional appeal because it seeks to get rid of the weapons we fear most first, but I do not think it is rational. As long as nationalistic tensions and technical knowhow exist, popguns can start conflicts that end up in nuclear holocaust. Furthermore, since nuclear weapons represent so much destructive capacity in such little packages, their existence is harder to inspect and control than is the massing and movement of conventional forces and weapons. I think that we must retain the minimum nuclear retaliatory capacity necessary for deterrence, *and* for security in limited risk taking, until international tensions have been reduced—reduced to a point where final elimination of the nuclear safeguards themselves can be achieved by successfully negotiated treaties.

(b) *Unilateral initiatives must not cripple our capacity to meet aggression by conventional weapons with appropriately graded conventional military responses.*

One of the main sources of resistance to nuclear disarmament comes from those who believe that if we were to remove this threat, the communists would continue to nibble away at the free world by other means until we were isolated. Actually, it is debatable whether our possession of nuclear weapons over a decade or more has done much to help us in the real war against communism around the world. This, of course, is the reason for recent emphasis upon strengthening our conventional capabilities. Unilateral initiatives on our part should not serve to weaken such capacity for conventional military operations directly, *but should create conditions in which the magnitude of such capability could be gradually reduced as part of the total policy.*

There are two main ways in which conventional forces and armaments can be reduced by GRIT. One is by direct initiative—that is, by using small steps in conventional disarmament, disengagement, or arms control as a means of reducing tensions. To the extent that these steps are reciprocated, our capacity to meet remaining sources of aggression by appropriately graded conventional response stays relatively the same—has not been "degraded," as the military phrase goes. The other is by transfer of conventional forces and armaments to an international police force under United Nations or similar auspices. This transfer of conventional capacity to the United Nations to counter aggression can be accomplished either by unilateral initiative (presumably, but not necessarily, with reciprocation) or by negotiated agreements. Both Soviet and United States disarmament proposals include phased transfer of conventional weapons to an international peace-keeping machinery.

At this point, no doubt, the Voice of the Dove is asking, "How can you say you are trying to reduce international tensions when you insist that we retain both our nuclear and our conventional armaments?" In the first place, this is not exactly what I have been saying; rather, I have argued that we should retain only the minimum nuclear capacity required for sufficient deterrence (and this only temporarily) and that we should gradually reduce our conventional forces by reciprocated initiatives and by transfer to the United Nations. In the second place, I would argue that there is no simple and direct relation between tensions and armaments; it is possible to modify the threat significance of armaments by a wide variety of actions that in themselves do not constitute disarmament. Then, in a less tense atmosphere, it should become easier to deal with armaments per se. And in the third place, I believe it would be disastrous from anyone's point of view—pacifist or otherwise—to take initiatives early in the game that would either openly invite aggression abroad or create extreme anxiety at home. We must begin by working within the requirements of the existing situation, even though we have the aim of gradually changing it. This is why we should not reduce our conventional forces abruptly and why we should not initiate actions that might endanger our "heartland." If taken advantage of, we might release full-scale nuclear retaliation and thereby write "finis" to this chapter of the human book.

(c) *Unilateral initiatives must be graduated in risk according to the degree of reciprocation obtained from opponents.*

This is the essential self-regulating characteristic of GRIT. It is the characteristic that makes it possible for us to keep within tolerable limits of total national security while continuing to apply pressure on an opponent to join our march toward peace. The size of the step taken at any particular time—the amount of security we are risking should reciprocation not be obtained or even should our step be taken advantage of—depends upon our own evaluation of what the other side has been doing up to that point in response to previous initiatives. If the Soviets had shown no signs of reciprocating, or had been offering what seemed to be only token reciprocations, we would keep right on moving, but with further small-risk initiatives. If, on the other hand, they had taken some verifiably significant, tension-reducing steps of their own, we would be in a position to increase the significance of our own next actions. The process can be slowed down or speeded up as the conditions of the moment require, but it should be kept going.

[*Editor's note:* In *An Alternative to War or Surrender* (1962), Osgood elaborates at some length on factors to be considered and precautions to be taken in implementing a GRIT strategy. Because of space limitations those designated by the letters (d)–(o) are simply listed here, with no elaboration.]

(d) Unilateral initiatives must be diversified in nature, both as to sphere of action and as to geographical locus of application.

(e) Prior to announcement, unilateral initiatives must be unpredictable by an opponent as to their sphere, locus, and time of execution.

(f) Unilateral initiatives must represent a sincere intent to reduce and control international tensions.

(g) Unilateral initiatives must be announced publicly at some reasonable interval prior to their execution and identified as part of a deliberate policy of reducing and controlling tensions.

(h) In their announcement, unilateral initiatives should include explicit invitation to reciprocation in some form.

(i) Unilateral initiatives that have been announced must be executed on schedule regardless of prior commitment by the opponent to reciprocate.

(j) Unilateral initiatives must be continued over a considerable period, regardless of immediate reciprocation or events of a tension-increasing nature elsewhere.

(k) Unilateral initiatives must, wherever possible, take advantage of mutual self-interests, mutual self-restraints, and opportunities for cooperative enterprise.

(l) Unilateral initiatives must be as unambiguous and as susceptible to verification as possible.

(m) Our initiatives and requested reciprocations should, wherever feasible, involve transfer of sovereignty from national to international auspices.

(n) Our initiatives and requested reciprocations should, wherever feasible, be designed to reduce the imbalance between "have" and "have-not" countries.

(o) Our initiatives and requested reciprocations should, wherever feasible, be designed to strengthen democratic as against totalitarian ways of life.

12.

The Kennedy Experiment: Unilateral Initiatives*

AMITAI ETZIONI

The pattern of events between June 10 and November 22, 1963, provided a partial test of a theory of international relations. The essence of the theory is that psychological gestures initiated by one nation will be reciprocated by others with the effect of reducing international tensions. This tension reduction, in turn, will lessen the probability of international conflicts and wars.

American Initiatives

The Kennedy experiment can be viewed as a test of a moderate version of the psychological theory that seeks to use symbolic gestures as unilateral initiatives to reduce tension to get at other factors, leading toward multilateral negotiations.

The first step was a speech by President John F. Kennedy at the American University on June 10, 1963, in which he outlined "A Strategy of Peace." While it is not known to what degree the president or his advisers were moved by a psychological theory, the speech clearly met a condition of this theory— it set the *context* for the unilateral initiatives to follow. As any concrete measure can be interpreted in a variety of ways, it is

* Excerpted from Amitai Etzioni, "The Kennedy Experiment: Unilateral Initiatives," *The Western Political Quarterly* 20, no. 2, part I (June 1967). Reprinted by permission of the University of Utah, Copyright Holder.

necessary to spell out the general state of mind these steps attempt to communicate.

The president called attention to the dangers of nuclear war and took a reconciliatory tone toward the Soviet Union in his address. He said that "constructive changes" in the Soviet Union "might bring within reach solutions which now seem beyond us." He stated that "our problems are man-made . . . and can be solved by man." Coming eight months after the 1962 Cuban crisis, when the United States and Russia stood "eyeball to eyeball," such statements marked a decisive change in American attitudes. Nor did the President imply that all the blame for the cold war rested with the other side; he called on Americans to "re-examine" their attitudes toward the cold war.

Beyond merely delivering a speech, the president announced the first unilateral initiative—the United States was stopping all nuclear tests in the atmosphere and would not resume them unless another country did. This, it should be noted, was basically a psychological gesture and not a unilateral arms limitation step. One can hold the psychological theory with varying degrees of strength. Osgood, in most of his writings on this subject, has advanced the stronger version, (1962), while I subscribe to the more moderate one (1962).

The steps that followed had much the same quality. Kennedy's speech, delivered on June 10, was published in full during the next few days in the Soviet government newspaper, *Izvestia,* as well as in *Pravda* with a combined circulation of 10 million, a degree of attention rarely accorded a Western leader. Radio jammers in Moscow were turned off to allow the Russian people to listen without interruption to the Voice of America's recording of the speech, a fact that was reported in the United States and, therefore, had some tension reduction effects on both sides. Premier Khrushchev followed on June 15 with a speech welcoming the Kennedy initiative. He stated that a world war was not inevitable and that the main danger of conflict stemmed from the arms race and the stockpiling of nuclear weapons. Khrushchev reciprocated on the psychological-military side by announcing he had ordered that the production of strategic bombers be halted. The psychological nature of this step is to be seen in that the bombers were probably about to be phased out anyway and that no verification was offered for cessation of production.

In the United Nations, the Soviet Union on June 11 removed its objection to a Western-backed proposal to send observers to war-torn Yemen. The United States reciprocated by removing, for the first time since 1956, its objection to the restoration of full status of the Hungarian delegation to the United Nations.

Although the United States had proposed a direct America-Russia communications link at Geneva in late 1962, the Soviets finally agreed to this measure on June 20, 1963. Next, attention focused on the test ban. Following the United States example, Russia reciprocated by not testing in the atmosphere, so that until the treaty was signed, both sides refrained from such testing under an understanding achieved without negotiation but rather through unilateral-reciprocal moves. This development, in line with the moderate version of the theory, led in July to multilateral negotiations and a treaty, signed on August 5, 1963.

On October 9, 1963, President Kennedy approved the sale of $250 million worth of wheat to the Soviet Union. The almost purely psychological nature of this step is not always understood. As the test-ban treaty had, for reasons mentioned above, a limited military significance, so the wheat deal had little commercial importance. The barriers to East–West trade were *not* removed; credit and license barriers were maintained. The main values of the deal were, hence, as a gesture and in the educational effect of the public debate which preceded the administration's approval of the deal.

October brought another transformation of a unilateral-reciprocal understanding into a binding, multilateral formal agreement. This time it concerned the orbiting of weapons of mass destruction and, once more, though it appeared to be a military measure, it was largely a psychological one.

Soviet Responses

One of the prevalent criticisms against the unilateral initiatives theory is that the Soviets might not respond to such initiatives. The Soviets, it is said, are Marxists and quite aware of the difference between real and symbolic moves. A policy of symbolic gestures would appeal only to people who think in Madison Avenue terms and not in political, military, and economic ones. The evidence on this point is fairly clear. For each move that was made, the Soviets reciprocated. Kennedy's "Strategy for Peace" speech was matched by a conciliatory speech by Khrushchev; Kennedy's unilateral declaration of cessation of tests was followed by a cessation of the production of strategic bombers; spies were traded for spies; and so forth. The Russians showed no difficulties in understanding the gestures and in responding to psychological initiatives; and they participated in a "you move–I move" sequence rather than waiting for simultaneous, negotiated, agreed-upon moves. Further, they shifted to multilateral-simultaneous arrangements once the appropriate mood was generated, as reflected in the test-ban treaty and outer space resolution.

References

Adelman, K. L. (1984–85). "Arms Control With and Without Agreements." *Foreign Affairs* 65 (2). Pp. 240–63.

Azar, E. and Burton, J., eds. (1985). *Facilitated Conflict Resolution—Theory and Practice* (Lebanon as a Case Example). Cambridge: Cambridge University Press.

Bundy, M.; Kennan, G.; McNamara, R. S.; and Smith, G. (1982). "Nuclear Weapons and the Atlantic Alliance." *Foreign Affairs* 60 (4).

—— (1984–85). "The President's Choice: Star Wars or Arms Control." *Foreign Affairs* 63 (2).

Burton, J. W. (1969). *Conflict and Communication: The Use of Controlled Communication in International Relations.* London: Macmillan.

—— (1979). *Deviance, Terrorism and War: The Process of Solving Unsolved Social and Political Problems.* NY: St. Martin's Press.

Cohen, S. P.; Kelman, H. C.; Miller, F. D.; and Smith, B. L. (1977). "Evolving Intergroup Techniques for Conflict Resolution: An Israeli-Palestinian Pilot Workshop." *Journal of Social Issues* 33 : 165–89.

Collins, Lt. Gen. A. S. (1976). "Theater Nuclear Warfare: The Battlefield." In J. F. Reichart and S. R. Sturm (1982), *American Defense Policy.* Baltimore: Johns Hopkins University Press. Pp. 356–65.

Cousins, N. (August 1945). "Modern Man Is Obsolete." *The Saturday Review.* Reprinted in *The Saturday Review,* Aug. 1, 1970.

Cox, A. (1982). *Russian Roulette: The Superpower Game.* NY: Times Books.

Davidson, W. D., and Montville, J. V. (Winter, 1981–82). "Foreign Policy According to Freud." *Foreign Policy.* Pp. 145–57.

Deutsch, M. (1973). *The Resolution of Conflict: Constructive and Destructive Processes.* New Haven: Yale University Press.

Doob, L. W., ed. (1970). *Resolving Conflict in Africa: The Fermeda Workshop.* New Haven: Yale University Press.

—— (1974). "A Cyprus Workshop: An Exercise in Intervention Methodology." *Journal of Social Psychology* 94 : 161–78.

Doob, L. W., and Foltz, W. J. (1973). "The Belfast Workshop: An Application of Group Techniques to a Destructive Conflict." *Journal of Conflict Resolution* 17 : 489–512.

Einstein, A. (1945). "Atomic War or Peace." *Atlantic Monthly,* Nov. 1948. In Nathan, O., and Norden, H., eds. (1960). *Einstein on Peace.* NY: Avenel. Pp. 347–51.

Etzioni, A. (1962). *The Hard Way to Peace.* NY: Collier Books.

Fisher, G. H. (1972). *Public Diplomacy and the Behavioral Sciences.* Bloomington, IN: Indiana University Press.

Ford, D. (1985). "A Reporter at Large: The Button." *The New Yorker* I. April 1, pp. 43–91; II. April 8, pp. 49–92.

Frye, A. (1983–84). "Strategic Build-Down: A Context for Restraint." *Foreign Affairs* 62 (2).

Gayler, Adm. N. (April 25, 1982). "How to Break the Momentum of the Nuclear Arms Race." *New York Times Magazine.* Pp. 48–88.

Kelman, H. C., ed. (1965). *International Behavior: A Social-Psychological Analysis.* NY: Holt.

——— (1972). "The Problem-Solving Workshop in Conflict Resolution." In R. L. Merritt, ed., *Communication in International Politics.* Urbana: University of Illinois Press. Pp. 168–204.

——— (1978). "Israelis and Palestinians: Psychological Prerequisites for Mutual Acceptance." *International Security* 3 : 162–86.

Kelman, H. C. and Cohen, S. P. (1976). "The Problem-Solving Workshop: A Social Psychological Contribution to the Resolution of International Conflicts." *Journal of Peace Research* 13 : 79–90.

——— (1979). "Reduction of International Conflict: An Interactional Approach." In W. G. Austin and S. Worschel, eds. *The Social Psychology of Inter-Group Relations.* Monterey, CA: Brooks/Cole. Pp. 283–303.

Kissinger, H. (1983). "A New Approach to Arms Control." *Time,* March 21, pp. 24–26.

Landau, D. (January 1984). "Citizen Diplomacy." *New Age.* Pp. 34–45, 93–97.

McNamara, R. S. (1983). "The Military Role of Nuclear Weapons." *Foreign Affairs* 62 (1).

Newhouse, J. (1985). "The Diplomatic Round." *The New Yorker,* July 22, pp. 37–55.

Osgood, C. E. (1962). *An Alternative to War or Surrender.* Urbana: University of Illinois Press.

Reves, E. (1945). *The Anatomy of Peace.* NY: Viking.

Rogers, C. L., and Ryback, D. (September 1984). "One Alternative to Nuclear Planetary Suicide." *The Counselling Psychologist.* 12 (2) : 2–12.

Saunders, H. (Summer, 1984). "When Citizens Talk." *Kettering Review.* 49–55.

Sharp, G. (1984). *Making the Abolition of War a Realistic Goal.* NY: World Policy Institute.

Walton, R. E. (1970). "A Problem-Solving Workshop on Border Conflicts in Eastern Africa." *Journal of Applied Behavioral Science* 6 : 453–89.

Wedge, B. (1972). "Mass Psychotherapy for Intergroup Conflict." In J. H. Masserman and J. J. Schwab, eds., *Man for Humanity.* Springfield, IL: Charles C. Thomas.

PART THREE

BASIC PSYCHOLOGICAL PROCESSES RELATED TO WAR

INTRODUCTION

Ralph K. White

Part Three discusses how several parts of what is seen by psychologists as "basic psychology" may be related to the causes and prevention of war: topics such as motivation, perception, misperception, and the organization of an individual personality. These topics represent roughly how psychologists and psychiatrists try to organize what they have learned from studying individual human beings living ordinary lives and interacting with others in small groups such as the family. There is much skepticism as to whether such knowledge can be directly applied, with any confidence, to nations interacting with nations or, rather, to the behavior of leaders and of ordinary citizens when they are thinking and feeling as citizens of a nation in an international context. The skepticism is justified. A human being becomes a somewhat different human being when he begins to think and feel in the "Hobbesian," anarchic context of international conflict and (sometimes) cooperation. But surely there are also resemblances between his behavior in other contexts and his behavior in that context, as Deutsch's discussion of "the malignant process of hostile interaction" in Chapter 8 has indicated. This is the "level of analysis problem" that for many years has plagued psychologists and others who have tried to explain war.

The approach taken here is that of open-minded empiricism. We need to discover, empirically, what the resemblances are between the two levels and what the differences are.

The contributors to Part Three hope that what they have done will contribute to that enterprise.

SECTION V

Two War-Related Motives: Pride and Fear

SECTION EDITOR: JEROME D. FRANK

INTRODUCTION

Ralph K. White

This section deals with questions of motivation. What do nations want? How are their goals related to war? Or, more precisely, what are the goals of the leaders, and of those who follow the leaders in paths that—often without either the majority of the leaders or the majority of the followers wanting it—actually lead to war?

Chapters 13–15 discuss a many-sided motive that Jerome Frank calls pride, while Andrew Schmookler speaks of "the ways of power" and Erich Fromm speaks of group narcissism. Those terms are obviously related to each other and also to what political scientists often refer to as the international competition for national power and prestige. Political scientists often describe power and prestige as ends in themselves, or as means to the end of security in an anarchic "Hobbesian" world, or as both ends and means. In Chapter 16, White, with his emphasis on fear (actually two quite different kinds of fear), comes close to this typical emphasis of the political scientists on security, since fear can be defined as an aroused desire for security.

This convergence of psychology and psychiatry with political science is noteworthy. From different points of view and using somewhat different terms the psychologists and psychiatrists (at least these particular ones) find themselves talking about essentially the same two major motives that are most stressed by political scientists. The similarity is in some degree a corroboration of both.

This common focus is, however, somewhat at variance with a strong tradition, in both psychiatry and psychology, that treats aggression as obviously the main motive behind all forms of violent conflict, including war. It is therefore worthwhile at this point to try to do some justice to the impulse of aggression as related to war and also to explain briefly why its importance as a cause of war is not, in this book, placed on a par with that of either pride or fear.

The psychiatrists' stress on an impulse of aggression (that is, a desire, conscious or unconscious, to kill or do harm to others, as an end in itself rather than as a means to some other end such as security) stems partly from Freud and is supported by much psychiatric experience. Anger and hate, the two terms in common usage that come closest to this definition of aggression, are often found by psychiatrists to be denied, suppressed, displaced, rationalized, or projected onto others. Projected hostility is in fact the common psychiatric interpretation of paranoid delusions of persecution. (This may or may not offer a clue to why nations develop paranoid feelings about each other.) Conscious anger is also an obvious aspect of international conflict.

Nevertheless, there are at least three reasons not to think aggression is primary as a cause of war, when compared with pride, especially wounded pride, or fear.

One reason is the very strong case that can be made for the primacy of both pride and fear, as the four chapters in this section will perhaps demonstrate. To give just one example: If nuclear war occurs because fear of preemption by the other side causes a given side to strike first, its fear of preemption is surely more potent than any anger the decision makers may feel. Their great preoccupation at such a moment is likely to be to limit, if possible, the nuclear damage to their own country.

Another reason is the historical record of the mood and behavior of decision makers at times of crisis, at least in the twentieth century. Snyder and Diesing, in their study of 16 war crises (1977, p. 291), found *no* instance in which war occurred because "tempers got out of control." The crisis of 1914 and the Cuban missile crisis are cases in point. Fear is prominent at such times: fear of appearing to be weak and irresolute (which is also pride), fear of a successful attack by the enemy if one's own country does not strike first, or fear that if war does not come now it will come later when the balance of power has shifted and one's own country is even less able to win. Pride is prominent. It is not only fear of appearing afraid, in the eyes of one's own countrymen, and therefore taking a "firm stand" that risks war, but also unwillingness (as the decision-makers see it) to allow their own country to be "pushed around." Anger is present, but less prominent.

Such examples suggest a third reason. When the leaders and people of a nation are full of anger at another nation their anger can often be traced back to wounded pride or fear or both. The Arab threat strikes fear into the hearts of Israelis; the existence and military expansion of Israel have deeply wounded the pride of the Arabs; and those two deeper roots largely account for the anger and hate that undoubtedly exist on both sides. To understand the deeper causes of war it is therefore necessary to consider primarily those roots.

13.

The Role of Pride*

JEROME D. FRANK

"Of the gods we believe, and of men we know, that by a necessary law of their nature they rule wherever they can. And it is not as if we were the first to make this law, or to act upon it when made; we found it existing before us, and shall leave it to exist forever after us; all we do is make use of it, knowing that you and everybody else, having the same power as we have, would do the same as we do."
—Thucydides, *The Peloponnesian War,* Book II

"Chief among the forces affecting political folly is lust for power, named by Tacitus as 'the most flagrant of all the passions.' "
—Barbara Tuchman, *The March of Folly from Troy to Vietnam* (1984)

While fear is undoubtedly a major psychological source of individual, group, and national violence, fear is itself a response to a perceived threat or attack. Hence, the interaction ending in war typically begins when one nation seeks to impose its will on another.

At a superficial level, nations attack others not only to protect themselves from external threats but also to gain more wealth, territory, slave labor, and for many other motives. At a deeper level, however, a major psychological drive behind all these reasons for aggression is the effort to maximize individual and group power, grounded in a pervasive human trait recognized

* Written for this volume.

as a source of trouble since antiquity. The Greeks called it hubris, the theologians pride, and modern psychiatrists narcissism. Although the human characteristics to which these terms refer differ in many respects, they have a common core—the individual's unrealistically high evaluation of the power and virtue of himself and his group, or excessive drive to achieve a *sense* of power and a sense of virtue.

The drive for national power is customarily cloaked by the euphemistic phrase, "protection of national interest," which in practice includes the nation's image of itself and its place in the world. Nations seem to have a "psychological need . . . to prove that they are bigger, better or stronger than other nations. Implicit in this drive is the assumption . . . that when a nation shows that it has the stronger army, it is also proving that it has . . . a better civilization" (Fulbright, 1966). Anything that threatens this drive toward power is seen as threatening the national "interest." Expanding nations feel their national interest to be threatened by an expansionist rival or even by weaker nations that resist domination. Nations whose preeminence is established regard as endangering their national interest threats to the status quo, including internal revolutions, based on nationalist and economic aspirations, that might possibly unseat subservient governments.

Leaders and nations often seek to conceal their drive for power from themselves by invoking moral pride—the duty to impose their superior world view and moral values on others. Past examples are the duty to take up the "white man's burden" or to bring Christianity to the heathen. Contemporaneous examples are the moral duty to combat godless communism or capitalist imperialism.

Individuals differ greatly in the strength of the drive for power. It is obviously strong in national leaders. They would not be leaders if they did not possess a strong drive to dominate others, and the very fact that they have pushed their way to the top reinforces their belief in their invincibility—a belief abetted by the adulation of their followers.

Since, driven by pride, national leaders and their societies can always find pretexts for attempting to extend their power, the hope of eliminating wars by removing obvious sources, such as fear of other nations or shortages of resources, is vain; and in a world loaded with engines of destruction capable of exterminating humanity, the future of the human race is problematical.

At the same time, since as social creatures humans can survive and flourish only in organized groups and these depend on hierarchies of leadership, not only is the drive for power inevitable, but it serves the interests of the group in some ways. The task, therefore, is not to eliminate power struggles but to preserve their constructive functions while holding their violent aspects to a tolerable level.

Hope that this task is achievable springs from the recognition that all organized societies, as the price of their continued viability, have devised ways of conducting internal power struggles by nonviolent rituals such as elections and litigation and, when violence does break out, ways of keeping it under control. This control is maintained by rules and laws enforced by the courts, the police, and the penal system.

An important psychological source of obedience to law is the sense of community of members of a society. Humans are social creatures who readily form bonds to others with whom they are in continuing contact. Andrew Schmookler (1984) and Erich Fromm (1964) place their hopes for survival on the historical process that they believe will lead to the formation of larger and larger groups until the sense of community is shared by all the earth's inhabitants. (See later chapters, this section.)

Since neither Schmookler nor Fromm specifies concrete steps toward this goal, it may be well to mention that conditions of modern life have created new positive as well as negative incentives for the attainment of a world community, in addition to new technologies that for the first time make such a community a realistic, if still distant, possibility.

The negative incentives spring from threats posed by the advent of monstrously destructive biological, chemical, and nuclear weapons, as well as by mounting pollution of the atmosphere and the oceans. On the positive side are the enormous potential benefits of, for example, elimination of worldwide plagues like smallpox and the possibility of worldwide climate control. Elimination of the threats and realization of the benefits both depend on international cooperation, which advances in electronic satellite communication and mass rapid transportation make possible on a hitherto undreamed-of scale. So, for the first time in history, the hope may not be entirely vain that the pride that "goeth before destruction" may yet be tamed by the growing sense of world community.

Some comments on the writings of others in relation to pride, including the books of Schmookler and Fromm from which the excerpts in this section were selected, are now in order.

Based on a broad cultural-anthropological perspective, Schmookler (1984) postulates that with the advent of civilization, marked by the shift from food gathering to food production, power came to dominate relations between groups. Freed from the constraints of scarcities, human groups became able to expand indefinitely, thereby shattering the biological limits that had imposed a crude order on group relations. In the resulting anarchy, the chief determinant of group relations is power. If for any reason one group decides to try to impose its will on another, the latter has no choice except to respond within the framework of power, which permits only four alternatives: withdrawal, destruction, transformation, and imitation. "No one is free to choose peace but anyone can impose on all the necessity for power," (1984, p. 21). Furthermore—a theme addressed also by Russell, Fromm, and Niebuhr—the drive for power is insatiable and, far from being restrained by morality, uses morality to justify itself. In a nuclear world, such an analysis seems to lead ineluctably to a prophecy of doom, which Schmookler seeks to counteract by voicing the hope that the growing interdependence of the world will eventually lead to a new order which "will control the actions of all to the degree needed to protect the well-being of the whole," (1984, p. 33).

The philosopher Bertrand Russell (1948), with characteristic incisiveness, comes right to the heart of the issue—the primacy of the drive for power and glory. Power, he asserts, is the fundamental concept of social science, just as energy is the fundamental concept in physics. Some penetrating comments on the psychology of leaders and followers are included in his book, as well as the dehumanizing effect on leaders of the mechanization of power.

To turn from the manifestations and consequences of the drive for power to its psychological causes, Robert W. White (1959) suggests that one such cause is the drive for competence, manifested from infancy and rooted in the biological need of all living creatures to control their environment. Supported by an extensive review of relevant theoretical and experimental literature, primarily from child psychology, White concludes that what he calls, "effectance motivation," which is on a par with other primary drives, is central to the child's learning to master its physical and human environment.

As the child grows to adulthood, effectance motivation, pressed into the service of pride, blossoms into the persistent, often maladaptive, self-aggrandizement of individuals and groups. To explain this unfortunate development, psychologists and psychiatrists, of whom Erich Fromm (1973) is representative, invoke narcissism, described by Fromm as "a state of experience in which only the person himself, *his* body, *his* needs . . . *his* property, everything and everybody pertaining to *him* are experienced as fully real."

Since some degree of narcissism is essential to survival, any "wound" to individual or group narcissism arouses anger and aggression.

Fromm's solution to the threat to human survival posed by narcissism, especially its group form, in a nuclear world is similar to that suggested by Schmookler. The individual must extend his narcissism to humanity itself. The motivation to make this leap is created by the need to combat threats to all mankind, such as hunger and disease; and allegiance to humanity as a whole is facilitated by the scientific attitude and the humanist tradition.

Reinhold Niebuhr's illuminating discussion of pride (1949)—of which narcissism may be seen as a special form—is a reminder that students of human nature, once they penetrate the barrier of terminology, have much to learn from religious thinkers, who, after all, wrestled with the puzzles of the human psyche for millennia before behavioral scientists existed.

From theologians, pride is the ultimate source of human destructiveness, the basic sin, a view consistent with Russell's exposition. Neibuhr's explanation of pride as the attempt to overcome the insecurity inherent in the human condition sheds light on the instability of individual and group aggrandizement—for the sense of the insignificance of life is grounded in existential fact. If, therefore, a person relies on the accumulation of power or wealth to overcome it, he can never accumulate enough.

Niebuhr's linking of self group aggrandizement to intellectual and moral pride and the pride of power, as well as his discussion of why groups are more aggrandizing than individuals, can be profitably compared with Fromm's.

Niebuhr's concept of intellectual pride is easily extrapolated to include the overconfidence of some nuclear weapons experts in their scenarios for fighting nuclear war. Since their scenarios are without any direct basis in experience, these experts' faith in them rests on nothing but intellectual pride.

Ralph K. White (1984, pp. 119, 128), views "macho pride" as a direct cause of war, second only to exaggerated fear of the adversary.

It may be noted in passing that Horney's distinction (referred to by White) between normal striving for power, based on strength, and its neurotic form, based on weakness, while useful for clinical purposes, is dubious in view of Niebuhr's reminder that existentially the strong are as insignificant as the weak, so that ultimately both healthy and neurotic power drives may have the same root.

Pride, finally, is not only a major psychological motivation for the onset of conflict but is also for its continuance beyond the point where either side can hope to achieve the goal for which it started to fight. As Barbara Tuchman documents in *The March of Folly* (1984), motives like "prestige," "face," "honor," all facets of pride, are major sources of leaders' and nations' folly—that is, persistence in policies contrary to their own interests.

While not using the word "pride," I make this point in the following passage:

> As military and civilian casualties mount, privation at home increases, and more and more resources are committed to the struggle, continuing the fight becomes a means of justifying past sacrifices. The predicament is somewhat like that of a gambler

who keeps raising his bets to recoup his past losses—the sacrifices would be justified only if the goal for which they were
made was really worthwhile, and the way to prove the goal
worthwhile is to redouble efforts to gain it. The gambler is
usually motivated in part by the need to show that his judgment
or his faith in his luck that led him to incur his original losses
is, after all, correct—the purpose of the effort now becomes to
protect his self-image, and achieving the goal becomes a means
to this end. In war the same process may lead to a shift in
motivation: proving one's courage and determination by continuing to fight becomes an end in itself, more important than
gaining the object of the fight, and the issue of who is tougher
becomes overriding. A tragic example was the terrible and
relentless struggle for Verdun in the First World War, which
continued after its ". . . strategic significance . . . had long
since passed out of sight; yet the battle had somehow achieved
a demonic existence of its own, far beyond the control of
generals of either nation. Honor had become involved to an
extent which made disengagement impossible." (Horne, 1966,
p. 42).

Blind commitment is made possible by the fact that the
prospect of defeat is for many people a worse alternative than
death. Death is not a real alternative for most people—each
of us, even the soldier in battle, has the illusion of personal
immortality; and since no one who has ever experienced it has
lived to tell the tale (modern medicine has created a handful
of apparent exceptions, but the generalization still holds), no
one really knows what it will be like. On the other hand, all
humans have suffered the mortification of defeat, so it is a very
real eventuality. The prospect of dying in defense of one's
country or its ideals, moreover, enhances one's self-image. The
soldier contemplating death in battle can identify himself with
the heroes whose glorious reputations brighten all history; but
surrender is linked to cowardice, a loathed human weakness.

In view of the degree of commitment, the size of the stakes,
and the heightened emotional tension, it is not surprising that
each combatant in war becomes increasingly wedded to his
course of action, and that filtering and reinterpreting information to support these courses reaches monumental proportions. [From Frank, *Sanity and Survival in the Nuclear Age.*
(New York: Random House, 1982), pp. 187–188.]

14.

Selection for the Ways of Power in Social Evolution*

ANDREW B. SCHMOOKLER

The Struggle for Power

In his classic, *Leviathan,* Thomas Hobbes describes what he calls "the state of nature" as an anarchic situation in which all are compelled, for their very survival, to engage in a ceaseless struggle for power. About this "war of all against all," two important points should be made: that Hobbes's vision of the dangers of anarchy captured an important dimension of the human condition and that to call that condition "the state of nature" is a remarkable misnomer.

In nature, all pursue survival for themselves and their kind. But they can do so only within biologically evolved limits. The living order of nature, though it has no ruler, is not in the least anarchic. Each pursues a kind of self-interest, each is a law unto itself, but the separate interests and laws have been formed over eons of selection to form part of a tightly ordered harmonious system. Although the state of nature involves struggle, the struggle is part of an order. Each component of the living system has a defined place out of which no ambition can extricate it. Hunting-gathering societies were to a very great extent likewise contained by natural limits.

* Excerpts from *The Parable of the Tribes: The Problem of Power in Social Evolution* (Berkeley: University of California Press, 1984). © 1984 The Regents of the University of California.

With the rise of civilization, the limits fall away. The natural self-interest and pursuit of survival remain, but they are no longer governed by any order. The new civilized forms of society, with more complex social and political structures, created the new possibility of indefinite social expansion: more and more people organized over more and more territory. All other forms of life had always found inevitable limits placed upon their growth by scarcity and consequent death. But civilized society was developing the unprecedented capacity for unlimited growth as an entity. (The limitlessness of this possibility does not emerge fully at the outset but rather becomes progressively more realized over the course of history as people invent methods of transportation, communication, and governance which extend the range within which coherence and order can be maintained.) Out of the living order there emerged a living entity with no defined place.

In a finite world, societies all seeking to escape death-dealing scarcity through expansion will inevitably come to confront each other. Civilized societies, therefore, though lacking inherent limitations to their growth, do encounter new external limits—in the form of one another. Because human beings (like other living creatures) have "excess reproductive capacity," meaning that human numbers tend to increase indefinitely unless a high proportion of the population dies prematurely, each civilized society faces an unpleasant choice. If an expanding society willingly stops where its growth would infringe upon neighboring societies, it allows death to catch up and overtake its population. If it goes beyond those limits, it commits aggression. With no natural order or overarching power to prevent it, some will surely choose to take what belongs to their neighbors rather than to accept the limits that are compulsory for every other form of life.

In such circumstances, a Hobbesian struggle for power among societies becomes inevitable. We see that *what is freedom from the point of view of each single unit is anarchy in an ungoverned system of those units.* A freedom unknown in nature is cruelly transmuted into an equally unnatural state of anarchy, with its terrors and its destructive war of all against all.

As people stepped across the threshold into civilization, they inadvertently stumbled into a chaos that had never before existed. The relations among societies were uncontrolled and virtually uncontrollable. Such an ungoverned system imposes unchosen necessities: civilized people were compelled to enter a struggle for power.

Power may be defined as the capacity to achieve one's will against the will of another. The exercise of power thus infringes upon the exercise of choice, for to be the object of another's power is to have his choice substituted for one's own. Power becomes important where two actors (or more) would choose the same thing but cannot both have it; power becomes important when the obstacles to the achievement of one's will come from the will of others. Thus, as the expanding capacities of human societies created an overlap in the range of their grasp and desire, the intersocietal struggle for power arose.

But the new unavoidability of this struggle is but the first and smaller step in the transmutation of the apparent freedom of civilized peoples into bondage to the necessities of power.

The Selection for Power: The Parable of the Tribes

The new human freedom made striving for expansion and power possible. Such freedom, when multiplied, creates anarchy. The anarchy among civilized societies meant that the play of power in the system was uncontrollable. In an anarchic situation like that, no one can choose that the struggle for power shall cease. But there is one more element in the picture: *no one is free to choose peace, but anyone can impose upon all the necessity for power.* This is the lesson of the parable of the tribes.

Imagine a group of tribes living within reach of one another. If all choose the way of peace, then all may live in peace. But what if all but one choose peace, and that one is ambitious for expansion and conquest? What can happen to the others when confronted by an ambitious and potent neighbor? Perhaps one tribe is attacked and defeated, its people destroyed and its land seized for the use of the victors. Another is defeated, but this one is not exterminated; rather, it is subjugated and transformed to serve the conqueror. A third seeking to avoid such disaster flees from the area into some inaccessible (and undesirable) place, and its former homeland becomes part of the growing empire of the power-seeking tribe. Let us suppose that others observing these developments decide to defend themselves in order to preserve themselves and their autonomy. But the irony is that successful defense against a power-maximizing aggressor requires a society to become more like the society that threatens it. Power can be stopped only by power, and if the threatening society has discovered ways to magnify its power through innovations in organization or technology (or whatever), the defensive society will have to transform itself into something more like its foe in order to resist the external force.

I have just outlined four possible outcomes for the threatened tribes: destruction, absorption and transformation, withdrawal, and imitation. *In every one of these outcomes the ways of power are spread throughout the system.* This is the parable of the tribes.

The parable of the tribes is a theory of social evolution which shows that power is like a contaminant, a disease, which once introduced will gradually yet inexorably become universal in the system of competing societies. More important than the inevitability of the struggle for power is the profound social evolutionry consequence of that struggle once it begins. *A selection for power among civilized societies is inevitable.* If anarchy assured that power among civilized societies could not be governed, the selection for power signified that increasingly the ways of power would govern the destiny of mankind. This is the new evolutionary principle that came into the world with civilization. Here is the social evolutionary black hole that we have sought as an explanation of the harmful warp in the course of civilization's development.

What is viable in a world beset by the struggle for power is what can prevail. What prevails may not be what best meets the needs of mankind. The continuous selection for power has thus continually closed off many humane cultural options that people might otherwise have preferred. Power therefore rules human destiny.

If the ambition of societies for power grew originally out of Malthusian necessities, it did not need to remain so. As the selection for power continued, it ultimately would favor those whose hunger for power exceeded their material need. In the beginning, people struggled because they truly needed room to live. As civilization developed, the struggle became more one for the kind of Lebensraum that represents a love of power for its own sake. The struggle for power developed a life of its own that would feed an unnatural growth in the "necessities" imposed by power upon humankind. The selective process ensured that it would most definitely not be the meek who inherited the earth.

Just as the freedom from the regime of nature brought upon mankind a new bondage to power, so also did the open-end-edness of possibilities prove not a release from but a part of the trap. Because the process of cultural innovation is open-ended, there can be no end point in the maximization of power. The evolution of civilization is therefore marked by a perpetual (though sometimes interrupted) escalation in the level of power a society must possess to survive intersocietal competition. The reign of power thus has no limit.

Heads I Win, Tails You Lose: The Nonalternatives of the Parable of the Tribes

The parable of the tribes begins: "Imagine a group of tribes living within reach of one another." It leads to the question: "What are the possible outcomes for those tribes threatened by a potent and ambitious neighbor?" We discover that the possibilities are quite limited. But more important, they all amount fundamentally to the same thing: the inescapable permeation of the entire system by the ways of power. It is, therefore, a parable about the theft of free human choice.

Let us look more closely at the four possibilities to which the threatened societies are confined. They are: (A) withdrawal, (B) destruction, (C) transformation, and (D) imitation.

A. Withdrawal

The only way to escape the compelling pressures of the intersocietal system is to escape from that system, that is, to remove one's social group beyond the reach of other societies. It is thus only in the least accessible regions of the earth that the most primitive of human societies have been able to survive into our times.

For societies already civilized the option of withdrawal is less open because of the logistics involved. A small group can run off into the mountains or the jungles. Even a tribe can retreat, as in the westward migration of some American Indian tribes as the Euro-American civilization threatened them from the east. But more settled and dense civilized societies are not so portable. They must stand and face the threat when it arrives.

B. Destruction

When the encounter comes, the weak are often at the mercy of the strong. And sometimes the strong show no mercy. Cultures have been obliterated, peoples exterminated.

The advance of modern imperialism left the more densely populated areas peopled by the natives, the conquerors lacking either the ruthlessness, the motive, or the means to carry out systematic genocide on such large groups. Ancient conquerors, however, were often fully prepared to slaughter whole peoples to make room for their own. We who live in the historical shadow of Auschwitz cannot rest secure in the belief that mass exterminations cannot accompany any future conquests, especially if, in the coming decades, a worsening imbalance between food and population leads to widespread famine.

Digression: The Moral Check?—But what of "rights" and "justice"? This is a question that inevitably recurs with the parable of the tribes. How can power have free reign when people are by nature concerned with the moral dimension of their conduct?

People are moral creatures. Unfortunately, although moral scruples can act as an obstacle to the unbridled pursuit of interest, they prove too often an easily surmountable barrier.

For one thing, people often use rationalization and hypocrisy to make moral principle a tool of rather than a check upon self-interest (as Marx so rightly pointed out). Beyond that, the jurisdiction of moral injunctions is often confined to relations within one's own group. The out-group is typically entitled to no such consideration. "Thou shalt not kill" was hardly intended as God's commandment to the Hebrews to be pacifists. The chronically dangerous "state of nature" among societies inevitably feeds intersocietal amorality. Also, the selection for power may select against moral sensitivity: nice guys are finished first.

The rule of power, the destruction of the innocent, are most ancient problems. Our vision of our own times will be clouded if we fail to recognize that. Some believe modern imperialism manifests the eruption of some new disease into human affairs. They are thus led to disparage Western civilization as uniquely corrupt and degraded. Some are aghast at the amorality of the Soviet Union which relentlessly presses forward its expansionist drive. They are led to regard that totalitarian regime as a nation unlike all others in its irremediable viciousness. But the disease lies not in any civilization, or race, or economic, or governmental system. The world has seen it all before, since history began.

C. Transformation

Even if a people and their culture survive conquest by a more powerful society, the option of continuing life as before may be stolen from them. They may be compelled to adopt the ways of their masters. The extent to which conquest results in cultural transformation can vary across a wide spectrum. Destruction might be seen as one extreme on this continuum, where the powerful replace the original people and their ways with their own. At the other extreme, the conqueror may simply seek to extract regular tribute or revenue from a society which otherwise is left unmolested. When the victor and the vanquished are on comparable levels of political and economic development, the change of rulers may have little impact on the society as a whole. If, however, the more powerful society has tapped wholly new springs of power, the most advantageous use of the new imperial acquisition may require transplanting the new more potent methods. In the first instance, the ruler's purposes are served simply by taking his "cut" of the action and letting the game go on as before. But when the new ruler knows a game that could yield a much bigger cut from the same underlying resources, he has practical reasons to impose his new game onto the old culture.

D. Imitation

In the first three outcomes, the ways of power spread when the mighty expand into areas where the weak have been. Resistance by the weak has been either absent or inconsequential in this picture. In actuality, resistance has counted for little when the advantage of the mighty has been overwhelming and when the threat has come so suddenly (in historic terms) that the weak have had little time to prepare to meet it.

Power can be resisted only with power. Potent breakthroughs thus require emulation. This is true not only within Europe, where modern power emerged in an intensively competitive international environment, but thence around the world as the omnivorous Western powers invaded other continents. The defensive imitation by the Japanese is noteworthy—"industrialize or be gobbled up like the rest."

The tyranny of power is such that even self-defense becomes a kind of surrender. Not to resist is to be transformed at the hands of the mighty. To resist requires that one transform oneself into their likeness. Either way, free human choice is prevented. *All ways but the ways of power are blocked.*

Hope

The parable of the tribes may seem to be an irredeemably pessimistic view of the dilemma of civilized peoples. It seems to say that civilized man is forever condemned to live in a condition in which some of his worst sins will be selected and magnified into laws of his cultural existence. But this is only partly true. There is indeed no way to return the dangerous djinni of human powers to the bottle. Even if we could, the parable of the tribes says we would only retrace the original, often nightmarish course of our history. Even if there is no turning back, there may be a way of moving forward.

The creation of a new order requires an end to the intersocietal anarchy that has been the overarching context of civilized life. Anarchy is the inevitable outcome of the fragmentation of mankind, and it was inevitable that civilized societies would emerge in a fragmented state. As long as the human cultural system was fragmented into a multiplicity of separate units, the problem of power remained insoluble. Even if any region of the world managed to solve the problem by extending unity and by living in peace, those people were still vulnerable to the reintroduction of the contaminant of power from outside its regional system. In our times, however, the possibility of an escape from this fragmented system is beginning to emerge. For the first time, the world is becoming a single interdependent system in which all the world's peoples are in contact. Meanwhile, the age-old struggle for power goes on and may annihilate us before we can create an order that controls power. But the centuries ahead give us the opportunity to place all human action within a structure that for the first time makes truly free human choice possible. Even so, it is far from clear how to get from here to there, or even what kind of world order "there" should be.

Having eaten the fruit of the tree of knowledge, we became as gods in power—and now must do so in wisdom. Having escaped the control of nature, mankind must create controls for itself, replacing the wholeness of nature with an artificial wholeness, substituting for the law of nature a human law. Here is another paradox: the laws of man require power, for power can be controlled only with power. The challenge, therefore, is to design systems that use power to disarm power. Only in such an order can mankind be free.

15.

Group Narcissism*

ERICH FROMM

Narcissism can be described as a state of experience in which only the person himself, *his* body, *his* needs, *his* feelings, *his* thoughts, *his* property, everything and everybody pertaining to *him* are experienced as fully real, while everybody and everything that does not form part of the person or is not an object of his needs is not interesting, is not fully real, is perceived only by intellectual recognition, while *affectively* without weight and color. A person, to the extent to which he is narcissistic, has a double standard of perception. Only he himself and what pertains to him has significance, while the rest of the world is more or less weightless or colorless, and because of this double standard the narcissistic person shows severe defects in judgment and lacks the capacity for objectivity.

Often the narcissistic person achieves a sense of security in his own entirely subjective conviction of his perfection, his superiority over others, his extraordinary qualities, and not through being related to others or through any real work or achievement of his own. He needs to hold on to his narcissistic self-image, since his sense of worth as well as his sense of identity are based on it. If his narcissism is threatened *he* is threatened in a vitally important area. When others wound his narcissism by slighting him, criticizing him, showing him up

* Excerpt from *The Anatomy of Human Destructiveness* (New York: Holt, Rinehart and Winston, (1973), Copyright © 1973 by Erich Fromm.

when he has said something wrong, defeating him in a game
or on numerous other occasions, a narcissistic person usually
reacts with intense anger or rage, whether or not he shows it
or is even aware of it. The intensity of this aggressive reaction
can often be seen in the fact that such a person will never
forgive someone who has wounded his narcissism and often
feels a desire for vengeance which would be less intense if his
body or his property had been attacked.

Among political leaders a high degree of narcissism is very
frequent; it may be considered an occupational illness—or as-
set—especially among those who owe their power to their influence over mass audiences. If the leader is convinced of his
extraordinary gifts and of his mission, it will be easier to convince
the large audiences who are attracted by men who appear to
be so absolutely certain. But the narcissistic leader does not use
his narcissistic charisma only as a means for political success;
he needs success and applause for the sake of his own mental
equilibrium. The idea of his greatness and infallibility is essentially based on his narcissistic grandiosity, not on his real achievements as a human being. And yet he cannot do without the
narcissistic inflation because his human core—conviction, conscience, love, and faith—is not very developed.

When, in group narcissism, the object is not the individual
but the group to which he belongs, the individual can be fully
aware of it, and express it without any restrictions. The assertion
that "my country" (or nation, or religion) is the most wonderful,
the most cultured, the most powerful, the most peace-loving,
etc., does not sound crazy at all; on the contrary, it sounds like
the expression of patriotism, faith, and loyalty. It also appears
to be a realistic and rational value judgment because it is shared
by many members of the same group. This consensus succeeds
in transforming the phantasy into reality, since for most people
reality is constituted by general consensus and not based on
reason or critical examination.

Group narcissism has important functions. In the first place,
it furthers the solidarity and cohesion of the group, and makes
manipulation easier by appealing to narcissistic prejudices. Second, it is extremely important as an element giving satisfaction
to the members of the group and particularly to those who

have few other reasons to feel proud and worthwhile. Even if
one is the most miserable, the poorest, the least respected
member of a group, there is compensation for one's miserable
condition in feeling "I am a part of the most wonderful group
in the world. I, who in reality am a worm, become a giant
through belonging to the group." Consequently, the degree of
group narcissism is commensurate with the lack of real satisfaction in life. Those social classes which enjoy life more are
less fanatical (fanaticism is a characteristic quality of group
narcissism) than those which, like the lower middle classes,
suffer from scarcity in all material and cultural areas and lead
a life of unmitigated boredom.

Those whose narcissism refers to their group rather than to
themselves as individuals are as sensitive as the individual
narcissist, and they react with rage to any wound, real or
imaginary, inflicted upon their group. If anything, they react
more intensely and certainly more consciously. An individual,
unless he is mentally very sick, may have at least some doubts
about his personal narcissistic image. The member of the group
has none, since his narcissism is shared by the majority. In case
of conflict between groups that challenge each other's collective
narcissism, this very challenge arouses intense hostility in each
of them. The narcissistic image of one's own group is raised to
its highest point, while the devaluation of the opposing group
sinks to the lowest. One's own group becomes a defender of
human dignity, decency, morality, and right. Devilish qualities
are ascribed to the other group; it is treacherous, ruthless, cruel,
and basically inhuman. The violation of one of the symbols of
group narcissism—such as the flag, or the person of the emperor,
the president, or an ambassador—is reacted to with such intense
fury and aggression by the people that they are even willing to
support their leaders in a policy of war.

Group narcissism is one of the most important sources of
human aggression, and yet this, like all other forms of defensive
aggression, is a reaction to an attack on vital interests. It differs
from other forms of defensive aggression in that intense narcissism in itself is a semipathological phenomenon. In considering the causes and the function of bloody and cruel mass
massacres as they occurred between Hindus and Moslems at

the time of the partition of India or recently between Bengali Moslems and their Pakistani rulers, group narcissism certainly plays a considerable role; this is not surprising if we appreciate the fact that we are dealing here with virtually the poorest and most miserable populations anywhere in the world.

In the development of the human race we find an ever increasing range of socialization; the original small group based on blood affinity gives way to ever larger groups based on a common language, a common social order, a common faith. The larger size of the group does not necessarily mean that the pathological qualities of narcissism are reduced. The group narcissism of the "whites" or the "Aryans" is as malignant as the extreme narcissism of a single person can be. Yet in general we find that in the process of socialization which leads to the formation of larger groups, the need for co-operation with many other and different people not connected among themselves by ties of blood, tends to counteract the narcissistic charge within the group. (Fromm, *The Heart of Man,* Random House: New York, 1964, p. 80.)

16

The Role of Fear*

RALPH K. WHITE

Realistic Fear and Deterrence

Sigmund Freud was aware of two different kinds of anxiety. He called them "objective" and "neurotic" anxiety. As he put it, objective anxiety is "a reaction to the perception of an external danger"; it "may be regarded as an expression of the instinct of self-preservation" (1924, p. 401). It is realistic and necessary as a basis for coping with real danger. However, in the case of those with neurotic anxiety,

> . . . we find a general apprehensiveness in them, a "free-floating" anxiety, as we call it, ready to attach itself to any thought which is at all appropriate, affecting judgments, inducing expectations, lying in wait for any opportunity to find a justification for itself. We call this condition *"expectant dread"* or "anxious expectation." People who are tormented with this kind of anxiety always anticipate the worst of all possible outcomes, interpret every chance happening as an evil omen, and exploit every uncertainty to mean the worst. (p. 405)

A distinction resembling this one is as necessary in the world's search for peace as Freud's distinction is in psychiatry and in the lives of ordinary individuals. It will be called here the distinction between realistic fear and exaggerated fear. Realistic

* Excerpted from *Fearful Warriors: A Psychological Profile of U.S.-Soviet Relations* (New York: The Free Press, 1984). Reprinted with permission of The Free Press, a Division of Macmillan, Inc. Copyright © 1984 by The Free Press.

fear is healthy and necessary, both in oneself and in any opposing country that is caught, with one's own, in the malignant process of hostile interaction. It is necessary in oneself both in order to face with clear eyes the unprecedented danger of nuclear war and in order to recognize honestly the genuine hostility in the opponent, which may combine with defensive fear to produce actual aggression. It is prudent, up to a point, to promote realistic fear of one's own arms in the minds of opponents, as a motive counteracting whatever other reasons they may have for starting a war. Exaggerated fear, on the other hand, is probably the number one psychological reason for war in the present-day world, since it not only fuels the arms race, with what Kennan calls the "grotesque redundancy" of the most lethal arms on both sides, but also increases greatly the danger of defensively motivated aggression by one side or the other.

Freud, by the way, would be one of the last to ignore the reality and intensity of aggressive impulses, especially subconscious, unacknowledged aggressive impulses, in opponents' minds as well as in one's own. His view of the human species is at the opposite pole from a Pollyanna optimism. He, much more than the majority of academic psychologists, has stressed the reality and intensity of aggressive impulses in human nature as such, the importance of acknowledging them honestly, and the importance of learning to cope with them in a constructive rather than a destructive way.

The distinction between the two kinds of fear becomes even clearer if we ask ourselves a simple question: In order to keep the peace should we ("we" in this case being either the West or the USSR) try to create fear of us in the minds of our adversaries? That question comes close to the heart of this book.

Those who stress deterrence much more than tension reduction (for brevity, and without prejudice, we can call them the deterrers, while recognizing that most of them favor some kinds of tension reduction also) are likely to have an unequivocal answer: yes, of course we should. The danger of war comes only from *them. They* understand only the language of force. Of course we should create a healthy fear, in them, of the harm they would suffer if they attack us or our allies.

Those who stress tension reduction much more than deterrence (for brevity, and without prejudice—which would be especially inappropriate, since this writer is one of them—we can call them the tension reducers) are likely to have an equally unequivocal answer: no, of course we shouldn't. There is entirely too much fear in the world already. Fear is what fuels arms races and an exaggerated preoccupation with power in order to be safe. It is a major cause of war. We should cultivate trust and friendship, not fear, if we want peace.

What both sides usually fail to realize is that the familiar little word "fear" encompasses two quite different things, and the answer to the crucial question depends very much on which of those meanings the speaker has in mind. A more adequate answer than either of the above would be that, to keep the peace, we should encourage realistic fear on both sides and discourage exaggerated fear on both sides. (Parenthetically, real harm is done when deterrers and tension reducers call each other names, rather than being courteous and listening to each other. Calling anyone a "hard-liner" or a "hawk" is name-calling, since both terms suggest unpleasant things such as machismo and bellicosity. Calling anyone a "soft-liner" or a "dove" is name-calling, since both suggest weakness of will and lack of courage if not also softness of mind. Deterrer and tension reducer are descriptive, not pejorative terms.)

Exaggerated Fear and Freud's "Neurotic Anxiety"

Freud's "neurotic anxiety," or something like it, is illustrated by a surprisingly large number of instances of aggression that have probably been mainly defensive in motivation. In recent history most of them have turned out badly for the aggressor, which raises sharply the question of how realistic the fear was in the first place:

• The German-Austrian attack on Serbia in 1914, probably motivated mainly by fear that if a "firm stand" against Serbia were not taken Austria-Hungary would disintegrate.

- The German attack on France through Belgium, motivated in large part by fear of a Russian invasion in the East.
- The "dismemberment" of Germany between 1918 and 1938, motivated mainly by France's fear of a third German invasion.
- The takeover of Eastern Europe by the USSR in 1944–48, motivated largely by fear of another invasion coming from the "capitalist West," comparable to Hitler's onslaught in 1941–45.
- The American action to restore the Shah in 1954, motivated mainly by fear of a Soviet absorption of Iran and domination of the Middle East.
- The concerted Arab attack on Israel in 1948, motivated by the feeling that "imperialism" had just implanted an expanding alien body in the heart of the Arab world and that Arab manhood demanded its destruction.
- Israel's attack on Egypt in 1956, growing out of Israel's perennial fear of being destroyed by the encircling Arabs.
- Israel's preemptive attack on Egypt in 1967, stemming from the same fear.
- The Soviet Union's crackdowns on Hungary and Czechoslovakia in 1956 and 1968, based mainly on fear of a domino process in Eastern Europe and a crumbling of the bulwark it had built against another attack from the West.
- The American war in Vietnam, based mainly on fear of a similar domino process, first in Southeast Asia and perhaps later in many Third World countries.
- Egypt's armed crossing of the Suez Canal in 1973, based mainly on the conviction that the Sinai was still part of Egypt, torn away by a still-expanding Israel in 1967.
- The Soviet intervention in Afghanistan, probably motivated (see Chapter 6) mainly by fear that the Soviet position in the entire Middle East, already unfavorable, would be made worse if a hitherto friendly border state were allowed to fall under hostile "imperialist" plus Chinese control.

The generalization that emerges from this list is both fundamental and seldom fully recognized. What emerges is the really startling importance of fear (sometimes realistic but usually exaggerated) as a cause of aggression and therefore of war. That generalization has great practical as well as theoretical importance, since it is the chief basis for the major practical upshot of this book: the primary importance of tension reduction—meaning chiefly the importance of reducing exaggerated fear on both sides—as a way of avoiding nuclear war.

Several of the twelve interpretations in the list are of course controversial. The historically informed reader will almost certainly question some of them in the necessarily oversimplified form in which they are presented here. (Such a reader will find the evidence for eight of them elaborated, to some extent, in Chapters 2 and 13–16 of White, *Fearful Warriors* [1984], and the other four, dealing with the Arab–Israeli conflict, in White, [1977]). The main point now, though, is that there are twelve of them and that they represent most of the acts of aggression in our century that are familiar to Americans (the chief ones not mentioned being Hitler's aggressions, Japan's, and North Korea's). If not enough to establish the proposition that exaggerated fear is the number one motive underlying twentieth-century acts of aggression, they are probably enough to establish fairly solidly the more modest proposition that exaggerated fear is *often* a major factor.

That statement does not challenge any established consensus among either historians or political scientists. Historians rarely make any generalizations of that sort, since by nature and training the ones who study war's causes focus intensively on the causes of a single war, or two or three at most, rather than extensively on many wars. As for political scientists, they are much more prone to generalize, and when they do their emphasis is usually on national security and on power as a means to security. The difference between them and this psychological approach is mainly a difference of words, not substance, since "fear" is a word for wanting security and not having it. The psychohistorical viewpoint of this book differs from theirs, not in any greater emphasis on fear, but in its sharper focus on exaggerated fear as distinguished from realistic fear, on the question of why fear of other nations is so often exaggerated, and on the question of how exaggerated fear can be reduced.

Why is fear of other nations so often exaggerated? The thought that the problem could be basically psychological is suggested by a nonpsychologist, George Kennan:

> We have gone on piling weapon upon weapon, missile upon missile, new levels of destructiveness upon old ones. We have done this helplessly, almost involuntarily, like the victims of some sort of hypnotism, like men in a dream, like lemmings heading for the sea, like the children of Hamlin marching along behind their Pied Piper. And the result is that we have achieved, we and the Russians together, in the creation of these devices and their means of delivery, levels of redundancy of such grotesque dimensions as to defy rational understanding. (1982, p. 176)

Again Freud, a specialist in irrational behavior, can help us. He interprets compulsive acts, such as the hand-washing compulsion, on the basis of their symbolic reassuring function; they serve to keep the underlying neurotic anxiety from reaching the surface of consciousness:

> [There are] patients whose symptoms take the form of obsessive acts, and who seem to be remarkably immune from anxiety. When we restrain them from carrying out their obsessive performances, their washing, their ceremonies, etc., or when they themselves venture an attempt to abandon one of their compulsions, they are forced by an appalling dread to yield to the compulsion and to carry out the act. (1924, p. 411)

There are at least some similarities between this and the arms-building compulsion that Kennan describes. In both cases there is an underlying intense anxiety; in both the anxiety is less acute, at least on the conscious level, when certain acts have been carried out; and in both there is much question as to whether in the real world those acts, judged rationally, are fulfilling a rational purpose. In both there is a kind of symbolic rationality if not an evidence-based rationality: handwashing presumably symbolizes getting rid of some kind of sin, the specific nature of which is more or less completely excluded from consciousness, and the piling up of redundant amounts of nuclear strength may symbolize extra reassurance against being hit first by the diabolical enemy. (It should be remembered that what we are now talking about is not all armed deterrence but the present redundancy of a particular kind of armed deterrence. A main thesis of this book is that, while an adequate second-strike capability and adequate conventional strength in Western Europe are rational enough, the redundancy—the excessiveness—of nuclear weapons, especially vulnerable nuclear weapons capable of a first strike, is not.)

Now, how can we, the peace-oriented people who constitute the immense majority of the people of the world, cope with our own compulsive tendency to build redundant nuclear arms?

At this point it is necessary to depart somewhat from Freud's analogy of a compulsively hand-washing neurotic person and to consider how the responsible foreign policymakers on both sides probably differ from compulsive neurotic hand washers.

One fairly obvious difference is that the national decision makers are more rational than the hand washers. Their fears have a more rational basis. Their positions in government show that they are at least somewhat intelligent and quite capable of coping with some aspects of the real world. Surely nothing so obviously irrational as washing their hands twenty times a day would come into their minds. Their minds would insist on some element of rationality even in their least rational public decisions. In this case at least one such element of rationality probably exists: the political value of seeming to be stronger, overall, in the eyes of potential opponents and of other countries who might be intimidated by the apparently stronger side. The side that other countries believe to be stronger would probably have a greater chance to prevail in tense controversies not only throughout the Third World but also in controversies involving Berlin, Yugoslavia, or Israel, and for those on each side who take it for granted that their side is always much more right than the other side that is an important consideration.

Those whose thinking is excessively anxiety-ridden may be prone to irrationality, though, in at least three other ways: (1) a failure to think candidly about whether the danger of nuclear war may be far greater than the danger of having a lower batting average in the many local controversies that crop up; (2) a failure to engage in the chessplayer's kind of empathy with the other reasons an opponent might have to refrain from starting either a nuclear or a large-scale conventional war; (3) an un-willingness to recognize the malignancy of the malignant process of hostile interaction and the likelihood that it is already making their own country, as well as its opponents, too belligerent and too ready to take serious risks of war.

What keeps so many intelligent people from thinking along those lines?

One answer is that their deeply ingrained diabolical enemy image—deeply ingrained partly for psychological reasons that have not yet been discussed here—fills their minds so fully that other thoughts, not based on it, are crowded out. Another answer is that the thought of a monsterlike enemy—an enemy who also has in his hands the most lethal weapons the world has ever seen—imperatively demands tangible reassurance, and the most tangible reassurance the present-day world offers is to have in one's own hands weapons as lethal and as numerous as his. (A more rational, more discriminating answer might be that one's own weapons should be as lethal as his but, because of overkill, could safely be much less numerous than his, with great profit from the standpoint of making him less of a monster.) Tangible symbols of reassurance are seized and clung to, with no effort to empathize with the enemy, partly because they are tangible—a kind of magic security blanket—and partly because the image of the opponent as a monster, with no human characteristics such as longing for peace or fear of oneself, precludes all empathy. How can anyone empathize with a monster?

If that is the case, it is obvious that there are great psycho-logical obstacles to rational thinking about nuclear weapons. Strong unconscious or subconscious emotional needs block the path. Etzioni was right in calling tension reduction "the hard way to peace." It will necessarily be long as well as hard.

The same analysis, though, suggests that a rational strategy for persuading the anxiety-ridden clingers to nuclear parity that they can relax their grip should contain two elements:

1. On the one hand, accepting their subconscious need for tangible symbols of safety and satisfying it, to a considerable

extent, by agreeing that both a second-strike capability and adequate conventional strength are needed
2. On the other hand, patiently and factually discussing the case against nuclear redundancy and the nature and value of realistic empathy with one's own worst enemy

References

Frank, J. D. (1982). *Sanity and Survival in the Nuclear Age.* NY: Random House.

Freud, S. (1924). *A General Introduction to Psychoanalysis.* London: Boni and Liveright. (Citations are from the American paperback edition, Doubleday Permabooks, 1953.)

Fromm, E. (1964). *The Heart of Man.* NY: Harper and Row.

——— (1973). *The Anatomy of Human Destructiveness.* NY: Holt, Rinehart and Winston.

Fulbright, J. W. (1966). *The Arrogance of Power.* NY: Random House.

Hobbes, T. (1940). *Leviathan.* New York: Dutton.

Horne, A. (Feb. 20, 1966). "Verdun—The Reason Why." *New York Times Magazine.*

Kennan, G. F. (1982). *The Nuclear Delusion: Soviet-American Relations in the Atomic Age.* NY: Pantheon.

Niebuhr, R. (1949). *The Nature and Destiny of Man.* Vol. 1. *Human Nature.* NY: Scribner's.

Rostow, W. W. (1971). *Politics and the Stages of Economic Growth.* Cambridge: Cambridge University Press.

Russell, B. (1948). *Power: A New Social Analysis.* London: Allen and Unwin.

Schmookler, A. B. (1984). *The Parable of the Tribes: The Problem of Power in Social Evolution.* Berkeley: University of California Press.

Snyder, G. and Diesing, P. (1977). *Conflict Among Nations.* Princeton: Princeton University Press.

Thucydides. (1972 trans.) *History of the Peloponnesian War.* Trans. Rex Warner. Harmondsworth: Penguin.

Tuchman, B. (1984). *The March of Folly from Troy to Vietnam.* NY: Knopf.

White, R. K. (1977). "Misperception in the Arab-Israeli Conflict." *Journal of Social Issues* 33 (1) : 190–221.

——— (1984). *Fearful Warriors: A Psychological Profile of the U.S.-Soviet Conflict.* NY: The Free Press.

White, R. W. (1959). "Motivation Reconsidered: The Concept of Competence." *Psychological Review* 66 : 297–331.

SECTION VI

Perception and Misperception in International Conflict

SECTION EDITOR: SUSAN T. FISKE

INTRODUCTION

RALPH K. WHITE

A major advance in social psychology during recent decades has been the large amount of experimentation and systematic theory building on social perception and misperception. The first chapter in this section, Chapter 17, by Philip E. Tetlock and Charles McGuire, Jr., illustrates that advance. Entitled "Cognitive Perspectives on Foreign Policy," it gathers together much of the best of what has been done and relates it to the subject matter of this book.

The word "cognitive" here is significant. On the one hand, in contrast with strict behaviorism, it implies a willingness to take seriously what goes on in a person's mind. The strict behaviorist's taboo on subjective terms such as feeling, wanting, believing, and expecting is quietly discarded; such terms are used whenever experimentation or common sense suggests that they are useful. On the other hand, in contrast with the often one-sided emphasis of psychoanalytically oriented psychologists on feeling and wanting, "cognitive" implies a primary focus on what is cognitive in a narrower sense: believing and expecting, for example, as distinguished from feeling and wanting. Perception in a very broad sense—a person's beliefs about the entire world around him, including especially the people in it— is the key concept.

This may or may not imply a diminished emphasis on how unconscious or semiconscious motives, such as a need to defend one's individual or group self-image, influence perception. Terms such as wishful thinking, denial, rationalization, projection, and selective inattention may or may not be stressed. There is a tendency, though, to give more attention to nonaffective, nonmotivational concepts such as the influence of preexisting beliefs on present perception, or the concept of "availability"—the readiness with which various ideas come into the mind as influenced, for instance, by recent vivid experiences.

The next two chapters, Chapter 18 by the political scientist Robert Jervis and Chapter 19 by the political psychologist Ralph White, illustrate that distinction, though the authors are not as far apart as some may suppose. Jervis's chapter, excerpted from the first chapter of his *Perception and Misperception in International Politics* (1976), which quickly became a classic within the new "behavioral" (i.e., psychological) movement in political science, is here entitled "A Critique of Early Psychological Approaches to International Misperception." We suggested the insertion of the word "early," which was not in his book when it was published (1976), in order to leave open the question of the extent to which psychology is still characterized by the neglect of cognitive factors (in the narrower sense of the word) that he saw at that time. It is not implied here that the neglect has ended, but I, for one, believe his critique contained much truth at the time it was written (it was a valid criticism of me, among others), and the chapter by Tetlock and McGuire confirms my impression that the shift of emphasis since then has been very marked and very wholesome.

Chapter 19, "Motivated Misperceptions," deals with the unconscious or semiconscious motivational factors in misperception, such as defense of the moral self-image and defense of the diabolical enemy image, that are not stressed by either Tetlock and McGuire or by Jervis.

17.

Cognitive Perspectives on Foreign Policy*

PHILIP E. TETLOCK and
CHARLES B. McGUIRE, JR.

The last fifteen years have witnessed an impressive expansion of cognitive research on foreign policy—on both methodological and theoretical fronts. On the methodological front, investigators have shown skill in drawing insights from a variety of research techniques, including laboratory experiments (reviewed by Holsti and George, 1975; Jervis, 1976); historical case studies (George and Smoke, 1974; Janis, 1982; Lebow, 1981); content analyses of archival documents (Axelrod, 1976; Falkowski, 1979; Hermann, 1980a, 1980b; Tetlock, 1983c), interview and questionnaire studies (Bonham, Shapiro, and Trumble, 1979; Heradstveit, 1974, 1981); and computer simulations of belief systems (Abelson, 1968; Anderson and Thorson, 1982). There are, moreover, numerous examples of multimethod convergence in the research literature: investigators from different methodological traditions have often arrived at strikingly similar conclusions concerning the roles that cognitive variables play in the foreign policymaking process. The theoretical diversity is equally impressive and healthy. In developing hypotheses linking cognitive and foreign policy variables, investigators have drawn upon a variety of intellectual traditions, including work on attribution theory (Heradstveit, 1981; Jervis, 1976; Tetlock, 1983b); cog-

* Excerpted from S. Long, ed., *Political Behavior Annual* (Boulder, Colo.: Westview Press, 1985).

nitive-consistency theory (Jervis, 1976); behavioral decision theory (Fischhoff, 1983; Jervis, 1982); the effects of stress on information processing (Holsti and George, 1975; Janis and Mann, 1977; Suedfeld and Tetlock, 1977), organizational principles underlying political belief systems (George, 1969; Holsti, 1977; Walker, 1983); and individual differences in cognitive styles (Bonham and Shapiro, 1977; Hermann, 1980a; Tetlock, 1981, 1983a, 1984). Each of these approaches has borne at least some empirical fruit.

We believe careful appraisal is now needed of what has been accomplished and of the directions in which theoretical and empirical work appears to be developing. We have divided our review chapter into four sections: "The Cognitive Research Program in Foreign Policy," "Representational Research," "Process Research," and "Conclusions."

I. The Cognitive Research Program in Foreign Policy

Cognitive research on foreign policy can be viewed as an incipient research program. The hard core of the cognitive research program is difficult to specify with confidence. (What fundamental assumptions do the overwhelming majority of investigators who work at this level of analysis share?) We believe, however, that the hard core consists of two key assumptions which deserve to be spelled out in detail:

(1) The international environment imposes heavy information-processing demands upon policymakers. It is very difficult to identify the best or utility-maximizing solutions to most foreign policy problems. Policymakers must deal with incomplete and unreliable information on the intentions and capabilities of other states. The range of response options is indeterminate. The problem consequences of each option are shrouded in uncertainty. Policymakers must choose among options that vary on many, seemingly incommensurable value dimensions (e.g., economic interests, international prestige, domestic political advantages, human rights, even lives). Finally, to compound the difficulty of the task, policymakers must sometimes work under intense stress and time pressure.

(2) Policymakers (like all human beings) are limited-capacity information processors who resort to simplifying strategies to deal with the complexity, uncertainty, and painful trade-offs with which the world confronts them (cf. Abelson and Levi, in press; Einhorn and Hogarth, 1981; George, 1980; Jervis, 1976; Nisbett and Ross, 1980; Simon, 1957; Taylor and Fiske, 1984). The foreign policy of a nation addresses itself, not to the external world per se, but to the simplified image of the external world constructed in the minds of those who make policy decisions (Axelrod, 1976; George, 1980; Holsti, 1976; Jervis, 1976). Policymakers may behave "rationally" (attempt to maximize expected utility) but only within the context of their simplified subjective representations of reality.

Implicit in these hard-core assumptions is the central research objective of the cognitive research program: to understand *the cognitive strategies that policymakers rely upon to construct and maintain their simplified images of the environment*. We find it useful to distinguish two basic types of cognitive strategies, both of which have received substantial attention: (a) reliance on cognitive or knowledge structures that provide frameworks for assimilating new information and choosing among policy options (belief systems, operational codes, cognitive maps, scripts); (b) reliance on low-effort judgmental and choice heuristics that permit policymakers to make up their minds quickly and with confidence in the correctness of their positions (e.g., "satisficing" decision rules, the availability, representativeness, and anchoring heuristics).

These two (by no means mutually exclusive) coping strategies correspond closely to the distinction cognitive psychologists have drawn between declarative knowledge (first category) and procedural knowledge (second category) of mental functioning (cf. Anderson, 1978, 1980). Research on declarative knowledge in the foreign policy domain—which we call representational research—is concerned with clarifying *what* policymakers think. What assumptions do they make about themselves, other states, the relationships among states, the goals or values underlying foreign policy, and the types of policies most instrumental to attaining those goals or values? Can typologies or taxonomies of foreign policy belief systems be developed? To what extent and in what ways do policymakers' initial beliefs or assumptions guide—even dominate—the interpretation of new evidence and the making of new decisions? The best-known examples of representational research are studies of the operational codes and cognitive maps of political elites (Axelrod, 1976; George, 1969, 1980; Heradstveit, 1981; Holsti, 1977). Research on procedural knowledge—which we call process research—is concerned with identifying abstract (content-free) laws of cognitive functioning that focus on *how* policymakers think about issues (the intellectual roots of process research can be directly traced to experimental cognitive and social psychology). The best-known examples of process research are studies of perception and misperception in international relations: the rules or heuristics that policymakers use in seeking causal explanations for the behavior of other states, in drawing lessons from history or in choosing among courses of action (cf. George, 1980; Jervis, 1976, 1982; Tetlock, 1983b).

Reasonable challenges can be raised to the hard-core premises of the program. One can question, for instance, the causal importance of policymakers' cognitions about the environment. Correlations between cognitions and actions are not sufficient to establish causality. The beliefs, perceptions, and values that people express may merely be justifications for policies they have already adopted as a result of other processes (e.g., psychodynamic needs and conflicts, bureaucratic role demands, domestic political pressures, international exigencies).

II. Representational Research

Psychologists and political scientists have invented an intimidatingly long list of terms to describe the cognitive structures that perceivers rely upon in encoding new information. These terms include "scripts" (Abelson, 1981; Schank and Abelson, 1977); "operational codes" (George, 1969; Holsti, 1977); "cognitive maps" (Axelrod, 1976); "stereotypes" (Allport, 1954; Hamilton, 1979); "frames" (Minsky, 1975); "nuclear scenes" (Tompkins, 1979); "prototypes" (Cantor and Mischel, 1979); as well as the more traditional and inclusive term "schemas"

(Nisbett and Ross, 1980). We do not propose a detailed classification of all possible cognitive structures in this chapter (for preliminary efforts in this area see Nisbett and Ross, 1980; Schank and Abelson, 1977; Taylor and Fiske, 1984). Our goals are more modest. We shall focus only on cognitive research specifically concerned with foreign policy. Within that domain, we further restrict our attention to two issues likely to be central to future theoretical developments in the field:

(1) What theoretical and methodological tools are at our disposal to describe the cognitive structures that influence foreign policy?
(2) To what extent is information processing in the foreign policy domain theory-driven (dominated by existing cognitive structures) as opposed to data-driven (responsive to external reality)?

Describing Foreign Policy Belief Systems

In principle, people can subscribe to an infinite variety of images of their own states, of other states, and of the relationships among states. We use the term "idiographic representational research" to describe case studies which present detailed descriptions of the foreign policy belief systems of individual decision makers. We use the term "nomothetic representational" research to describe studies in which the primary goal is the development and testing of general theoretical statements that apply to large populations of individuals. The focus thus shifts from the uniqueness of particular policymakers to underlying similarities or themes that permit cross-individual and cross-situational comparisons. We discuss three lines of nomothetic representational research: the work on operational codes, cognitive mapping, and personality correlates of foreign policy belief systems.

Operational Code Research

Operational codes impose badly needed cognitive order and stability on an ambiguous and complex international environment (George, 1969). They do so in multiple ways: by providing norms, standards, and guidelines that influence (but do not unilaterally determine) decision makers' choices of strategy and tactics in dealings with other nations. George proposed that the essence of an operational code can be captured in its answers to a number of "philosophical" questions concerning the "nature of the political universe" and a number of "instrumental" questions concerning the types of policies most likely to achieve important objectives (see also Holsti, 1977).

Operational codes are organized hierarchically such that central or core beliefs exert more influence on peripheral beliefs than vice versa. One strong "belief candidate" for a central organizing role in operational codes is whether the decision maker believes the political universe to be essentially one of conflict or one of harmony (Holsti, 1977). People who view the world in Hobbesian, zero-sum terms (a war of all against all) are likely to differ on a variety of belief dimensions from those who see the world as potentially harmonious. These two groups will tend to appraise the motives and goals of opponents differently and disagree on the best strategies for pursuing policy goals. Another strong candidate for a central organizing role in operational codes is the decision-maker's belief concerning the root causes of international conflict. People who attribute conflict to different root causes (e.g., human nature, attributes of nations, the international system) will tend to have different views on the likelihood of, and necessary conditions for, long-term peace.

Tetlock (1983b) notes that both sides seem to possess an unlimited capacity to view international events in ways that support their initial positions ("aggressive" Soviet acts can always be construed as defensive responses to external threats; "conciliatory" Soviet acts can always be construed as deceptive maneuvers designed to weaken Western resolve). This is consistent with the "principle of least resistance" in the attitude change literature (McGuire, in press). Those beliefs most likely to "give in" to contradictory evidence are beliefs that have the fewest connections to other beliefs in the cognitive system.

COGNITIVE MAPPING

Cognitive mapping is a methodological technique for capturing the causal structure of policymakers' cognitive representations of policy domains (Axelrod, 1976). Cognitive maps consist of two key elements: concept variables, which are represented as points, and causal beliefs linking the concepts, represented as arrows between points. A concept variable is defined simply: something that can take on different values (e.g., defense spending, American national security, balance of trade). Causal beliefs exist whenever decision makers believe that change in one concept variable leads to change in another variable.

Axelrod and other investigators have constructed a number of cognitive maps based on detailed content analyses of archival documents (e.g., Hitler-Chamberlain negotiations at Munich, the British Far Eastern Committee deliberations on Persia) and interviews with policymakers (e.g., State Department officials, energy experts). These studies demonstrate, at minimum, that: (1) cognitive mapping can be done with acceptable levels of intercoder reliability; (2) policymaking deliberations are saturated with causal arguments and that maps of these deliberations tend to be large and elaborate (in the sense that many different concept variables are causally connected with each other). (See Axelrod, 1976; Bonham and Shapiro, 1976; Bonham, Shapiro, and Trumble, 1979; Levi and Tetlock, 1980; Ross, 1976.)

Systematic analysis of cognitive maps has, however, provided more than descriptive information; it has also deepened our understanding of the cognitive bases of foreign policy. For instance, although cognitive maps are large and causally elaborate, they also tend to be simple, in that maps do not usually include trade-off relationships. Preferred policies usually have only positive consequences; rejected policies, only negative ones (cf. Jervis, 1976). This obviously makes decision making much easier; competing, difficult-to-quantify values do not have to be weighed against each other. Maps also rarely include reciprocal causal relationships (feedback loops) among variables: causality flows in only one direction. Axelrod summarizes the cognitive portrait of the decision-maker that emerges from his work in this way:

one who has more beliefs than he can handle, who employs a simplified image of the policy environment that is structurally easy to operate with, and who then acts rationally within the context of his simplified image. (1976)

Our confidence in this summary portrait is reinforced by the very similar conclusions that have emerged from laboratory research on judgment and decision making (Abelson and Levi, in press; Einhorn and Hogarth, 1981; Kahneman, Slovic, and Tversky, 1981).

INDIVIDUAL DIFFERENCE RESEARCH ON BELIEF SYSTEMS

Even the most prominent advocate of the realist school of international politics—Henry Kissinger—concedes that foreign policymakers "work in darkness"; they make choices not only without knowledge of the future but usually even without adequate knowledge of what is happening in the present (Kissinger, 1979). This "structural uncertainty" (Steinbruner, 1974) of foreign policy problems has led many analysts to propose an analogy between international politics and projective tests used in personality assessment: the international scene, in much the same way as a good projective test, evokes different psychologically important response themes from national leaders. Foreign policy belief systems do not emerge in a psychological vacuum; they emerge as plausible self-expressive responses to the situations in which policymakers find themselves (Etheredge, 1978). From this standpoint, it is essential to study the personality background or context out of which belief systems evolve.

Evidence on relations between personality and foreign policy preferences comes from the full range of methodological sources, including laboratory experiments, surveys, content analyses of archival documents, expert ratings of policymakers, and case studies (Christiansen, 1959; Eckhardt and Lentz, 1967; Etheredge, 1978; Lasswell, 1930; McClosky, 1967; Terhune, 1970; Tetlock, 1981; Tetlock, Crosby, and Crosby, 1981). The similarity in results across methodologies is, moreover, impressive.

These lines of research remind us that foreign policy belief systems do not exist in isolation from broader dimensions of individual differences in interpersonal style, cognitive style, and basic motivational variables. To paraphrase Lasswell (1930), foreign policy beliefs may sometimes serve as rationalizations for psychological needs and tendencies that have been displaced onto the international scene. A critical challenge for future theory will be to resolve the tension between purely cognitive analyses of foreign policy (which grant "functional autonomy" to belief systems) and motivational analyses of foreign policy (which view belief systems as subservient to other psychological variables and systems).

A COMMENT ON THEORY-DRIVEN VERSUS DATA-DRIVEN PROCESSING

We turn from the nature of foreign policy belief systems to the impact of belief systems on the policymaking process. A casual reader of the literature might easily walk away with the impression that foreign policy is overwhelmingly "theory-driven" (i.e., that the preconceptions policymakers bring to decision-making situations are much more important determinants of the actions taken than is the objective evidence). Both experimental and case study evidence appear to support this conclusion. The laboratory evidence comes from multiple sources, including research on primary effects in impression formation, the resistance of political attitudes and stereotypes to change (Hamilton, 1979; Lord, Ross, and Lepper, 1979); rigidity or set effects in problem solving (Luchins, 1942); and the persistence of causal attributions even after the discrediting of the information on which the attributions were initially based (Nisbett and Ross, 1980). The evidence from actual foreign policy settings comes most importantly from the pioneering work of Jervis (1976). He notes that the historical record contains many references to government leaders who have treated belief-supportive information uncritically while simultaneously searching for all possible flaws in belief-challenging information.

We need to be careful, however, in discussing the theory-driven nature of foreign policy. Reliance on prior beliefs and expectations is not irrational per se (one would expect it from a "good Bayesian"); it becomes irrational only when perseverance and denial dominate openness and flexibility. Cognitive models of foreign policy—like cognitive models generally—must acknowledge the coexistence of theory-driven and data-driven processing. Each is necessary; neither will suffice alone (see Bennett, 1981).

III. Process Research

The previous section examined representational research on the beliefs and assumptions decision makers bring to policy problems and on the impact of those beliefs and assumptions on foreign policy. In this section, we focus on the rules or procedures that people may use in making policy decisions: the rules vary widely in form, in complexity, and in the "mental effort" required for their execution (Newell and Simon, 1972; Payne, 1982).

In practice, however, the laboratory and field evidence of the last ten years indicates that people do not rely equally on effort-demanding and top-of-the-head procedural rules. People appear to be "cognitive misers"—effort savers who show a marked preference for simple, low-effort heuristics that permit them to make up their minds quickly, easily, and with confidence in the correctness of the stands they have taken (see Abelson and Levi, in press; Einhorn and Hogarth, 1981; Fischhoff, 1981; Nisbett and Ross, 1980; Taylor and Fiske, 1984).

This "cognitive miser" theme helps to unify research on cognitive processes in foreign policy. We examine here five lines of research: work on the fundamental attribution error, extracting lessons from history, avoidance of value trade-offs, the policy-freezing effects of commitment, and crisis decision making. In each case, the cognitive miser image of the decision maker serves as leitmotif: policymakers often seem unwilling or unable to perform the demanding information-processing tasks required by normative models of judgment and choice.

THE "FUNDAMENTAL ATTRIBUTION ERROR"

The fundamental attribution error has been described as a pervasive bias in social perception (Jones, 1979; Nisbett and Ross, 1980; Ross, 1977). Numerous experiments indicate that, in explaining the actions of others, people systematically underestimate the importance of external or situational causes of behavior and overestimate the importance of internal or dispositional causes (Kelley and Michela, 1980; Jones, 1979; Nisbett and Ross, 1980). The most influential explanation for the fundamental attribution error focuses on people's tendency to rely on low-effort judgmental heuristics (as opposed to more demanding procedural rules) in interpreting events. Jones (1979), for instance, argues that in many settings the most cognitively available (first-to-come-to-mind) explanation for behavior is some intrinsic property or disposition of the person who performed the behavior.

Do the laboratory studies describe judgmental processes that also operate in foreign policy settings? Our answer is a tentative yes. Two important qualifications should, however, be noted. First, the natural unit of causal analysis for foreign policymakers is often the nation-state, not the individual human actor used in laboratory experiments. With this caveat, though, much seems to fall into place. Jervis (1976) argues that policymakers tend to see the behavior of other states as more centralized, planned, and coordinated than it is. He notes, for instance, a number of historical situations in which national leaders have ascribed far too much significance to movements of military forces that were routine, accidental, or responses to immediate situational variables (e.g., the North Vietnamese interpretation of reduced American air attacks on Hanoi and Haiphong in 1966 as support for a peace initiative, not a reaction to inclement weather). Jervis also notes historical situations in which policymakers have seriously overestimated the internal coherence of the foreign policies of states. National policies are not always the result of long-term planning; sometimes they are reactions to immediate opportunities or setbacks or the products of miscalculation, miscommunication, bureaucratic infighting, or domestic political pressures. Observers often attribute Machiavellian intentions to

policies that are the cumulative result of many unrelated causes
(e.g., the Allies exaggerated the coordination among German,
Italian, and Japanese moves in the late 1930s and early 1940s;
the Soviets saw the failure of the Western powers to invade
France in 1943 as part of a well-calculated effort to make the
Soviet Union bear the brunt of the war against Nazi Germany).

A second qualification is also, however, necessary to our
discussion of the fundamental attribution error. As with belief
perseverance, we should refrain from strong normative judgments. We rarely know the true causes of the behavior of other
states. In a world in which policymakers are motivated to make
or misrepresent their intentions (Heuer, 1981), the truth tends
to emerge slowly and rarely completely.

EXTRACTING LESSONS FROM HISTORY

Analogical reasoning can be defined as "the transfer of knowledge from one situation to another by a process of mapping—
finding a set of one-to-one correspondences (often incomplete)
between aspects of one body of information and other" (Gick
and Holyoak, 1983, p. 2). Many psychologists regard analogical
reasoning as fundamental to human intelligence and problem
solving (e.g., Newell and Simon, 1972; Sternberg, 1982). People
try to categorize and structure unfamiliar problems in terms of
familiar ones.

Students of foreign policy have also paid attention to analogical reasoning—in particular, to how policymakers use historical precedents to justify current policies (George, 1980; Jervis,
1976; May, 1973). Case studies of foreign policy decisions are
filled with references to policymakers who were determined to
profit from what they think were the lessons of the past (e.g.,
Stanley Baldwin, Adolf Hitler, Harry Truman, Charles de Gaulle,
John F. Kennedy, Lyndon Johnson). For instance, when the
Korean War broke out unexpectedly in 1950, Harry Truman
perceived parallels with totalitarian aggression in the 1930s and
quickly concluded that the North Korean invasion had to be
repelled (Paige, 1968). Similarly, Lyndon Johnson's fear of "another Castro" shaped his perceptions of the unrest in the Do-

minican Republic in 1965 and his judgment of the need for American intervention (Lowenthal, 1972).

There is nothing wrong with trying to learn from the past. Unfortunately, policymakers often draw simplistic, superficial, and biased lessons from history. Various lines of evidence are revealing in this connection:

(1) One's political perspective heavily colors the conclusions one draws from history. In a survey of American opinion leaders, Holsti and Rosenau (1979) examined the lessons that supporters and opponents of American involvement drew from the Vietnam War. Prominent lessons for hawks were that the Soviet Union is expansionist and that the United States should avoid graduated escalation and honor alliance commitments. Prominent lessons for doves were that the United States should avoid guerrilla wars (e.g., Angola), that the press is more truthful on foreign policy than the administration, and the civilian leaders should be wary of military advice. Interestingly, *no one lesson* appeared on both the hawk and dove lists (cf. Zimmerman and Axelrod, 1981).

(2) If contending states learn anything from one crisis experience to the next, it may be simply to become more belligerent in their dealings with adversaries. Lessons of history are often assimilated into Realpolitik belief systems that emphasize the importance of resolve and toughness when "vital interests" are at stake (Leng, 1983).

(3) Policymakers rarely consider a broad range of historical analogies before deciding which one best fits the problem confronting them. They rely on the most salient or cognitively available precedent (usually a precedent that policymakers have experienced at firsthand or that occurred early in their adult lives).

(4) Policymakers often draw sweeping generalizations from preferred historical analogies and are insensitive to differences between these analogies and current situations (history, after all, never repeats itself exactly). One rarely hears policymakers, privately or publicly, conceding the partial relevance of several analogies to a problem and then attempting to draw contingent rather than universal generalizations. For example, instead of "If a military buildup (or appeasement), then a nuclear holo-

caust," one could ask, "Under what conditions will one or the other policy increase or decrease the likelihood of war?"

AVOIDANCE OF VALUE TRADE-OFFS

In many decision-making situations, there are no clear right or wrong answers. Each policy option has both positive and negative features (e.g., lower inflation is accompanied by higher unemployment; greater military strength is accompanied by greater budget deficits). Available experimental and historical evidence indicates that decision makers find trade-offs unpleasant and tend to avoid them (Abelson and Levi, in press; Einhorn and Hogarth, 1981; Gallhofer and Saris, 1979; George, 1980; Jervis, 1976; Slovic, 1975; Steinbruner, 1974). Trade-offs are unpleasant for cognitive reasons (it is very difficult to "net out" the positive and negative features of alternatives—What common units can be used to compare the value of human lives and one's national credibility as an ally?) and for motivational reasons (it is very difficult to justify to oneself and to others that one has sacrificed one basic value in favor of another). To avoid trade-offs, decision makers rely on a variety of "noncompensatory choice heuristics" (Montgomery and Svenson, 1976). For instance, according to Tversky's (1972) elimination-by-aspects rule, people compare response alternatives on one value dimension at a time, with the values being selected with a probability proportional to their perceived importance. All alternatives not having satisfactory loadings on the first (most important) value are eliminated. A second value is then selected with a probability proportional to its importance, and the process continues until only one option remains.

Experimental data have repeatedly demonstrated the importance of noncompensatory choice heuristics in decision making (Bettman, 1979; Montgomery and Svenson, 1976; Payne, 1976; Tversky, 1972; Wallsten, 1980). In the words of Hammond and Mumpower (1979): "We are not accustomed to presenting the rationale for the choice between values. . . . When our values conflict, we retreat to a singular emphasis on our favorite value."

Research in foreign policy settings supports this generalization. As already noted, cognitive maps of policymaking deliberations make few references to value trade-offs (i.e., policy options typically are not seen as having contradictory effects on "utility"). Similarly, Jervis (1976) has used the term "belief system overkill" to describe the tendency of policymakers in historical situations to avoid trade-offs by generating a plethora of logically independent reasons in support of the stands they have taken. Jervis (1976, p. 137) describes the phenomenon in this way: "decision-makers do not simultaneously estimate how a policy will affect many values. Instead, they look at only one or two most salient values. As they come to favor a policy that seems best on these restricted dimensions, they alter their earlier beliefs and establish new ones so that as many reasons as possible support their choice." (See also George, 1980).

THE FREEZING EFFECTS OF COMMITMENT

Once people have committed themselves to a course of action, they find it very difficult to retreat from that commitment. These "attitude-freezing" effects of commitment have been studied extensively in experimental social psychology and organizational behavior (e.g., Deutsch and Gerard, 1955; Helmreich and Collins, 1968; Janis and Mann, 1977; Kiesler, 1971; Staw, 1980). Public announcement of an attitudinal position increases later resistance to persuasive attacks on the attitude and motivates people to generate cognitions supportive of the attitude. The more irreversible the commitment, the stronger the effects tend to be (Janis and Mann, 1977; Staw, 1980). The most influential explanation for these findings is in terms of cognitive dissonance theory (Festinger, 1964). People seek to justify their commitments (and their self-images as rational, moral beings) by protraying actions they have freely chosen as reasonable and fair.

In addition to the laboratory evidence, many foreign policy examples exist of the "freezing" effects of commitment on the attitudes of national leaders. Jervis (1976) has offered the most comprehensive analysis of such effects. He identifies many plausible examples, including: the unwillingness of the pre–World War II Japanese government to compromise the gains achieved as a result of its large military losses in China, President Wilson's abandonment of his serious reservations about entering World War I after making the crucial decision, and the reluctance of American officials committed to the Diem regime in South Vietnam to acknowledge the regime's shortcomings. To some extent, such postcommitment bolstering of decisions is adaptive (little would be accomplished if we abandoned commitments in the face of the first setback). Postcommitment bolstering becomes "irrational" only when the desire of decision makers to justify their commitments (and to recoup "sunk costs"— Staw, 1980) blinds them to alternative policies with higher expected payoffs. Assessing exactly when postcommitment bolstering becomes irrational is, of course, a tricky judgment call.

CRISIS DECISION MAKING

Policymakers fall prey to the previously discussed biases and errors even under favorable information-processing conditions. Policymakers do not, however, always work under favorable conditions. They must sometimes function in highly stressful crisis environments in which they need to analyze large amounts of ambiguous and inconsistent evidence under severe time pressure, always with the knowledge that miscalculations may have serious consequences for their own careers and vital national interests (Brecher, 1979; C. Hermann, 1969; Holsti, Brody and North, 1969; Holsti and George, 1975; Lebow, 1981).

Converging evidence—from laboratory experiments and simulations, historical case studies, and content analyses of decision makers' statements—supports this "disruptive-stress" hypothesis. The experimental literature on the effects of stress is enormous (for reviews, see Janis and Mann, 1977; Staw, Sandelands, and Dutton, 1981). There is basic agreement, though, that high levels of stress reduce the complexity and quality of information processing. The impairment includes a lessened likelihood of accurately identifying and discriminating among unfamiliar stimuli (Postman and Bruner, 1948); rigid reliance on old, now inappropriate problem-solving strategies (Cowen, 1952); reduced search for new information (Schroder et al., 1967); and heightened intolerance for inconsistent evidence (Streufert and Streufert, 1978).

Case studies and content analyses of historical records point to similar conclusions. As crises intensify, particularly crises that culminate in war, images of environment and policy options appear to simplify and rigidify. Policymakers are more likely to ignore alternative interpretations of events, to attend to a restricted range of options, and to view possible outcomes of the conflict in terms of absolute victory or defeat (C. Hermann, 1972; Holsti, 1972; Holsti and George, 1975; Lebow, 1981; Raphael, 1982; Suedfeld and Tetlock, 1977; Tetlock, 1979, 1983b, 1983c).

Simplification effects are not, however, an automatic reaction to international crises (see Tanter, 1978, for a detailed review). We need a theory—similar to the Janis and Mann (1977) conflict model of decision making—that allows for the possibility that threats to important values do not always disrupt, and sometimes even facilitate, complex information processing. The effects of crises may depend on many factors: individual difference variables (self-image as effective coper, track record of performance in previous crises) and situational variables (the reversibility and severity of existing threats).

IV. Concluding Remarks

How successful has the cognitive research program been? Many positive signs exist. There is no shortage of theoretical speculation and hypotheses on how cognitive variables influence foreign policy. Considerable research has been done. There are impressive indications of multimethod convergence in the work to date. A cumulative body of knowledge appears to be developing. Perhaps most important, the research program continues to be "heuristically provocative" in the sense of suggesting new avenues of empirical and theoretical exploration.

But all is not well within the cognitive research program. Current theory is seriously fragmented. Consensus is lacking on the extent to which and the ways in which cognitive variables influence foreign policy. Contradictory examples can be identified for most, if not all, of the theoretical generalizations offered earlier on the role that cognitive variables play in foreign policy. Consider the following claims:

- Policymakers are too slow in revising their initial impressions of an event.
- Policymakers overestimate the importance of long-term planning and underestimate the importance of chance and immediate situational pressures as causes of the behavior of other states.
- Policymakers avoid difficult value trade-offs.
- Policymakers draw simple and biased lessons from history.
- Policymakers rigidly defend and bolster past commitments.
- Policymakers analyze information in especially simplistic and superficial ways under high-stress crisis conditions.

Although the preponderance of the evidence is consistent with the above generalizations, the exceptions cannot be glibly dismissed. One can point to laboratory and historical situations in which the generalizations do not hold up well (e.g., Abelson and Levi, in press; Janis, 1982; Jervis, 1976; Maoz, 1981; McAllister, Mitchell, and Beach, 1979; Payne, 1982; Tetlock, 1983b,).

The cognitive research program must ultimately come to grips with these anomalies. We believe a viable cognitive theory will have to take the form of a "contingency theory" of political information processing—one that acknowledges the capacity of people to adopt different modes of information processing in response to changing circumstances. From a contingency theory perspective, the search for immutable laws of cognitive functioning is misguided (Jenkins, 1981; McAllister et al., 1979; Payne, 1982; Tetlock, in press). The appropriate question is not "What kind of machine is the human information processor?" but rather "What kinds of machines do people become when confronted with particular types of tasks in particular types of environments?" No single cognitive portrait of the policymaker is possible. Under some conditions, people rely on complex information-processing rules that approximate those prescribed by normative models of judgment and choice. Under other conditions, policymakers rely on simple top-of-the-head rules that minimize mental effort and strain. The major objective of the positive heuristic of the research program should not be to arrive at a global characterization of the information processor; rather, it should be to identify the personality and situational boundary conditions for the applicability of different characterizations of the information processor.

18.

A Critique of
Early Psychological Approaches
to International Misperception*

ROBERT JERVIS

What are the causes and consequences of misperception? What kinds of perceptual errors commonly occur in decision making? How are beliefs about politics and images of other actors formed and altered? How do decision makers draw inferences from information, especially information that could be seen as contradicting their own views?

These questions have not been adequately discussed by specialists in either psychology or international relations. The latter have assumed that decision makers usually perceive the world quite accurately and that those misperceptions that do occur can only be treated as random accidents. This book seeks to demonstrate that this view is incorrect. Perceptions of the world and of other actors diverge from reality in patterns that we can detect and for reasons that we can understand. We can find both misperceptions that are common to diverse kinds of people and important differences in perceptions that can be explained without delving too deeply into individuals' psyches. This knowledge can be used not only to explain specific decisions but also to account for patterns of interaction and to improve our general understanding of international relations.

If scholars trained in international relations have paid little attention to perceptions, the same cannot be said for psychologists. But while their work is extremely valuable for showing the importance of the subject it is marred by five major faults. First, more attention is paid to emotional than to cognitive factors. Wishful thinking, defense mechanisms, and other motivated distortions of reality are focused on to the relative exclusion of the problem of how even a perfectly unemotional and careful person would go about drawing inferences from highly ambiguous evidence in a confusing and confused world. As Robert Abelson has noted, "there are plenty of 'cold' cognitive factors which produce inaccurate world-views" (Abelson, 1973).

Second, almost all the data supporting the theories are derived from laboratory experiments. Whether these settings and the manipulations that are employed reveal processes that are at work in the real world is hard to determine. Even harder to gauge is whether the influences discovered in the laboratory are strong enough to make themselves felt, and felt in the same way, when they are intermixed with the other powerful variables that affect political decision making. For example, very few experiments give the subjects incentives to perceive accurately, yet this is the prime concern of decision makers.

Third, a strong policy bias pervades most of the analysis—the element of conflict of interest is played down in international relations in general and in the cold war in particular.

Fourth, and related to the last point, the structure of the international system and the dangers and opportunities peculiar to this setting are often overlooked or misunderstood. As a result of these four weaknesses, this literature contains a great deal of "overpsychologizing"; explanations, usually highly critical of the decision maker, involving many psychological variables are given for behavior that can be explained more convincingly by political analysis. More specifically, there is little comprehension of the consequences of the lack of a sovereign in the international realm and little analysis of the reasons why even highly rational decision makers often conclude that they must be extremely suspicious and mistrustful. These biases also lead psychologists to analyze only the views of those statesmen with whom they have little sympathy and to refrain from using their theories to treat the policy preferences of those with whom they agree. Thus images and reasoning drawn from the "hard-line" approach to foreign policy are examined to show the operation of emotional influences and cognitive processes that inhibit intelligent decision making, but arguments and belief systems that support conciliation are never analyzed in these terms.

As grave as these defects are, they are less troubling and less hard to rectify than the fifth: most psychological theories, and especially those that have been applied to international relations, do not account for the ways that highly intelligent people think about problems that are crucial to them. And few of the experiments that provide the bulk of the empirical evidence for the theories have been directed to this question. Rather, theories about the formation and change of beliefs have been constructed around beliefs that are relatively unimportant to the person, about which he has little information, and for which the consequences of being right or wrong are only minor. One reason for this is that the desire to construct theories that are rigorous and parsimonious has meant that only simple beliefs can be analyzed. Although this may be the best way to produce theories that eventually will be able to explain complex thinking, there is little reason to expect that at their present stage of development such theories will provide much assistance in understanding the ways that competent people go about making important decisions. Thus, Abelson admits that a significant criticism of the theory that he coauthored and that often has been applied to foreign policy decision making is that "it gives too little scope to the possibilities of human thought, even as practiced by mediocre thinkers, and, on the other side of the same coin, that it imputes the drawing of certain . . . conclusions which are manifestly absurd by any standard" (Abelson, 1968, p. 119).

I have studied a large number of cases from different historical periods and analyzed only those misperceptions that occur with great frequency. I have also searched for instances of misperceptions that would be inconsistent with the explanations I was developing. For many of the propositions, there were almost no cases that were the opposite of what was expected. But even if this makeshift method of gathering evidence has not led to false conclusions, it has inhibited the testing of complex explanations and the discovery of patterns of perception that are subtle or masked by confounding variables. Thus the lack of an appropriate sample of cases is less apt to mean that my arguments are incorrect than that they are limited to the more obvious relationships.

Given the complexity and ambiguity of information about international relations, perceptual and other decision making errors will always be common. But steps could be taken to increase the degree to which disciplined intelligence can be brought to bear and decrease the degree to which decision makers hold images and reach conclusions without thinking carefully about what they are doing. Indeed if judgment is distinguished from perception by the criterion that the latter is automatic and not under conscious control, then these proposals are designed to increase explicit and self-conscious judgment and decrease the extent to which decision makers perceive without being aware of the alternatives that are being rejected.

If these criticisms mean that we cannot take any existing psychological theories as they are and apply them to political decision making, they definitely do not mean that we should ignore all these theories. To do so would be to overlook a large amount of invaluable work and would make it difficult to detect, and almost impossible to explain, patterns of misperception. Indeed it is partly because most international relations scholars have paid no attention to psychology that they have failed to recognize the importance of misperception, let alone deal with it adequately.

Complementing the problem of diverse theories that were not developed to deal with problems with which we are concerned is the difficulty of mustering solid evidence. I have chosen an approach that is broad and eclectic—too eclectic for some tastes, perhaps—and have borrowed from theories and experimental findings in diverse parts of psychology. In drawing on studies of attitude change, social psychology, cognitive psychology, and visual perception, one faces the danger of mixing incommensurable theories or incompatible assumptions and failing to do justice to the theories themselves. The former danger is outweighed by the dual advantages of gaining a wider variety of insights and greater confidence in our explanations by finding that they are supported by theories in such different realms as, for example, attitude change and visual perception. The second cost—failing to discuss in detail the psychological theories in their own right—is worth paying because my goal is to understand politics.

19.

Motivated Misperceptions*

RALPH K. WHITE

How Motives and Perceptions Combine

If a person *wants* something and *believes* that a certain kind of behavior will help him to get it, he is likely to tend to engage in that kind of behavior. This is the obvious, everyday, commonsense proposition that describes roughly how motives (wants) and perceptions (beliefs) combine to produce behavior. It justifies this chapter's emphasis on motives and perceptions. (In these words or others, this proposition is implicit or explicit in the great bulk of modern psychology, as well as in common sense. In "decision theory" it is axiomatic, with the word "utility" substituted for "motive" and "perceived consequences" substituted for "perception.")

Which is more important, to understand the motives related to nuclear war, as we tried to do in the last chapter, or to understand the perceptions related to it?

In my judgment, understanding the perceptions is more important, if only because they are much more varied. Hawks and doves in the West both want peace. Both are, with rare exceptions, convinced of the horrors of nuclear war. Both also, with rare exceptions, want very much to preserve the independence of their country and its NATO allies. There are differences of emphasis on those two goals, but as a rule the differences

* Excerpted from *Fearful Warriors: A Psychological Profile of U.S.-Soviet Relations* (New York: The Free Press, 1984). Reprinted with permission of The Free Press, a Division of Macmillan, Inc. Copyright © 1984 by The Free Press.

are not great. Both hawks and doves want both. They differ greatly, though, in their beliefs as to what policies are most likely to preserve peace and independence at the same time, and those differences in turn depend greatly on widely different perceptions of the men in the Kremlin—their power, relative to ours, and their primary foreign policy goals and intentions. As the statisticians might put it, the variance of perceptions on this subject is considerably greater than the variance of motives and therefore contributes much more to the variance of attitudes and behavior.

How They Influence Each Other

Although motives and perceptions are different in their essence, they are so closely intertwined that as a rule neither can be understood without some reference to the other.

Consider, for instance, the deceptively simple little word "fear." Fear is an extremely potent motive in international affairs and can be an extremely destructive one. It is probably the chief motive, surpassing even macho pride, that pushes forward the nuclear arms race, causing its grotesque redundancy on both sides; as history has shown, it also underlies a great many of the aggressive actions that directly cause war. Is it a motive or a perception? Obviously, it is both. It has a motivational side and a perceptual side. When we speak of exaggerated fear we are focusing on its perceptual side; we are calling it a misperception, or rather a partial misperception, which is what nearly all misperceptions are. The perception of danger naturally comes first, but almost simultaneously with it there is an urge to avoid the danger either by escape or by attack. The perception and the impulse to action are so intimately, inextricably bound together that we naturally speak of them together as fear. But, if we want to diminish the exaggerated fear in ourselves or our opponents, we need to focus on its perceptual side and treat it as a problem in perception.

Or consider another deceptively simple and familiar word, "anger." Ordinarily we focus on its motivational side, the desire a person has to hurt the object of his anger. But it, like fear, also has a perceptual side. The object of the anger is perceived as deserving to be hurt. In the word "anger" there is a strong connotation of reactiveness. A person who is angry is assumed to be angry because of something another person has done that is so hurtful or so wrong (as he perceives it) that it deserves retaliation or punishment.

That can be a mistake, or a partial mistake, and if so the retaliation or punishment that occurs can be called an over-reaction. As a rule, we do not speak of exaggerated anger, but we often should, because very often the perceptual side of it is exaggerated.

The father who comes home glowering because of a humil-iation at his office and lashes out at his son because of a trivial misdeed really believes, at the moment, that the son's misdeed was not trivial but serious. His overreaction is the direct result of a misperception—not a cold, cognitive misperception but a hot misperception suffused with an emotional sense of the outrageousness of what his son has done. The Austrians and Hungarians who, with strong German backing, precipitated World War I by declaring war on Serbia had a similarly hot misper-ception that an atrocious murder, the murder of the archduke and his wife, committed by one Serbian fanatic in the name of national independence, was necessarily the result of a dia-bolical plot against the beneficent Austro-Hungarian Empire by the government of Serbia, probably backed by Russia. In their minds the attribution of evil, which was realistic enough when evil was attributed to one murderer, Princip, and his two ac-complices, had spread to include, automatically and without evidence, the government of Serbia and the entire nation it represented. Austria, in their eyes, was being attacked by *Serbian* subversion and assassination. The danger represented by that attack had to be fought off, and the crime had to be punished. But what came first in their minds was their perception of the danger and their perception of the nature and source of the crime.

The psychologists (Dollard, Doob, Miller, Mowrer, and Sears, 1939) who have conceived of "aggression" or "instigation to aggression" as a direct response to an external stimulus or as a direct response to frustration have not seen all of the psychological picture. They have not clearly seen that, between the stimulus and the response, there is a necessary "intervening variable" consisting of perception of danger, of evil deserving punishment, or of both. Nor have they clearly seen how importantly those intervening variables can be influenced by factors within the person, such as the "floating anxiety" Freud talks about or the floating anger and hostility that we ourselves should be talking about. Their term "frustration" covers some of those factors within the person but not all of them. As a minimum, we need to recognize the great perception-determining importance of a long-term, deeply ingrained diabolical image of a national enemy. Among the many forms of what Jervis calls "preexisting beliefs," this is the one that most powerfully and directly influences the specific perceptions that directly mobilize the motives and cause the actions that cause war.

Jervis's Motivated and Unmotivated Errors

It is clear, then, that perceptions often influence motives. It is also clear that motives, including subconscious and unconscious motives, can influence perception.

In his book *Perception and Misperception in International Politics* (1976), now a classic, and in subsequent writings, Robert Jervis makes a fundamental distinction between the subconscious motives that influence and often greatly distort perception, on the one hand, and on the other hand the nonmotivational cognitive factors, such as preexisting beliefs, that can also have major distorting effects.

The rest of this chapter deals with errors (i.e., misperceptions) that seem to be due mainly to subconscious motives.

Subconsciously or unconsciously motivated misperception has already been referred to at several points: the process of rationalization, presumably motivated by a need to think well of oneself or one's own group (the extended self); the process of projection of blame, presumably motivated largely by a need, when someone has to be blamed, to blame persons other than oneself or one's own group; and the Adlerian process of compensation for inferiority feelings by exaggerating the power or the toughness of the self, motivated largely, once again, by a need to think well of the self. The importance of various kinds of self-deluding pride in all of these is obvious. The distorting influence of Freud's "free-floating anxiety" as a factor in the origin of exaggerated fear and of worst-case military thinking has also been mentioned. In that case the unconscious motive presumably is not a need for self-esteem but a need to find a tangible, specific external resting place for an internally generated diffuse anxiety. As Freud put it, the anxiety is "lying in wait for any opportunity to find a justification for itself."

More systematically, we shall now consider five kinds of motivated misperceptions that are especially related to the causes of war:

1. A diabolical enemy image
2. A moral self-image
3. A "pro-us" illusion
4. Overconfidence and worst-case thinking (omitted in this excerpt)
5. Overlapping territorial self-images (omitted in this excerpt)

A Diabolical Enemy Image

People tend to assume that what is familiar is also understood. A case in point is the black-and-white picture (or better, since black is not bad, the Good Guys–Bad Guys picture). It is extremely familiar. Everyone who has read a cheap thriller or seen a cheap western movie knows about it and is prepared to smile benignly about it, as if he understood it.

He probably does not. There is a mystery in it that very few people have thought much about but that lies close to the heart of the problem of how to prevent nuclear war. The mystery lies in the question: Why do intelligent people torment themselves by imagining a monsterlike enemy, or at least imagining that their human enemies are more monsterlike than they actually are? Why do they wantonly *increase* their own fear?

The Good Guys part of the picture seems immediately understandable as a form of wishful thinking. People would like to think they are good, and by various psychological devices, including trying to be really good in their behavior, manage to believe that they are. Rationalization helps too. The urge to think well of oneself is so obvious and universal that we feel we have explained a psychological process when we have attributed it to that urge. The mystery lies far more in the Bad Guys part of the picture. Is *that* wishful thinking? For instance, do people on both sides of the East–West conflict *want* to believe that their opponents, now armed with the most lethal weapons the world has ever seen, are also incurably evil in all respects, including foreign policy, and implacably aggressive? Do they want to believe it, when there is so much evidence that it is far from true?

The fact itself has been discussed on the descriptive level at several points in this book, under names such as exaggerated fear, worst-case thinking, and—most disturbing at all—defensively motivated aggression. Not only the nuclear arms race but also the possible actual outbreak of another major war, which could be or become nuclear, seem likely to be due to the diabolical enemy image more than to any other single factor.

On a more explanatory level the thought has been advanced that there could be obscure unconscious or partly conscious satisfactions in creating and clinging to the monster image. Freud's concept of projection of guilt has been invoked, namely that when blame has to be attributed to someone it is usually attributed to someone or something other than the self. Freud's concept of free-floating anxiety "lying in wait for any opportunity to find a justification for itself" has also been invoked. Are those explanations adequate?

Probably not. Both seem tenuous when compared with the anxiety we *create* for ourselves by picturing human opponents, who are probably as frightened of us as we are of them, as villains or monsters.

There is very little reason to think that most of us in the United States carry around with us a deep or unconscious sense of national guilt that has to be projected onto another nation. Why should we? Objectively speaking, it is true, our nation has done its share of bad things, but *we* didn't do them. Our government did. At the time they were done our government leaders probably seemed to have pretty good reasons for doing them. Perhaps we then felt a certain amount of vicarious guilt, semiconsciously if not consciously, because it was our country acting and we felt identified with it; but that could be handled either by the universal process of rationalization (which our leaders and the mass media helped us to perform satisfactorily) or by consciously blaming our leaders themselves, perhaps projecting what was left of our sense of guilt on them but not on the enemy. After that, very little would be left.

Floating anxiety seems like a somewhat more plausible explanation but not much more. Most of us *are* anxious a good deal of the time; sometimes we feel just generally anxious without knowing why. Few of us, though, have the kind of clearly neurotic anxiety on which Freud was focusing, and those of us who are not so neurotic usually have a fairly good idea of what we are anxious about—meeting next month's bills, for instance, what will happen to interest rates, an unfriendly remark by a friend, or the chance of nuclear war. It does not seem plausible that many of us have any great need to find a tangible justification for diffuse internally generated anxiety of the type Freud was talking about.

The mystery deepens when a puzzled psychologist notices how often intelligent people, many of them liberal on domestic issues and normally skeptical of the rightness of their government's foreign policies, relax their skepticism when it comes to accepting the conventional wisdom with regard to the implacable aggressiveness of the Soviet rulers. Worse, they often do not seem properly curious or thoughtful at that point. They make no effort to imagine how the world looks to the men in the Kremlin or what defensive reasons those men might have for actions such as Afghanistan or the big arms buildup. It seems not to occur to them that they themselves might be indulging in the kind of Bad Guys imagery that they smile about when they see their children drinking it in at a Western movie.

It may sound naive to a psychiatrist, but my own hunch is that our best single clue lies precisely there—in the pleasurable excitement that many people, especially children, get from drinking in an absorbing melodrama. For a good reason our films, television, comics, and video games are full of it. Conflict is always exciting. Football and basketball games are exciting but they do not usually have the extra punch that is provided by a hero who is fighting for Good against Evil and with whom we as individuals can identify. The more evil and the more powerful and threatening the enemy can be made to seem, the better. It is only then that the righteousness and the virility of the hero and his inevitable ultimate triumph can fully stand out in contrast.

I would call this macho pride. We come back to macho pride, glorified by an intense sense of righteousness, on a semifantasy level. It is wonderfully satisfying to those who are psychologically able to give themselves up to it, unless it comes *too* close to home, as the danger of nuclear war now does.

Could we melodrama-lovers dramatize ourselves, with comparable satisfaction, as Good Guys fighting valiantly against nuclear war itself? Some are doing it now.

The other best clue, in my judgment, lies in the satisfaction of feeling more grimly "realistic" about an enemy than others are.

There is nothing wrong or conducive to misperception in getting satisfaction from feeling realistic. That is an appropriate reward and reinforcement for *being* realistic. There is often something conducive to misperception though (and akin to macho pride) in feeling more *grimly* realistic than other people. Realism actually calls for nothing but great respect for evidence and for orderly, honest thinking on the basis of evidence. Grimness and feeling superior to others should have nothing to do with it—any more than wanting to be benevolent and peaceful should have anything to do with it. For some reason, though, many people apparently assume that there is something hard, virile, and automatically realistic about totally condemning an out-group that their own group condemns and putting the worst possible interpretation on anything it does. An American who thinks he sees anything good about the Soviet Union (or, formerly, Communist China) is dismissed as "soft" on Communism, and there is no more potent verbal weapon with which to handle heretics than the word "soft." (The opposite is more plausible. It takes more courage to disagree with one's own group than to agree with it.) Perhaps the line of association is that seeing an out-group as diabolical connotes readiness for violent conflict, and readiness for violent conflict connotes virility. It is a fighting stance. In any case, an association between the diabolical enemy image and a macho self-image does seem to exist, and to distort realistic judgment.

In this way, again, we come back to macho pride. On a subconscious level it is hard to give it up.

Even those two reasons, however—macho melodrama and supposedly grim realism—do not seem fully adequate to explain the hold that the diabolical enemy image has on our minds. Some of the mystery remains.

A Moral Self-Image

The nearly universal tendency to a moral self-image is obvious. Probably no modern nation (including Germany and Japan) that was embarking on what its neighbors regarded as aggression has talked about it in those terms or even, apart from some lone dissenters, seemed to wonder whether that was what it was doing. The process of rationalization, when most of the members of a group join in reinforcing each other's rationalizations, is obvious and powerful in defending their collective Good Guys image.

There is also a fairly obvious reason for rationalization: a need to think well of one's own group, at least in comparison with others. Group pride is a gratifying thing, and by various psychological ego-serving devices (rationalization, projection, denial, selective inattention) groups usually succeed in achieving it.

There are interesting and not yet answered questions, though: What harm does it do? Does it make war more likely? Since nations serving their own self-interest will do what they want to do anyway (one might argue), why deny them the innocent satisfaction of believing that what they do is right? The war-promoting nature of the diabolical enemy image is relatively clear: It fuels the arms race on both sides, and it increases the chances of defensively motivated aggression on both sides. Does the moral self-image do anything that bad?

Probably not, but bad enough. In the first place, the cynics who say that nations always act in a completely selfish, conscienceless way may be going too far. Although Niebuhr is probably right in his book *Moral Man and Immoral Society* (1960) to picture nations as morally worse in dealing with other nations than most individuals are in dealing with other individuals, that does not necessarily mean that they act with total disregard for the demands of conscience. Therefore, if a nation that has some conscience left narcotizes its conscience by rationalization and proceeds to aggression or other war-promoting actions that it would not have engaged in if it had honestly recognized how bad they were, the harm done is clear. Rationalization after an action has occurred may do no harm; it is then too late to reconsider. But rationalization when contemplating a future action that might not occur if its wrongness were recognized in time is a different story.

The Vietnam War is a case in point. A great many Americans came around eventually to thinking it was morally wrong as well as expensive in lives, money, and the future soundness of the American economy. Whether all of that was true or not, the great majority now wish they had never gone into it. From their standpoint, wouldn't they have been wiser to recognize all the counts against it, including the moral ones, before rather than after getting thoroughly involved? We Americans were rationalizing in a highly efficient way during the early years of the war (as many of us see it in retrospect). Couldn't our rationalization then be regarded as a cause of the war? It supplied little if any of the motive power behind our fighting, but perhaps it took some of our brakes off when they should have been on.

How about the USSR? Do the Soviet people feel as innocent as we in the West do?

There is abundant evidence that the great majority do, even in the face of such seemingly obvious instances of Soviet aggression as the takeover of Eastern Europe and the invasion of Afghanistan, and even in the minds of people who are in other ways deeply discontented and disillusioned. George Feifer, along with many detailed reports of discontent and disillusionment in recent years, says that the threat to the world is all the greater because disillusionment in the Soviet system rarely carries over into opposition to Moscow's foreign policy. Even Russians brimming with discontent still tend, with their villagelike patriotism, to rally around the Motherland when it appears to be in trouble. . . . Most Russians are content to believe that their tanks went to the aid of an Afghan people menaced by imperialist interference, as they rescued the Czechoslovak people from a similar danger in 1968. (1981, p. 55)

As for Afghanistan, Robert Kaiser's description of Soviet perceptions is strikingly at variance with typical American perceptions of what happened:

When the Soviets realized that they had caused an international furor much stronger than they had expected, they reacted bitterly, if also typically. Dr. Freud could have had the Russian nation in mind when he devised his theory of projection. Our fault? How could this be our fault? Clearly the Americans were to blame for the unhappy change in the international atmosphere brought on by the Soviet Union's fraternal help for the people of Afghanistan. This was the Party line, and because it so suited the national personality, a great many Russians obviously accepted it. Like people everywhere the Russians are gifted at presuming their own benevolence. (1981, p. 511)

It is obviously impossible to tell how fully the top Party people, as distinguished from the general public, believe their own propaganda about America's guilt and their own innocence, but there are psychological reasons (White, 1965, pp. 242–44, 269–74) for thinking that probably most of them do believe most of it.

Like our own, their rationalizations of outright aggression are truly frightening. The brakes are off when they should be most firmly on.

The "Pro-Us" Illusion

Another war-promoting misperception, much less often recognized than the two that have just been discussed, can be called the "pro-us" illusion (White, 1969, pp. 34–38; 1970, pp.

29–30) and can be defined as the tendency to perceive others as more friendly to one's own country—*or less hostile*—than they actually are.

That is, or at least appears at first sight to be, the exact opposite of the diabolical enemy image. That image normally includes the idea that another country is implacably, aggressively hostile to one's own country, while the pro-us illusion pictures others as more friendly or less hostile than they are. It is suggested here that both forms of perceptual distortion exist, that both promote war more often than not, and that to some extent they do conflict with each other, but that to a larger extent they apply to different things and can coexist without conflict as parts of a larger psychological pattern.

The following examples will give substance to the idea:

• Hitler in 1939 greatly underestimated the massive shift of British and French opinion against him which had just occurred as a result of his takeover of the Czech part of Czechoslovakia, breaking the promises he had made at Munich. He therefore imagined he could get away with his attack on Poland without having to fight a major war. He was wrong.

• The Japanese, in deciding to attack Pearl Harbor, underestimated the intensity of the wounded pride and the tenacity of the anger their action would create in the United States. They realized that America would fight but clung to the hope that after several initial defeats the fighting spirit of Americans would fade. It did not.

• President Kennedy and his chief advisers appear to have half-expected that a landing at the Bay of Pigs would touch off a popular pro-American rebellion in Cuba against Castro. It did not. And they should have known better. State Department intelligence, under Roger Hilsman, knew better, and the last honest opinion poll in Cuba (by Lloyd Free; see Cantril, 1967) had indicated a considerable majority favoring Castro at that time.

• For many years the United States fought in Vietnam, not really imagining that most of the people were on our side and against the Vietcong but believing that the majority "couldn't care less" about the outcome of the war, and vaguely assuming that those who were strongly on our side were as numerous as those strongly against us. The outcome, and other evidence (White, 1970, pp. 37–103), suggest that on the latter point we were mistaken and that if we had judged more realistically the actual state of Vietnamese opinion in 1962–65, we would not have fought in that war.

• For several years after 1917 the Bolshevik leaders, especially Trotsky, clung to the hope that the successes of the Red Army would touch off revolutions in border countries such as Finland and Poland and that Europe as a whole, exhausted and disillusioned by World War I, was ripe for communist revolution. With some exceptions they were mistaken.

• For many years a great many people in the West clung to the hope that the common people of the USSR were their "secret allies" (Lyons, 1954) against the men in the Kremlin. There is evidence that that was never very true and that it is emphatically not true now.

The pro-us illusion evidently takes several forms: underestimating the chance that certain potential opponents will become actual opponents and therefore initiating a war in a spirit of overconfidence (Hitler in 1939); underestimating the tenacity and fighting spirit of an actual or expected opponent (Japan in 1941); believing that the people in an opposing country are more acutely discontented and in a more revolutionary mood than they are (the United States and Cuba in 1961, the Bolshevik leaders and the rest of Europe in 1917–20, the West and the USSR for many years thereafter); and believing that a rebellion in some other country—a rebellion opposed to one's own interests—is less formidable and has less popular support than it does (the United States in Vietnam and, it should be added immediately, the Soviets in Afghanistan). In all of these cases the warriors have not been too fearful. They have been *not fearful enough.*

Probably the main factor is the moral self-image, combined with a tendency to assume that others see our behavior in as favorable a light as we ourselves do. To assume that others see things as we do is a very common tendency. John Foster Dulles, for instance, once said, "Khrushchev does not need to be convinced of our good intentions. He knows we are not aggressors and do not threaten the security of the Soviet Union"

(Jervis, 1976, p. 68). Another example: We Americans in Vietnam—most of us—had by 1965 rather thoroughly rationalized our intervention, glossing over the corruption and other sins of the military oligarchy and perhaps unduly demonizing the Vietcong leaders on the village level, who then were doing their best to win over the peasants. We persuaded ourselves that we were really helping, not hurting, the peasants. We did not persuade ourselves totally by any means but probably enough to make us underestimate the peasants' hostility to us as invading foreigners and to our Saigon allies as corrupt city-based usurers and exploiting landowners. If we had had more empathy with their anger at us and fear of us, or less self-righteousness to start with, we might not have sent our troops there in the first place or kept them there for so long.

References

Abelson, R. P. (1968). "Psychological Implication." In R. P. Abelson et al., eds., *Theories of Cognitive Consistency: A Sourcebook.* Chicago: Rand-McNally.

———— (1973). "The Structure of Decision." In R. C. Schank, and K. M. Colby, eds., *Computer Models of Thought and Language.* San Francisco: Freeman.

———— (1981). "Psychological Status of the Script Concept." *American Psychologist* 36 : 715–29.

Abelson, R. P., and Levi, A. (3d ed., in press). "Decision-Making and Decision Theory." In G. Lindzey and E. Aronson, eds., *Handbook of Social Psychology.* Reading, MA: Addison-Wesley.

Allison, G. (1972). *Essence of Decision.* Boston: Little, Brown.

Allport, G. W. (1943). "The Ego in Contemporary Psychology," *Psychological Review* 50 : 451–78.

———— (1954). *The Nature of Prejudice.* Garden City, NY: Doubleday/Anchor.

Anderson, J. (1976). *Language, Memory and Thought.* Hillsdale, NJ: Erlbaum.

———— (1978). "Arguments Concerning Representations for Mental Imagery." *Psychological Review* 85 : 249–77.

———— (1980). *Cognitive Psychology and Its Implications.* San Francisco: Freeman.

Anderson, P. A., and Thorson, S. J. (1982). "Systems Simulation: Artificial Intelligence Based Simulations of Foreign Policy Decision Making." *Behavioral Science* 27 : 176–93.

Axelrod, R. (1976). *Structure of Decision.* Princeton: Princeton University Press.

Bennett, W. L. (1981). *Perception and Cognition: An Information Processing Framework for Politics.* In S. Long, ed., *Handbook of Political Behavior.* NY: Plenum.

Bettman, J. R. (1979). *An Information Processing Theory of Consumer Choice.* Reading, MA: Addison-Wesley.

Bonham, G. M., and Shapiro, M. J. (1976). "Explanation of the Unexpected: The Syrian Intervention in Jordan in 1970." In R.

P. Axelrod, ed., *Structure of Decision.* Princeton: Princeton University Press.

———— (1977). "Foreign Policy Decision Making in Finland and Austria: The Application of a Cognitive Process Model." In G. M. Bonham and M. J. Shapiro, eds., *Thought and Action in Foreign Policy.* Basel: Birkhauser Verlag.

Bonham, G. M.; Shapiro, M.; and Trumble, T. (1979). "The October War: Changes in Cognitive Orientation Toward the Middle East Conflict." *International Studies Quarterly* 23 : 3–44.

Brecher, M. (1979). "State Behavior in a Crisis: A Model." *Journal of Conflict Resolution* 23 : 446–80.

Cantor, N., and Mischel, W. (1979). "Prototypes in Person Perception." In L. Berkowitz, ed., *Advances in Experimental Social Psychology.* Vol. 2. NY: Academic Press.

Cantril, H. (1967). *The Human Dimension: Experiences in Policy Research.* New Brunswick: Rutgers University Press.

Christiansen, B. (1959). *Attitudes Toward Foreign Affairs as a Function of Personality.* Oslo: Oslo University Press.

Converse, P. E. (1964). "The Nature of Belief Systems in Mass Publics." In D. Apter, ed., *Ideology and Discontent.* NY: The Free Press.

Cowen, E. L. (1952). "Stress Reduction and Problem Solving Rigidity." *Journal of Consulting Psychology* 16 : 425–28.

Deutsch, M., and Gerard, H. (1955). "A Study of Normative and Informational Social Influences upon Individual Judgment." *Journal of Abnormal and Social Psychology* 15 : 629–36.

Dollard, J.; Doob, L.; Miller, N.; Mowrer, O. H.; and Sears, R. (1939). *Frustration and Aggression.* New Haven: Yale University Press.

Eckhardt, W., and Lentz, T. (1967). "Factors of War/Peace Attitudes." *Peace Research Reviews* 1 : 1–22.

Einhorn, H., and Hogarth, R. M. (1981). "Behavioral Decision Theory." *Annual Review of Psychology* 31 : 53–88.

Etheredge, L. S. (1978). *A World of Men: The Private Sources of American Foreign Policy.* Cambridge: MIT Press.

———— (1981). "Government Learning: An Overview." In S. Long, ed., *Handbook of Political Behavior.* NY: Plenum.

Falkowski, L. S., ed. (1979). *Psychological Models in International Politics.* Boulder, CO: Westview Press.

Feifer, G. (February 1981). "Russian Disorders: The Sick Man of Europe." *Harpers.* Pp. 41–55.

Festinger, L. (1964). *Conflict, Decision and Dissonance.* Stanford: Stanford University Press.

Fischhoff, B. (1975). "Hindsight and Foresight: The Effects of Outcome Knowledge on Judgment Under Uncertainty." *Journal of Experimental Psychology: Human Perception and Performance* 1 : 288–99.

———— (1981). "For Those Condemned to Study the Past: Heuristics and Biases in Hindsight." In D. Kahneman, P. Slovic, and A. Tversky, eds., *Judgment Under Uncertainty.* Cambridge: Cambridge University Press.

———— (1983). "Strategic Policy Preferences: A Behavioral Decision Theory Perspective." *Journal of Social Issues* 39 : 133–60.

Gallhofer, I. N., and Saris, W. E. (1979). "Strategy Choices of Foreign Policy-Makers." *Journal of Conflict Resolution* 23 : 425–45.

George, A. L. (1969). "The 'Operational Code': A Neglected Approach to the Study of Political Leaders and Decision-Making." *International Studies Quarterly* 13 : 190–222.

———— (1980). *Presidential Decisionmaking in Foreign Policy: The Effective Use of Information and Advice.* Boulder, CO: Westview Press.

George, A. L., and Smoke, R. (1974). *Deterrence in American Foreign Policy: Theory and Practice.* NY: Columbia University Press.

Gick, M., and Holyoak, K. (1983). "Schema Induction and Analogical Transfer." *Cognitive Psychology* 15 : 1–38.

Hamilton, D. (1979). "A Cognitive-Attributional Analysis of Stereotyping." In L. Berkowitz, ed., *Advances in Experimental Social Psychology.* Vol. 12. NY: Academic Press.

Hammond, D., and Mumpower, J. (1979). "Risks and Safeguards in the Formation of Social Policy." *Knowledge: Creation, Diffusion, Utilization* 1 : 245–58.

Helmreich, R., and Collins, B. (1968). "Studies in Forced Compliance: Commitment and Magnitude of Inducement to Comply as Determinants of Opinion Change." *Journal of Personality and Social Psychology* 10 : 75–81.

Heradstveit, D. (1974). *Arab and Israeli Elite Perceptions.* Oslo: Universitatforlaget.

———— (1981). *The Arab-Israeli Conflict: Psychological Obstacles to Peace.* Oslo: Universitatsforlaget.

Hermann, C. (1969). *Crises in Foreign Policy.* Indianapolis: Bobbs-Merrill.

———— (1972). *International Crises: Insights from Behavioral Research.* NY: The Free Press.

Hermann, M. G. (1980). "Assessing the Personalities of Soviet Politburo Members." *Personality and Social Psychology Bulletin* 6 : 332–52.

—— (1980). "Explaining Foreign Policy Behavior Using the Personal Characteristics of Political Leaders." *International Studies Quarterly* 24 : 7–46.

Heuer, R. (1981). "Strategic Deception and Counter-Deception." *International Studies Quarterly* 25 : 294–327.

Hitch, C., and McKean, R. (1965). *The Economics of Defense in the Nuclear Age.* NY: Atheneum.

Holsti, O. R. (1972). *Crisis Escalation War.* Montreal: McGill-Queen's University Press.

—— (1976). "Foreign Policy Formation Viewed Cognitively." In R. Axelrod, ed., *Structure of Decision.* Princeton: Princeton University Press.

—— (1977). "The 'Operational Code' as an Approach to the Analysis of Belief Systems." *Final Report to the National Science Foundation.* Grant No. SOC 75–15368. Duke University.

Holsti, O. R.; Brody, R. A.; and North, R. C. (1969). "The Management of International Crisis: Affect and Action in American-Soviet Relations." In D. G. Pruitt and R. C. Snyder, eds., *Theory and Research on the Causes of War.* Englewood Cliffs, NJ: Prentice-Hall.

Holsti, O. R., and George, A. L. (1975). "Effects of Stress Upon Foreign Policymaking." In C. P. Cotter, ed., *Political Science Annual.* Indianapolis: Bobbs-Merrill.

Holsti, O. R., and Rosenau, J. (1979). "Vietnam, Consensus, and the Belief Systems of American Leaders." *World Politics* 32 : 1–56.

Janis, I. (2d ed., 1982). *Groupthink.* Boston: Houghton Mifflin.

Janis, I., and Mann, L. (1977). *Decision Making.* NY: The Free Press.

Jenkins, J. (1981). "Can We Have a Fruitful Cognitive Psychology?" In J. H. Flowers, ed., *Nebraska Symposium on Motivation.* Lincoln: University of Nebraska Press.

Jervis, R. (1976). *Perception and Misperception in International Politics.* Princeton: Princeton University Press.

—— (1982). "Perception and Misperception in International Politics: An Updating of the Analysis." Paper presented at the Annual Meeting of the International Society of Political Psychology, Washington, D.C., June 24–27, 1982.

Jones, E. E. (1979). "The Rocky Road from Acts to Dispositions." *American Psychologist* 34 : 107–17.

Kahn, H. (1961). *On Thermonuclear War.* Princeton: Princeton University Press.

Kahneman, D.; Slovic, P.; and Tversky, A., eds. (1981). *Judgment Under Uncertainty: Heuristics and Biases.* Cambridge: Cambridge University Press.

Kaiser, R. (1981). "U.S.-Soviet Relations: Goodbye to Détente." *Foreign Affairs.* Special issue, "America and the World, 1980" 59 (3) : 500–21.

Kelley, H. H., and Michela, J. (1980). "Attribution Theory and Research." *Annual Review of Psychology* 31 : 457–501.

Kiesler, C., ed. (1971). *The Psychology of Commitment.* NY: Academic Press.

Kissinger, H. A. (1979). *White House Years.* NY: Knopf.

Lakatos, I. (1970). "Falsification and the Methodology of Scientific Research Programs." In I. Lakatos and A. Musgrave, eds., *Criticism and the Growth of Knowledge.* Cambridge: Cambridge University Press.

Lasswell, H. (1930). *Psychopathology and Politics.* Chicago: University of Chicago Press.

Lebow, R. N. (1981). *Between Peace and War.* Baltimore: Johns Hopkins University Press.

Leng, R. J. (1983). "When Will They Ever Learn?: Coercive Bargaining in Recurrent Crises." *Journal of Conflict Resolution* 27 : 379–419.

Levi, A., and Tetlock, P. E. (1980). "A Cognitive Analysis of the Japanese Decision to Go to War." *Journal of Conflict Resolution* 24 : 195–212.

Lord, C.; Ross, L.; and Lepper, M. (1979). "Biased Assimilation and Attitude Polarization: The Effects of Prior Theory on Subsequently Considered Evidence." *Journal of Personality and Social Psychology* 37 : 2098–2108.

Lowenthal, A. F. (1972). *The Dominican Intervention.* Cambridge: Harvard University Press.

Luchins, A. S. (1942). "Mechanization in Problem-Solving: The Effects of Einstellung." *Psychological Monographs* 54 : 1–95.

Lyons, E. (1954). *Our Secret Allies.* NY: Duell, Sloan and Pearce.

Maoz, Z. (1981). "The Decision to Raid Entebbe." *Journal of Conflict Resolution* 25 : 677–707.

May, E. (1973). *Lessons of the Past.* NY: Oxford University Press.

McAllister, P. W.; Mitchell, T. R.; and Beach, L. R. (1979). "The Contingency Model for the Selection of Decision Strategies: An Empirical Test of the Effects of Significance, Accountability, and Reversibility." *Organizational Behavior and Human Performance* 24 : 228–44.

McClosky, H. (1967). "Personality and Attitude Correlates of Foreign Policy Orientation." In J. N. Rosenau, ed., *Domestic Sources of Foreign Policy*. NY: The Free Press.

McGuire, W. J. (3d ed., in press). "The Nature of Attitudes and Attitude Change." In G. Lindzey and E. Aronson, eds., *Handbook of Social Psychology*. Reading, MA: Addison-Wesley.

Minsky, M. (1975). "A Framework for Representing Knowledge." In P. H. Winston, ed., *Psychology of Computer Vision*. NY: McGraw-Hill.

Montgomery, H., and Svenson, O. (1976). "On Decision Rules and Information Processing Strategies for Choice Among Multiattribute Alternataives." *Scandinavian Journal of Psychology* 17 : 283–91.

Newell, A., and Simon, H. A. (1972). *Human Problem Solving*. Englewood Cliffs, NJ: Prentice-Hall.

Niebuhr, R. (1960). *Moral Man and Immoral Society*. NY: Scribner's.

Nisbett, R., and Ross, L. (1980). *Human Inference: Strategies and Shortcomings of Social Judgment*. Englewood Cliffs, NJ: Prentice-Hall.

Paige, G. D. (1968). *The Korean Decision*. NY: The Free Press.

Payne, J. W. (1976). "Task Complexity and Contingent Processing in Decision-Making: An Information Search and Protocol Analysis." *Organizational Behavior and Human Performance* 16 : 366–87.

——— (1982). "Contingent Decision Behavior." *Psychological Bulletin* 92 : 382–402.

Postman, L., and Bruner, J. S. (1948). "Perception Under Stress." *Psychological Review* 55 : 314–23.

Putnam, R. (1971). *The Beliefs of Politicians*. New Haven: Yale University Press.

Raphael, T. D. (1982). "Integrative Complexity Theory and Forecasting International Crises: Berlin 1946–1962." *Journal of Conflict Resolution* 26 : 423–50.

Ross, L. (1977). "The Intuitive Psychologist and His Shortcomings: Distortions in the Attribution Process." In L. Berkowitz, ed., *Advances in Experimental Social Psychology*. Vol. 10, NY: Academic Press.

Ross, S. (1976). "Complexity and the Presidency: Gouverneur Morris in the Constitutional Convention." In R. Axelrod, ed., *Structure of Decision.* Princeton: Princeton University Press.

Schank, R. C., and Abelson, R. P. (1977). *Scripts, Plans, Goals and Understanding: An Inquiry into Human Knowledge Structures.* Hillsdale, NJ: Erlbaum.

Schelling, T. (1963). *The Strategy of Conflict.* Cambridge: Harvard University Press.

Schroder, H. M.; Driver, M.; and Streufert, S. (1967). *Human Information Processing.* NY: Holt, Rinehart and Winston.

Simon, H. A. (1957). *Models of Man: Social and Rational.* NY: Wiley.

Slovic, P. (1975). "Choice Between Equally Valued Alternatives." *Journal of Experimental Psychology: Human Perception and Performance* 1 : 280–87.

Staw, B. M. (1980). "Rationality and Justification in Organizational Life." In B. M. Staw and L. Cummings, eds., *Research in Organizational Behavior.* Vol. 2. Greenwich, CT: JAI Press.

Staw, B. M.; Sandelands, L. E.; and Dutton, J. E. (1981). "Threat-Rigidity Effects in Organizational Behavior: A Multilevel Analysis." *Administrative Science Quarterly* 26 : 501–24.

Steinbruner, J. (1974). *The Cybernetic Theory of Decision.* Princeton: Princeton University Press.

Steinbruner, J., and Carter, B. (1975). "The Organizational Dimension of the Strategic Posture: The Case for Reform." *Daedalus* (Summer) Issued as Vol. 4, No. 3, of *The Proceedings of the American Academy of Arts and Sciences.*

Sternberg, R. J. (1982). *Handbook of Human Intelligence.* NY: Cambridge University Press.

Streufert, S., and Streufert, S. (1978). *Behavior in the Complex Environment.* Washington, D.C.: Winston and Sons.

Suedfeld, P., and Tetlock, P. E. (1977). "Integrative Complexity of Communications in International Crises." *Journal of Conflict Resolution* 21 : 168–78.

Tanter, R. (1978). "International Crisis Behavior: An Appraisal of the Literature." In M. Brecher, ed., *Studies of Crisis Behavior.* New Brunswick, NJ: Transaction.

Taylor, S., and Fiske, S. (1984). *Social Cognition.* Reading, MA: Addison-Wesley.

Terhune, K. (1970). "The Effects of Personality on Cooperation and Conflict." In R. G. Swingle, ed., *The Structure of Conflict.* NY: Academic Press.

Tetlock, P. E. (1979). "Identifying Victims of Groupthink from Public Statements of Decision Makers." *Journal of Personality and Social Psychology* 37 : 1314–24.

——— (1981). "Personality and Isolationism: Content Analysis of Senatorial Speeches." *Journal of Personality and Social Psychology* 41 : 737–43.

——— (1983). "Accountability and Complexity of Thought." *Journal of Personality and Social Psychology* 45 : 74–83.

——— (1983). "Policy-Makers' Images of International Conflict." *Journal of Social Issues* 39 : 67–86.

——— (1983). "Psychological Research on Foreign Policy: A Methodological Overview." In L. Wheeler, ed., *Review of Personality and Social Psychology.* Vol. 4. Beverly Hills, CA: Sage.

——— (in press). "Accountability: The Neglected Social Context of Judgment and Choice." In B. Staw and L. Cummings, eds., *Research in Organizational Behavior.* Vol. 6. Greenwich, CT: JAI Press.

Tetlock, P. E.; Crosby, F.; and Crosby, T. (1981). "Political Psychobiography." *Micropolitics* 1 : 193–213.

Tompkins, S. S. (1979). "Script Theory: Differential Magnification of Affects." In H. E. Howe and R. A. Dienstbier, eds., *Nebraska Symposium on Motivation.* Vol. 26. Lincoln: University of Nebraska Press.

Tuchman, B. (1962). *The Guns of August.* NY: Macmillan.

Tversky, A. (1972). "Elimination by Aspects: A Theory of Choice." *Psychological Review* 79 : 281–99.

Walker, S. (1983). "The Motivational Foundations of Political Belief Systems: A Re-analysis of the Operational Code Construct." *International Studies Quarterly* 27 : 179–201.

Wallsten, T. (1980). "Processes and Models to Describe Choice and Inference." In T. Wallsten, ed., *Cognitive Processes in Choice and Behavior.* Hillsdale, NJ: Erlbaum.

White, R. K. (1965). "Soviet Perceptions of the U.S. and the U.S.S.R." In H. C. Kelman, ed., *International Behavior.* NY: Holt, Rinehart and Winston.

——— (1969). "Three Not-so-Obvious Contributions of Psychology to Peace." Lewin Memorial Address, *Journal of Social Issues* 25 (4) : 23–29.

——— (rev. ed., 1970). *Nobody Wanted War: Misperception in Vietnam and Other Wars.* NY: The Free Press.

——— (1977). "Misperception in the Arab-Israeli Conflict." *Journal of Social Issues* 33 (1) : 190–221.

Wohlstetter, A. (1959). "The Delicate Balance of Terror." *Foreign Affairs* 37 : 211–35.

Zimmerman, W., and Axelrod, R. P. (1981). "The Lessons of Vietnam and Soviet Foreign Policy." *World Politics* 34 : 1–24.

SECTION VII

Personalities of the Decision Makers

SECTION EDITOR: OLE R. HOLSTI

INTRODUCTION

Ole R. Holsti

In recent years social scientists and historians have tended to deemphasize the impact of the individual leader on foreign policy. The image of a powerful leader astride events has often been replaced by one who is caught up in complex organizational and bureaucratic webs with only a limited ability to wield the levels of power. Who has not read Harry Truman's prediction of what his successor would experience?: "He'll sit here, and he'll say, "Do this! Do that!" And nothing will happen. Poor Ike—it won't be a bit like the Army. He'll find it very frustrating."

To the extent that these developments represent a more sophisticated understanding of the complex causes of war and conditions of peace, they are to be welcomed. But in some cases the pendulum may have swung too far in reaction against "great man" approaches to history.

The two essays in this section illustrate the political impact of leadership personality and belief systems. Robert Tucker presents an analysis of the totalitarian dictator as a personality type. Building upon some of Harold Lasswell's insights, Tucker draws evidence from the careers of Stalin and Hitler. The implications of his essay are sobering. The totalitarian personality may occur infrequently at the top levels of government, but only a Pangloss would believe that the type became extinct with the deaths of Hitler and Stalin. Given the almost certain proliferation of nuclear weapons, the ability to inflict millions of deaths may well rest in the hands of a totalitarian dictator of even a small nation.

Tucker's essay depicts important aspects of a relatively rare personality type. In contrast, the study of John Foster Dulles focuses on a more general psychological attribute. His case illustrates how firmly held beliefs affected his interpretations of Soviet behavior. In at least some instances, his assessments were not only inadequate guides to policy, but they were also politically costly. For example, his frequent predictions of "Soviet collapse" did little to enhance his credibility among key members of the Senate.

Taken together, then, these two essays illustrate two rather different points of intersection between psychology and war. Stalin and Hitler were psychopathological personalities whose "displacement of private affects upon public objects" (to use Lasswell's phrase) resulted in millions of deaths. Dulles, in contrast, was highly educated, intelligent, and normal. His tendency to interpret the actions of adversaries in ways that rendered his beliefs self-confirming is surely not unique. To the extent that it is shared among political leaders, it illustrates an important constraint on stabilizing relations between adversaries.

20.

The Dictator and Totalitarianism: Hitler and Stalin*

ROBERT C. TUCKER

I

Significantly, we have few if any studies of the totalitarian dictator as a personality type. It may be that we are little closer to a working psychological model of him than Plato took us with his brilliant sketch of the ideal type of the "tyrant" in *The Republic.* The purpose of the present chapter is to argue the need for one, and to do this in the context of a critical reexamination of the theory of totalitarianism.

First, a word on the use of the term "totalitarianism." Starting in the late 1930s and 1940s, a number of thinkers, mostly of European origin, evolved a theory of "totalitarianism" or the "total state" in an effort to account for the new type of dictatorship that had made its appearance in Germany under Hitler, Russia under Stalin, and perhaps also in Italy under Mussolini.[1] Hitler's Germany and Stalin's Russia were viewed as the two principal and indubitable manifestations of the novel political phenomenon. It was not so much a form of political organization as a form of outlook and action, a peculiar mode of political life. Thus Hannah Arendt, whose *Origins of Totalitarianism* was in many ways a culminating synthesis of this entire trend

* Excerpted from Robert C. Tucker, *The Soviet Political Mind: Stalinism and Post-Stalin Change* (New York: Norton, 1971). By permission of the author and the publisher, W. W. Norton, Inc. Copyright © 1971 by W. W. Norton, Inc.

of theory in the first stage, did not treat Lenin's Russia as genuinely totalitarian. She saw the original Bolshevik system as a "revolutionary dictatorship" rather than as a totalitarian one, and 1929, the year of Stalin's advance to supreme power and the start of the great collectivization campaign, as "the first year of clearcut totalitarian dictatorship in Russia" (Arendt, 1951, p. 391). Accordingly, Soviet totalitarianism was treated as preeminently a phenomenon of the Stalin era. I intend to follow this usage here, meaning by "totalitarianism" the special kind of dictatorship or political phenomenon that existed in Germany under Hitler; in Russia under Stalin; and, though perhaps only marginally, in Italy under Mussolini. The possibility that this special political phenomenon may have existed or may yet come into existence elsewhere is not, however, meant to be excluded.

There is a large biographical literature on the totalitarian dictators. These works are typically political biographies that tell the story of the subject's life and career against the background of his time and the politics of his country. A notable exception to this rule is Alan Bullock's *Hitler: A Study in Tyranny* (1962), which essays, in its well-known chapter on "The Dictator," an extended character portrait of the mature Hitler. Bullock depicts Hitler's obsessive hatred of the Jews, his craving to dominate, his need for adulation, his grandiose fantasies, and his extraordinary capacity for self-dramatization and self-deception. But he also sees Hitler as an astute practical politician of very great ability and suggests that the defining characteristic of his political personality lay in the "mixture of calculation and fanaticism" (Bullock, 1962, p. 375). Some elements of this characterization of Hitler may be of use in defining the totalitarian dictator as a personality type. But it is notable that the biographer does not view his subject in comparative perspective or note the broader implications of his analysis of Hitler's personality.

We should not underestimate either the difficulty of "typing" the totalitarian dictator or the resources available to us for dealing with this task. On the first point, it is clear that the dictators significantly differ from one another. Thus, Hitler lacked Stalin's administrative talent and associated psychological traits, whereas Stalin was lacking in Hitler's remarkable oratorical powers and the qualities of personality that went along with them. A conception of the totalitarian dictator as a personality type would have to be sufficiently broad to transcend these differences and embrace only those decisively important characteristics that were shared. On the other hand, it would have to be sufficiently specific to enable us, in principle, to discriminate between the authentic totalitarian dictator on the order of Hitler or Stalin, and others, such as Lenin, Tito, Franco, and Perón, who may belong to different dictatorial classifications. The requisite combination of breadth and specificity will obviously not be easy to achieve. On the other hand, the present-day social scientist has impressive resources of data and ideas to draw upon in dealing with this problem. A rich store of factual information on the totalitarian dictators and others is available to us now. And work done in recent decades on personality and politics has yielded general concepts that may serve as useful tools of analysis. In his classic study of *Psychopathology and Politics,* to take the most important example, Harold Lasswell laid the groundwork for a "functional" politics that would focus prime attention not on political office as such but on political personality types, such as the "agitator," "theorist," and "administrator." Lasswell has enunciated concepts and propositions that may be of great help in this enterprise. Notable among them is the proposition that "Political movements derive their vitality from the displacement of private affects upon public objects," and the closely related thesis that such displacement involves certain "processes of symbolization" whereby collective symbols are made proxy for self-symbols (Lasswell, 1960, pp. 173, 186). We shall have occasion in what follows to apply these ideas.

Also noteworthy in the present context is the literature that has developed around the theme of the "authoritarian personality." Having originated in Germany, this idea was introduced to the English-speaking public by Erich Fromm in his *Escape from Freedom* (1941). Fromm's thesis was that German National Socialism and other fascist movements in Europe derived much of their mass appeal from the widespread incidence among the lower middle classes in these countries of a personality that he labeled "sado-masochistic" or "the authoritarian character." The

authoritarian character combined a craving for power over others
with a longing for submission to an overwhelmingly strong
outside authority. Hitler himself, as revealed in *Mein Kampf,*
was treated as an example, an "extreme form," of the authoritarian character. Continued research in this field led to the
pathfinding work by T. W. Adorno and his associates,[2] *The
Authoritarian Personality,* which presented as a central theoretical construct the notion of an "F-syndrome" or potential
fascism in the personality.

The great importance of the problem is undeniable. But it
cannot be taken for granted that the motives or personality
traits that lead some persons to become followers of a totalitarian
movement are the same as those which cause others to become
its organizers and leaders. In this connection it appears to be
a defect of Fromm's study mentioned above that it fails to
reckon explicitly with the possibility that the personality needs
which cause some people to want to lose their freedom are not
the same as those which cause a Hitler, for example, to want
to take it away from them. The relationship between the needs
of the leader and the needs of the followers might well be one
of complementarity rather than similarity.

II

Hardly less significant than the absence of a clear idea of the
totalitarian dictator as a personality type is the absence of any
resulting widespread sense that a need of political science is
going unfulfilled. For evidence that this is so, and also for an
explanation of why it is so, we may profitably turn to the
literature of the recent past on the totalitarian dictatorship as
a political system.

Turning to the question of the dictator, it cannot be said that
the theorists of totalitarianism have overlooked his presence in
the system. Friedrich and Brzezinski (1956, pp. 17, 18, 26), for
example, refer to the Nuremberg trials and Khrushchev's secret
speech of 1956 as sources of evidence for the view that Mussolini,
Hitler, and probably Stalin too were "the actual rulers of their
respective countries," and they conclude that the totalitarian

dictator "possesses more nearly absolute power than any previous type of political leader." Much earlier Sigmund Neumann (1942, p. 43) described the dictator as the "moving spirit" of the total state, and Arendt writes of "the absolute and unsurpassed concentration of power in the hands of a single man" who sits in the center of the movement "as the motor that swings it into motion" (1951, pp. 361, 392).

But "chief cogwheel" would have expressed more accurately the way in which she and others among the theorists actually seem to conceive the dictator's role. She ascribes to the Leader's lieutenants the view that he is "the simple consequence of this type of organization; he is needed, not as a person but as a function, and as such he is indispensable to the movement" (1951, p. 374). This also seems to be Arendt's own view, arising out of the general conception of the totalitarian system as a mechanistic leviathan operating under pressure of its own system needs and the "supersense." The system needs remain basic, according to this way of thinking; *Führers* are functional requisites of totalitarianism as a peculiar kind of system.

"Not as a person but as a function"—this phrase takes us to the heart of an issue that particularly needs pursuing. We cannot say that the dictator is missing from the model of the totalitarian state that has been elaborated. But he is present in it rather as a function than as a person. This helps to explain why the theorists, while taking cognizance of the dictator, accord him no more than secondary importance in the theory of totalitarianism. He is seen as fulfilling certain needs of the system, which of course he does. But the system, or its politics, is not in turn seen as fulfilling certain personal needs of his. Insofar as the theorists take a psychological view of him at all, they see him simply as sharing with the rest of the leadership the postulated supersense or totalitarian mystique. The assumption of a generalized ideological fanaticism takes the place of psychological analysis of the dictator as an individual personality. His political motivations consequently are not really appraised in psychological terms; his manner of displacing "private affects" upon "public objects" remains outside the purview of the theory of totalitarianism. And this, in my view, is a very great deficiency of the theory.

III

When we confront the theoretical model of a totalitarian polity with what we now know about the factual situation in Hitler's Germany and Stalin's Russia, it appears that the model was seriously deficient in its omission of the personal factor from the dynamics of totalitarianism, its obliviousness to the impact of the dictator's personality upon the political system and process. For not only do Hitler and Stalin turn out to have been, as already indicated, autocrats who at many crucial points individually dominated the decision-making process and behavior of their governments. The factual evidence likewise supports the further conclusions that (1) in both instances we have to do with individuals whose personalities would be classified somewhere on the continuum of psychiatric conditions designated as paranoid; and (2) in both instances the needs of the paranoidal personality were a powerful motivating factor in the dictatorial decision making. The dictator did not, so to speak, confine the expression of his psychopathological needs to his private life while functioning "normally" in his public political capacity. Rather, he found a prime outlet for those needs in political ideology and political activity. In terms of Lasswell's formula, his psychopathological "private affects" were displaced onto "public objects." As a result, the dynamics of totalitarianism in Hitler's Germany and Stalin's Russia were profoundly influenced by the psychodynamics of the totalitarian dictator. The Soviet case is particularly instructive in this regard. For while our factual knowledge is less complete, we have here a system that survived the totalitarian dictator and thus some possibility of assessing the impact of his personality by studying the difference that his death made.

Before coming to power Hitler set forth in *Mein Kampf,* with its doctrine about a worldwide Jewish conspiracy to subvert the master race, a private vision of reality showing very strong parallels with psychiatric descriptions of a paranoid delusional system. Subsequently the vision began to be acted out inside Germany in the anti-Jewish terror, of which Hitler himself was the single most powerful driving force. Still later, when World War II was precipitated by the German invasion of Poland in

1939, it was Hitler's furiously insistent determination to (as he put it) "annihilate my enemies" that drove him, in the face of widespread apathy toward war in his own society and even in his own government, to push the world over the brink; and the story of his actions and reactions on the eve and in the uncertain early days of the conflict is like a page out of a case history of paranoia, save that this was likewise a page of world history. During the war the internal terror continued, now on the scale of occupied Europe as a whole. It was Hitler's own will to genocide that generated the relentless pressure under which Himmler's terror machine proceeded during the war to carry out the murder of European Jewry: "Himmler organized the extermination of the Jews, but the man in whose mind so grotesque a plan had been conceived was Hitler. Without Hitler's authority, Himmler, a man solely of subordinate virtues, would never have dared to act on his own" (Bullock, 1962, p. 403).

Stalin's career differed from Hitler's, among other ways, in that he did not come to power as the recognized leader of his own movement but gradually took over from above a movement that had come to power much earlier under other leadership, mainly Lenin's. Certain other differences flowed from this. Whereas Hitler's personal dictatorship was established rather easily through the blood purge of June 1934, which took no more than a few hundred lives, Stalin's arose through the veritable conquest of the Communist party and Soviet state in the Great Purge of 1936–38, in which an estimated five to nine million persons were arrested on charges of participation in an imaginary great anti-Soviet counterrevolutionary conspiracy. In this case the dictator's private vision of reality was not set forth in advance in a bible of the movement but was woven into the preexisting Marxist-Leninist ideology during the show trials of 1936–38, which for Stalin were a dramatization of his conspiracy view of Soviet and contemporary world history. The original party ideology was thus transformed according to Stalin's own dictates into the highly "personalized" new version of Soviet ideology that was expressed in the Moscow trials and in Stalin's *Short Course* of party history published in 1938. Contrary to the above-reviewed theory of totalitarianism, the Great Purge of 1936–38 was not a product of the needs of Soviet totalitarianism as a system. Not system needs but the needs of Stalin, both political and psychopathological, underlay to a decisive degree the terror of 1936–38.

As in Hitler's case, we see in Stalin's the repetitive pattern, the subsequent reenactment in foreign relations of psychopathological themes and tendencies expressed earlier in the internal sphere. It was mainly in the postwar era of Soviet cold war against the West, against Tito, and so forth, that Stalin's psychological needs and drives found relatively uninhibited outlet in the field of external relations. Contributing factors included, on the one hand, the fact that an older and more deeply disordered Stalin was now less able to exercise restraint save in the face of very grave external danger, and, on the other hand, the capacity of a relatively more strong and less threatened Soviet Union to make its weight felt internationally with a large degree of impunity. We have the testimony of Khrushchev in the 1956 secret report that now "The willfulness of Stalin showed itself not only in decisions concerning the internal life of the country but also in the international relations of the Soviet Union" and that Stalin "demonstrated his suspicion and haughtiness not only in relation to individuals in the U.S.S.R., but in relation to whole parties and nations." The latter point is illustrated with a vivid recollection of Stalin in 1948 deciding on the break with Tito in a state of blind fury, exclaiming: "I will shake my little finger—and there will be no more Tito. He will fall" (Khrushchev, 1956, p. S48). Other postwar Soviet acts or policies that were influenced, if not directly caused, by Stalin's psychological needs include the imperious demands upon Turkey in 1945; the shutting down of cultural contacts and general isolationism of the 1947–53 period; the extension of blood purges and show trials to Soviet-dominated Eastern Europe; the suspicion shown toward nationalist revolutions in Asia and elsewhere; and the unprecedentedly extreme Soviet psychological warfare of 1949–53 against the West as manifested, in particular, in the savage propaganda campaign about alleged American germ warfare in Korea. There was, finally, the extraordinarily significant affair of the Kremlin doctors in January–February 1953, which had a vital bearing upon Soviet foreign policy as well as upon internal affairs.

In both Germany and Russia, then, the dictatorial personality exerted its impact originally in ideology and the internal life of the country, and later found a major field of expression in foreign relations as well. The internal impact was felt, among other ways, in the form of terror; the external, in a special sort of aggressiveness that may best be described, perhaps, as an externalization of the terror. In other words, domestic terror, which may be viewed under the aspect of "internal aggression" against elements of the population, was followed by foreign aggression, which may be viewed as a turning of the terror outward upon the world. Parenthetically, since this temporal order of priority was and generally would be conditioned by objective factors in the situation (e.g., the necessity for the dictator to capture complete control of his own society before he can channel his personality needs into foreign policy), there may be a basis for relatively early identification of a rising totalitarian dictator of the type of Stalin or Hitler. This suggests, moreover, that the international community might possibly develop a politics of prevention based on stopping the dictatorial personality at the stage of "internal aggression." However, this would necessitate a modification of the traditional doctrine of nonintervention insofar as it sanctions the unlimited right of a nation-state to deal with its own population as the ruler or regime sees fit, provided only that it continues to observe the accepted norms of international law in relations with other states. Upon the willingness and ability of the international community to recognize this problem, and to institute means of preventing individuals of paranoid tendency from gaining or long retaining control of states, may hang the human future. Were Hitler and Stalin, for example, dictators of their respective countries in the 1970s instead of the 1930s, the probability coefficient of civilization's survival would be very low.[3]

The evidence disclosed by the Stalin and Hitler cases on the connection between dictatorial psychopathology and the politics of totalitarianism strongly suggests that the personal factor should be included in the theoretical model of a totalitarian system. On the basis of the factual record in these cases, as just summarized, the contribution of the dictator's personality to the dynamics of totalitarianism should be recognized as one of the regular and important components in the "syndrome." Such a conclusion appears all the more compelling in view of the extremely heavy emphasis that the theory has placed, as noted earlier, upon pervasive and permanent terror as the very essence of totalitarianism. For in the Soviet and Nazi cases, the dictators themselves, driven by pathological hatred and fear of what they perceived as insidiously conspiratorial enemy forces operating at home and abroad, were responsible to a very significant extent for the totalitarian terror that did in fact exist in Hitler's Germany and Stalin's Russia. The Soviet case is especially instructive, since it reflects the relation of Stalin to the Stalinist terror, not only positively in the form of direct evidence of his determining role, but also negatively in the form of the decline of terror that began to be felt almost immediately after his death and has since continued. As late as January–February 1953, it may be said on the basis of the present writer's personal observations in Russia at that time, Soviet society was almost paralyzed with terror as preparations for another great purge developed to the accompaniment of ominous official charges that an anti-Soviet conspiracy, with threads leading to foreign intelligence services, was or had been abroad in the land. Stalin's death at that time not only cut short the purge operation but inaugurated the subsiding of the internal terror that had developed in a wavelike movement of advance and partial retreat ever since his rise to supreme power in 1929. Insofar as terror has continued to exist in post-Stalin Soviet society, it has become, to use Arendt's distinction, terror of the "dictatorial" rather than the "totalitarian" variety.

Given these facts and the premises of the theory of totalitarianism, certain conclusions concerning both Russia and totalitarianism would seem to follow. First, if total terror is the essence of totalitarianism, then a Soviet political system in which such terror has ceased to exist and in which terror generally has greatly subsided over a substantial period of years should be pronounced, at least provisionally, post-totalitarian. Second, if the terror in Hitler's Germany was connected in considerable degree with Hitler as a personality, and that in Stalin's Russia with Stalin as a personality, then the explanations of totalitarian terror in terms of functional requisites of totalitarianism as a system or a general ideological fanaticism in the ruling elite would appear to have been basically erroneous—a conclusion which derives further strength from the fact that the ruling elite in post-Stalin Russia remains committed to the communist ideology. Third, the theory of totalitarianism should not only bring the dictator and his personality into the "syndrome," but also should give specific recognition to the role of the dictatorial personality in the dynamics of totalitarian terror.

IV

Some of the very psychological characteristics that might tend to incapacitate an individual for a major role in other kinds of organizations may be potent qualifications for leadership of a fighting organization.

This organizational milieu is, in particular, favorable for the emergence in leadership positions of individuals of a type that may be called the "warfare personality." Hitler and Stalin were examples who also happened to be, in their respective ways, men of outstanding leadership ability. The warfare personality shows paranoid characteristics as psychiatrically defined, but what is essential from the standpoint of this discussion is that it represents a *political* personality type. The characteristically paranoid perception of the world as an arena of deadly hostilities being conducted conspiratorially by an insidious and implacable enemy against the self finds highly systematized expression in terms of political and ideological symbols that are widely understood and accepted in the given social milieu. Through a special and radical form of displacement of private affects upon public objects, this world image is politicalized. In the resulting vision of reality, both attacker and intended victim are projected on the scale of large human collectivities. Consequently, in proclaiming the imperative need to fight back against an enveloping conspiratorial menace, the warfare personality identifies the enemy not as simply his own but as the society's and, in particular, the organization's. His particular vision of reality may therefore furnish potent ideological inspiration for a fighting organization, especially at a time of acute social malaise and crisis when conspiracy-centered outlooks show a certain plausibility and have an appeal to very many in the membership of the organization and in its wider social constituency. There is thus a possible close "fit" between the needs of a fighting organization qua organization for militant orientation and leadership and the needs of a warfare personality qua personality for a leadership role and a life of unremitting struggle against enemies. Paradoxically, the very enemy fixation that would help incapacitate the individual for leadership of most other organizations is here the key to the confluence of organizational and personal needs.

There are other ways too in which psychopathological tendencies may prove highly "functional" for the warfare personality, both on the road to power in a fighting organization and also in his possible subsequent position as political ruler in a system of totalitarian character. Especially noteworthy is an extraordinary capacity for self-dramatization and self-deception. The presence of this quality in Hitler's personality has been mentioned above. We see it also in Stalin, and it appears to be a basic attribute to the warfare personality who is sufficiently gifted to qualify as a totalitarian dictator. He shows an outstanding ability, as it were, to project *mein Kampf* as *unser Kampf,* to pass himself off as merely the spearhead of the endangered group's resistance in a countrywide and ultimately worldwide struggle against the conspiratorial menace (however the latter is defined). What enables him to be so convincing in this capacity is his self-dramatization, which in turn is serious rather than playful. He carries conviction because he has conviction. He is like an actor who lives his role while in the process of playing it, with the difference that he rarely if ever stops playing it. He is—if the cases of both Hitler and Stalin as subsequently documented are indicative—extremely egocentric as a personality, yet able to project himself with signal success as utterly group-centered, as a person for whom self is nothing and the organization or the movement or the system is all; and he can do this because he himself is so persuaded of the fact, being the first to believe in himself in his own role. He thus appears, but deceptively, as a peculiarly selfless prisoner of an abstract "ideological supersense" or "totalitarian mystique." The psychological reality is much more complex. We may, then, hypothesize that a capacity for what may be called sincere simulation, for effective masking of his own psychological needs as those of the organization or system, is a characteristic of the totalitarian dictator as a personality type. And it may be in part for this reason that scholarly students of totalitarianism have, as argued earlier here, unduly emphasized "system needs" as motivating forces of totalitarianism and left out of account the impact of the needs of the dictatorial personality. They too have been deceived by him.

In the career of a totalitarian dictator a time may come, of course, when his vision of reality loses its persuasive power within the leadership of the movement, when he can no longer successfully project his psychological needs as needs of the system, when simulation fails. This is what appears to have happened toward the close of Stalin's life, and it is one of the reasons why his case is so extraordinarily instructive for theoretical analysis. Owing to his psychological rigidity on the one hand and postwar changes in objective conditions of the Soviet state on the other, a rift opened up in his last years between his policy views and those held by others in the inner circle of top leaders. By about 1949 the Soviet state could no longer really be said to exist in a hostile external environment, and even the world beyond the limits of the great new surrounding belt of communist-dominated states remained dangerously hostile only insofar as Soviet acts and attitudes served to sustain the prevalent fear, suspicion, and unfriendliness. To some forces high in the leadership it appeared that these new circumstances permitted, and Soviet interests dictated, a diplomacy of international détente in the cold war. In presenting this view to Stalin, they apparently argued that the old "capitalist encirclement" was a thing of the past now that the USSR had a "socialist borderland" composed of friendly states. However, Stalin, who for psychological reasons was obsessed with the omnipresence of "enemies" and convinced of the need to press the cold war in perpetuity, saw a diplomacy of détente as criminal folly, and relaxation of East–West tension, save on a momentary tactical basis, as out of the question.

In rejecting the détente policy, he put forward the psychologically very significant argument that the ideological postulate of a hostile capitalist encirclement must not be understood in "geographical" but rather in "political" terms, meaning that Soviet Russia must be seen as ringed with hatred and hostility even under the new circumstances when she had a "socialist borderland." And largely in order to demonstrate graphically that the hostile capitalist encirclement "still exists and operates," as the Soviet press put it at the time, he staged in the last year of his life the affair of the Kremlin doctors, which must be seen not simply as an "internal affair" but in its connection with Stalin's foreign policy. Analysis of this final (and probably fatal) episode in Stalin's political career shows that he was using the alleged Anglo-American–Jewish conspiracy for medical murder of Soviet leaders as a telling riposte against the high-level Soviet advocates of relaxation of international tension, and also as a basis for getting rid of these men and others with a new blood purge. The doctors' trial, which was apparently about to start at the very moment when Stalin providentially became "gravely ill," was to have dramatized—as the propaganda buildup for its January–February 1953 showed—the continuing hostile machinations of what Stalin saw as a diabolical external enemy whose agents were operating internally in Russia, and even in the Kremlin, in the guise, for example, of Soviet doctors. All talk of a decrease of international tension, of improving relations with adversaries, would thus be exposed as a political absurdity. This interpretation of the affair is, incidentally, supported by Khrushchev's statement in the 1956 secret speech that Stalin, after distributing protocols of the doctors' confessions to members of the politburo, told them: "You are blind like young kittens; what will happen without me? The country will perish because you do not know how to recognize enemies." Stalin's politics of the "doctors' plot" were politics of paranoia. They represented the desperate effort of an aged warfare personality to continue acting out his private vision of reality and his bellicosity in the politics of his regime at a time when the vision had lost its credibility among the dictator's own entourage and the bellicosity endangered the system and all its beneficiaries.

Notes

1. The important earlier contributions include Sigmund Neumann, *Permanent Revolution* [1942], Emil Lederer, *State of the Masses* [1940], Franz Neumann, *Behemoth* [1942], and Hannah Arendt, *The Origins of Totalitarianism* [1951].

2. Editor's note: The frequent practice of referring to "Adorno et al." is unfair to the other authors of this very important work. Its unique combination of quantitative and psychometric expertise with clinical insight was primarily the work of Else Frenkel-Brunswik, Nevitt Sanford and Daniel Levinson at the University of California, Berkeley. (Adorno's name was put first only because the authors were listed in alphabetical order.)

3. The menace of the paranoid in the nuclear age has been strongly emphasized by Lasswell. Pointing out that "All mankind might be destroyed by a single paranoid in a position of power who could imagine no grander exit than using the globe as a gigantic funeral pyre," he goes on: "Even a modicum of security under present-day conditions calls for the discovery, neutralization and eventual prevention of the paranoid. And this calls for the overhauling of our whole inheritance of social institutions for the purpose of disclosing and eliminating the social factors that create these destructive types" (Lasswell, 1948, p. 184).

The official handbook of the American Psychiatric Association describes paranoia as "characterized by an intricate, complex, and slowly developing paranoid system, often logically elaborated after a false interpretation of an actual occurrence," and adds: "The paranoid system is particularly isolated from much of the normal stream of consciousness, without hallucinations and with relative intactness and preservation of the remainder of the personality, in spite of a chronic and prolonged course" (*Mental Disorders,* 1952, p. 28).

21.

The Belief System and National Images: John Foster Dulles*

OLE R. HOLSTI

I. The Belief System and National Images

Even a cursory survey of the relevant literature reveals that in recent years—particularly in the decade and a half since the end of World War II—students of international politics have taken a growing interest in psychoattitudinal approaches to the study of the international system. It has been proposed, in fact, that psychology belongs at the "core" of the discipline (Wright, 1955, p. 506). Two related problems within this area have become particular foci of attention.

1. A number of studies have shown that the relationship between "belief system," perceptions, and decision making is a vital one (Rokeach, 1960; Smith et al., 1956; Snyder et al., 1954).[1] A decision maker acts upon his "image" of the situation rather than upon "objective" reality, and it has been demonstrated that the belief system—its structure as well as its content—plays an integral role in the cognitive process (Boulding, 1956; Festinger, 1957; Ray, 1961).

2. Within the broader scope of the belief system–perception–decision-making relationship there has been a

* Ole R. Holsti, "The Belief System and National Images: John Foster Dulles," *Conflict Resolution*, Vol. 6, No. 3 (September 1982), pp. 244–52. Reprinted by permission of Sage Publications, Inc.

heightened concern for the problem of stereotyped national images as a significant factor in the dynamics of the international system (Bauer, 1961; Boulding, 1959; Osgood, 1959b; Wheeler, 1960; Wright, 1957). Kenneth Boulding, for example, has written that "The national image, however, is the last great stronghold of unsophistication. . . . Nations are divided into 'good' and 'bad'—the enemy is all bad, one's own nation is of spotless virtue" (Boulding, 1959, p. 130).

The relationship of national images to international conflict is clear: decision makers act upon their definition of the situation and their images of states—others as well as their own. These images are in turn dependent upon the decision maker's belief system, and these may or may not be accurate representations of "reality." Thus it has been suggested that international conflict frequently is not between states, but rather between distorted images of states (Wright, 1957, p. 266).

The purpose of this chapter is to report the findings of a case study dealing with the relationship between the belief system, national images, and decision making. The study centers upon one decision maker of unquestioned influence, John Foster Dulles, and the connection between his belief system and his perceptions of the Soviet Union.

The analytical framework for this study can be stated briefly. The belief system, composed of a number of "images" of the past, present, and future, includes "all the accumulated, organized knowledge that the organism has about itself and the world" (Miller et al., 1960, p. 16). It may be thought of as the set of lenses through which information concerning the physical and social environment is received. It orients the individual to his environment, defining it for him and identifying for him its salient characteristics. National images may be denoted as subparts of the belief system. Like the belief system itself, these are "models" which order for the observer what will otherwise be an unmanageable amount of information (Bauer, 1961).

In addition to organizing perceptions into a meaningful guide for behavior, the belief system has the function of the establishment of goals and the ordering of preferences. Thus it actually has a dual connection with decision making. The direct relationship is found in that aspect of the belief system which tells us "what ought to be," acting as a direct guide in the establishment of goals. The indirect link—the role that the belief system plays in the process of "scanning, selecting, filtering, linking, reordering, organizing, and reporting" (McClelland, 1962, p. 456)—arises from the tendency of the individual to assimilate new perceptions to familiar ones, and to distort what is seen in such a way as to minimize the clash with previous expectations (Bronfenbrenner, 1961; Ray, 1961; Rokeach, 1960). Like the blind men, each describing the elephant on the basis of the part he touches, different individuals may describe the same object or situation in terms of what they have been conditioned to see. This may be particularly true in a crisis situation: "Controversial issues tend to be polarized not only because commitments have been made but also because certain perceptions are actively excluded from consciousness if they do not fit the chosen world image" (Rapoport, 1960, p. 258).

The belief system and its component images are, however, dynamic rather than static; they are in continual interaction with new information. The impact of this information depends upon the degree to which the structure of the belief system is "open" or "closed." According to Rokeach,

> At the closed extreme, it is new information that must be tampered with—by narrowing it out, altering it, or constraining it within isolated bounds. In this way, the belief-disbelief system is left intact. At the open extreme, it is the other way around: New information is assimilated *as is* . . . thereby producing "genuine" (as contrasted with "party-line") changes in the whole belief-disbelief system. (1960, p. 50)

Thus, while national images perform an important function in the cognitive process, they may also become dysfunctional. Unless they coincide in some way with commonly perceived reality, decisions based on these images are not likely to fulfill expectations. Erroneous images may also prove to have a distorting effect by encouraging the reinterpretation of information that does not fit the image; this is most probable with rigid "models" such as "totalitarian communism" or "monopolistic capitalism" which exclude the very types of information that might lead to a modification of the models themselves (Bauer, 1961; Wheeler, 1960).

II. John Foster Dulles and the Soviet Union

The selection of John Foster Dulles as the central figure for my study fulfilled a number of historical and research requirements for the testing of hypotheses concerning the relationship between the belief system and perceptions of other nations. He was acknowledged as a decision maker of first-rate importance, and he held office during a period of dramatic changes in Soviet elites, capabilities, and tactics. In addition, he left voluminous public pronouncements and writings on both the Soviet Union and on the theoretical aspects of international politics, thus facilitating a reconstruction of salient aspects of both his belief system and his perceptions of the Soviet Union.

The sources used in this study included all of Dulles's publicly available statements concerning the Soviet Union during the 1953–59 period, derived from a content analysis of 434 documents, including congressional testimony, press conferences, and addresses.[2] These statements were transcribed, masked, and quantified according to the "evaluative assertion analysis" technique devised by Charles E. Osgood and his associates (Osgood et al., 1956; Osgood, 1959a).[3]

All of Dulles's statements concerning the Soviet Union were translated into 3,584 "evaluative assertions" and placed into one of four categories:

1. *Soviet Policy:* assessed on a friendship-hostility continuum (2,246 statements).
2. *Soviet Capabilities:* assessed on a strength-weakness continuum (732 statements).
3. *Soviet Success:* assessed on a satisfaction-frustration continuum (290 statements).
4. *General Evaluation of the Soviet Union:* assessed on a good-bad continuum (316 statements).

The resulting figures, when aggregated into time periods, provide a record of the way in which Dulles's perceptions of each dimension varied. From this record inferences can be made of the perceived relationship between the dimensions.

Dulles's image of the Soviet Union was built on the trinity of atheism, totalitarianism, and communism, capped by a deep belief that no enduring social order could be erected upon such foundations.[4] He had written in 1950, for example, that: "Soviet Communism starts with an atheistic, Godless premise. Everything else flows from that premise" (Dulles, 1950, p. 8). Upon these characteristics—the negation of values at or near the core of his belief system—he superimposed three dichotomies.

1. The "good" Russian people versus the "bad" Soviet leaders.[5]
2. The "good" Russian national interest versus "bad" international communism.[6]
3. The "good" Russian state versus the "bad" Communist party.[7]

That image of the Soviet Union—which has been called the "inherent bad faith of the Communists" model (Kissinger, 1962, p. 201)—was sustained in large part by his heavy reliance on the study of classical Marxist writings, particularly those of Lenin, to find the keys to all Soviet policies (Dulles, 1958b).

In order to test the general hypothesis that information concerning the Soviet Union tended to be perceived and interpreted in a manner consistent with the belief system, the analysis was focused upon the relationship Dulles perceived between Soviet hostility and Soviet success, capabilities, and his general evaluation of the Soviet Union. Specifically, it was hypothesized that Dulles's image of the Soviet Union would be preserved by associating decreases in perceived hostility with:

1. Increasing Soviet frustration in the conduct of its foreign policy.
2. Decreasing Soviet capabilities.
3. No significant change in his general evaluation of the Soviet Union.

Similarly, it was hypothesized that increasing Soviet hostility would be correlated with the success and the strength attributed to the USSR.

The results derived through the content analysis of Dulles's statements bear out the validity of the hypotheses. These strongly suggest that he attributed decreasing Soviet hostility to the necessity of adversity rather than to any genuine change of character.

In a short paper it is impossible to include all of the evidence and illustrative material found in the full-length study from which this paper is derived. A few examples may, however, illuminate the perceived relationship in Dulles's mind (see Table 21.1).

The 1955–56 period, beginning with the signing of the Austrian State Treaty and ending with the dual crises in Egypt and Hungary, is of particular interest. Dulles clearly perceived Soviet hostility to be declining. At the same time, he regarded that decline as symptomatic of a regime whose foreign policy had been an abysmal failure and whose declining strength was forcing Soviet decision makers to seek a respite in the cold war. That

Table 21.1
Dulles's Assessment of the USSR

Period	Hostility	Success	Capabilities	General Evaluation
1953: Jan–Jun	+2.01	−1.06	+0.33	−2.81
Jul–Dec	+1.82	−0.40	−0.30	−2.92
1954: Jan–Jun	+2.45	+0.46	+2.00	−2.69
Jul–Dec	+1.85	−0.25	+1.93	−3.00
1955: Jan–Jun	+0.74	−1.81	−0.80	−2.83
Jul–Dec	+0.96	−1.91	−0.20	−2.33
1956: Jan–Jun	+1.05	−1.68	+0.37	−2.91
Jul–Dec	+1.72	−2.11	−0.22	−3.00
1957: Jan–Jun	+1.71	−2.10	−0.28	−2.79
Jul–Dec	+2.09	−1.01	+0.60	−2.93
1958– Jan–Jun 1959	+2.03	+0.02	+1.47	−2.86
Jul–Feb	+2.10	−1.20	+1.71	−2.90

Rank-Order Correlations:

	N	τ	P
Hostility–Success (Friendship–Failure):	12	+0.71	0.01
Hostility–Strength (Friendship–Weakness):	12	+0.76	0.01
Hostility–Bad (Friendship–Good):	12	+0.03	n.s.

he felt there was a causal connection between these factors can be suggested by numerous statements made during the period.[8]

The process of how Soviet actions were reinterpreted so as to preserve the model of "the inherent bad faith of the Communists" can also be illustrated by specific examples. Dulles clearly attributed Soviet actions which led up to the Geneva "Summit" Conference—notably the signing of the Austrian State Treaty—to factors other than good faith. He proclaimed that a thaw in the cold war had come about because "the policy of the Soviet Union with reference to Western Europe has failed" (U.S. Senate, 1955, p. 15), subsequently adding that "it has been their [Soviet] system that is on the point of collapsing" (U.S. House of Representatives, 1955, p. 10).

A year later, when questioned about the Soviet plan to reduce their armed forces by 1.2 million men, he quickly invoked the theme of the bad faith of the Soviet leadership. After several rounds of questions, in which each reply increasingly deprecated the value of the Soviet move in lowering world tensions, he was asked, "Isn't it a fair conclusion from what you have said this morning that you would prefer to have the Soviet Union keep these men in their armed forces?" He replied, "Well, it's a fair conclusion that I would rather have them standing around doing guard duty than making atomic bombs." In any case, he claimed, the reduction was forced by industrial and agricultural weakness: "I think, however, that what is happening can be explained primarily by economic factors rather than by a shift in foreign policy intentions" (U.S. Senate, 1956, pp. 884–85).

There is strong evidence, then, that Dulles "interpreted the very data which would lead one to change one's model in such a way as to preserve that model" (Bauer, 1961, p. 227). Contrary information (a general decrease in Soviet hostility, specific non-hostile acts) were reinterpreted in a manner which did not do violence to the original image. In the case of the Soviet manpower cuts, these were attributed to necessity (particularly economic weakness) and bad faith (the assumption that the released men would be put to work on more lethal weapons). In the case of the Austrian State Treaty, he explained the Soviet agreement in terms of frustration (the failure of its policy in Europe) and weakness (the system was on the point of collapse).

The extent to which Dulles's image of the Soviet Union affected American decision making during the period cannot be stated with certainty. There is considerable evidence, however, that he was the primary, if not the sole architect of American policy vis-à-vis the Soviet bloc (Adams, 1961; Morgenthau, 1961; Davis, 1961). Moreover, as Sydney Verba has pointed out, the more ambiguous the cognitive and evaluative aspects of a decision-making situation, and the less a group context is used in decision making, the more likely are personality variables to assert themselves (Verba, 1961, pp. 102–3). Both the ambiguity of information concerning Soviet intentions and Dulles's modus operandi appear to have increased the importance of his image of the Soviet Union.[9]

III. Conclusion

These findings have somewhat sobering implications for the general problem of resolving international conflict. They suggest the fallacy of thinking that peaceful settlement of outstanding international issues is simply a problem of devising "good plans." Clearly, as long as decision makers on either side of the cold war adhere to rigid images of the other party, there is little likelihood that even genuine "bids" (North et al., 1960, p. 357) to decrease tensions will have the desired effect. Like Dulles, the Soviet decision makers possess a relatively all-encompassing set of lenses through which they perceive their environment. Owing to their image of "monopoly capitalism," they are also preconditioned to view the actions of the West within a framework of "inherent bad faith."

To the extent that each side undeviatingly interprets new information, even friendly bids, in a manner calculated to preserve the original image, the two-nation system is a closed one with small prospect for achieving even a desired reduction of tensions. If decreasing hostility is assumed to arise from weakness and frustration, and the other party is defined as inherently evil, there is little cause to reciprocate. Rather, there is every reason to press further, believing that added pressure will at least ensure the continued good conduct of the adversary, and perhaps even cause its collapse. As a result, perceptions of low hostility are self-liquidating and perceptions of high hostility are self-fulfilling. The former, being associated with weakness and frustration, do not invite reciprocation; the latter, assumed to derive from strength and success, are likely to result in reactions which will increase rather than decrease tensions.

There is also another danger: to assume that the decreasing hostility of an adversary is caused by weakness (rather than, for example, the sense of confidence that often attends growing strength) may be to invite a wholly unrealistic sense of complacency about the other state's capabilities.

In such a closed system—dominated by what has been called the "mirror image"—misperceptions and erroneous interpretations of the other party's intentions feed back into the system, confirming the original error (Ray, 1961).[10]

If this accurately represents the interaction between two hostile states, it appears that the probability of making effective bids to break the cycle would depend upon at least two variables:

1. The degree to which the decision makers on both sides approach the "open" end of Rokeach's scale of personality types (Rokeach, 1960).
2. The degree to which the social systems approach the "pluralistic" end of the pluralistic-monolithic continuum. The closer the systems come to the monolithic end, the more they appear to require the institutionalization of an "external enemy" in order to maintain internal cohesion (North, 1962, p. 41; Wheeler, 1960).

Notes

1. Although in the literature the terms "belief system" (Rokeach, 1960, pp. 18–9), "image" (Boulding, 1956, pp. 5–6), and "frame of reference" (Snyder et al., 1954, p. 101) have frequently been used synonymously, in this chapter "belief system" will denote the complete world view, whereas "image" will denote some subpart of the belief system.

2. The author has corresponded with a number of Dulles's close associates. They almost unanimously stated that Dulles's public assessments of various characteristics of the Soviet regime were identical with his private beliefs.

3. The method involves the translation of all statements into one of two common sentence structures:

1. Attitude Object One/Verbal Connector/Common-meaning Evaluator
2. Attitude Object One/Verbal Connector/Other Attitude Object(s)

For example, the sentence, "The Soviet Union is hostile, opposing American interests," is translated to read:

1. The Soviet Union/is/hostile (form 1).
2. The Soviet Union/opposes/American interests (form 2).

The relevance of such sentences to evaluation of Attitude Object One is estimated on the basis of values assigned to the other elements in these sentences. They range from +3 to −3.

4. "Dulles was an American Puritan very difficult for me [Albrecht von Kessel], a Lutheran, to understand. This partly led him to the conviction that Bolshevism was a product of the devil and that God would wear out the Bolsheviks in the long run, whereas many consider it a perversion of Russian qualities" (Drummond and Coblentz, 1960, p. 15).

5. "There is no dispute at all between the United States and the peoples of Russia. If only the Government of Russia was interested in looking out for the welfare of Russia, the people of Russia, we would have a state of non-tension right away" (Dulles, 1958a, p. 734).

6. "The time may come—I believe it will come—when Russians of stature will patriotically put first their national security and the welfare of their people. They will be unwilling to have that security and that welfare subordinated to the worldwide ambitions of international communism" (Dulles, 1955a, p. 329).

7. "The ultimate fact in the Soviet Union is the supreme authority of the Soviet Communist Party. . . . That fact has very important consequences, for the State and the Party have distinctive goals and they have different instruments for getting those goals. . . . Most of Russia's historic goals have

been achieved. . . . But the big, unattained goals are those of the Soviet Communist Party" (Dulles, 1948, pp. 271–72).

8. "It is that [United States] policy, and the failure of the Soviet Union to disrupt it, and the strains to which the Soviet Union has itself been subjected which undoubtedly require a radical change of tactics on the part of the Soviet Union" (Dulles, 1955c, p. 914).

"Today the necessity for [Soviet] virtue has been created by a stalwart thwarting of efforts to subvert our character. If we want to see that virtue continue, I suggest that it may be prudent to continue what produced it" (Dulles, 1955b, p. 8).

"The fact is, [the Soviets] have failed, and they have got to devise new policies. . . . Those policies have gradually ceased to produce any results for them. . . . The result is, they have got to review their whole creed, from A to Z" (U.S. Senate, 1956, p. 19).

9. "Nor was the Secretary of State, in either his thinking or his decisions, much affected by what the Department of State knew and did. Dulles devised the foreign policies of the United States by drawing upon his own knowledge, experience and insight, and the Department of State merely implemented these policies" (Morgenthau, 1961, p. 305).

"He was a man of supreme confidence within himself. . . . He simply did not pay any attention to staff or to experts or anything else. Maybe in a very subconscious way he did catalogue some of the information given him but he did not, as was characteristic of Acheson and several others of the Secretaries of State with whom I have worked, take the very best he could get out of his staff" (Anonymous. Letter to author by an associate of Dulles—undated).

10. "Herein lies the terrible danger of the distorted mirror image, for *it is characteristic of such images* that they are self-confirming; that is, each party, often against its own wishes, is increasingly driven to behave in a manner which fulfills the expectations of the other. . . . Seen from this perspective, the primary danger of the Soviet-American mirror image is that it impels each nation to act in a manner which confirms and enhances the fear of the other to the point that even deliberate efforts to reverse the process are reinterpreted as evidence of confirmation" (Bronfenbrenner, 1961, p. 51).

References

Adams, S. (1961). *Firsthand Report*. NY: Harper and Row.

Adorno, T. W.; Frenkel-Brunswik, E.; Levinson, D. J.; and Sanford, R. N. (1950). *The Authoritarian Personality*. NY: Harper and Row.

American Psychiatric Association (1952). *Mental Disorders* (a handbook). Washington, D.C.

Arendt, H. (1951). *The Origins of Totalitarianism*. NY: Harcourt, Brace.

Bauer, R. A. (1961). "Problems of Perception and the Relations Between the United States and the Soviet Union." *Journal of Conflict Resolution* 5 : 223–29.

Boulding, K. E. (1956). *The Image*. Ann Arbor: University of Michigan Press.

——— (1959). "National Images and International Systems." *Journal of Conflict Resolution* 3 : 120–31.

Bronfenbrenner, U. (1961). "The Mirror Image in Soviet-American Relations: A Social Psychologist's Report." *Journal of Social Issues* 17 : 46–56.

Bullock, A. (rev. ed., 1962). *Hitler: A Study in Tyranny*. NY: Harper and Row.

Davis, S. R. (1961). "Recent Policy Making in the United States Government." In D. G. Brennan, ed., *Arms Control, Disarmament, and National Security*. NY: George Braziller.

Drummond, R. and Coblentz, G. (1960). *Duel at the Brink*. Garden City, NY: Doubleday.

Dulles, J. F. (1948). "Not War, Not Peace." *Vital Speeches* 14 : 270–73.

——— (1950). *War or Peace*. NY: Macmillan.

——— (1955). "Our Foreign Policy in Asia." *Dept. of State Bulletin*. Pp. 327–32.

——— (1955). "Tenth Anniversary of the U.N." *Dept. of State Bulletin* 33 : 6–10.

——— (1955). Transcript of News Conference, May 24, 1955. *Dept. of State Bulletin* 32 : 914.

——— (1958). "Interview." *Dept. of State Bulletin* 39 : 733–39.

—— (1958). "Reply to Bertrand Russell." *Dept. of State Bulletin* 38 : 290–93.

Festinger, L. (1957). *A Theory of Cognitive Dissonance.* Evanston, IL: Row, Peterson.

Friedrich, C. J., and Brzezinski, Z. (1956). *Totalitarian Dictatorship and Autocracy.* Cambridge: Harvard University Press.

Fromm, E. (1941). *Escape from Freedom.* NY: Holt, Rinehart and Winston.

Khrushchev, N. S. (July 16, 1956). *The Crimes of the Stalin Era.* Special Report to the Twentieth Congress of the Communist Party of the Soviet Union (published as Section Two of the *New Leader*).

Kissinger, H. (1962). *The Necessity of Choice.* Garden City, NY: Doubleday.

Lasswell, H. (1948). *Power and Politics.* NY: Norton.

—— (rev. ed., 1960). *Psychopathology and Politics.* NY: Harper and Row.

Lederer, E. (1940). *State of the Masses.* NY: Norton.

McClelland, C. A. (1962). "General Systems and the Social Sciences." *Etc.: A Review of General Semantics* 18 : 449–68.

Miller, G. A.; Galanter, E.; and Pribram, K. H. (1960). *Plans and the Structure of Behavior.* NY: Holt, Rinehart and Winston.

Morgenthau, H. J. (1961). "John Foster Dulles." In N. A. Graebner, ed., *An Uncertain Tradition.* NY: McGraw-Hill.

Neumann, F. (1942). *Behemoth.* NY: Oxford University Press.

Neumann, S. (1942). *Permanent Revolution.* NY: Harper.

North, R. C.; Koch, H.; and Zinnes, D. (1960). "The Integrative Functions of Conflict." *Journal of Conflict Resolution* 4 : 353–74.

North, R. C. (1962). "Some Informal Notes on Conflict and Integration." Unpublished manuscript.

Osgood, C. E.; Saporta, S.; and Nunnally, J. C. (1956). "Evaluative Assertion Analysis." *Litera, Studies in Language and Literature.* Istanbul: English Dept., University of Istanbul.

Osgood, C. E. (1959). "The Representational Model." In I. Pool, ed., *Trends in Content Analysis.* Urbana: University of Illinois Press.

—— (1959). "Suggestions for Winning the Real War with Communism." *Journal of Conflict Resolution* 3 : 311–25.

Rapoport, A. (1960). *Fights, Games, and Debates.* Ann Arbor: University of Michigan Press.

Ray, J. C. (1961). "The Indirect Relationship Between Belief System and Action in Soviet-American Interaction." M.A. thesis, Stanford University.

Rokeach, M. (1960). *The Open and Closed Mind.* NY: Basic Books.

Smith, M. B.; Bruner, J. S.; and White, R. W. (1956). *Opinions and Personality.* NY: Wiley.

Snyder, R. C.; Bruck, H. W.; and Sapin, B. (1954). *Decision-Making as an Approach to the Study of International Politics.* Princeton: Princeton University Press.

U.S. House of Representatives. (June 10, 1955). Committee on Appropriations. *Hearings.* Washington, D.C.

U.S. Senate. (May 5, 1955). Committee on Foreign Relations. *Hearings.* Washington, D.C.

———— (Feb. 24, 1956). *Hearings.* Washington, D.C.

Verba, S. (1961). "Assumptions of Rationality and Non-Rationality in Models of the International System." *World Politics* 14 : 93–117.

Wheeler, H. (1960). "The Role of Myth System in American-Soviet Relations." *Journal of Conflict Resolution* 4 : 179–84.

Wright, Q. (1955). *The Study of International Relations.* NY: Appleton-Century-Crofts.

———— (1957). "Design for a Research Project on International Conflict and the Factors Causing Their Aggravation or Amelioration." *Western Political Quarterly* 10 : 263–75.

PART FOUR

INTERACTIVE PROCESSES
RELATED TO WAR

INTRODUCTION

Ralph K. White

Part Four covers three major topics—deterrence, government decision making and crisis management, and escalation—that have obvious relevance to the prevention or limitation of war. They also represent interactive processes in which there is clear interaction between individuals, parts of a government bureaucracy, or nations.

In contrast with Part Three we are now operating on the level on which historians and political scientists normally operate, though from a somewhat psychological point of view. Consequently the level-of-analysis problem that was serious in Part Three is no longer serious. That is of course to be expected, since all of the writers except Irving Janis are historically and psychologically oriented political scientists (Richard Ned Lebow, Alexander George, Richard Smoke and Ole Holsti), and Janis, the psychologist, is decidedly oriented toward history and political science.

Section VIII

Deterrence

section editor: Richard Ned Lebow

INTRODUCTION

Ralph K. White

The word "deterrence" covers two rather different things that should be carefully distinguished, since the arguments for and against them are quite different. One is the amount of armed strength that a country may build up over a period of years, ordinarily with the avowed purpose of deterring a potentially aggressive opponent from attacking the country or its allies. It can be called deterrence through strength. The other consists of the threats a country makes, explicitly or implicitly, in words or in actions such as military mobilization, designed to induce a threatening attacker to desist or refrain from attacking. It can be called deterrence through demonstrating resolve.

As the reader may now be well aware, there is some consensus among the contributors to this volume, notably in Section IV, that both kinds are *sometimes* desirable if done in the right way. That is clearly true in the case of deterrence through strength. Even Charles Osgood (Chapter 11), who presents a plan for graduated and reciprocated but ultimately drastic tension reduction and disarmament, insists that an adequate second-strike nuclear capability and adequate conventional forces should always be retained. While there is much room for discussion of how much armed strength and what kinds of armed strength are "adequate," no author in this volume rejects them on principle.

Deterrence through resolve is another story. Each of the two chapters in this section deals primarily with it, and each shows skepticism about it in many ways and on many grounds. For example, there is the basic proposition that what is intended as deterrence by a frightened defender, such as the mobilizations at the outset of World War I, may be interpreted by a frightened attacker (yes, attackers *are* often frightened) as clear preparation for attack and as justification for intensified military action. The danger of imprudent preemption and of too rapid escalation is obvious.

Chapter 22, an excerpt from the classic work, *Deterrence in American Foreign Policy: Theory and Practice,* by Alexander L. George and Richard Smoke, is one of several recent examples of criticism of orthodox deterrence theory, chiefly on the ground that it is deductive in nature, lacking a solid inductive, empirical basis. The excerpt is useful also in urging consideration of methods of international influence other than, or in addition to, traditional forms of armed deterrence and demonstration of resolve.

"Deterrence Reconsidered: The Challenge of Recent Research," by Richard Ned Lebow (Chapter 26), is an even sharper critique of conventional deterrence theory, with more systematic presentation of instances in which it has not worked as the theory would predict; for example, the failure of Israel to deter Egypt in 1973 and the failure of the United States to deter Japan in 1941.

22.

From Deterrence to Influence in Theory and Practice*

ALEXANDER L. GEORGE and RICHARD SMOKE

The Narrowness of Deterrence Theory and Practice

From the dual perspective of theory and practice, we have examined deterrence as it applies to crisis and limited-war situations—a rather different case from strategic deterrence. Some opinions to the contrary notwithstanding, policymakers can indeed benefit, perhaps greatly, from theory about deterrence of this kind. Properly formulated, theory can assist in diagnosing emergent situations and in determining how best to apply a deterrence strategy. Perhaps more important, the diagnosis can, with the assistance of theory, determine whether a deterrence strategy is really applicable and desirable in any given situation.

We have discussed the special characteristics a theory must have to be relevant to policy and the problems the investigator encounters in attempting to develop more valid policy-relevant theory. We have found that deterrence theory to date has been seriously deficient in the requirements for policy relevance. It is in the nature of any theory that it must simplify some aspects of the reality it seeks to comprehend. But if policy use is to be made of a theory, those elements of the real-life phenomenon that were left out or oversimplified in the formulation of the

* Excerpted from Chapter 2 of *Deterrence in American Foreign Policy: Theory and Practice* (New York: Columbia University Press, 1974).

theory must be identified, and their implications for the theory's content and its use by policymakers must be noted. This is just what has not been done with deterrence theory. Reasoning deductively from decision theory, and especially from game theory, investigators have offered a relatively abstract theory of deterrence which has received little testing against historical reality. Moreover, this theory has been presented in the prescriptive mode—that is, as a guide for policy—despite the fact that it does not in actuality meet the requirements for policy relevance.

In order to identify the existing theory more fully and to rectify some of its deficiencies, we have examined in detail some historical experiences with the use of deterrence in American foreign policy. By looking inductively at the problem of deterrence in concrete historical situations, we have been able to identify many factors that affect the uses and limitations of deterrence strategies in foreign policy—factors that were not taken into account properly, or at all, in previous formulations of deterrence theory. Using these case studies we have developed an explanatory—not primarily prescriptive—theory of the conditions under which deterrence succeeds or fails, becomes applicable or inapplicable.

We have not confined our critical appraisal to deterrence theory. Nor have we restricted our examination of American foreign policy to showing how systematic study of history can assist in developing a better theory of deterrence. We have also been critical of certain aspects of American foreign policy itself during the cold war period. We felt that the critical appraisal of deterrence theory that we were undertaking would benefit from, and in fact required, a critical stance toward the use of deterrence strategy in American foreign policy. The reason for this is a simple one: since deterrence is an instrument of foreign policy, its uses and limitations are very much affected by the nature of that foreign policy and by the sophistication and skill with which policymakers use all instruments of policy, of which deterrence is but one, on behalf of national goals.

Rather than presenting a more detailed summary of our findings to this point, we will now focus attention on a fundamental shortcoming of both the theory and the practice of deterrence since World War II. Deterrence theorists have erred, we submit, in regarding deterrence as a separable, self-contained phenomenon about which a useful general prescriptive theory could be developed. The work of early theorists was flawed by the evident assumption that a viable theory of deterrence could be developed independently of a broader theory of internation influence, one that would encompass the utility of positive incentives as well as threats of negative ones. American policymakers erred in a similar manner by relying on deterrence strategy too heavily and making insufficient use of other means of influencing and controlling the conflict potential in their relations with other states. For understandable reasons the narrowness of this focus on deterrence was not readily apparent to policymakers and scholars at the time. It seemed a necessary corrective to the earlier overreliance of the Western powers on more conciliatory diplomatic approaches to adversaries—first toward Hitler in the 1930s, then toward Stalin during the latter part of World War II and immediately thereafter. As a result of these events, "appeasement" fell into such disrepute as to discredit more generally the traditional reliance of classical diplomacy upon negotiation and conciliation for adjusting conflicting interests and for reconciling change in the international system with the requirements for stability.

A major conclusion of this study, therefore, is that deterrence should be viewed, not as a self-contained strategy, but as an integral part of a broader, multifaceted influence process. Concerning theory, what is needed is not merely a better deterrence theory per se but rather a broader theory which encompasses deterrence as one of a number of means that can be employed, separately or in some combination, to influence conflict processes and to control the conflict potential in interstate relations. Concerning practice, policymakers need to recapture the perspective of classical diplomacy at its best, which emphasized flexible, discriminating use of a variety of means for influencing adversaries and avoiding conflict. Whether deterrent threats are necessary and useful in a particular historical situation cannot be judged either in theory or in practice on the basis of a prescriptive theory that narrowly confines itself to indicating how to make threats: threats that are credible and potent enough to force an opponent to conclude that it is not in his self-interest to encroach on the defender's interests.

These criticisms of the narrowness of deterrence theory and of the overreliance of American foreign policy on deterrence strategy apply, we maintain, even to the height of the cold war. One of the limitations of deterrence theory noted repeatedly in different ways throughout this study is that it did not attempt to define the scope and relevance of deterrence strategy in American foreign policy. Throughout the years of the cold war, therefore, deterrence theory offered no help (to say the least!) in curbing a tendency to globalize and rigidify the policy of containment; it offered no criteria for making selective, discriminating use of deterrence.

In noting the decline of fundamental cold war premises, let us recall that containment policy rested on a particular image of Soviet behavior as expansionist. It attributed to Soviet rulers a strong, almost compulsive desire to expand into any vacuum in order to enhance Soviet power and influence, and to bring the rest of the world under some kind and degree of Soviet control. The Soviet Union was seen as at the head of a monolithic international communist movement, either behind any challenge to the status quo or poised to exploit ruthlessly any takeover by a noncommunist reformist or revolutionary group. This "devil image" of the opponent, which attributed malevolence and ruthless efficiency to Soviet rulers, gave way gradually as experience showed that the Soviet Union was often quite cautious and unsuccessful in expanding its influence. Moreover, the rulers and peoples of many new countries proved themselves able to accept Soviet economic, military, and diplomatic support without losing their independence.

Following the Cuban missile crisis, Kennedy and Khrushchev moved quickly to a détente. What was significant in this development was that American leaders began to view the Soviet Union as a limited adversary rather than as a total enemy. Similarly, the nature of the conflict with the Soviet Union was now perceived in non-zero-sum terms rather than, as in the acute cold war era, in terms of a zero-sum contest. This change was dramatically signaled in President Kennedy's eloquent American University address of June 10, 1963, when he called upon the American people to reexamine their views on the cold war and warned his listeners "not to see only a distorted and desperate view of the other side, not to see conflicts as inevitable, accommodation as impossible and communication as nothing more than an exchange of threats. No government or social system is so evil that its people must be considered lacking in virtue" (*New York Times,* June 11, 1973, p. 16).

From Deterrence to Inducement

The rapidly shifting context of United States foreign policy [in 1974] provides greater room—and a newly receptive audience—for analysis of the broader problem of "influence" among nations.

At its most general, of course, "influence" encompasses all or nearly all aspects of relations among nations, and its study is virtually coextensive with the entire discipline of international relations and with the entire conduct of foreign policy. But it is not to this level of generality that we urge attention. Rather, it is "influence" in the context of conflict reduction which, we believe, demands fresh study, especially for its applications to the post–cold war world of the 1970s and beyond. In theory, there are major devices besides threats for reducing or preventing overt conflict. For example, a contingent promise may be more appropriate in some situations than a contingent threat.

All influence devices including deterrence may be thought of analytically as falling into two broad, not wholly distinct categories according to the time horizon to which they apply. Devices other than deterrence are potentially available for dealing with short-term problems of crisis or with a threat of crisis. One such is appeasement in its original and honorable sense of giving the opponent his minimum, essential demands in the interests of peace. This device, perhaps now better named "conciliation," is appropriate under two circumstances: (1) where there are grounds for believing that the opponent's objectives are in fact limited and can be satisfied at a reasonable cost; or (2) where one needs to appease a greedy opponent in order to buy time in order to prepare ways of deal with him more effectively.

But when we turn to the long-term development of the international system we find greater reasons still for examining the entirety of internation influence—including deterrence but not limited to it and indeed, deemphasizing it. It is in this respect that American foreign policy is likely to be particularly weak and in need of help from specialists in international relations. For, obviously, it is inadequate merely to deter unfavorable change; one must also create and/or guide change in favorable directions.

These two categories are not rigidly distinct. Strategies aimed at dealing with short-term problems in ways substituting for or supplementing deterrence can also be a part of one's longer-term plans. But the distinction is useful because in the two categories the policymaker's roles and activities differ. In one case he begins with the immediate situation and searches for means to cope with it; while in the other he begins with a model or image of his desired future international reality and deductively reasons back from it toward the present, in order to devise appropriate strategies or means for pursuing the longer-range objectives. The latter task is the more difficult of the two, especially for the United States. Inevitably, the United States in important respects is a status quo power. Less inevitably, the United States also lacks, except in the vaguest terms, any vision of how it wishes world politics to develop over the long run. (Stanley Hoffmann addresses himself to this in detail in Chapter 5, Part III, of *Gulliver's Troubles* [1968].) The result is the widely observed "reactive" character of U.S. foreign policy, a tendency to do little until a challenge to the status quo arises, and then to deal with it as a threat. Deterrence is an influence policy peculiarly appropriate to these attitudes.

For this reason and doubtless others as well, deterrence has been singled out by American theorists and policymakers for special attention, with other kinds of influence policies left in the hazy background. But appreciation of the importance of supplementing deterrence theory has been growing among specialists in international relations. Roger Fisher in his *International Conflict for Beginners* (1969) notes that "in this era of nuclear weapons and deterrence the Department of Defense has become quite sophisticated about making threats [but] we have no comparable sophistication regarding the making of offers." And he believes that "this is an important way of exerting influence on which there has been far too little organized consideration." (Fisher [1969, p. 106] carries the analysis of influence processes further in his book, *Dear Israelis, Dear Arabs* [1973].)

Probably many theorists would agree that the time is overripe for deterrence theory to be supplemented with what might be called "inducement theory," the two together forming an important ingredient of the broader inter-nation influence theory to which we have referred. Under the circumstances of the 1970s, and foreseeably the 1980s, not only must deterrence be comprehended and executed in more subtle ways than in the past, as discussed earlier in this chapter; but deterrence increasingly must be supplemented with inducement policies as well.

23.

Deterrence Reconsidered:
The Challenge of
Recent Research*

RICHARD NED LEBOW

The principal theme of *Psychology and Deterrence* is disenchantment with deterrence as both a theory of state behavior
and a strategy of conflict management. Deterrence is inadequate
as an explanatory theory of international relations because the
growing body of empirical evidence indicates that neither leaders
contemplating challenges nor leaders seeking to prevent them
necessarily act as the theory predicts. We are also critical of
deterrence as a prescriptive strategy because it can provoke the
very behavior it seeks to prevent.

The major strengths and weaknesses of deterrence can both
be said to derive from the theory's most fundamental characteristic: it is a system of abstract logic all of whose principal
postulates have been derived deductively. This contributed to
the theory's appeal as it facilitated the development of coherent,
elegant, and seemingly powerful explanations for important
aspects of interstate behavior. For statesmen and scholars alike,
deterrence theory held out the promise of a pathway through
the forbiddingly complex and increasingly dangerous maze of
international relations, a pathway that began with one's own
national interest and led in the end to enhanced security. This

* Excerpted from Robert Jervis, Richard Ned Lebow, and Janice Gross Stein,
Psychology and Deterrence (Baltimore: The Johns Hopkins University Press, 1985).

was particularly attractive in a world of nuclear weapons because it encouraged statesmen to believe that efforts on their part to reduce any uncertainties surrounding a state's willingness to defend its commitments could prevent miscalculation by an adversary and forestall the kinds of challenges that had so often led to war in the past. For this reason, deterrence continues to be seen as the principal intellectual and policy bulwark against nuclear holocaust.

Despite the obvious appeal of deterrence theory, its sometimes sophisticated but always abstract rationality fails to provide an adequate description of how states actually behave. Case studies indicate that states are both more cautious *and* more prone to risk-taking than the theory predicts (Lebow, 1984). They also suggest that judgments of the credibility of another state's commitment may have little to do with its bargaining reputation. In addition, there is some evidence that the timing of foreign policy challenges may be independent of the relative military balance between the parties involved.

Any critique of deterrence must in all fairness acknowledge that deterrence sometimes seems to have been a successful strategy for preserving one's interests while avoiding war. Unfortunately, successes are much more difficult to document than failures because they generally result in inaction. In the absence of evidence detailing the deliberations of a state's leaders, it is impossible to know whether they actually contemplated a challenge of another state's commitment and, if they did, whether they decided against it because of perceptions of its military capability and resolve.

Likely examples of successful deterrence in the post-1945 period include West Berlin in the 1960s, Taiwan in the 1950s, and South Korea after 1953. Taiwan and South Korea probably would have been invaded and taken over by hostile neighbors in the absence of vigilant efforts on their part to develop the means to defend themselves. In all three cases, success also depended upon the continuing commitment of the United States to protect their independence, or existing status in the case of Berlin. It also seems evident that mutual possession of nuclear weapons has made both superpowers more cautious of each other than might have otherwise been the case. However, it is by no means clear that nuclear deterrence has succeeded in preventing a Soviet invasion of Western Europe, as is sometimes alleged. Moscow may have shied away from such an adventure even in the absence of the threat of nuclear retaliation. Nor is it apparent that the obvious reluctance of the superpowers to transgress upon each other's vital interests is in any way attributable to their respective strategic doctrines, force structures, or public statements about those interests.

There is also a class of situations in which deterrence might have worked if it had been applied. Munich is commonly cited in this regard, the assumption being that Hitler would have backed down had France and Britain remained unequivocal in their commitment to defend Czechoslovakia. Hitler, however, was furious that Chamberlain was so accommodating and even raised new demands at the last moment in the hope of forestalling an agreement (Weinberg, 1970–80, p. 663). By 1938, Hitler *wanted* war. Resolve on the part of his adversaries would have been no more successful than appeasement in preventing it. Had Britain and France stood firm a few years earlier, then the future of Europe might have been quite different.

Berlin in 1948 and Korea in 1950 seem better examples of confrontations which might have been averted if deterrence had been practiced. Studies of the Berlin crisis have documented the series of contradictory measures and public statements that characterized American policy toward that city prior to the imposition of the blockade. They have suggested that this indecision and confusion encouraged Soviet leaders to conclude that the United States was unwilling to risk war to defend its position in that city (Clay, 1950; Howley, 1950; Davison, 1958, pp. 71–78). An even more compelling case has been made that American disengagement from South Korea in 1949–50 led the North Koreans to conclude that Washington would not intervene militarily to prevent their conquest of the South (Truman, 1955, 2,355–65; McLellan, 1976, 267–70). Unambiguous American policies which demonstrated the depth of the American commitment to the status quo *prior* to both challenges might well have forestalled them.

Finally, there are a number of conflicts in which deterrence was tried but failed. The Cuban missile crisis is the most obvious example. Graham Allison called John F. Kennedy's efforts to put the Soviet Union on notice that the United States would not tolerate the introduction of "offensive weapons" into Cuba "a textbook case of responsible diplomacy" (Allison, 1971, p. 42). However, Kennedy's efforts failed to deter Khrushchev from surreptitiously attempting to deploy ballistic missiles on that island capable of striking at the United States. The year 1962 also witnessed the failure of patient Chinese efforts to deter India from pursuit of its "Forward Policy" in territory contested by the two countries. Deterrence also failed in the Middle East in 1967, 1969–70, and 1973. Arab states provoked or started a war with Israel in all three instances despite Israeli military superiority and unquestioned Israeli resolve to use that superiority in defense of its interests.

The states whose commitments were challenged in the examples cited above appear to have carried out the four operations held to be essential for deterrence. They (1) defined their commitments with some precision; (2) communicated the existence of these commitments to adversaries well in advance of any challenge; (3) possessed the military capability to defend their commitments or to punish severely any adversary who challenged them; and (4) demonstrated their resolve to use force if necessary to do this. It would be a mistake to focus only on the behavior of the defender in these instances in order to find out why deterrence failed (Lebow, 1981, pp. 82–97). The analyst must also inquire into the motives of the challengers in question and seek to understand how and why they misjudged the capability or resolve of their adversaries.

Case studies analyzed in *Psychology and Deterrence* and in other publications by its several authors suggest two principal explanations for these kinds of deterrence failures. The first is the existence of numerous and diverse barriers to interstate communication which can distort, transform, or altogether block out the signals states send to each other. The second is the apparent failure of states practicing deterrence to identify and address, at the same time, what may be the most important causes of foreign policy aggression.

Barriers to Signaling

The success of deterrence as a strategy of conflict avoidance depends not only upon the capability and resolve of the defender of a commitment but just as much upon his ability to communicate that capability and resolve to adversaries. When difficulties arise in this regard, deterrence theorists usually attribute them to structural causes, among them the past military weakness, internal political division, or poor reputation for resolve of the state in question. When deterrence is predicated upon nuclear reprisal, they also stress the difficulty of making this threat credible when it would entail war with another nuclear power.

Deterrence theorists tend to ignore the difficulties that are associated with the signaling process itself (Jervis, 1970, pp. 18–40). They assume that adversaries, who usually speak different languages, nevertheless share common symbols that facilitate effective communication. Everyone is thought to understand, so to speak, the meaning of fierce guard dogs, barbed wire, and "No Trespassing" signs. In practice, however, this may not be so. Statesmen, moreover, frequently adopt complex and finely calibrated strategies of coercion which make quite unrealistic demands on their adversaries' interpretative abilities. A striking example of this was the American decision in 1965 to send ashore a "light" marine division instead of a "heavy" army division in order to signal to Hanoi Washington's limited objectives. The intended significance of the type of unit deployed was undoubtedly lost to the North Vietnamese for whom the salient fact was that of the deployment itself (Rosen, 1982, pp. 83–113; Gaddis, 1982, pp. 246–53).

A second, and probably equally common cause of insensitivity to signals, arises from the failure to understand the context in which they are made and in terms of which they take on meaning. A signal can easily be missed if it is not recognized as a significant deviation from the norm. Allen Whiting describes several such occurrences preceding the Chinese entry into the Korean War in November 1950. Peking increased both the frequency of newspaper articles on Korea and the strength of the language used to indicate Chinese interests on that peninsula.

There is no evidence that the Americans picked this up or, if they did, were in any way aware of the manner in which the foreign language press especially was being used to signal intensified Chinese concern with developments in Korea (Whiting, 1960).

Signals can also be misunderstood if they are interpreted in an inappropriate context. The international relations literature abounds with examples of such distortion. In 1961 Chinese soldiers surrounded Indian outposts which had been set up in contested areas of Ladakh. Having demonstrated their ability to cut off several Indian outposts, the Chinese subsequently withdrew, leaving the Indian pickets unharmed. Peking intended the action as a demonstration of resolve but one that would allow Indian leaders to back down without loss of face because violence had been avoided. However, government officials in New Delhi interpreted the Chinese withdrawal as a sign of timidity. They reasoned that Chinese forces had failed to press their tactical advantage because Peking feared the consequences of a wider conflict with India. As a result, Indian leaders became even bolder in their efforts to occupy as much of the disputed territory, east and west, as was possible (Whiting, 1975, pp. 42–106).

The reason why the Chinese signal failed to have its intended effect was the belief on the part of Nehru, Menon, and their military advisers that Peking was loath to start a war with India because it feared defeat. They were also convinced that China wished to avoid being branded as the aggressor by the nonaligned bloc. As later events demonstrated, these Indian assessments were based on serious misjudgments about both the political and the military consequences of a Sino-Indian conflict. The Chinese, who were unaware of the nature and extent of these Indian illusions, behaved in a way damaging to deterrence by reinforcing in Indian minds the very expectations about themselves they sought to forestall (Lebow, 1981, pp. 57–95).

Chinese awareness of the unrealistic nature of Indian estimates of the military balance would have required an intimate and detailed knowledge of privileged communications of the Indian government, something not normally at the disposal of other states, especially adversaries. For this reason, the problem posed to effective communication by assymetrical assessment seems to be all but insurmountable in cases in which such assessments cannot be inferred from diplomatic discussions, public statements, or actual policies.

Even analysts sensitive to this problem would no doubt face great difficulties in convincing their own governments that adversarial assessments of the military or political balance were completely at variance with their own. Take the case of Pearl Harbor. The Japanese attack was predicated upon the erroneous assumption that the American reaction to destruction of its Pacific fleet would be to withdraw from the western Pacific. As Japanese leaders wanted to avoid an all-out war against the United States, a struggle they knew they could never win, their attack would make sense only if the resulting war could indeed be kept limited and short. Imagine, if you will, the difficulties of an American intelligence analyst who had succeeded in second-guessing this scenario in trying to convince his superiors of Japanese intentions. The premise upon which the attack rested—that the United States would accommodate itself to loss of its fleet instead of fighting back—would have struck American officials as so patently absurd that they would have been likely to have dismissed out of hand any warning based on it.

The Falklands conflict provides a recent and even more dramatic example of the importance of the adversary's understanding of the context as a determinant of a willingness to take risks (Lebow, 1983a, pp. 5–36). There were many causes of miscalculation in both capitals, but one important one was surely the fact that Buenos Aires and London conceived of the conflict in quite different terms. From the Argentine perspective the Malvinas were national territory that had been occupied by a colonial power since 1833. British sovereignty over the islands was an atavism in a world that had witnessed numerous wars of national liberation that had all but brought the age of colonialism to an end. Viewed in this light, it seemed a farfetched notion indeed that a colonial power in the year 1982 would try to reimpose, let alone succeed, in reimposing its rule on a "liberated colony" by force of arms. World opinion, international morality, and most important of all, the constellation of international political forces all seemed to militate against it.

The analogies that sprung into Argentine minds were Goa and Suez—an early invasion scenario concocted by the navy was actually called Plan Goa. The original Goa operation resulted in the colonial power, Portugal, accommodating itself to the loss of its colonial enclave on the Indian subcontinent when it was overrun by India. Suez, of course, remains the best example of how an attempt to reimpose colonial domination failed for all the reasons mentioned above.

The British conceived of the Falklands controversy in an altogether different light. Politicians, the press, and public opinion for the most part dismissed the colonial metaphor as inappropriate because the population of the islands was of British stock and wished to remain under the protection of the Crown. Majority opinion did not see the Argentine invasion as an example of national liberation but rather as an act of naked aggression carried out by a brutal dictatorship against a democratic and peaceful people. For the British, the relevant historical analogy was Hitler and the origins of World War II. Newspapers made frequent references to the events and lessons of that period. Chief among the lessons was the need to stand up to aggression lest failure to do so whet the appetites of would-be aggressors everywhere. The Thatcher government pursued this line of reasoning: it justified the need to retake the Falklands with the twin arguments that "aggression must not be allowed to succeed" and that "freedom must be protected against dictatorship."

If it was inconceivable for Argentina that Britain would go to war to regain the Falklands, it was equally inconceivable to most Britons that they would not if it proved the only way to effect an Argentine withdrawal. The different cognitive contexts in terms of which the two countries understood the conflict led not only to contrasting visions of justice but also to quite different imperatives for action. Unfortunately, policymakers in both London and Buenos Aires, while not altogether ignorant of the others' conceptualization of the conflict, seemed unable to grasp its implications for that country's behavior.

Statesmen could be educated to the importance of trying to conceptualize conflicts as they are experienced by their adversaries. This does not mean that they would succeed in doing so. The obstacles that stand in their way are both self-imposed, consisting of all the personal, political, as well as cultural obstacles to the development of empathy, and also structural obstacles, involving a function of differing conceptual contexts and of asymmetries in assessment. There is already quite a literature in psychology on empathy and techniques of encouraging it. Some of it has been useful in sensitizing people to the manifestations and effects of prejudice, thereby easing racial tensions in various institutional settings. In theory, policymakers could also be taught empathy. In practice, this is unlikely to happen, as most policymakers will have neither the time nor the inclination for such training. Their political needs are probably an even bigger barrier to empathy as the difficult kinds of decisions that political office entails would not be facilitated (quite the reverse) by greater understanding of the needs and motivations of political opponents or other groups whose interests were about to be sacrificed.

The external impediments that hinder proper interpretation of an adversary's signals are probably even more difficult to overcome. This may require an intimate familiarity with the political culture in question. However, leaders of countries themselves rarely possess any special area expertise. American presidents in particular are unlikely to have very much foreign experience. This does not mean that they lack firm opinions about foreign policy, especially when it concerns the motives of their country's principal adversary. They also tend to surround themselves with advisers who hold similar views. While this may be a lamentable practice, leaders may be no better informed when they rely on the advice of "experts." Familiarity with a country or culture is in itself no guarantee of accurate insight or prescience. It can even be a hindrance to the extent that the "old Russia hand," Arabist, or what-have-you, is the prisoner of deeply held but not necessarily accurate opinions about what goals motivate that country's policymakers or what factors they weigh when they make decisions. For all these reasons, misunderstandings and incomprehension will always be rife. Given this unpleasant fact of international political life, a strategy of conflict management based upon the premise that clear, unambiguous signaling is readily attainable seems quite unrealistic.

The Causes of Aggression

Deterrence theory assumes that commitments are most often challenged because the states responsible for them appear to lack the capability or will to defend them. Case studies of actual conflicts contradict this depiction of international relations in important ways. They indicate that the existence of a vulnerable commitment is neither a necessary nor a sufficient condition for a challenge. Vulnerable commitments may never be challenged, while credible ones may be. This phenomenon points to the existence of serious misperceptions on the part of challengers and to the presence of different, or at least additional, causes of aggression.

My own study of brinkmanship crises analyzed a class of acute international crises whose defining characteristic was the expectation on the part of the initiator that the adversary would back down when challenged (Lebow, 1981, pp. 57–95). I found that much more often than not brinksmanship challenges were initiated in the absence of any good reasons indicating that the adversary lacked either the capability or the resolve to defend this commitment. Not surprisingly, almost all these challenges resulted in setbacks for the initiators, who were themselves compelled to back down or go to war.

Faulty judgment on the part of initiators could most often be attributed to their perceived need to carry out a brinkmanship challenge. This compulsion arose from a combination of grave foreign and domestic problems which policymakers believed could only be overcome through the successful challenge of an adversary's commitment. Brinkmanship was conceived of by them as a necessary and forceful response to danger, as a means of preserving national strategic or domestic political interests before time ran out.

When policymakers believed in the necessity of challenging commitments of their adversaries, they became predisposed to see their objectives as attainable. They convinced themselves that they would succeed without provoking war. Because they knew the extent to which they were powerless to back down, they expected that their adversaries would accommodate them by doing so. Some of the policymakers involved also took comfort in the illusion that their country would emerge victorious at little cost to themselves if the crisis got out of hand and led to war.

The extent to which would-be challengers are inner-directed and inwardly focused is also a central theme of the work of Janice Stein (in Jervis, Lebow, & Stein, 1985). In her analysis of the five occasions between 1969 and 1973 when Egyptian leaders seriously contemplated the use of force against Israel, Stein found that decision making departed significantly from the postulates of deterrence theory. All five decisions revealed a consistent and almost exclusive fixation by Egyptian leaders on their own political interests. They spoke in almost apocalyptic terms of Egypt's need to liberate the Sinai: to uphold the rights of Palestinians; and, above all, to wipe out the humiliation of 1967 by waging a successful military campaign. By contrast, Israel's interests, and the imperatives for action that could be expected to flow from them, were not at all salient for Egyptian leaders.

The Egyptian failure to consider the relative interests of both sides resulted in a flawed estimate, not of Israel's credibility, but rather of the scope of Israel's military response. In 1969 Egyptian leaders attached a very low probability to the possibility that Israel would carry the war of attrition onto Egyptian territory in order to maintain its position in the Sinai, a miscalculation of major proportions, given the magnitude of the punishment Israel in fact inflicted upon Egypt. In 1973 the Egyptians never even considered the possibility that Israel would invade Egypt proper as a means of reasserting its authority along the Canal and then refused until it was too late to give credence to reports that such an operation was under way.

Egypt's inability to understand that Israel's leaders believed that defense of the Sinai was important both for its own sake and as an indicator of resolve was merely one cause of its miscalculation in 1969. Stein demonstrates that Egyptian leaders overestimated their own capacity to determine the course of a war of attrition and underestimated that of Israel. They also developed a strategy to fight the war, to culminate in a crossing of the Canal, that was predicated on a fatal inconsistency: the belief that Egypt could inflict numerous casualties on Israel in the course of a war of attrition but that Israel would refrain from escalating that conflict in order to reduce its casualties.

Stein describes these self-indulgent assessments and also Egypt's toleration of logical contradictions in its expectations as evidence of pervasive wishful thinking. She believes that this was a response to the strategic dilemma faced by Egyptian planners in 1969. Egypt could neither accept the status quo nor sustain the kind of military effort that would have been necessary to alter it. Instead, Egypt embarked upon a poorly conceived limited military action. The wishful thinking and the biased estimates associated with it were a form of bolstering the means by which Egyptian leaders convinced themselves that their strategy would succeed. Once again Israel's deterrent failed, not because of any lack of capability or resolve, but because Egypt's calculations, in the words of Stein, "were so flawed that they defeated deterrence."

Egyptian decision making in 1969 provides one more example of the phenomenon that my study of brinkmanship identified as the most frequent cause of serious miscalculation in international crisis: the inability of leaders to find a satisfactory way of reconciling two clashing kinds of threat. The psychological stress that arises from this decisional dilemma is usually relieved by the adoption of defensive avoidance as a coping strategy. Leaders commit themselves to a course of action and deny information that indicates that their policy might not succeed. As has been true in many cases of crisis decision making, the Egyptian decisional dilemma that prompted defensive avoidance was the result of incompatibility between domestic imperatives and foreign realities. The domestic threat—political and economic losses—was the overriding consideration for Egyptian policymakers as it was for the Argentines.

The primacy of domestic political concerns may not be entirely attributable to the self-interest of the policymakers involved, although this factor should not be discounted. It may also be related to their ability to foresee and visualize domestic disasters more vividly than foreign ones. Because of this the domestic costs of passivity in these cases probably appeared greater and more probable than a more detached assessment might have indicated and certainly also more difficult to deny.

Foreign catastrophe, by contrast, depended upon the behavior of adversaries whose political systems were less well understood than one's own and whose policies were accordingly more difficult to predict. It was simply much easier for policymakers to delude themselves that somehow their foreign ventures would succeed than it was for them to convince themselves that the domestic price of restraint would be less than horrendous. Not surprisingly, they chose to avoid what appeared to be certain loss in favor of a policy that held out the prospect of at least lower costs in the Egyptian case and the chance of substantial gain in the case of Argentina.

If deterrence theory describes an adversary's vulnerability as the catalyst for aggression, it prescribes credible, defensive commitments as the most important means of discouraging it. The empirical evidence marshaled in this study once again challenges the validity of the theory's assumptions. This is most apparent with respect to the role of military capability, and adversarial restraint is both more uncertain and more complex than deterrence theory allows.

Stein found that Egypt went to war in 1973 in spite of its leaders' adverse estimate of the military balance. The same domestic political considerations that compelled Egyptian leaders to challenge Israel also provided the incentives for Egyptian military planners to devise a strategy that compensated for their military weakness. Human ingenuity and careful organization succeeded in exploiting the flexibility of multipurpose conventional weaponry to circumvent many of the constraints of military inferiority. The Egyptians achieved a defensive superiority in what they planned to keep a limited battle zone.

According to Stein, two other considerations were crucial catalysts for the Egyptian decision to challenge Israel in 1973. These were the twin assumptions made by Sadat and his advisers that there was no chance of regaining the Sinai by diplomacy and that the longer they postponed war the more the military balance would favor Israel. Both assumptions helped to create a mood of desperation in Cairo, so much so that Sadat repeatedly purged the Egyptian military command until he found generals who were optimistic of finding a way around Israel's awesome air and armored capability.

The Japanese decision to attack the United States in December 1941 seems analogous in almost every important respect to the Egyptian decision of 1973. Like the Egyptians, the Japanese fully recognized the military superiority of their adversary, in this instance based on greater naval power and a vastly superior economic base. The Japanese nevertheless felt compelled to attack the United States in the forlorn hope that a limited victory would facilitate a favorable settlement of their festering and costly conflict with China. As the Egyptians were to do more than thirty years later, the Japanese military planners devised an ingenious and daring strategy to compensate for the adversary's advantages; they relied on air power and surprise in the hope of neutralizing American naval power in the Pacific in one sharp blow. They too deluded themselves into believing that their foe would reconcile itself to the political consequences of a disastrous initial defeat instead of fighting on to regain the initiative, a miscalculation for which they were to pay a truly monumental price. The Japanese strategy was also an act of desperation. Tokyo opted for war only after it became clear that it could not attain its objectives by diplomacy. Japanese leaders were also convinced that the military balance between themselves and their adversaries would never again be so favorable as it was in 1941 (Butow, 1961; Borg and Okamoto, 1973).

These two cases suggest that the military balance, even when correctly assessed, is only one of several considerations taken into account by policymakers contemplating war. They are also influenced by domestic and foreign political pressures which push them to act, frustration with the low probability of achieving their goals by peaceful means, and their judgments about future trends in the military balance. As we have just seen, these considerations can prove decisive.

If there is any single example that drives home the point that challenges may be unrelated to the military balance it is the recent war in the Falkland Islands. The Argentine decision to invade in March 1982 was a result in the first instance of the faltering legitimacy of the military junta and its increasingly desperate need to do something to shore up its public support. Like the Japanese and the Egyptians, the Argentines had also lost all faith in the prospect of achieving their external goal, sovereignty over the islands, by diplomacy. Disenchantment with negotiations was all the more a catalyst for military action, as peaceful resolution of the dispute had appeared a very real possibility until the failure of the so-called lease-back proposal in the late fall of 1981. A transfer of sovereignty had seemed so likely that the junta, both as a bargaining tactic and as a means of drumming up domestic support for itself, had actively encouraged public expectations to this effect. The Argentine military now became the prisoner of the very passions it had helped to arouse.

Had a military appraisal of the situation dominated Argentine deliberations, the junta would almost certainly have waited another year before launching its invasion of the Falklands. It was public knowledge that in the interim HMS *Invincible* would have gone to the Australian navy. *Intrepid* and *Fearless,* the two amphibious assault ships, would have been scrapped together with some of the supporting frigates. Britain, which barely possessed sufficient naval assets to retake the Falklands in 1982, would almost certainly have been unable to do so in the absence of these vessels. The junta, composed of generals and admirals, deemed political considerations more important than calculations of relative military balance, with results that were nothing short of disastrous.

Most of the twenty-odd cases examined by Lebow (1984) and Stein (1985) in their most recent studies support the conclusion that policymakers who risk or actually start wars pay more attention to their own strategic and domestic political interests than they do to the interests and military capabilities of their adversaries. Their strategic and political needs appear to constitute the principal motivation for a resort to force. When these needs are paramount, policymakers are prone to disregard the ways in which the same kinds of strategic and political needs might compel adversaries to stand firm in defense of their commitments. They may discount an adversary's resolve even when the state involved has gone to considerable lengths to demonstrate that resolve and to develop the military capabilities needed to defend its commitment.

Deterrence theory can be accused of standing reality on its head. It assumes a constant level of hostility between adversaries the expression of which is a function of the opportunity to act. Our cases point to just the reverse causation: the principal incentive for aggressive foreign policy appears to be a state's own perceived vulnerabilities which lead its policymakers to challenge an adversary even when external opportunity to act, in the form of an opponent's vulnerable commitment, is absent. Domestic and strategic needs and the perceptual distortions they engender may actually constitute the greatest threat to peace in the contemporary world. This finding has obvious and important policy implications.

Deterrence dictates that the defender attempt to manipulate the adversary's calculus of cost and gain in order to reduce the adversary's incentive to attack or to challenge an important commitment. The research described in *Psychology and Deterrence* suggests that one important reason why deterrence often fails is that defenders attempt to manipulate attributes of the situation, especially adversarial perceptions of resolve and relative military capability, that may not be critical to the calculations of the would-be aggressor. Efforts to influence the adversary may require attention to the *adversary's* strategic dilemmas, domestic political costs of inaction, and assessment of achieving at least some objectives by nonviolent means. All these factors must be considered by defenders as proper and productive targets for manipulation.

If weakness is an equal or even more important source of confrontational foreign policies than strength, it calls for a corresponding shift in the focus of efforts to prevent the use of force. Too much attention is probably devoted in theory and practice to making commitments credible and not nearly enough to trying to understand what might prompt an adversary to challenge them. A more sophisticated approach to conflict management would make use of both deterrence and reassurance. Leaders must seek to discourage an adversary's challenges by attempting to reduce both the adversary's opportunity and its perceived need to carry them out. They ought to avoid situations in which their own state is perceived as so weak or irresolute as to invite challenge but at the same time be careful not to make an adversary feel so weak or threatened that it has the need to do so.

It may be that to avoid war a status quo power has to pursue two distinct and not easily reconcilable objectives. It must maintain its own power and credibility while at the same time working to forestall the development of the kind of unstable conditions that lead to a security dilemma. In the words of Jack Snyder, the status quo power "must worry about everyone's security, not just its own" (Snyder, in Jervis, Lebow, and Stein, 1985). The ideal way to accomplish this may be to deploy the kinds of forces which convey no serious threat of offensive advantage and thus avoid bringing about a situation of strategic instability. Policymakers should also shun commitments and alliances that can be defended only by forces and strategies that pose a threat to the adversary's ability to provide for its own defense and that of its allies.

Conclusions

Deterrence purports to describe an *interactive* process between the defender of a commitment and a would-be challenger. The defender is expected to define and publicize its commitment and do its best to make it credible in the eyes of his adversary. Would-be challengers are expected to update frequently their assessment of their opponents' commitments and to probe for weaknesses with regard to their capability and resolve. The repetitive cycle of test and challenge is expected to provide both sides with an increasingly sophisticated understanding of each others' interests, propensity for risk-taking, threshold of provocation, and style of foreign policy behavior.

Several of the cases analyzed or referred to in our study cast doubts upon the expectation that repetitive interaction between adversaries contributes to a better understanding of their respective intentions and modus operandi. From the perspective of the challenger, one reason for this may be the inner-directed focus of policymakers. Leaders contemplating challenges of other states' commitments were remarkably insensitive to external realities. The Americans in Korea in the fall of 1950, Sadat's

Egypt in 1973, and the Argentine junta in 1982, to mention only three examples, initiated challenges primarily in response to their domestic political needs. These internal imperatives, not their external opportunities to act, were decisive to their decisions to proceed. In the Egyptian and Argentine cases, domestic political pressures determined the timing of the challenge as well. In the Egyptian decision, the putative resolve and capability of the adversary did not figure prominently in the policy debate. When external military and political realities were considered, as in the Korean and Falklands decisions, they were on the whole subordinated to political needs; the information available was distorted or processed selectively in order to make a challenge appear feasible. Policymakers in these cases can hardly be said to have based their challenges on their judgments of the credibility of their adversaries' commitments. Their process of risk assessment differed markedly from that described by deterrence theory.

From the perspective of the defender, the picture appears much the same; repeated clashes can fail to lead to any better understanding of adversarial motivations or foreign policy style. Soviet-American relations can be cited as a case in point. The "lessons" American policymakers have drawn from the series of cold war confrontations can only in the loosest sense be said to derive from the behavior of their adversary. They seem more the result of a largely subjective learning process whereby American policymakers tended to interpret Soviet behavior in terms of their preexisting notions of the motivations behind Soviet foreign policy. I have tried to document elsewhere how the Cuban missile crisis provides a striking illustration of the way in which assumptions about adversaries can misleadingly seem to be confirmed and thereby increase their grip over the minds of the policymakers who approach international affairs in terms of them (Lebow, 1983b, pp. 431–58). Afghanistan seems to have had the same effect.

The image of adversarial relationships that emerges from our study is one in which the expectations that the two sides have of each other may bear little relationship to reality. Challengers tend to focus on their own needs and do not seriously consider— or if they do, often distort—the needs, interests, and capabilities of their adversaries. Defenders in turn may interpret the motives or objectives of a challenger in a manner consistent with their expectations whether those expectations are in any way warranted. Both sides may also prove insensitive to each other's signals for a variety of political, cultural, or other reasons. In such circumstances, recurrent deterrence episodes may not facilitate greater mutual understanding. Experience may actually hinder real learning to the extent that it encourages apparent confirmation of misleading or inappropriate "lessons."

The inner direction of policymakers points to one of the ironies of international life: much of the effort made by defenders to impart the appearance of credibility to their commitments is probably wasted as challengers may not pay much attention to them. Even when they do, they may deny or simply not understand the signals being directed their way. Cultural, contextual, and organizational barriers to interpretation abound, not to speak of motivated biases on the part of policymakers already committed to proceeding with a challenge.

Partisans of deterrence admit that it may not always succeed in discouraging aggressive behavior. But they insist that it is unfair to assess the efficacy of nuclear deterrence on the basis of conventional cases. They describe deterrence between nuclear adversaries as far more effective in regulating conflict because the prospect of nuclear war is so terrifying as to frighten policymakers into behaving more or less rationally in crisis situations. Both Bernard Brodie and Thomas Schelling have at one time or another advanced this line of argument (Brodie, 1973, pp. 313–14, 375–432; Schelling, 1966, pp. 96–111, 246–47). Schelling's argument is worth describing because it has become something of a party line for deterrence theorists. He describes the threshold to war as generally ambiguous and difficult to define. Escalation is characterized by uncertainty, as neither side can really know just what action on its part will trigger war. It becomes an exercise in competitive risk-taking with diplomatic victory going to the side willing to take the greatest risks, assuming that war is avoided. But the devastating nature of nuclear war and the uncertainty of the threshold encourage prudence and caution on both sides. Adversaries, Schelling argues, atttempt to avoid war by taking small, carefully controlled, and, whenever possible, reversible steps up the rungs of the escalation ladder (Schelling, 1966, pp. 96–97).

There is another side to the nuclear coin. According to a number of scholars, nuclear weapons have had the effect of raising the "provocative threshold," that is, of increasing the number of actions that now come within the purview of coercive bargaining, but which in the prenuclear age might have precipitated war (e.g., Kahn, 1965, pp. 94–131; Osgood, R. E., and Tucker, R. W., 1967, pp. 150–57; Snyder, G. H., and Diesing, P., 1977, pp. 451–54). Snyder and Diesing point out that the observable lengthening of the crisis escalation ladder somewhat contradicts the assertion that nuclear adversaries behave more cautiously because of their fear of war: "The paradox is that the nuclear fear faces two ways; it induces caution in oneself but also the thought that the opponent is cautious too, and therefore will tolerate a considerable amount of pressure and provocation before resorting to acts that seriously risk nuclear war" (1977). The obvious danger here is that one side or the other, convinced that the step it is about to take is acceptable to the adversary, and perhaps even likely to compel the adversary to concede, will instead push the confrontation beyond the point of no return. In Premier Khrushchev's metaphor, the "knots of war" will become tied too tightly for either side to undo them.

Our own findings lend credence to the fear that such a miscalculation could occur. We saw that policymakers are prone to distort reality in accord with their needs even in situations that appeared relatively unambiguous. The more numerous and ambiguous the signals are, the easier it becomes to do this, for uncertainty is often a breeding ground, not of restraint, but of irrational confidence. It is questionable whether any situation can be so salient and stark as to preclude wishful thinking. It may be, as many deterrence theorists allege, that the most obvious kinds of vital interests backed up by a credible second-strike capability constitute such a barrier to misperception. Certainly, this a comforting belief. It is nevertheless apparent that the variety of complex signals that constitute crisis bargaining possess no such clarity. Many of these signals are subtle or intentionally vague. Others require a sophisticated understanding of the adversary's political process or culture to be properly understood. It is in this kind of situation, when the outcome of the crisis may unwittingly hang in the balance, that wishful thinking or miscalculation is most likely to occur.

References

Allison, G. T. (1971). *Essence of Decision: Explaining the Cuban Missile Crisis.* Boston: Little, Brown.

Borg, D., and Okamoto, S., eds. (1973). *Pearl Harbor as History: Japanese-American Relations, 1931–1941.* NY: Columbia University Press.

Brodie, B. (1973). *War and Politics.* NY: Macmillan.

Bueno de Mesquita, B. (1981). *The War Trap.* New Haven: Yale University Press.

Butow, R. (1961). *Tojo and the Coming of the War.* Stanford: Stanford University Press.

Clay, L. (1950). *Decision in Germany.* Garden City, NY: Doubleday.

Davison, W. P. (1958). *The Berlin Blockade: A Study in Cold War Politics.* Princeton: Princeton University Press.

Fisher, R. (1969). *International Conflict for Beginners.* NY: Harper and Row.

——— (1973). *Dear Israelis, Dear Arabs: A Working Approach to Peace.* NY: Harper and Row.

Gaddis, J. L. (1982). *Strategies of Containment.* NY: Oxford University Press.

George, A. L., and Smoke, R. (1974). *Deterrence in American Foreign Policy: Theory and Practice.* NY: Columbia University Press.

Hoffmann, S. (1968). *Gulliver's Troubles.* NY: McGraw-Hill.

Howley, F. L. (1950). *Berlin Command.* NY: Putnam.

Huth, P., and Russett, B. (July 1984). "What Makes Deterrence Work? Cases from 1900 to 1980." *World Politics* 36 (4) : 496–526.

Ienaga, S. (1978). *The Pacific War, 1931–1945.* NY: Pantheon.

Jervis, R. (1970). *The Logic of Images in International Relations.* Princeton: Princeton University Press.

Jervis, R.; Lebow, R. N.; and Stein, J. G. (1985). *Psychology and Deterrence.* Baltimore: Johns Hopkins University Press.

Kahn, H. (1965). *On Escalation: Metaphors and Scenarios.* NY: Praeger.

Kennedy, J. F. (July 11, 1963). "American University Address." *New York Times.*

Kennedy, P. (1981). *The Realities Behind Diplomacy: Background Influences in British External Policy, 1865–1980.* London: Allen and Unwin.

Lebow, R. N. (1981). *Between Peace and War: The Nature of International Crisis.* Baltimore: Johns Hopkins University Press. Pp. 270–71.

——— (March 1983). "Miscalculation in the South Atlantic: The Origins of the Falkland War." *Journal of Strategic Studies* 6 : 5–35.

——— (Fall 1983). "The Cuban Missile Crisis: Reading the Lessons Correctly." *Political Science Quarterly* 98 : 431–58.

——— (Summer 1984). "Windows of Opportunity: Do States Jump Through Them?" *International Security* 8 : 147–86.

Mack, A. (January 1975). "Why Big Nations Lose Small Wars." *World Politics* 27 : 175–200.

Maxwell, N. (1972). *India's China War.* Garden City, NY: Doubleday.

McLellan, D. S. (1976). *Dean Acheson: The State Department Years.* NY: Dodd, Mead.

New York Times, Index to (1900–1980). NY: The New York Times.

Osgood, R. E., and Tucker, R. W. (1967). *Force, Order, and Justice.* Baltimore: Johns Hopkins University Press.

Rosen, S. P. (Fall 1982). "Vietnam and the American Theory of Limited War." *International Security* 7 : 83–113.

Russett, B. (1967). "Pearl Harbor: Deterrence Theory and Decision Theory." *Journal of Peace Research* 4 (4) 89–105.

Schank, R. C. and Colby, K. M., eds. (1973). *Computer Models of Thought and Language.* San Francisco: Freeman.

Schelling, T. C. (1963). *The Strategy of Conflict.* Cambridge: Harvard University Press. Pp. 3–20.

——— (1966). *Arms and Influence.* New Haven: Yale University Press.

Singer, J. D.; Bremer, S.; and Stuckey, J. (1972). "Capability Distribution, Uncertainty, and Major Power War, 1820–1965." In B. Russett, ed., *Peace, War and Numbers.* Beverly Hills, CA: Sage.

Snyder, G., and Diesing, P. (1977). *Conflict Among Nations.* Princeton: Princeton University Press.

Snyder, J. L. (1985). "Perceptions of the Security Dilemma in 1914." In R. Jervis, R. N. Lebow, and J. G. Stein, *Psychology and Deterrence.*

Stein, J. G. (1985). "Calculation, Miscalculation and Conventional Deterrence: The View from Cairo;" and "Calculation, Miscalculation and Conventional Deterrence II: The View from Jerusalem." In R. Jervis, R. N. Lebow, and J. G. Stein, *Psychology and Deterrence*. Baltimore: Johns Hopkins University Press.

Truman, H. S. (1955). *Memoirs*. Garden City, NY: Doubleday. Vol. 2 : 355–65.

Weinberg, G. (1970–80). *The Foreign Policy of Hitler's Germany*. 2 vols. Chicago: University of Chicago Press.

Whiting, A. S. (1960. *China Crosses the Yalu: The Decision to Enter the Korean War*. NY: Macmillan.

——— (1975). *The Chinese Calculus of Deterrence: India and Indochina*. Ann Arbor: University of Michigan Press.

SECTION IX

Government Decision Making and Crisis Management

SECTION EDITOR: IRVING L. JANIS

INTRODUCTION

Ralph K. White

The importance of wise government decision making as a way of preventing war, especially at times of crisis, is obvious. And the need for it is overwhelmingly demonstrated by history.

Barbara Tuchman, in her recent book *The March of Folly: From Troy to Vietnam* (1984), paints a picture of the preponderance of "folly" in the affairs of governments down through the ages, including the heedless starting of wars that often ended in disaster. It makes shocking reading, especially when the reader stops to wonder whether present-day governments are any less prone to folly than those of the past.

The Australian historian Geoffrey Blainey, in his little-known but important work, *The Causes of War* (1973), surveys a great many wars from 1700 to the present and comes to a similar conclusion. The factor he stresses most is military overconfidence, which he sees as the most frequent single differentiating factor in the background of war. The political scientist John Stoessinger in *Why Nations Go to War* (1974, pp. 223–24) makes a related generalization: "no nation that started a major war in this century emerged a winner." The litany is startling: not Germany or Austria-Hungary in World War I, not Tsarist Russia in World War I (to the extent that Russia started it), not Germany in World War II, and not Japan in World War II. All were disastrously defeated. Folly! (Add, for good measure, both sides in Korea, our Bay of Pigs, our Vietnam experience, the Soviet Union in Afghanistan, Israel in Lebanon, and perhaps the United States in Nicaragua.)

This section, Section IX, contains two highly relevant chapters. Chapter 24, "International Crisis Management in the Nuclear

Age," is by the social psychologist Irving L. Janis, well known for his "group-think" concept and for his systematic theoretical exploration of the dynamics of group decision making (Janis and Mann, 1977). Both are well represented here. He also introduces his chapter with a broad-brush treatment of the world's present nuclear predicament, including the nuclear winter—a description that is not paralleled anywhere else in this volume.

Chapter 25, "Decision Making in Crises," is by the political scientist Richard Ned Lebow. In a surprising disagreement with the revered Greek historian Thucydides, he makes a strong case for the importance of the immediate causes of war—that is, what happens in a war crisis—even when compared with the underlying causes, which have quite generally been regarded as more important and more worthy of study. The chapter is excerpted from his book *Between Peace and War* (1981), a historical study of 26 crises that did or did not eventuate in war, and focuses especially on what he calls "brinkmanship crises." From these he concludes that two kinds of fears are predominant in such crises: fear of a future adverse balance of power if something decisive is not done in the present, and fear of a domestic backlash and a possible overturning of the government if it does not act decisively. (That of course raises a deeper question that does have to do with underlying causes: Why are elites and publics so often nationalistically self-assertive and insistent on decisive action?)

24.

International Crisis Management in the Nuclear Age*

IRVING L. JANIS

The Nuclear Arms Race

During the past few years, large numbers of people have become aware of the enormous disparity between what needs to be done to avert the danger of nuclear war, according to sensible commentators, and what is actually being done by political leaders in Washington, Moscow, and other national capitals. Among the sensible commentators are prominent ex-statesmen who have held high leadership positions in the United States government— men like McGeorge Bundy, George Kennan, and Robert McNamara. They repeatedly call attention to the danger that the nuclear arms race will end up with a nuclear holocaust that will destroy our entire civilization (see, e.g., Bundy, Kennan, McNamara, and Smith, 1982; Kennan, 1982). And they, along with many other former governmental leaders, repeatedly urge a number of fundamental steps toward reducing the danger— a nuclear freeze as a first step toward working out comprehensive disarmament agreements, the development of an international system for controlling nuclear weapons and for negotiating disputes, the full implementation of antinuclear proliferation

* Excerpts from a paper presented at a Conference on Applied Social Psychology at Claremont Graduate School, which will be published in *Applied Social Psychology Annual*. This paper includes material from Janis's forthcoming book, *Crisis Management and Mismanagement in the Nuclear Age* (in preparation).

treaties, and the reorientation of technological research. The technological reorientation they recommend involves moving away from developing more destructive weapons toward constructing effective safety devices to reduce the chances of accidental nuclear explosions, misreadings of monitored radar screens, and inadvertent launching of nuclear missiles.

But, as we all know, these sensible recommendations continue to be ignored. Year after year the nuclear arms race has continued to accelerate, not just at the increasing pace of the Reagan Administration, but also during the Carter Administration and all the preceding administrations since the end of World War II.

So the big question that confronts us is: Whence lies our hope for survival? One common answer repeatedly given by government spokesmen is that we can rely upon deterrence. But deterrence from mutually assured destruction does not seem to offer any real hope for the long run. Leading scientists and experts on international relations have become increasingly critical of deterrence theory (see George and Smoke, 1974; Gottfried, Bethe, Garwin, Lebow, Gayler, Sagan, and Weisskopf, 1984; Jervis, Lebow, and Stein, 1985; Lebow, 1981; Morgan, 1977). Many of them argue that sooner or later the thousands of poised nuclear missiles are very likely to be released, either as a result of human error or as a result of deliberate decisions during an international crisis, at a time when one or another group of national leaders believe that their own country is about to be attacked and that they can somehow cut down on the amount of destruction by launching their own missiles first.

Faint Rays of Hope

So whence lies our hope? Let me give you my personal answer. Like most other psychologists and social scientists concerned about the arms race, I am not optimistic. But I think I can discern a few faint rays of hope that might gradually be augmented and combined to become a brilliant beam. One of those faint rays is the spread of pro-peace movements that have arisen in America and in many European countries. Those movements at the very least provide some political incentives to help induce policymakers in their respective countries to take meaningful steps toward disarmament and control of nuclear weapons.

Another very faint ray of hope has to do with the reality-testing capabilities of the policymakers themselves. If the dangers of an all-out nuclear war are as horrendous as practically everyone I know thinks they are, then national leaders in the United States, the Soviet Union, and all the other countries that have nuclear weapons—or are about to have them—ought to become highly motivated to take preliminary steps to lessen those dangers. Of course, they might go in the direction of planning to win a nuclear war by a preemptive-strike strategy designed to prevent the enemy from launching a full-scale nuclear attack. But that option could become less and less attractive, especially if Paul Ehrlich, Carl Sagan, and the numerous other scientists who collaborated with them are correct in the analysis they published in December 1983 in *Science,* forecasting a hitherto unsuspected consequence of extensive nuclear explosions. According to their forecasts, even a limited nuclear war involving only a few hundred of the tens of thousands of existing nuclear warheads would lead to many months and possibly a year or more of subzero temperatures throughout the entire earth (Ehrlich, Sagan, Kennedy, and Roberts, 1984; Turco, Toon, Ackerman, Pollack, and Sagan, 1983). This prolonged "nuclear winter" would freeze all water supplies and destroy almost all food supplies, which might lead to the extinction of all human life. If those forecasts turn out to be based on sound assumptions and come to be accepted by the scientific community, policymakers will realize that launching a nuclear strike will be completely sucidal even if the enemy does not retaliate at all. If so, they will become strongly motivated to move toward genuine arms control and to favor negotiation procedures for handling international conflicts.

At present, when practically none of the fundamental steps to control nuclear weapons and to prevent international disputes from escalating into all-out war are being taken, there is still another very faint ray of hope left, it seems to me. That third slight ray of hope has to do with conflict management. The top policymakers of the major nuclear powers show many signs of being highly motivated to avoid miscalculations and erroneous assumptions in making crucial decisions, especially in crises where there is a relatively high risk of inadvertent outbreak of nuclear war. Isn't it realistic, therefore, to expect policymakers to be in the market for improving their decision-making procedures in order to become more efficient crisis managers?

Now, you will notice that each of the three faint rays of hope I have mentioned involve attitude changes, decision making, and behavioral change. They involve overcoming psychological resistances to new courses of action, avoiding misperceptions, and preventing various other sources of error that make for maladaptive behavior. These are topics that fall squarely within the domain of social-psychological theory and research. It seems to me that social psychologists can offer a little something to strengthen each of these very faint rays of hope, to help magnify them perhaps to such an extent that they could become a dependable beam to dispel the bleak gloominess of the future as most of us now view it.

Research on International Crises

A few years ago I came to the conclusion that social psychologists, along with other behavioral and social scientists, should give top priority to research problems that have some potentiality for contributing useful guidelines for preventing nuclear war. And I began redirecting my own research to concentrate on problems of crisis management in international conflicts—to focus on that third faint ray of hope. The main questions I am trying to answer are: What are the major psychological sources of error that give rise to ill-conceived policy decisions during international crises? What are the major situational factors that are determinants of each of the sources of error?

One of the first requirements essential for starting to carry out research on defective policymaking is to specify criteria that can be used as dependent variables. In my earlier research (Janis, 1972; Janis and Mann, 1977), I reviewed the extensive literature on decision making and extracted seven major criteria to use in judging whether a decision made by a person or group is of high versus low quality. Such judgments pertain to the problem-solving procedures that lead up to the act of commitment to a final choice (see Etzioni, 1968; Maier, 1967; Simon, 1957; Taylor, 1965; Wilensky, 1967; Young, 1966). As applied to decision making groups, the seven procedural criteria or requirements are as follows: to the extent that time and available resources permit, the group (1) thoroughly canvases a wide range of policy alternatives; (2) takes account of the full range of objectives to be fulfilled and the values implicated by the choice; (3) carefully weighs whatever is found out about the costs or drawbacks and the uncertain risks of negative consequences, as well as the positive consequences, that could flow from each alternative; (4) intensively searches for new information relevant for further evaluation of the policy alternatives; (5) conscientiously takes account of any new information or expert judgment to which the members are exposed, even when the information or judgment does not support the course of action they initially prefer; (6) reexamines the positive and negative consequences of all known alternatives, including those originally regarded as unacceptable, before making a final choice; and (7) makes detailed recommendations or provisions for implementing the chosen policy, with special attention to contingency plans that might be required if various known risks were to materialize.

These criteria or requirements can be used to judge the quality of decision-making activities even when the outcome of the decision is too complex or too ambiguous to be evaluated as successful or unsuccessful. Although systematic data are not yet available on this point, it seems plausible to assume that, when national leaders make consequential policy decisions, their failures to meet the criteria are symptoms of defective decision making that increase the chances of undesirable outcomes, such as unintended military escalation. In order to assess the frequency and intensity of such symptoms displayed by members of a policy-planning group for any given decision, it is necessary to examine the available records and memoirs bearing on the group's formal and informal meetings.

So far in my comparative case studies of crisis management and mismanagement, I have been using the seven criteria for assessing the quality of decision making in an impressionistic way by making qualitative clinical judgments based on the available case materials. In a systematic study that I have just started in collaboration with Greg Herek, we are using a standard rating procedure for each of the seven criteria and separate rating procedures for short-term and long-term outcomes. This study is designed to investigate the assumption that often the outcomes are partly determined by the quality of decision-making procedures. In subsequent studies we plan to check further on the expected relationship by obtaining ratings of the seven criteria from trained research assistants who are kept as blind as possible with regard to the outcome of the decisions and all other variables under investigation. The ratings will be used to select examples for intensive case studies focusing on psychological sources of error that lead to poorly worked out decisions.

Groupthink as a Source of Defective Decision Making

One of the theoretical models of defective decision making that I am examining in my present research on international crises since World War II is derived from my prior research on fiascoes resulting from foreign policy decisions made by top-level governmental advisory groups (Janis, 1972, 1982). In that earlier research, I called attention to a concurrence-seeking tendency among moderately or highly cohesive groups, which I refer to as "groupthink." When this tendency is dominant, the members use their collective cognitive resources to develop rationalizations in line with shared illusions about the invulnerability of their organization or nation and display other symptoms of concurrence-seeking (referred to as "the groupthink syndrome").

A number of historic fiascoes appear to have been products of defective decision making on the part of misguided government leaders who obtained social support from their in-groups of advisers. My analysis of case studies of historic fiascoes suggests that among the groups of policy advisers dominated by "groupthink" are: President Harry S. Truman's advisory group, whose members supported the decision to escalate the Korean War in 1950 despite firm warnings by the Chinese communist government that United States entry into North Korea would be met with armed resistance from the Chinese; President John F. Kennedy's advisory group, whose members supported the decision to launch the Bay of Pigs invasion of Cuba in May 1961 despite the availability of information indicating that it would be an unsuccessful venture and would damage United States relations with other countries; and President Lyndon B. Johnson's "Tuesday luncheon group," whose members supported the decision to escalate the war in Vietnam during the mid-1960s despite intelligence reports and other information indicating that this course of action would not defeat the Vietcong or the North Vietnamese and would entail unfavorable political consequences within the United States.

In all these "groupthink"-dominated groups, there were strong internal pressures toward uniformity, which inclined the members to avoid raising controversial issues, even in their own minds, or calling a halt to softheaded thinking, even when they were keenly aware that the group was moving toward an ill-conceived course of action. "In the months after the Bay of Pigs," Arthur Schlesinger, Jr., wrote in *A Thousand Days* (1965), "I bitterly reproached myself for having kept so silent during those crucial discussions in the cabinet room. . . . I can only explain my failure to do more than raise a few timid questions by reporting that one's impulse to blow the whistle on this nonsense was simply undone by the circumstances of the discussion" (p. 258). Schlesinger adds, "Had one senior advisor opposed the adventure, I believe that Kennedy would have canceled it. No one spoke against it. . . . Everyone around him thought he had the Midas touch and could not lose. Despite himself, even this dispassionate and skeptical man may have been affected by the soaring euphoria of the new day" (p. 259).

Eight main symptoms of groupthink run through the case studies (Janis, 1972, 1982). Each symptom can be identified by a variety of indicators, derived from historical records, observers' accounts of conversations, and participants' memoirs. The eight symptoms of groupthink are:

1. An illusion of invulnerability, shared by most or all the members, which creates excessive optimism and encourages taking extreme risks;
2. An unquestioned belief in the group's inherent morality, inclining the members to ignore the ethical or moral consequences of their decision;
3. Collective efforts to rationalize in order to discount warnings which might lead the members to reconsider their assumptions before they commit (or recommit) themselves to a policy decision;
4. Stereotyped views of rivals and enemies as too evil to warrant genuine attempts to negotiate, or as too weak and stupid to counter whatever risky attempts are made to defeat their purposes;
5. Self-censorship of deviations from the apparent group consensus, reflecting each member's inclination to minimize to himself the importance of his doubts and counterarguments;
6. A shared illusion of unanimity concerning judgments conforming to the majority view (partly resulting from self-censorship of deviations, augmented by the false assumption that silence means consent);
7. Direct pressure on any member who expresses strong arguments against any of the group's stereotypes, illusions, or commitments, making clear that this type of dissent is contrary to what is expected of all loyal members;
8. The emergence of self-appointed mindguards—members who protect the group from adverse information that might shatter their shared complacency about the effectiveness and morality of their decisions.

Taking account of prior research findings on group dynamics, I have formulated a set of hypotheses concerning the conditions that foster concurrence-seeking on the basis of inferences from my case studies of groupthink and from comparative case studies of well-worked-out decisions made by similar groups whose members made realistic appraisals of the consequences. One of these counterpoint case studies is of the main decision made by the Kennedy Administration during the Cuban missile crisis in October 1962. Another deals with the hardheaded way that planning committees in the Truman Administration evolved the Marshall Plan in 1947. These two case studies indicate that policymaking groups do not always suffer the adverse consequences of group processes, that the quality of the group's decision-making activities depends upon current conditions that influence the group atmosphere, including leadership practices.

My main hypotheses concerning the causes of groupthink specify that the main antecedent conditions involve a group that is *cohesive,* functioning as decision makers in an organization charcterized by certain types of *structural faults.* Among the major organizational faults that contribute to the groupthink tendency are: (1) insulation of the decision-making group; (2) lack of tradition of impartial leadership; (3) lack of norms requiring methodical decision-making procedures; and (4) homogeneity of the members' social background and ideology. Also included among the antecedent conditions that promote groupthink in cohesive groups are certain types of *provocative situations* that temporarily lower the members' level of self-esteem, such as encountering moral dilemmas in which the only alternatives that apper to be feasible are ones that violate ethical or humanitarian standards.

In order to determine whether groupthink is one of the sources of error that helps to account for any given policy fiasco, it does not suffice merely to see if a few of the symptoms can be detected. Rather, it is necessary to examine all the available evidence to determine whether the entire groupthink pattern is present. Before concluding that groupthink affected the decision-making process, the investigator must ascertain that most of the symptoms were manifested, that the group cohesiveness and other antecedent conditions were present, and that the expected immediate consequences (the symptoms of defective decision making) also were observed (see Janis, 1982).

Not all cohesive groups suffer from groupthink, though all may be vulnerable from time to time. A cohesive group of competent people is not only characterized by high commitment to the group's decisions and conscientious implementation but is also generally capable of making better decisions than any individual in the group who works on the problem alone (see

Hatvany and Gladstein, 1982; Steiner, 1982). And yet the advantages of having policy decisions made by a cohesive group are often lost when the leader and the members are subjected to stresses that generate a strong need for unanimity. An unrestrained striving for concurrence fosters lack of vigilance, unwarranted optimism, sloganistic thinking, and reliance on shared rationalizations that bolster the alternative seen as least objectionable (Janis and Mann, 1977). That alternative is often the one urged by the leader of the policymaking group at the outset of the group's deliberations about a strategic decision. When groupthink remains dominant throughout all the meetings, the leader's initial biases are likely to remain uncorrected despite the availability of impressive evidence against them.

In order to prevent groupthink, I have suggested a set of interrelated recommendations. In my book on *Victims of Groupthink,* I discuss in detail ten prescriptive hypotheses which involve counteracting the conditions that foster groupthink (Janis, 1982):

1. Information about the causes and consequences of groupthink given to policy makers well before the onset of a crisis will have a beneficial deterring effect, if presented in a way that is neither unduly optimistic nor pessimistic.

2. The leader, when assigning a policy-planning mission to a group, should be impartial instead of stating preferences and expectations at the outset. This practice is likely to be effective, however, only if the leader consistently allows the conferees the opportunity to develop an atmosphere of open inquiry and to explore impartially a wide range of policy alternatives. '

3. The leader of a policy-forming group at the outset should assign the role of critical evaluator to each member, encouraging the group to give high priority to airing objections and doubts. This practice will not be successful, however, unless it is reinforced by the leader's acceptance of criticism of his or her own judgments in order to discourage the members from soft-pedaling their disagreements.

4. At every meeting devoted to evaluating policy alternatives, one or more members should be assigned the role of devil's advocate. In order to avoid domesticating and neutralizing the devil's advocates, however, the group leader will have to give each of them an unambiguous assignment to present the opposing arguments as cleverly and convincingly as he or she can, as a good lawyer would, challenging the testimony of those advocating the majority position.

5. One or more outside experts or qualified colleagues within the organization who are not core members of the policy-planning group should be present at each meeting on a staggered basis and should be encouraged to challenge the views of the core members.

6. Each member of the policy-planning group should discuss periodically the group's deliberations with trusted associates in his or her own unit of the organization and report back their reactions.

7. Whenever the policy issue involves relations with a rival organization or out-group, a sizable block of time (perhaps an entire session) should be spent surveying all warning signals from the rivals and constructing alternative scenarios of the rival's intentions.

8. After reaching a preliminary consensus about what seems to be the best policy alternative, the policy-planning group should hold a "second chance" meeting at which every member is expected to express as vividly as he or she can all residual doubts and to rethink the entire issue before making a definitive choice.

9. Throughout the period when the feasibility and effectiveness of policy alternatives are being surveyed, the policy-planning group should from time to time divide into two or more subgroups to meet separately, under different chairpersons, and then come together to hammer out their differences.

10. The organization should routinely follow the administrative practice of setting up several independent policy-planning and evaluation groups to work on the same policy question, each carrying out its deliberations under a different chairperson.

392 Interactive Processes Related to War

All these and related prescriptive hypotheses, such as the procedures recommended by Alexander George (1980) for ensuring "multiple advocacy," must be validated by systematic social psychological research before they can be applied with any confidence. Research designed to test these prescriptive hypotheses, which has already been started by investigators using laboratory experiments and systematic field studies, can contribute to our basic theoretical understanding of group decision-making processes as well as to practical guidelines for crisis management (see Courtwright, 1978; Flowers, 1977; Fodor and Smith, 1982; Janis, 1982, pp. 302–38; Tetlock, 1983). Many of the antigroupthink procedures might also prove to be helpful for counteracting initial biases of the members, preventing pluralistic ignorance, and eliminating other sources of error that can arise independently of groupthink.

Defective Patterns of Coping with Stress

Another conceptual model I am using in my research on sources of error in international crises pertains to patterns of coping with the stresses of decision making. In my collaborative work with Leon Mann (*Decision Making,* 1977), the groupthink syndrome is treated as a special case of one particular defective coping pattern—defensive avoidance. Our work focused on a major problem that requires theoretical analysis and empirical research: Under what conditions does stress have favorable versus unfavorable effects on the quality of decision making? Our conflict-theory analysis attempted to answer this question as well as broader questions concerning the conditions under which people will use sound decision-making procedures to avoid arriving at ill-conceived choices that they soon regret. We described, on the basis of the extensive research on psychological stress, the different ways people deal with stress when they are making vital decisions. When a person is preoccupied with a decisional conflict, the main sources of stress include fear of suffering from the known losses that will be entailed by whichever alternative is chosen, worry about unknown things that could go wrong when vital consequences are at stake, concern about making a fool of oneself in the eyes of others, and losing self-esteem if the decision works out badly. Vital decisions often involve conflicting values, which make the decision maker realize that any choice he or she makes will require sacrificing ideals. As a result, the decision makers' anticipatory anxiety, shame, or guilt is increased, which adds to the level of stress.

In assuming that stress itself is frequently a major cause of errors in decision making, we do not deny the influence of other common causes, such as ignorance, defective use of analogies, prejudice, and bureaucratic politics. We maintain, however, that a major reason for many ill-conceived and poorly implemented decisions has to do with the motivational consequences of decisional conflict, including attempts to ward off the stresses generated by agonizingly difficult choices.

Our analysis deals with five basic patterns of coping with any threat or opportunity requiring a person to make a vital choice. These patterns were derived mainly from an analysis of the research literature on psychological stress bearing on how people react to warnings that urge protective action to avert disasters. The five coping patterns are:

1. *Unconflicted adherence (or inertia):* The decision maker complacently decides to continue whatever he or she has been doing, ignoring information about the risks.
2. *Unconflicted change:* The decision maker uncritically adopts whichever new course of action is most salient or most strongly recommended, without making any contingency plans and without psychological preparation for setbacks.
3. *Defensive avoidance:* The decision maker evades the conflict by procrastinating, shifting responsibility to someone else, or constructing wishful rationalizations that bolster the least objectionable alternative, minimizing the expected unfavorable consequences and remaining selectively inattentive to corrective information. (This pattern usually seems to be dominant among the members of a policy-planning group when they display the symptoms of groupthink.)
4. *Hypervigilance;* The decision maker in a paniclike state searches frantically for a way out of the dilemma, rapidly shifting back and forth between alternatives, and impulsively seizes upon a hastily contrived solution that seems to promise

immediate relief. He or she overlooks the full range of consequences of the choice because of emotional excitement, repetitive thinking, and cognitive constriction (manifested by reduction in immediate memory span and simplistic ideas).

5. *Vigilance:* The decision maker searches painstakingly for relevant information, assimilates information in an unbiased manner, and appraises alternatives carefully before making a choice.

While the first two patterns are occasionally adaptive in saving time, effort, and emotional wear and tear, especially for routine or minor decisions, they often lead to defective decisions when decision makers must make a choice that has serious consequences for themselves or for their organization or nation. Similarly, defensive avoidance and hypervigilance may occasionally be adaptive in certain extreme situations but generally reduce the decisionmakers' chances of averting serious losses. Consequently, all four are regarded as defective patterns of decision making in major crises or whenever important values are at stake. The fifth pattern, vigilance, although occasionally maladaptive if danger is imminent and a split-second response is required, generally facilitates a problem-solving approach that meets the main criteria for sound decision making.

Among the main questions we addressed were: What are the conditions that make for vigilance? How do they differ from those that make for each of the four defective coping patterns? Preliminary answers to these questions are presented in Figure 24.1, which is a schematic summary of the Janis and Mann (1977) conflict model of decision making. This model, based on the research literature on psychological stress, specifies the psychological conditions that mediate the five coping patterns and the level of stress that accompanies them.

Our analysis of the pertinent research literature (Janis and Mann, 1977, Chap. 3) indicates that the coping patterns are determined by the presence or absence of three conditions: (1) awareness of serious risks for whichever alternative is chosen (i.e., arousal of conflict); (2) hope or optimism about finding a better alternative; and (3) belief that there is adequate time in which to search and deliberate before a decision is required.

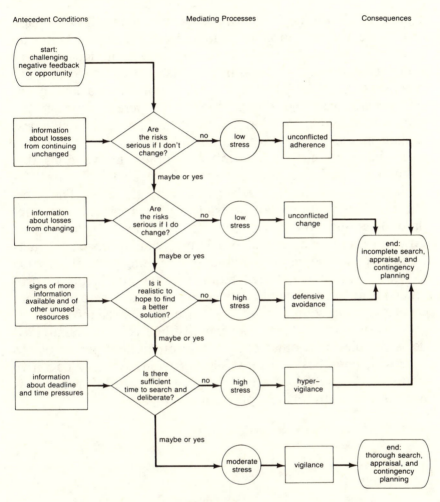

Figure 24.1
The conflict–theory model of decision making (after Janis and Mann, 1977).

Although there may be marked individual differences in preference for one or another of the coping patterns, all five patterns are assumed to be in the repertoire of every person when he or she functions as a decision maker. In different circumstances the same person will use different coping patterns depending on which of the three crucial conditions are present or absent.

In our review of social-psychological studies bearing on premature closure, postdecisional regret, and a number of other aspects of decisional behavior (Janis and Mann, 1977, chaps. 4–12), we call attention to scattered findings consistent with predictions about the behavioral consequences of vigilant versus nonvigilant coping patterns, from which we conclude that our theoretical analysis is plausible. We also describe a few of our own social-psychological experiments that were designed to test prescriptive hypotheses derived from our conflict model. These include studies of the effectiveness of a balance sheet procedure, stress inoculation, and a number of other interventions that counteract the beliefs and perceptions specified in Figure 24.1 as being responsible for defective coping patterns. The most effective interventions can probably be incorporated into standard operating procedures to be followed by policymakers in order to promote a vigilant problem-solving approach to international crises. Some of the standard operating procedures, such as the balance sheet, which requires systematic listing of pros and cons for each available alternative, might also help to prevent other common sources of error—for example, reliance on stereotypes of opponents; the availability heuristic, oversimplified decision rules; and other cognitive shortcuts that people use to deal with complicated issues. These various types of cognitive errors are likely to increase if the person's motivational state is not conducive to vigilant problem solving.

25.

Decision Making in Crises*

RICHARD NED LEBOW

Underlying versus Immediate Causes of War

Following the example of Thucydides, students of war have distinguished between underlying and immediate causes of war. The former refer to the long-term causes of hostility and tension between states; the latter, to the proximate issues or crises that actually trigger war. For Thucydides the underlying causes were the ones that really mattered. This is made clear in his treatment of the origins of the Peloponnesian War. Thucydides attributed the conflict to the growth of the Athenian Empire, its need for expansion, and the fear this inspired among other *Poleis*, especially Sparta. In his view, this situation made war inevitable. If it had not come in 431 B.C., touched off by Athenian involvement in the war between Corinth and Corcyra, some other event would sooner or later have brought the two hegemons of ancient Greece to blows. The proximate causes of war were important only insofar as they determined the timing of the conflict (Thucydides, trans. 1972, esp. pp. 124–36).

The logic and clarity of Thucydides' exposition has left its imprint upon the development of Western thought about conflict. Subsequent students of war have not only distinguished between underlying and immediate causes of war but have also

* Excerpted from Richard Ned Lebow, *Between Peace and War* (Baltimore and London: The Johns Hopkins University Press. 1981).

generally followed Thucydides in treating the underlying causes as the more important of the two. Hobbes, Kant, Rousseau, and Marx all represent this tradition. For a contemporary example of the pervasive influence of this conception one need only look at the historiography of World War I. Historians hotly debate the responsibility of the various nations for the war but are in surprising agreement about the overriding importance of the underlying causes of the conflict. The prevailing view is that the assassination of the archduke was merely one of many events that could have triggered a war that would have been extremely difficult to avoid.

Psychological experiments support the hypothesis that people tend to increase their estimates of the probability of an outcome once it has occurred. Baruch Fischhoff, a psychologist, speculates that one cause of this is that "it is quite flattering to believe, or lead others to believe, that we would have known all along what we could only know with outcome knowledge, that is, that we possess hindsightful foresight" (Fischhoff, 1975).

The Thucydidean analysis of conflict unquestionably encourages whatever predisposition exists to describe events as more unavoidable than they were. By emphasizing the importance of long-term or underlying causes of conflict it prompts investigators to identify and highlight the particular strands of development that appear to have led to the events whose origins they wish to explain. Other strands of development that might have led to different outcomes are often ignored. According to R. H. Tawney, this problem is endemic to the historical discipline. "Historians," he writes, "give an appearance of inevitability to an existing order by dragging into prominence the forces which have triumphed and thrusting into the background those which they have swallowed up" (Tawney, 1912). The treatment of futures that might have been is relegated to science fiction.

The extent to which "creeping determinism," as Fischhoff calls it, colors our thinking can be seen by examining the outcome and significance of the Cuban missile crisis. Had that crisis led to war the next generation of historians, assuming there was one, would have portrayed the crisis and the war that followed as the natural, even inevitable result of almost twenty years of cold war between the Soviet Union and the United States. Ideology, the nuclear arms race, competition for spheres of influence, and domestic payoffs of aggressive foreign policies would all have been described as important underlying causes of the war. In restrospect, World War III would appear as unavoidable as World War I.

Fortunately, the Cuban confrontation did not lead to war. It may actually have been a catalyst of détente, a sobering lesson for both superpowers that encouraged them to seek less dangerous ways of coping with mutual tensions. If Soviet-American relations continue to improve, future historians may even see the crisis as the turning point of the cold war. The Cuban crisis might thus have lent itself to two radically different historical interpretations depending on its outcome, an outcome according to most students of the crisis that was touch-and-go (Allison, 1971; Kennedy, 1969). A different man at the helm in either Washington or Moscow (what if Nixon had won the 1960 election?), the choice of the air-strike option instead of the blockade, yet another act of insubordination by either military establishment—a change in any one of a hundred conditions could have led to a different outcome.

The fact that the management of the Cuban crisis determined whether or not the United States and the Soviet Union went to war and may also have influenced the subsequent pattern of relations between them indicates that the immediate cause of war, and crisis in particular, is an important independent variable in international relations. The proximate causes of conflict may even be as important as the underlying ones if a crisis can determine whether long-standing tensions are ultimately eased or lead to war.

The premise that crises can be turning points in international conflicts is the overarching theme of this book. By examining the relationship between crisis and war we shall seek to determine the extent to which crisis influences the course of a conflict as well as the manner in which this occurs. In keeping with this objective, three specific areas of investigation were selected. The first of these, the *origins of crisis,* is perhaps the most difficult problem to come to grips with analytically as crises are the outgrowth of national and international developments whose roots may go back years if not decades. Just where should the researcher limit his search for the causes of a particular conflict? Take the case of World War I. Should we begin our analysis with the formation of the Franco-Russian alliance, an event that intensified German fears of encirclement, or with the independence of Serbia, an important catalyst of Slavic nationalism, or even further back with the economic and social changes that gave rise to nationalism and ultimately threatened the very existence of multiethnic dynastic states? Each is a valid starting point depending upon the approach and level of analysis that is adopted.

The second focus of research is the *outcome of crisis.* The central question here is why some crises are resolved by diplomacy while others result in war. Are such outcomes determined by the particular nature of crisis? To what extent are they a function of decisions made during the course of the crisis itself? We should also like to know just how crises lead to war. When is war the result of a deliberate decision to advance the nation's vital interest by force of arms? When is it the result of miscalculation? Is miscalculation associated with particular underlying organizational structures and patterns of policymaking? If so, is it possible to predict the performance of a political system in crisis or suggest ways of improving crisis performance?

The final focus of research pertains to *crisis and international relations,* that is the relationship between crisis and underlying patterns of conflict. In what ways do crises affect the long-term relations between protagonists? In what circumstances do they act to inteinsfy or ameliorate the conflicts which they reflect? Crises are the most salient points of conflict between states short of war. They are likely to bring such conflicts into sharper focus by providing policymakers with insights into the state of mind and objectives of both adversaries and allies. Acute crises probably also produce a kind of collective trauma in that leaders on both sides usually face grave challenges to their personal and national interests during the course of a crisis and are not likely to regain their sangfroid readily even after successful mastery of such challenges.

The data for this study have been drawn from twenty-six historical cases of crisis. But the book is not organized around case studies. It is structured in terms of a conceptual framework, and particular cases are described only so far as they are useful or necessary to document theoretical propositions. When I began research in 1971, this approach was something of a departure from other studies of crisis, which consisted of individual case studies or analyses of crisis decision making based on several cases at best. In the course of the last few years two important and truly comparative studies have appeared: Alexander L. George and Richard Smoke, *Deterrence in American Foreign Policy* (1974), and Glenn H. Snyder and Paul Diesing, *Conflict Among Nations* (1977). George and Smoke generalize about deterrence on the basis of eleven cases of crisis between 1948 and 1962 in which the United States was a major participant. Snyder and Diesing make use of sixteen cases of crisis, from Fashoda in 1898 to the Middle East crisis of 1973, to analyze international bargaining. Both sets of authors approached their data with a list of explicit variables, thus ensuring a degree of uniformity in the analysis of their respective cases. Both had samples large enough to encourage some confidence in their ability to distinguish between what was idiosyncratic and what was of general importance. George and Smoke observe: "With this [comparative] method the investigator is able . . . to uncover similarities among cases that suggest possible generalizations, but he is also able to investigate the differences among cases in a systematic manner" (George and Smoke, 1974, pp. 95–96). On this basis they justify "contingent generalizations" about the efficacy of deterrence.

My approach closely parallels that of these two studies. I examined a large number of crises in terms of a prepared set of explicitly formulated analytical questions in an initial effort to devise a framework in terms of which crisis and crisis politics might fruitfully be described. Subsequently, I sought to formulate hypotheses with respect to the three research foci described earlier. The fundamental assumption underlying this approach is that the broader perspective made possible by the use of the comparative method will be more useful in furthering our understanding of crises than yet another case study. The intensive analysis of single cases has unquestionably generated a wide range of insights into crisis behavior, but it has begun to come up against the limitations inherent in such an approach. The most serious of these limitations is the inability of the researcher to discern *patterns* of behavior which are dependent upon the observation of a class of events. Instead, generalizations must be based on the internal structure of the case. Hypotheses formulated in such a manner must have pretensions of universality or at least of wider applicability, but claims to this effect can be validated only through the analysis of other cases. The case-study approach, therefore, runs the risk of failing to distinguish between what is unique to the case and what is common to the class of events as a whole. As a result, generalizations based on a single case or even a small sample run the risk of being incorrect and misleading. The emphasis on severe time constraints in a number of recent studies of crisis is a case in point. This no doubt derives from the frequent choice of the July 1914 and Cuban missile crises as the subjects of case studies. Both crises were of extremely short duration but are in fact typical of crises as a whole.

The limitations of case studies by no means invalidate their utility. Rather, they point to the need for parallel studies undertaken from a comparative perspective. The two approaches can readily complement each other. Case studies can suggest hypotheses which lend themselves to testing in carefully selected cases. The comparative method is used here with this end in mind: to provide structure to a class of events, and by doing so helping researchers to formulate problems and hypotheses with greater sophistication. Three types of crisis will be analyzed in this study: *justification of hostility, spinoff,* and *brinkmanship* crises.

Table 25.1.
Justification-of-Hostility Crises

July (1914) [Austria vs. Serbia]
Second Lusitania (1915–16)
Manchuria (1931)
Poland (1939)
Gulf of Tonkin (1964)

Justification-of-hostility crises are unique in that leaders of
the initiating nation make a decision for war *before* the crisis
commences. The purpose of the crisis is not to force an accommodation but to provide a casus belli for war. Initiators of
such crises invariably attempt to make their adversary appear
responsible for the war. By doing so they attempt to mobilize
support for themselves, both at home and abroad and to un-
dercut support for their adversary. . . .

Spinoff Crises

This section concerns the origins and politics of our second
category of crisis. The term "spinoff" was chosen to refer to
these crises because they are secondary confrontations arising
from a nation's preparations for, or prosecution of, a primary
conflict. They are outgrowths of wars in which the initiator is
or expects to be a participant. War can prompt extraordinary
actions on the part of the belligerents. Spinoff crises develop
when such actions, designed to advance the initiators' interests
in primary conflicts, provoke confrontations with third parties.
Those included in our sample are listed in Table 25.2.

Table 25.2.
Spinoff Crises

Spanish-American (1898–99)
July (1914) (Germany vs. Belgium)
 (Germany vs. Britain)
German-American U-boat crises (1915–17)
 First *Lusitania* (1915)
 First and Second *Arabic* (1915)
 Sussex (1916)
 Unrestricted U-boat warfare (1917)
Russo-Finnish (1939)

. . .

Brinkmanship Crises

Brinkmanship crises can be said to develop when a state
knowingly challenges an important commitment of another state

in the hope of compelling its adversary to back away from his commitment. The initiator's expectation that his adversary will back down rather than fight is the defining characteristic of brinkmanship crises. The initiator is not attempting to start a war, as in a justification-of-hostility crisis, but rather aims to achieve specific political objectives (see Table 25.3).

What kinds of threats encourage policymakers to provoke confrontations which may result in war? Judging from the cases, the most important external threat is the *expectation by policymakers of a dramatic impending shift in the balance of power in an adversary's favor.* In seven of thirteen cases of brinkmanship the crisis was preceded by the widely shared perception among policymakers of the initiator that a dramatic and negative shift in the balance of political-military power was imminent. (These cases are Korea 1903–4, First Morocco, Agadir, Bosnian Annexation, July [Austria-Hungary and Germany vs. Russia and France], Berlin [1948–49], and Cuba [1962].) Brinkmanship in these cases was conceived of as a forceful response to this acute impending danger—as a means of preventing or redressing the shift in the balance of power before time ran out and such a response became unrealistic.

A second motivation for brinkmanship derives from the *weakness of the initiator's political system.* In four of our cases, Korea (1903–04), Bosnia (1908–09), July (1914), and the Middle East (1967), domestic political instability or the frangibility of the state itself was instrumental in convincing leaders to provoke a confrontation. They resorted to the time-honored technique of attempting to offset discontent at home by diplomatic success abroad. . . .

Conclusions

THUCYDIDES REBUTTED

The introduction raised the question of the relative importance of the *underlying* and *immediate* causes of war. Are the underlying causes, as most historians suggest, the more important

Table 25.3
Brinkmanship Crises

Crisis	Commitment	Initiator's Objectives
Fashoda (1898)	Britain's commitment to deny France any presence in the Sudan	British recognition of French interests in Egypt; colonial concessions in West Africa
Korea (1903–4)	Japan's commitment to economic and political dominance in Korea	Japanese recognition of Russian interests in Korea
First Morocco (1905–6)	France's claim to primacy in Morocco	Expose French military weakness vis-à-vis Germany; force a change of government in France; destroy the Anglo-French Entente
Bosnia (1908–9)	Russia's commitment to oppose unilateral Austrian expansion in the Balkans	Reduce the threat to Austria-Hungary posed by pan-Slavism
Agadir (1911)	France's claim to primacy in Morocco	Weaken or destroy the Anglo-French Entente
July (1914)	Russia's commitment to maintain Serbian independence	Strengthen Austria-Hungary; weaken the Franco-Russian alliance; escape encirclement by hostile powers
Rhineland (1936)	The demilitarization of the Rhineland	Free Germany from the restrictions imposed by the Treaty of Versailles
May and Munich (1938)	France's commitment to Czechoslovak independence and territorial integrity	Destroy Czechoslovakia; achieve a free hand in Eastern Europe
Berlin (1948)	The American, British, and French commitment to preserve their position in Berlin and influence in Germany	Forestall economic reforms and the unification of the Western zone; expel the Western allies from Berlin
Korea (1950)	China's commitment to resist the penetration of United Nations forces beyond the 38th parallel	Unify Korea under a pro-American government
Sino-Indian (1962)	China's commitment to the territorial status quo in the Himalayas	Compel Chinese withdrawal from territory claimed by India

Crisis	Commitment	Initiator's Objectives
Cuba (1962)	To keep missiles capable of carrying nuclear warheads out of Cuba	Compensate for nuclear inferiority; demonstrate resolve to Cuba and China
Arab-Israeli (1967)	Maintain free passage through the Straits of Tiran	Preserve Nasser's position in the Arab world; humiliate Israel

determinant of war, or can the proximate causes play an equally significant role?

Our investigation of acute international crisis has demonstrated that immediate causes of war can exercise an important and even decisive influence on the course of a conflict. Acute international crises were found to be significant in two respects. They can determine whether war breaks out or peace is maintained. They can also intensify or ameliorate the underlying sources of conflict in cases where war is averted.

The extent to which a crisis influences the course of conflict depends upon the generic nature of the crisis in question. In justification-of-hostility crises, where the purpose of the crisis is to mobilize support for a war, the independent role of crisis is not very great, because the decision for war precedes the crisis. Even so, the crisis may be instrumental in forestalling war to the extent that it convinces policymakers that they have misjudged the degree of domestic or foreign support for their action.

The independent role of crisis is also minimal in spinoff crises. This kind of confrontation is characterized by an extensive search for accommodation on the part of both protagonists, neither of whom wants war. Although none of the spinoff crises we studied were resolved peacefully, it is conceivable that such a crisis may prompt the nations involved to find an acceptable compromise. The Russo-Finnish crisis might have been resolved had the Soviets not mismanaged the confrontation.

The independent role of crisis is greatest in brinkmanship crises. Initiators of brinkmanship crises enter into such confrontations with the expectation that their adversaries will back down when the commitments of these adversaries are challenged. When such crises lead to war it is the result of decisions made during the course of the confrontation. These decisions, we discovered, are most often the result of the same kinds of miscalculations that lead initiators to conclude in the first place that their adversaries would back down.

Judging from our cases, leaders felt compelled to pursue aggressive foreign policies in response to pressing foreign and domestic problems. The most common external catalyst of brinkmanship was the perception that decisive action was required to prevent a significant adverse shift in the strategic or political balance of power. The need to shore up a regime, the political system, or the state itself constituted important domestic incentives for brinkmanship. In most cases, several such incentives were present and reinforced one another, bringing about widespread support within the policymaking elite for a confrontatory foreign policy.

When leaders felt themselves compelled to pursue brinkmanship challenges, they frequently rationalized the conditions for their success. Once committed to brinkmanship, they became insensitive in varying degrees to information that challenged the prospect of its success. They often devised elaborate personal and institutional defenses to avoid having to come to terms with this information. However, in the many brinkmanship scenarios based on erroneous perceptions of an adversary's resolve, it was imperative for initiators to remain sensitive to cues from their environment about the validity of their expectations. When initiators recognized and corrected for initial misjudgments, they usually succeeded in averting war, although this often required a major cooperative effort, as in the Fashoda and Cuban missile crises. When little or no learning occurred, usually because leaders found the truth too threatening, the protagonists remained on a collision course, as was the case in the July 1914, Korean (1950), and Sino-Indian crises.

Crisis management is certainly crucial to the outcome of brinkmanship crises. Our investigation of crisis policymaking nevertheless suggests that a narrow research focus on techniques of crisis management is not likely to lead to improved performance. Good crisis management depends upon a number of underlying political conditions. It requires the existence of a relatively open decision-making environment, a cohesive political elite, and a serious commitment on the part of policymakers to avoid war. As we have seen, these conditions cannot simply be created by fiat during the course of a crisis. If present, they are organic qualities of the political system and culture. The ability of even the most imaginative and forceful leaders to guide their policies through crisis situations is largely determined by important attributes of the political system over which they may exercise no control or very little control in the short run.

This finding indicates that much of the focus of contemporary research on crisis management is misplaced. To emphasize unduly the actions of leaders and their policies during the crisis is to look only at the tip of the proverbial iceberg. Of greater importance for understanding crisis behavior is the process by which such decisions are reached and implemented, for this process ultimately decides the substance of actual policy. Successful crisis management is therefore a function of cultural, organizational, and personal behavioral patterns established long before the onset of any crisis. These patterns and the expectations they create largely determine the performance of a system in crisis. It follows that leaders must also be evaluated in terms of their precrisis decisions, that is, the extent to which they were effective in creating a policymaking environment conducive to successful crisis management within the limitations imposed by the political culture in which they operated. This study has attempted to define and analyze some of the most important of these underlying conditions affecting crisis performance. In this sense, we have come full circle by finding the most important attributes of the immediate causes of war to be themselves a function of underlying causes, albeit of a domestic nature.

The second way in which crisis is important is in terms of its impact upon the underlying causes of conflict. Underlying tensions give rise to a variety of manifestations, among them arms races, alliances, and competition for influence. These visible manifestations of tension are likely to aggravate the clash between the protagonists in particular arenas of conflict. The resulting confrontations can lead to war, although war can also come about in the absence of crisis.

The links between these stages of conflict are extremely important. The progression from underlying tension to crisis and possible war can be described as an amplifying feedback network (see Figure 25.1). Each stage tends to magnify the intensity of the previous stages and thereby the probability of a renewed cycle of conflict. This process characterized Anglo-German relations in the period 1895–1914 and Soviet-American relations during the cold war. In all three instances, the level of hostility between protagonists dramatically intensified through a process of reinforcement learning.

Feedback need not always be positive (i.e., having the effect of increasing tension). An agreement to limit armaments or a negotiated settlement of an outstanding territorial dispute, to cite just two tension-reducing acts, can generate "negative" feedback in the sense that it diminishes mutual perceptions of underlying tensions and thereby dampens the manifestations of these tensions. Depending upon their course and outcome, international crises can accordingly intensify or diminish the level of underlying tension and hostility.

Crises are especially important in this regard because an important characteristic of amplifying feedback networks is that exacerbation in one element of the system is not merely transmitted throughout the system but is magnified in the process. Crisis, the penultimate step in the progression from underlying hostility to war, can profoundly affect leaders' assessments of their adversaries' intentions. It can lead policymakers on both sides to see war as more likely and prompt them to initiate policies in preparation for such a conflict, which may have the effect of making their expectations of war self-fulfilling. It is arguable that the series of crises prior to World War I had such an effect. Conversely, a crisis whose resolution succeeds in

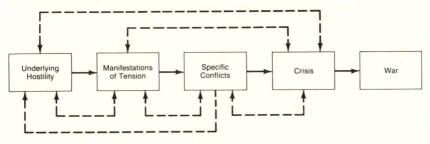

Figure 25.1

removing outstanding sources of friction can dramatically reduce long-standing hostility between the protagonists. The Fashoda crisis appears to have had this effect. Fashoda marked the high point of Anglo-French colonial rivalry but also led to mutual efforts to reduce the tension characterizing relations between them in the entente of 1904. The Cuban missile crisis might be examined in the same light. It marked the most dangerous point of the cold war and was followed by mutual efforts to reduce the tension characterizing relations between the super-powers. The Cuban confrontation did not really resolve any serious political issue, but it did have an important shock value. By raising a very real prospect of nuclear war for the first time, it led both the United States and the Soviet Union to see the need for some kind of accommodation. It is still too early to tell how successful the superpowers will be in defusing the tensions of the cold war, but there can be no question that Cuba was an important catalyst of détente. Crises therefore not only play an important role in international conflicts but can be turning points, for better or worse, of such conflicts.

References

Allison, G. T. (1971). *Essence of Decision: Explaining the Cuban Missile Crisis.* Boston: Little, Brown.

Blainey, G. (1973). *The Causes of War.* NY: The Free Press.

Bundy, M. G.; and Kennan, G. F.; McNamara, R. S.; and Smith, G. (Spring 1982). "Nuclear Weapons and the Atlantic Alliance." *Foreign Affairs.*

Courtwright, J. A. (1978). "A Laboratory Investigation of Groupthink." *Communication Monographs* 45 : 229–46.

Ehrlich, R. R.; Harre, J.; Harwell, M. A.; Raven, P. H.; Sagan, C.; Woodwell, G. M.; Berry, J.; Ayensu, E. S.; Ehrlich, A. H.; Eisner, T.; Gould, S. J.; Grover, H. D.; Herrera, R.; May, R. M.; Mayr, E.; McKay, C. P.; Mooney, H. A.; Myers, N.; Pimentel, D.; and Teal, J. M. (1983). "Long-Term Biological Consequences of Nuclear War." *Science* 222 : 1293–1300.

Ehrlich, P. R.; Sagan, C.; Kennedy, D.; and Roberts, W. O. (1984). *The Cold and the Dark: The World After Nuclear War.* NY: The Free Press.

Etzioni, A. (1968). *The Active Society.* NY: The Free Press.

Fischhoff, B. (1975). "Hindsight/Foresight: The Effect of Outcome Knowledge on Judgment Under Uncertainty." *Journal of Experimental Psychology: Human Perception and Performance* 3 (1) : 288–99.

Flowers, M. (1977). "A Laboratory Test of Janis' Groupthink Analysis." *Journal of Personality and Social Psychology* 42 : 178–85.

Fodor, E. M., and Smith, T. (1982). "The Power Motive as an Influence on Group Decision Making." *Journal of Personality and Social Psychology* 42 : 178–85.

George, A. (1980). *Presidential Decisionmaking in Foreign Policy: The Effective Use of Information and Advice.* Boulder, CO: Westview Press.

George, A., and Smoke, R. (1974). *Deterrence in American Foreign Policy: Theory and Practice.* NY: Columbia University Press.

Gottfried, K.; Bethe, H.; Garwin, R.; Lebow, R. N.; Gayler, N.; Sagan, C.; and Weisskopf, V. (1984). *Anti-Satellite Weapons and Ballistic Missile Defense.* NY: Random House.

Hatvany, N. G., and Gladstein, D. (1982). "A Perspective on Group Decision Making." In D. A. Nadler, M. L. Tushman, and N. Hatvany, eds., *Approaches to Managing Organizational Behavior.* Boston: Little, Brown.

Janis, I. L. (1972, rev. ed., 1982). *Victims of Groupthink: Psychological Studies of Policy Decisions and Fiascoes.* Boston: Houghton Mifflin.

Janis, I. L., and Mann, L. (1977). *Decision-Making: A Psychological Analysis of Conflict, Choice and Commitment.* NY: The Free Press.

Jervis, R.; Lebow, R. N.; and Stein, J. G. (1985). *Psychology and Deterrence.* Baltimore: Johns Hopkins University Press.

Kennan, G. (1982). *The Nuclear Delusion: Soviet-American Relations in the Atomic Age.* NY: Pantheon.

Kennedy, R. F. (1969). *Thirteen Days: A Memoir of the Cuban Missile Crisis.* NY: Norton.

Lebow, R. N. (1981). *Between Peace and War.* Baltimore: Johns Hopkins University Press.

Maier, N. (1967). "Group Problem Solving." *Psychological Review.* 74 : 239–49.

Morgan, P. (1977). *Deterrence: A Conceptual Framework.* Beverly Hills, CA: Sage.

Schlesinger, A. Jr. (1965). *A Thousand Days.* Boston: Houghton Mifflin.

Simon, H. A. (1957). *Models of Man: Social and Rational.* NY: Wiley.

——— (3d ed., 1976). *Administrative Behavior: A Study of Decision-Making Processes in Administrative Organization.* NY: The Free Press.

Snyder, G., and Diesing, P. (1977). *Conflict Among Nations.* Princeton: Princeton University Press.

Steiner, I. (1982). "Heuristic Models of Groupthink." In H. Brandstetter, J. H. Davis, and G. Stocker-Kreichgauer, eds., *Contemporary Problems in Group Decision-Making.* New York: Academic Press.

Stoessinger, J. (1974). *Why Nations Go to War.* NY: St. Martins.

Tawney, R. H. (1912). *The Agrarian Problem in the Sixteenth Century.* London: Longmans, Green.

Taylor, D. W. (1965). "Decision Making and Problem Solving." In J. March, ed., *Handbook of Organizations.* Chicago: Rand-McNally.

Tetlock, P. E. (1983). "Psychological Research on Foreign Policy. A Methodological Overview." In L. Wheeler, ed., *Review of Personality and Social Psychology*. Vol. 4. Beverly Hills, CA: Sage.

Thucydides. (1972). *History of the Peloponnesian War*. Trans. Rex Warner. Harmondsworth: Penguin.

Tuchman, B. (1984). *The March of Folly: From Troy to Vietnam*. NY: Knopf.

Turco, R. P.; Toon, O. B.; Ackerman, T. P.; Pollack, J. B.; and Sagan, C. (1983). "Nuclear Winter: Global Consequences of Multiple Nuclear Explosions." *Science* 222 : 1283–92.

Wilensky, H. L. (1967). *Organizational Intelligence*. NY: Basic Books.

Young, S. (1966). *Management: A Systems Analysis*. Glenview, IL: Scott, Foresman.

SECTION X

Escalation

SECTION EDITOR: RICHARD SMOKE

INTRODUCTION

Richard Smoke

Escalation is at once one of the most important, most intriguing, and most intractable of all the psychopolitical problems of war and peace. The risk that some crisis or small conflict might escalate "out of control" may be the greatest danger we face in today's nuclear world. Experts are generally agreed that neither the USSR nor the United States would deliberately launch a nuclear war "out of the blue," because leaders on both sides know the retaliation they would face. It is in that sense that "deterrence works." The real hazards of nuclear war lie in the possibility of a sheer technical breakdown (such as a computer malfunction leading to a missile launch) and in the possibility of a crisis escalating into war. During the Cuban missile crisis of 1962, President Kennedy is said to have estimated the chances that a global nuclear war might erupt from the crisis to be "somewhere between one in three and even."

Hence, many specialists are concerned to understand how crisis and escalation processes can be controlled and halted. Yet the factors that make up a crisis, and the dynamics of escalation, turn out to be highly complex. They involve intricate and ever changing combinations of psychological, political-diplomatic, domestic political, military-strategic, technical-military, and other elements.

Two specialists who have focused on the intersection of psychological with political and military elements in escalation are represented in this section. Ole Holsti's 1972 book, *Crisis Escalation War* (excerpted in Chapter 26) develops an in-depth analysis of the crisis of July and August 1914 that triggered World War I. Richard Smoke's 1977 book, *War: Controlling*

Escalation (excerpted in Chapter 27), comparatively analyzes five other "low-level" clashes, some of which did and some of which did not escalate into major wars. Many important similarities appear in their conclusions (these similarities are not stated twice in the excerpts presented here). Some complementarities also appear, deriving largely from differences from the authors' foci. Holsti's study is of an intense crisis of fairly short duration (for that era) and draws particular attention to such important factors as stress and fatigue. Smoke's study is of longer-duration escalation processes in which some hostilities are already going on, and it focuses on the interactive effects back and forth of actual and potential military events.

26.

Crises, and Ways to Keep Them from Escalating*

OLE R. HOLSTI

Crisis, Stress, and Decision Making

Clearly the assumptions of deterrence are valid most of the time and under most circumstances, even in relations of considerable enmity such as "cold wars." Otherwise, we would be at war almost continuously. Nevertheless, there is a substantial element of truth in one critic's assertion that "the theory of deterrence . . . first proposes that we should frustrate our opponents by frightening them very badly and that we should then rely on their coolheaded rationality for our survival" (K. Deutsch, 1963, p. 70).

The more general question is how crisis—defined here as *a situation of unanticipated threat to important values and restricted decision time*—is likely to affect policy processes and outcomes. What are the probable effects of crisis upon abilities which are generally considered essential to effective decision making? These include the ability to:

Identify major alternative courses of action.
Estimate the probable costs and gains of each alternative course.
Resist premature cognitive closure.

* Excerpts from *Crisis Escalation War* (Montreal and London: McGill–Queen's University Press, 1972).

Distinguish between the possible and the probable.
Assess the situation from the perspective of other parties.
Discriminate between relevant and irrelevant information.
Tolerate ambiguity.
Resist premature action.
Make adjustments to meet real changes in the situation (and, as a corollary, to distinguish real from apparent changes).

The most important aspect of crises for our purposes is that these situations are characterized by high stress for the individuals and organizations involved. That a threat to important values is stress inducing requires little elaboration. The element of surprise is also a contributing factor; there is evidence that unanticipated and novel situations are generally viewed as more threatening. Finally, crises are often marked by almost around-the-clock work schedules, owing to both the severity of the situation and to the absence of extended decision time. During the Cuban missile confrontation, for instance, many American officials slept in their office for the duration of the crisis: "We had to go on a twenty-four hour basis here in the Department of State," (Rusk, 1963). Premier Khrushchev also appears to have had little sleep during that week: "I must confess that I slept one night in my studio fully dressed on the sofa. I did not want to be in the position of one western diplomat who, during the Suez crisis, rushed to the telephone without his trousers" (1970, p. 497; see also p. 436).

STRESS AND PERFORMANCE: THE EVIDENCE FROM PSYCHOLOGY

The central concern here is to explore the possible consequences of crisis-induced stress on those aspects of individual and organizational performance that are most likely to affect the processes and outcomes of foreign policymaking. In this book stress is viewed as *the result of a situation that threatens important goals or values.* For reasons to be discussed later, we shall measure stress by subjective responses to the situation rather than by attributes of the situation itself.

As a starting point, we shall turn to the rich and voluminous body of theory and evidence from experimental psychology. The advantages of precise measurement, easy replication, and tight control over the experimental variables have permitted psychologists to probe many aspects of human performance in various types of situations.

Some degree of stress is an integral and necessary precondition for individual or organizational problem solving; in its absence we lack any motivation to act. Low levels of pressure alert us to the presence of a situation requiring our attention, increase our vigilance and our preparedness to cope with it. If the problem is qualitatively simple and performance is measured by quantitative criteria, stress can increase output. The threat of a severe flood may result in exceptional physical performance by emergency work crews who are filling and stacking sandbags, and a severe international crisis might give rise to improved output by foreign office clerical staffs.

Our present concern, however, is not with the effects of crisis on persons engaged in manual or clerical tasks but with its consequences on the performance of top-ranking foreign policy officials. Foreign policy issues are nearly always marked by complexity, ambiguity, and the absence of stability; they usually demand responses which are judged by qualitative rather than quantitative criteria. It is precisely these qualitative aspects of performance that are most likely to suffer under high stress.

Most research findings indicate a curvilinear relation between stress and the performance of individuals and groups. A moderate level of anxiety can be beneficial, but at higher levels it disrupts decision processes. On the basis of a series of experiments, Birch determined that intermediate—rather than high or low motivation—was most conducive to the efficient solution of problems requiring both high and low insight. A related finding is that persons with moderate fear were better able to cope with the problems arising from major surgery than were those with high or low fear (Janis, 1958). These results have been supported by other studies (Birch, 1945; Yerkes, 1934). Lanzetta, in an analysis of group behavior, found that "under increased stress there was a decrease in initiating behaviors, mainly in terms of 'diagnoses situation, makes interpretation' kinds of behavior; and an increase in more 'general discussions of the task' kind of behavior," (Lanzetta, 1955). Following their analysis of the effects of stress on perception, Postman and Bruner (1948) concluded: "Perceptual behavior is disrupted, becomes less well controlled than under normal conditions, and hence is less adaptive. The major dimensions of perceptual function are affected: selection of percepts from a complex field becomes less adequate and sense is less well differentiated from nonsense; there is maladaptive accentuation in the direction of aggression and escape; untested hypotheses are fixated recklessly".

Other effects of stress which have been found in experimental research include: increased random behaviour; increased rate of error; regression to simpler and more primitive modes of response; problem-solving rigidity; diminished focus of attention, across both time and space; reduced ability to discriminate the dangerous from the trivial; diminished scope of complex perceptual activity; loss of abstract ability; disorientation of visual-motor coordination; and loss of complexity in the dimensions of political cognition. A finding of special relevance for international crises is that tolerance for ambiguity is reduced when there is high stress. Under these conditions individuals made decisions before adequate information was available, with the result that they performed much less capably than those working under normal conditions. The combination of stress and uncertainty leads some persons to feel that "the worst would be better than this" (Smock, 1955).

To summarize, in situations of high stress "there is a narrowing of the cognitive organization at the moment; the individual loses broader perspective, he is no longer able to 'see' essential aspects of the situation and his behavior becomes consequently less adaptive" (Krech and Crutchfield, quoted in Korchin, 1964, p. 63).

Some experimental studies have been criticized on both conceptual and methodological grounds, but the general conclusion that high stress inhibits rather than facilitates most aspects of human performance appears to be unassailable. Moreover, the capabilities which may be enhanced by moderate-to-high stress tend to have limited relevance in formulating foreign policy, whereas the skills inhibited under these conditions are usually crucial for such complex tasks.

Conclusion: Some Thoughts on Policy Implications

INFERRING MOTIVES AND INTENTIONS

One critical aspect of policymaking in a crisis is inferring the motives and intentions of others. The range and nature of alternatives that will be given a serious hearing will depend significantly on images of other nations. Individuals and bureaucracies that are wedded to "inherent good faith," "inherent bad faith," or similar one-dimensional models of others are likely to consider a very limited repertoire of options. Compounding the problem is the very real difficulty of gaining hard and verifiable evidence about such elusive and sometimes mercurial attributes as motivations. History is not barren of instances in which disaster arose from faulty assessments of others' capabilities—witness the American estimates of Japanese and Chinese military strength in 1941 and 1950, respectively (R. Wohlstetter, 1962; McLellan, 1968)—but the decidedly more difficult task of adducing intentions has no doubt created far more problems. George Kennan has observed that "in everything that can be statistically expressed—expressed, that is, in such a way as not to imply any judgment on our motivation—I believe the Soviet Government to be excellently informed about us. I am sure that their information on the development of our economies, on the state of our military preparations, on our scientific progress, etc., is absolutely first-rate. But when it comes to the analysis of our motives, to the things that make our life tick as it does, I think this whole great system of intelligence-gathering breaks down seriously" (Kennan, 1957, pp. 21–22).

This disability is not, of course, limited to the Soviet Union, or even to totalitarian nations. Munich, Pearl Harbor, Korea, and Suez are a few of the more dramatic cases in which leaders of democratic nations seriously misread the situation. During the months prior to the Cuban missile crisis American and

Soviet leaders also provided vivid evidence of their limited abilities to estimate each other's willingness to take risks.

Soviet leaders ignored all evidence and warnings that the Nazis would invade in 1941, as did the Americans with respect to the Tet offensive in 1968. A systematic study of thirty-two crises revealed that "warning signs are seldom decoded properly before threats of violence" (Haas, 1969, p. 73). The reverse situation in which conciliatory actions are dismissed as tricks may occur equally often, especially under crisis conditions. Even between allies of long standing there may be difficulties in adducing motives properly, as Neustadt has noted with respect to Anglo-American diplomacy during the Suez crisis of 1956 and the Skybolt incident six years later (1970, pp. 67, 71).

At minimum, sound judgments about intentions and motives require adequate information. In 1914 the volume of diplomatic communication increased steadily as war approached; the same appears to be true of most crises. The problem of information, then, is more likely to be qualitative than quantitative; there may be an immense flow of diplomatic correspondence, but the information contained therein may lend itself to multiple inferences.

Thus, perhaps even more important than raw information is a valid theory to give it meaning and relevance; rarely do "the facts speak for themselves." A single fact or even a set of data is usually consistent with several theories. It is quite probable that most international disasters can be traced, not to the inadequate information, but rather to the absence of adequate models into which to place the facts. Throughout the summer of 1939, for example, London and Paris received warnings from diverse sources that a Nazi agreement with the USSR was in the offing. These were dismissed with such comments as "highly improbable" (Mosely, 1969, p. 229). The facts were not at issue—for example, Hitler's recent speeches had been devoid of their usual anti-Bolshevik diatribes and Vyacheslav Molotov had replaced Maxim Litvinov as Soviet foreign minister. The missing ingredient was a frame of reference which could assimilate and properly evaluate clues that the apparently implacable ideological enemies might find it expedient to join forces. A similar conclusion emerges from Roberta Wohlstetter's detailed analysis of the attack on Pearl Harbor: "If our intelligence system and all our other channels of information failed to produce an accurate image of Japanese intentions and capabilities, it was not for want of the relevant materials. Never before have we had so complete an intelligence picture of the enemy." She goes on to point out that too much information, bureaucratic rivalries, and normal limitations on human perceptions were at the root of the failure. If there is any antidote to these problems, it is to be found in a "willingness to play with materials from different angles and in the context of unpopular as well as popular hypotheses" (1962, pp. 302, 382).

These examples illustrate the need for a set of alternative premises and theories against which the evidence can be tested. Well-established psychological principles suggest that few persons can effectively examine evidence from more than one or two views of reality. And although the complex bureaucracies that characterize all modern governments are intended to reduce the effects of idiosyncratic elements, even organizations can become single-minded advocates of a preferred viewpoint.

The advice that every foreign office needs "devil's advocates" is often given (Jervis, 1968; de Rivera, 1968, pp. 61–64, 209–11) but is apparently hard to implement. It appears that the ability to create a decision-making environment receptive to both "popular and unpopular" hypotheses is a rare talent. That dissenters in totalitarian systems rarely enjoy long public careers is a point that requires little elaboration.

It is however, far more instructive to illustrate how easy it is even in a nontotalitarian political system to exclude unpopular ideas from policymaking councils, especially in crises.

Recent American administrations provide further examples of how easily open debate may be discouraged. In some respects, the problem can be traced to the isolation of national leaders and the size and complexity of contemporary governments. Most American presidents have come to office vowing that they will avoid the isolation of their predecessors, that theirs will be an "open administration." None has been very successful in this respect; the gap between aspiration and performance has been especially notable during some recent foreign policy crises.

Johnson himself contributed to the problem by being less than vigorous in seeking advice on Vietnam which may have challenged his own premises about the war. For example, he appointed his close friend Clark Clifford as secretary of defense in part because Clifford was seen as a staunch supporter of administration policies in Vietnam. Clifford began doubting the wisdom of those policies when the Joint Chiefs of Staff were unable to provide satisfactory answers to the most basic questions about the conduct of military operations and their consequences. After that the president refused ever again to meet privately with his secretary of defense. In the salty language of one participant, "The President was colder than a whore's heart." Earlier, Vice-President Humphrey had suffered virtual banishment from top-level policy discussions for questioning administration policy on the war. Whether or not the doubts entertained by Clifford and Humphrey were valid, incidents such as this are bound to affect other advisers. Only the most courageous—or foolhardy—would have failed to draw the conclusion that unpopular opinions are neither welcomed nor rewarded.

MILITARY ADVISERS

The views of military advisers almost always take on special importance during international crises—and legitimately so. But in the absence of broad consultation with persons who represent a variety of personal and bureaucratic viewpoints, all too often technical military considerations will prevail over diplomatic and political ones. Brodie's assessment of World War I generals—"It was their horizons rather than their skills which proved so disastrously limited" (1959, p. 59)—may have relevance for other times and places. The missile confrontation illustrated the tendency of military advisers to view crises from a purely military perspective. The Joint Chiefs of Staff stood solidly in favor of bombing the [Cuban] missile sites rather than using a minimal level of force—the blockade—as a lever with which to seek a political solution of the situation. Indeed, use of atomic weapons was urged by at least one of the service chiefs.

In the face of a suspected mobilization by the adversary in the near future, the "safe" course from the perspective of one who may be called upon to fight a war is to alert or mobilize his forces. This may, in turn, be precisely the action which tips the balance in favor of mobilization by the other side, thereby setting the stage for another round of escalation. The soldier may tend to view crisis developments from the perspective of gaining an advantageous military position should diplomacy fail to resolve the situation. But the very actions which may advance that end may also impede crisis management efforts by *increasing time pressure* even further and by *restricting policy options.*

ALLIANCE COMMITMENTS

Policy options may also be reduced materially by initiating or increasing alliance commitments during a crisis, especially with partners who cannot be depended upon to view the resulting obligations as reciprocal. Such pledges may ultimately force a choice between two unpalatable alternatives: reducing the commitment under threat, thereby seriously eroding one's credibility in the future; or backing the promise to the hilt, with the possibility of becoming a prisoner of the ally's policies. New or expanded pledges of support to small allies may also complicate rather than facilitate the resolution of crisis situations by introducing further—and often irrelevant—issues into crisis negotiations. Fidel Castro attempted to inject such issues into Soviet-American bargaining during and immediately after the resolution of the missile crisis. It is probably fortunate that Soviet leaders, who had serious and probably justified doubts about the quality and volatility of Cuban leadership (A. and R. Wohlstetter, 1968, pp. 69–91), did not irrevocably commit Soviet policy and prestige to whatever demands may have emerged from Havana.

The American experience in Vietnam further underscores the danger of increasing commitments made under crisis conditions to weak and not wholly responsible allies.

The tragedy of British and French policies during the late 1930s is that they failed to honor their commitments to Czechoslovakia, a nation possessed of a large and well-trained army;

a powerful armaments industry; superb geographical location; and strong popular support, except among Sudeten Germans. Having assisted in the destruction of this ideal ally, Britain then undertook a frantic and poorly conceived pledge of support to Poland, called by some the most romantic and corrupt nation in Europe.

Wise parents, labor and management negotiators, and skilled diplomats know that in a conflict situation one should not abandon a previously established position under the threat of force. Perhaps an equally valuable corollary is: exercise caution in making new commitments or increasing existing ones in the heat of a crisis.

THE ADVERSARY'S OPTIONS

The danger of war is never greater than when a nation's leaders define the situation as one in which the options are reduced to a war or humiliation with a crippling loss of "face." By the end of July 1914, most leaders in Berlin, Vienna, St. Petersburg, Paris, and London had come to the conclusion that this was precisely the situation in which they found themselves. It is, on the one hand, necessary to avoid appeasing the adversary's illegitimate demands and to impress on him the dangers of pressing them; on the other, it is equally important to avoid placing the opponent in a position where large-scale violence is perceived as the least distasteful, or perhaps the sole, alternative. The task, in short, is to demonstrate to the adversary by actions and words that the adversary's self-interest can best be served in choosing the path of de-escalation. The trick, of course, is to map this path in clear terms and to make it appear as the most attractive alternative. Among the crisis management techniques which may enhance the likelihood of success are the following.

Perhaps the first prerequisite is a sensitivity to the adversary's frame of reference. To assume, as many statesmen came to believe in 1914, that only leaders of the opposing nations were free to end the crisis by taking appropriate steps is a convenient and self-serving rationalization, but it also amounts to abdicating responsibility for future developments. This is *not* to say, however, that one must agree with the opponent or appease his demands; empathy is not synonymous with sympathy. Rather, the point is that one can scarcely hope to influence others without a realistic image of the situation they find themselves in, of the hopes and fears which may motivate them, of the intra- and inter-bureaucratic pressures which may impinge on them, and of the "operational codes" which may dictate their strategies and tactics. It also pays never to forget that the opponents, too, are making choices under highly stressful conditions. Firsthand accounts of the missile crisis reveal that President Kennedy and his advisers exhibited an unusual ability to place themselves in the shoes of the men in the Kremlin.

Make every effort to slow the pace of crisis events. Intense time pressure is rarely consistent with calculated decision making.

During a crisis responsible policymakers should be in control, not only of broad strategic decisions, but also of the details of implementations. It is especially important that efforts to deescalate or slow the pace of events are not sabotaged, inadvertently or otherwise, by subordinates. In 1914 Russian and German officers effectively undermined last-minute—and at best not overly promising—efforts by the two monarchs to avoid a European war. These are by no means isolated incidents. Until his dismissal in 1951, General Douglas MacArthur repeatedly made public policy statements which were in direct conflict with Washington's diplomatic stance on the Korean War and general Far Eastern policy. In contrast to the almost unbelievable tolerance exhibited by President Truman, Secretry Acheson, and the Joint Chiefs of Staff toward MacArthur, President Kennedy and Defense Secretary McNamara maintained fairly effective control over the minutest details of strategy and tactics during the missile crisis, even in the face of the intense displeasure of Naval Chief George W. Anderson.

ATTRIBUTES OF WEAPONS

Although the distinction between "offensive" and "defensive" weapons lives on in debates about strategy and disarmament, it is not very useful for our purposes because most defensive weapons can also be used to attack. Nevertheless, it is a mistake to assume that "a weapon is a weapon." Some armaments convey such clear implications of "first strike" that they draw everyone's finger a little closer to the trigger, especially in crisis situations. The German army in 1914 did precisely this. It was widely recognized that Germany hoped to offset the disadvantages of a possible two-front war by rapid mobilizations; a quick victory over France while the ponderous Russian army was being mobilized; and, after France was defeated, a decisive deployment of German forces to the Russian front. A delay of hours, or even minutes, might make the difference between being able to retaliate and having one's military capabilities destroyed. Compressed decision time and the need for a hair-trigger on retaliatory forces thus significantly increase the probabilities of accidental war. Consider, for example, the situation of a single nuclear explosion over an American or Soviet city. Without adequate time for investigation of its causes, it might be impossible to determine whether it was the result of an accident, forerunner of an all-out attack, or some other cause. In these circumstances the pressures for immediate retaliation against the presumed attacker might become irresistible.

Conversely, invulnerable strategic forces—those which cannot be eliminated, even by the most severe attack that the enemy can mount—*may* mitigate some of the more severe time pressures attending a crisis. Knowledge that one's forces are secure reduces the motive to "shoot first and ask questions later." The temptation to launch a first strike should diminish as the certainty and probable costs of devastating retaliation increase. Equally important, when retaliatory systems are invulnerable the incentive to undertake a preemptive attack in the absence of complete information (as in the example of the explosion of unknown origin) declines as the ability to delay response increases decision time.

The speed, range, and destructive capacity of modern weapons may under some circumstances provide a potential attacker with the opportunity and temptation to destroy the adversary's military forces with a surprise attack. If one nation's leaders believe that a surprise attack will permit quick victory without much likelihood of retaliation, because the enemy nation's weapons can be destroyed before they are used, the two countries have an inherently unstable relationship. Virtually all European leaders in 1914 defined the situation as one in which great—and possibly decisive—advantages would accrue to the nation or alliance which struck the first military blow. The same belief was held by several persons during the missile crisis; fortunately, the president was not among them. Vulnerable military capabilities not only invite a possible enemy attack but, even worse, that knowledge creates immense pressures to use them before they are destroyed (A. Wohlstetter, 1959). And, of course, the adversary will realize the implications of this dilemma for his own planning: in order to forestall the possibility of a preemptive blow, the only "safe" option may be to unleash a desperate last-minute effort to blunt the other side's attack. Under these circumstances, the "conservative" strategy is to assume the worst and to act as if an attack were imminent.

Vulnerable forces greatly magnify time pressures on policy makers because they provide no incentive to delay response. Knowledge that the opponent can launch a crippling surprise attack reduces decision time and increases pressure to launch a preemptive strike at the first signal (which may turn out to be false) that such an attack is imminent. When both nations' deterrent forces are vulnerable, the situation is even less stable, as neither side can afford to delay.

27.

The Nature and Control
of Escalation*

RICHARD SMOKE

A. Introduction

[Beginning in America in the 1950s, some national security specialists and other analysts have tried to develop ideas about escalation and its companion concept, limited war.] Some analysts recognized very early (although not until later was there widespread agreement) that atomic weapons are not "just another weapon" but are qualitatively different. Nuclear weapons, even those of relatively small explosive power, are generally considered to be more like chemical and biological warfare in their strangeness and horror than they are like chemical explosives. Because they are felt to be bizarre and special, politically they *are,* no matter how limited their strictly military effects might be in some cases. Gradually it was recognized that the deliberate nonuse of nuclear weapons is the most obvious, most certain, and most important firebreak, as it came to be called, for keeping a war contained.

[In other ways as well, analysts were able to identify some aspects of how wars could be kept limited.] But for some years there was no general theoretical framework for these and related

* Reprinted by permission from Richard Smoke, *War: Controlling Escalation* (Cambridge: Harvard University Press, 1977). Copyright © 1979 by Richard Smoke. Except as otherwise indicated, brackets in this chapter are the author's.

ideas. This framework, and with it the single most significant intellectual advance in our understanding of limited warfare, was contributed at the end of the 1950s in a series of articles by Thomas C. Schelling. Gathered into a book (*The Strategy of Conflict*) in 1963 and expanded in a subsequent book (*Arms and Influence*) in 1966, Schelling's ideas now dominate the literature on limited warfare and escalation and have undoubtedly been absorbed into government thinking also, in the United States and to some extent abroad. Because of their influence, as well as their intellectual merit, they require brief summation.

The fundament of Schelling's analysis is the distinction between those aspects of action that are oriented toward gaining direct goals in a conflict and those aspects that are oriented toward "bargaining" with one's opponents over the nature of the conflict, including its "ground rules." Since explicit communication between the two sides is mostly or entirely absent, the bargaining is essentially by moves—by each party's actions. "Communication is by deed rather than by word." Hence, the mutually recognized limits in any war "are generally found by a process of tacit maneuver" (1966, p. 262).

Schelling begins his analysis with the case where a war is beginning and each side, faced with a potentially chaotic situation, is searching for a set of limits that both can agree on. He points out that "the best choice for either depends on what he expects the other to do, knowing that the other is similarly guided." Schelling calls this "the problem of coordinating expectations," and he suggests that belligerents should, and usually do, pick out salient aspects of the objective situation to highlight by their actions. "Because the bargaining tends to be tacit, there is little room for fine print." Each side picks points of uniqueness in the situation, which because they are objective and noticeable, each can reasonably hope the opponent will also notice and appreciate. "The proposals have to be simple; they must form a recognizable pattern; they must rely on conspicuous landmarks; and they must take advantage of whatever distinctions are known to appeal to both sides" (1966, p. 137).

Geographic physiognomy is the most obvious kind of saliency. Holding one's actions within an area bounded by a range of mountains, a river, or a minor political boundary clearly signals a new limit that is being offered for both sides to observe. In Korea, for instance, the United Nations conspicuously halted all operations (including air operations) at the Yalu River; the communists did not attack UN forces or their supporting logistic systems outside the Korean peninsula and its immediate air and water environs.

A saliency does not have to be geographic, however. Whether the weapons employed are nuclear or not is a particularly obvious saliency. Traditional conventions of war, and other conventions of a legal, historical, cultural, or intellectual nature, can also be used. The critical conditions establishing saliencies are, first, that they be in some sense "objective," so that both sides know that each is aware of them or can easily be made aware of them; and second, that they be in some sense discrete or discontinuous—qualitative and not matters of degree" (Schelling, 1966, p. 138).

B. The Many Meanings of Escalation

Another approach is to analyze various related images, or meanings, that escalation may have. Let us begin with two simple images of escalation that are especially frequent in general discourse about escalation and war. I shall call them the *actor image* and the *phenomenal image* of escalation. The actor image presents escalation as being a unilateral *act* of specifiable individuals and institutions, an independent and conscious decision to commit a certain kind of action and the deliberate execution of that decision. The phenomenal image presents escalation as being a natural *phenomenon* of war, a process that seems to get started and keep going on its own, partly outside the control of any participant. In other words, wars "naturally" tend to expand.

Each image has a number of implications which, if followed consistently, add up to an *implicit model* of escalation. The phenomenal model includes the concepts that escalation tends to happen automatically in war; that it is almost a kind of force; that this tendency or force is constantly present; and that it may get out of control, and indeed is likely to do so. The actor model includes the ideas that escalation is a neutral possibility, which may be decided upon and may not; that it sometimes is decided upon and carried out, and otherwise is absent; and that control is a tangential or nonproblematical issue. The phenomenal model is a continuous model, focusing on a process that works over time. A sequence of events is the paradigm case. The actor model is a discontinuous model, focusing on a decision that is made (or not made) in a particular moment. A single situation at a given point in the war is the paradigm case.

An implicit phenomenal model is commonplace in popular discussions of escalation, such as newspaper editorials and columns of opinion. Antiwar polemics nearly always rely heavily upon an implicit phenomenal model. An implicit actor model is frequently found in strategic analyses performed by military and national security specialists; it is also common in accounts written long after a war by diplomatic and military historians. During an ongoing war, polemics that urge an aggressive strategy and emphasize the prospects of victory almost always rely heavily upon an implicit actor model.

Yet the difference between the two models, if each is followed through consistently, is fundamental. In the phenomenal model, escalation is something that *happens,* in which the participants are caught up. In the actor model, escalation is something that some government unilaterally *does.*

IMAGES OF ESCALATION: IS THERE AN UPWARD DYNAMIC?

[Perhaps the most important question, buried within the complex interplay of the actor and phenomenal images, is whether escalation includes an innate upward dynamic.] Some treatments of escalation, which emphasize the actor aspect almost exclusively, suggest that there are no greater forces that favor escalation than favor deescalation. "No movement" is the natural state of a conflict. Escalation in this image is without causes. The *reasons* for making decisions to escalate will be as many and varied as the tactical situations in which escalation can appear useful.

The majority of contemporary discussions adopt the image of escalation that includes some degree of innate upward dynamic. This presupposition is not limited to discussions that heavily emphasize the phenomenal aspect of escalation but is found in more balanced treatments as well.

There are several reasons why this assumption is popular and plausible. Of course, there are a great many reasons why an upward thrust might be found in particular wars. But there seem to be six general sources for an upward dynamic that are likely to be relevant to *all* wars and to be, in fact, part of the nature of war. They do not conflict with one another but are mutually reinforcing.

The first and most obvious source of an upward dynamic is the desire to take a step that will contribute greatly to winning the war, perhaps even win it. As William Kaufmann has written, "Because of its competitive character war places a heavy premium upon the attainment of an advantage, however fleeting; and this in turn invites imitation. As the belligerents strive to gain a comparative advantage, the conflict undergoes an expansion" (1958, see Refs. pp. 477, 479).

A second general source of escalation is the desire not to lose. This is not the same thing as the desire to win but is almost equally basic. A nation trying to stave off complete defeat is likely to seize on any feasible way of escalating the war—perhaps to spin out the conflict in the hope that circumstances will change for the better, perhaps to attain some kind of stalemate, perhaps to convert a developing disaster into only a modest loss. If a way can be found to do it, a nation with declining hopes of winning may be very highly motivated to commit an escalation that promises some outcome other than a disastrous defeat.

A third source of an upward dynamic supplements the first two with an analogy drawn from poker: as the stakes rise, so does the desire to do more to win the whole pot (and so does the fear of losing the whole pot). There is a kind of escalation of the stakes—which is distinguishable from, but is one of the causes of, decisions to escalate operations. For example, after the death or maiming of millions of young men and after colossal economic costs, neither side in World War I was able to settle for the modest objectives with which it had begun. After Great Britain in World War II realized its extreme peril, it found itself escalating its means of warfare to include a punitive weapon, terror bombing of cities, which it had previously considered horrible and immoral. As the stakes rise, the costs one is willing to pay and the risks one is willing to run also tend to rise. So do the objectives one wants to set as the appropriate reward for incurring these costs and risks.

Yet the mere fact that nations by this time are warring violently tends to threaten larger stakes than were in dispute at the outbreak of hostilities. Kaufmann observes that "the interests that become jeopardized once a war starts . . . are numerous and complex, and their protection and/or enhancement may seem worth very considerable sacrifices," (Kaufmann, 1958, p. 595). In sum, belligerents' *motivation* to win, and not to lose, is a *variable* that is almost sure to rise after actual war has broken out and begun to jeopardize additional interests. It may rise still higher as the war drags on, imposing ever higher casualties and costs, and if the war escalates, threatening still greater values. Thus escalation can feed on itself: earlier escalations threaten wider and deeper interests, which heighten the motivation on both sides to win—and hence the motivation on both sides to escalate.

A fourth and related source of escalation concerns the personal motives and psychology of high-level decision makers. In wartime it is normal for decision makers to set aside other policy goals they may have entertained for their country and concentrate upon winning. Achieving victory becomes the perceived prerequisite for nearly all other policy objectives. (For example, President Lyndon Johnson in 1966 and 1967 believed that resuming his effort to create a Great Society demanded a victory in Vietnam first.) High-level decision makers and their immediate staffs may also feel that victory, or at least the clear prospect of victory, is necessary if they are not to be thrown out in the next election—or, in nondemocratic countries, in a coup or revolt. Decision makers in wartime also usually conclude that, whatever their other achievements or other goals, their place in history will be importantly determined by whether or not they won their war.

For these and other similar reason, policymaking individuals and groups tend in wartime to identify their own personal position, success, and the like with the success of their nation in the war. This conscious and unconscious identification with victory creates a psychological and political climate at the upper levels of governments that is receptive to escalation options that seem to promise a quicker and more certain victory (or a less likely or less serious defeat). Organizational and bureaucratic incentives reinforce this, for in wartime it tends to be the military services (and other agencies whose mission is victory) that move to the center of the policymaking process.

A fifth source of an intrinsic upward bias concerns the tactical or purely military requirements of war. In most war situations there will seem to be military reasons for crossing whatever salient barriers may exist, particularly if one does not try hard to be imaginative about possible enemy countermoves.

The desired military action need not seem decisive, although it may. This motive for escalation is not the same as the hope of winning. Rather, the action may simply seem (like wiping out the Cambodian sanctuaries) important if not critical, very tempting, and frustrating to forgo.

These are five rationales that seem to offer a persuasive basis for a study like this one to adopt the image of escalation as an innate tendency, a built-in upward dynamic. Adopting this image also preserves one of the original, and evidently appealing, implications of the word "escalation": an escalator, unlike a ladder, carries its riders up. Furthermore, to acknowledge this tendency provides a more significant and realistic challenge to those who seek to control escalation than to disavow most of the problem by denying any inherent upward tendency. There is a sixth rationale, though, which comprises the most intriguing, and from one point of view the most fundamental, source of escalation's upward dynamic. It is worth discussing in a little more depth.

Many discussions impute to warfare a kind of "action-reaction effect," in which an escalation by one belligerent triggers a counterescalation by the other as a reaction, which may then trigger another counterescalation by the first as its reaction, and so on. It is this reciprocal feature that gives escalation much of its complexity and that provides a compelling reason for postulating an upward dynamic. (It is reminiscent of the action-reaction effect that many specialists have thought to be one of the causes of arms races.)

Certainly escalation does not have to have a back-and-forth character. There are many historical instances of a single escalatory act by a belligerent, which went unanswered by the opponent. Indeed, there are instances of repeated escalations by the same power, all of which failed to call forth a significant response, often because of simple incapability on the part of the opponent. The Spanish-American War was like this. Once it became clear, as it very quickly did, that Spain's frantic diplomatic efforts to find European allies would come to nothing, the Americans could escalate the war as much as they pleased.

But in most situations, particularly in the contemporary world, both sides in a war retain options for escalating the conflict. Or one side may be able to appeal to a powerful ally if it is in danger of losing too heavily (as Egypt, for instance, did in the 1973 Yom Kippur War).

There are two main images of action and responses in escalation. One presents a two-step process of action and reaction—tit for tat. One belligerent escalates to achieve an advantage, whereupon the opponent counterescalates in reply. Let us call this *reciprocal escalation.*

The other main image emphasizes the improbability of stability; it posits that escalation can go on indefinitely. An original escalation triggers a reaction, which in turn leads to a counterreaction, and so on, with no clear, necessary, or definite end to the cycle. Let us call it *cyclical-sequence escalation.*

Escalation in this image is *interactive* in nature. The consequences of the original escalation and its reply create a new situation, which has two important qualities. First, it is likely to encourage additional escalations. Second, the new situation is not entirely foreseeable in advance because the consequences of different players' moves have interacted. For these reasons players are likely to underestimate how much the situation, after a few escalations back and forth, is likely to encourage still further escalation.

The essence of this image of escalation is that the action-reaction phenomenon interactively creates situations which cannot be fully calculated before embarking on the process and which typically will involve unexpected new pressures for (or unexpectedly strong pressures) for further escalation.

Another important feature of the cyclical-sequence image is its strong emphasis upon escalation's *potentially open-ended* character. This feature distinguishes it sharply from the reciprocal-escalation image. One could construct variations on the two-step theme wherein the expectation in a given case might be that escalation would go three, or four, or any small number of steps; these would be only variations on the theme, because they would still employ its essential premise—that after a specific number of events, a plateau of stability will be reached and the process will halt. The cyclical-sequence image differs sharply from this in its implication that the process may not halt, but continue indefinitely. To be sure, the cyclical-sequence image presents escalation only as *potentially* open-ended: unless the phenomenal aspect of escalation is being emphasized very heavily, there is no necessary implication that escalation must actually continue to the limit of the belligerents' capabilities. Uncertainty plays a large role in this image. The emphasis, however, is upon the probability of additional escalation.

IMAGES OF ESCALATION: STEPPED VERSUS HOMOGENEOUS

[A further significant issue is:] Does escalation proceed gradually and homogeneously, or in steps? And, if in steps, how big a step must one take to be really escalating? Some analysts restrict the meaning of escalation to steps that are very large indeed.

Toward the opposite pole is a frequently recurring image of escalation, often called gradualist or graduated escalation: escalation proceeding in a very large number of indefinitely small steps. In its logically extreme form, this image presents escalation as a homogeneous, undifferentiated process—a continuous curve with infinite gradations in the level of violence.

Much of the basis for this rather popular image may be the suspicion that escalation is dangerous precisely because it comes as the cumulative effect of many small acts, rather than as the predictable consequence of a deliberate decision. Certainly this image tends to be found in polemic antiwar speeches and literature, and in its extreme form can easily be married to an extreme phenomenal model of escalation. Somewhat paradoxically, a homogeneous image of escalation probably also tends to be the image held by many professional military officers, who often seem to have little objection to describing almost any new battlefield operation or any introduction of new weapons as an escalation.

I believe that for most analytic purposes this is also too narrow an image, and one freighted with many difficulties. It retards analysis by falsely suggesting that there is little that can be observed, pinned down, and identified. It tends to overlook the many known historical instances where a single identifiable step or set of steps had definable consequences, clearly different from the consequences of any other new battlefield action. It contradicts the decision makers' frequent perception that when escalating they are making serious, meaningful decisions of high policy. And, if it includes the idea of inevitability, it is intrinsically pessimistic with respect to controlling escalation.

[Since history provides examples of all sorts of escalation, and many gradations between, the most useful approach is to define escalation, not in terms of absolute magnitude, but contextually.] We recall that for Schelling, by no means can anything at all be an effective limit to a limited war. Rather, limits are saliencies that are objective, hence noticeable by all parties in the situation, and that are in some fashion discrete or discontinuous. For Schelling, to escalate is to cross such a saliency.

A major advantage of this criterion is that it is entirely contextual. It dispenses with any attempt to find an a priori, noncontextual size for escalations. According to circumstances, a step may or may not need to be "big" to cross a salient limit. This corresponds to a commonsense appraisal of the matter. Let us adopt this criterion. *Escalation* here will mean crossing the limits of any less than all-out war, *limits* being defined in Schelling's way. Escalation as the term is used in this book is not a homogeneous growth curve, nor a step of any foreordained magnitude, but *a step of any size that crosses a saliency.*

A useful working concept of escalation, then, has the following main features. It presents escalation as consisting in the crossing of saliencies, which are taken as defining the limits of a conflict. As a war escalates, it moves upward and outward through a pattern of saliencies that are provided situationally. What defines a saliency is that it is objective, and hence noticeable by all parties, and that it is in some way discrete or discontinuous.

The model assumes that war by its nature favors escalation. The analytically most distinctive reason for this is the potential, usually present in war, for an open-ended action-reaction sequence, where the consequences of the various steps interact to create situations that cannot be fully foreseen. Because of this potential for *cyclical-sequence escalation,* and for other important reasons that have been discussed, there is an inherent upward tendency in warfare. Escalation is not a mere possibility—something that may happen or may not, like a rainstorm over the battlefield. It is an ever present "pressure" or temptation or likelihood, something that requires more deliberate thought and action to stop and reverse than to start. It is certainly not inevitable, however, nor do we assume that an automatic, uncontrollable process leading to all-out war can be triggered easily.

[*Editor's note:* Dr. Smoke's study proceeds to analyze, for about 200 pages, three historical wars in which escalation did not occur but might have been expected (the Spanish Civil War, and the Austro-Prussian and Franco-Prussian wars) and two in which escalation did occur but well might not have (the Crimean War and the North American portion of the Seven Years' War). Historical cases from the era prior to the invention of nuclear weapons were chosen deliberately, for reasons explained in his book. The cases are studied both individually and comparatively. Extracts from some of his conclusions follow.]

C. On the Assessment of Conflicts

Two Dimensions of Escalation

Both the limits that constrain wars, and the escalations that create new and wider limits, have at least two intricately related aspects or dimensions. One is their bargaining and demonstrative aspect. Thomas Schelling (followed by many others) has shown that both the process of fixing stable limits and the process of executing controlled escalations are, in a very important way, bargaining processes. Limits that last for any time represent a tacit agreement by the belligerents on the rules of the game. Similarly a controlled escalation (to less than all-out war) represents a tacit proposal by one belligerent for new ground rules. Often a controlled escalation also represents a demonstration of will, commitment, or motivation, which is part of the bargaining and which may heighten the risk for everyone involved.

Much of the evidence collected here reconfirms this well-established view. In the escalations of the Spanish Civil War, the Crimean War, and the Seven Years' War, there is ample evidence of decision makers bargaining tactily with their opponents to find advantageous ground rules, yet constrain the fighting and forestall the much bigger wars that all recognized as possible and few desired. Many of these escalations were also executed as demonstrations of will and commitment.

Besides their bargaining aspect, limits and escalations clearly have a direct or intrinsic significance also. This includes the vital matter of the immediate military implications for each side of a particular limit or escalation. But it is by no means limited to these implications.

Latencies

One of the ways in which escalation gets out of control— one that is not always apparent—is a seemingly careful step that activates some nation's previously latent motive or interest.

A classic example is the Russian attack on the Turkish naval flotilla in Sinope Bay. Although this attack may have been within a very technical reading of what the British had previously communicated they would tolerate, the overwhelming margin of the victory was not within its spirit. By annihilating the Turkish squadron so easily and completely, the Russians activated an extremely important British security interest: general naval supremacy. The interest previously had been entirely latent. It had not been challenged or engaged by events up to that point, and neither the British nor anyone else expected it to be challenged. Their complete surprise, almost as much as their estimate of the significance of the challenge itself, accounted for the vehemence of their reaction. This is a particularly vivid example, because the interest activated here was the kind Ernest May (1962) calls *axiomatic* rather than *calculated*—that is, an interest so fundamental that it is part of the bedrock of foreign policy, not a quantity handled, and perhaps shifted up or down in value, in the day-by-day and month-by-month calculations of policymakers.

Less sudden but equally profound was the process in the early 1750s by which the latent goals of the British and French not to allow each other hegemony over the North American continent were gradually activated by the conflict over the Ohio territory. In its latent form the motive here was somewhat abstract and diffuse. But the mounting conflict in that region focused the attention of policymakers in London and Paris on the Ohio and, with the assistance of somewhat biased information from the supporting bureaucracies, led to the crystallization of the latent concerns on both sides.

A striking aspect of the five studies presented here is the number of times it was necessary to identify *failures of analysis,* as they were termed, on the part of policymakers and their staffs. Some were failures to identify the kind of factors just discussed. But a number of them represent more fundamental failures to comprehend how the world looked to others. More formally, they consisted in inattentiveness to, or outright unawareness of, the basic assumptions and presuppositions of decision makers in other capitals and their overall perspectives on the situation; their underlying goals (as opposed to immediate objectives); and their full range of options as these appeared in the context of *their* presuppositions, perspectives, and goals. Such lapses can be regarded as failures of imagination, failures of empathy, or failures of conceptualization and analysis. Since what is needed can, to a large extent, be obtained through high-quality analysis. I shall call them *conceptual failures,* a term that may have been used first in this sense by George Kennan (1960).

All of our cases include such conceptual failures, and they play a dominating role in those where escalation got out of control. During the sequence leading to the Seven Years' War, for instance, the French apparently did not appreciate what their preparations for a massive reinforcement of Canada would suggest to the English about the possible extent of French objectives. In the two wars of German unification, lapses of this kind by the Austrians and French played an essential role in their permitting, by default, the initial war contexts desired by the Prussians to emerge. During the Spanish Civil War, it was a failure of this kind that led officials in London and Paris to overlook available strategic warnings—of not one but several kinds—of the most dramatic escalation, the Italian submarine campaign.

There is an additional category: failures to *reassess* opponents' presuppositions, perspectives, and the like in the wake of an event that may have changed them.

In all these instances, the deficiency did not lie in intelligence failures in the ordinary sense: failures by working-level officers to uncover vital information, or report it upward high enough for its significance to be assessed by officials aware of "the big picture." Nor did the deficiency lie in the inevitable limitation on what governments can find out in times of crisis and war. All or nearly all the necessary information could have been available to policymakers—or could have been made available if lower-ranking officials had been appropriately queried and directed. The deficiency lay at the policymaking level itself, in inadequate conceptualization of the information at hand and in the absence of accessible information which, also because of inadequate conceptualization, was not sought out. To put it colloquially, at the highest levels the big picture wasn't big enough.

The evidence of the cases studied here is plentiful and consistent. One must conclude that *conceptual failures in this sense contribute substantially to many instances of escalation getting out of control.* Events can begin to get out of hand when one side does not adequately comprehend the other's basic *frame of reference* (as these conceptual ingredients may be termed for brevity).

And conversely, one must conclude that high attentiveness to other capitals' basic frames of reference contributes substantially to controlling escalation. The outstanding examples among the cases studied here are the Prussian performances of 1866 and 1870. The next general theme to be struck, then, is that, in controlling escalation, attentiveness to others' basic frames of reference really matters.

Not surprisingly, a number of scholars have come to similar conclusions in studying foreign policy disasters of various sorts. Many officials experienced in foreign and national security decision making also appreciate the importance of this kind of attentiveness. It is usually taken as axiomatic at the working level of state departments and foreign ministries, where officials have responsibility for just this sort of effort. At high policy-making levels, too, the need to "appreciate the other side's point of view" is an idea that usually commands policymakers' assent.

Assenting to the idea, though, is not the same as initiating a conscious, active effort to bring to light the basic frames of reference of their counterparts in other capitals. The attention that decision makers nearly always pay to their counterparts' *immediate objectives* does not substitute for this deeper conceptual understanding. And often they may not be aware of the extent of the conceptual deficiency.

[Some of the subtler questions in controlling escalation involve cognitive psychology: the role of perceptions and especially of expectations.] Officials evidently make major decisions not only on the basis of perceptions of present events and their immediate consequences but also on the basis of more general *expectations* about the future progress and outcome of the war (Expectations may be regarded as a special kind of perceptions—perceptions about the probable future.)

To illustrate this simple idea, let us take as an example an event that was extraordinarily dramatic and that in many ways made for unusually clear perceptions: the atomic bombing of August 1945. Even in this case expectations, not just immediate perceptions, played a crucial role. The Japanese policymakers' decision to surrender shortly after the bombing was not based primarily upon their perception and assessment of the sudden, complete loss of one or even two cities. It was based primarily upon their expectation that the United States would be able promptly to destroy every Japanese city in the same fashion. (In fact, the United States at the time did not have nearly enough fissionable material in hand to do this, a closely guarded secret which, if penetrated by the Japanese, might well have led to a different decision.)

With a few rare exceptions, the main significance of an escalation does not lie in its direct, tangible consequences that impact almost immediately. *The main significance of an escalation lies in its effect on the expectations of policymakers in all the nations concerned.* Escalations quickly shift the policymakers' field of expectation about the course and outcome of the war, and this will generally be more significant in subsequent decision making than the action's direct, physical results.

[It turns out to be important not to assume that different capitals hold similar expectations.] Often the fields of expectation on different sides are *not* similar; or a rough resemblance may mask important variations in particulars. For example, near the beginning of the Spanish Civil War, French policymakers, on the one hand, and German and Italian ones, on the other, each expected that their own de facto ally in Spain would win the civil war. In fact, both sides expected that their own ally would win it quickly!

This leads to a general remark. The evidence of the cases studied here suggests that policymakers tend to underestimate this dissimilarity in wartime expectations from one capital to another. They appreciate that, naturally, their opponents' objectives are radically different from their own. But the evidence suggests that policymakers tend to underestimate how much *their opponents' expectations also differ from their own.*

For instance, in the escalation sequence leading to the Seven Years' War, British and French policymakers each understood the other side's objective of controlling the Ohio region relatively early. Only much later did each understand the other's expectation that historical tends in America would "naturally" assure this control unless the opponent took violent initiatives. Only then—too late—was each able to comprehend that the other had been acting defensively all along.

It is crucial in controlling escalation that policymakers realize that in the other capitals the expectations, not just the objectives, may be radically different from their own. This can be a difference that really matters, because others are making their decisions on the basis of their own expectations. Hence the conceptual attentiveness to the frames of reference of policymakers abroad, discussed earlier, needs to include prominent attention to their expectations. Examining other's expectations, indeed, will lead one automatically toward attending to their underlying presuppositions, their basic perspectives, and other ingredients in their frame of reference.

There is no simple formula for controlling escalation. Yet if just one "quick-and-dirty" idea were to be demanded from this study, one simple rule of thumb that in practice would lead one to many of the points being made, it should probably be this: pay attention to others' expectations, not just their objectives. . . .

[As an escalation sequence continues and the stakes rise for all participants, cognitive dissonance starts to come into play.] A sense of threat and anxiety may develop among *all* high-ranking officials. The extent to which the reality-simplifying effect is invoked may or may not depend on where in the government an official is located or on his policy biases. In 1853 Lord Aberdeen, the prime minister and long an advocate of concessions to the Russians, was apparently affected by reality-simplifying about as much as the cabinet hawks like Lord Palmerston were. (Possibly more, although hawk opinion also simplified as the escalation sequence proceeded.)

This psychological effect of rising stakes is significant, partly because there is a tendency in the literature about escalation and limited war for analysts to discuss "the rising stakes" as an analytically clear and calculable process. There is an implicit suggestion that as escalation reaches a higher rung, the costs and risks being incurred are higher, naturally, but the way in which costs and risks are weighed and evaluated has not changed. To put it in the language of decision theory, although some of the numbers in the payoff matrices have gone up and are still going up, one continues to perform the probability calculations in the same way.

This is true mainly in the abstract, hypothetical world of strategic analysis. In the concrete world of actual policymaking, the progressive rise in stakes may well generate a progressive rise in feelings of threat and anxiety among decision makers. In this state of mind they cannot really contemplate all possibilities in an identical neutral spirit, as is implicitly required in formal strategic analysis. They may, as Bernard Brodie has pointed out, "yield to emotions like rage or fear" (1966, p. 119). Even if they do not simply yield to their emotions, an unconscious cognitive dissonance is created whenever they turn to options such as making a new and generous negotiating offer to the other side. The dissonance makes it more difficult to explore and weigh such possibilities carefully and creatively.

In a state of great anxiety and with a deep sense of threat, in fact, *a truly imaginative and creative approach* to the question, "What generous new offers can we make to the other side in a renewed negotiating effort?" could be so dissonant as to be psychologically almost impossible. Yet a renewed negotiating effort, and some generosity on at least some issues, might be the only thing that could control the future escalation of the conflict.

The psychological effect of rising stakes is not the only reason why a sequence of escalation cumulatively narrows policymakers' subjective fields of expectation. Another reason involves the well-known psychological process called *reinforcement*. Many researchers have pointed to a feedback process between hostile behavior and perceptions of hostility. It occurs in relations between individuals and groups as well as between nations.

Hostile behavior by one party tends to reinforce others' perception of that party as hostilely motivated, and this arouses hostility in the others. How does this work in escalation?

Consider, for the sake of clarity, an action-reaction escalation cycle beginning at a low level of violence and perhaps also involving military demonstrations and signals short of violence. At this point, policymakers on both sides still are entertaining a relatively wide range of images about plausible futures and expectations about potentially useful lines of policy.

Now one side escalates. Particularly if this escalation is not accompanied by a very visible negotiating effort, it tends to shift the perceptions of policymakers on the other side: their image of the opponent as potentially reasonable has *not* been reinforced; their image of the opponent as potentially hostile and aggressive *has* been reinforced.

If, then, the other side counterescalates in its turn, the perceptions of decision makers on the first side tend to be shifted in the same way. Particularly if the counterescalation is not accompanied by a negotiating initiative, their perceptions too are reinforced in the direction of seeing the other side as more hostile and aggressive. As the sequence of action and reaction proceeds, this cross-reinforcement continues. The effect does not have to be great at any one step for the cumulative effect over a sequence of steps to be quite significant. More and more, each side sees the other as an enemy and the conflict as an acute one.

For that matter, escalation does not need to proceed in an action-reaction cycle for reinforcement to come into play. There is also a *self-reinforcement* effect when a policy departure in one direction is not balanced by a policy departure in the contrary direction. The foregoing analysis suggests several reasons why escalation sequences result in a cumulative narrowing of decision makers' fields of expectation. There is self-reinforcement that results from a series of unbalanced policy departures. There is cross-reinforcement that results from a hostile action-reaction cycle. And there is reality-simplifying that results from deepening feelings of anxiety and threat.

As escalation continues, decision makers' subjective universes of perceptions and images become steadily narrower. The range of expectations tightens: fewer and fewer possibilities seem plausible. Policymakers begin to feel that the future is closing in on them. This sense of a closing future—the sense that the worst possibilities are the only ones to expect—then becomes its own additional source of anxiety. Policymakers, unaware of the cognitive effects being created by the sequence of events, attribute their sense of the future closing in to the enemy's actions and to his intolerable objectives—simultaneously wondering, perhaps, why the future seems to be closing in so fast. The subjective future closes in faster than one anticipates it should because it is closing in for psychological, not just objective, reasons. And as the cycle feeds on itself, the closing future is confirmed and made real by the policy decisions that are made.

References

Aronson, E. (March-April 1966). "Threat and Obedience." *Transaction* 3 : 25–27.

Birch, H. G. (1945). "Motivational Factors in Insightful Problem-Solving." *Journal of Comparative Psychology* 37 : 295–317.

Brodie, B. (1959). *Strategy in the Missile Age.* Princeton: Princeton University Press.

——— (1966). *Escalation and the Nuclear Option.* Princeton: Princeton University Press.

de Rivera, J. (1968). *The Psychological Dimension of Foreign Policy.* Columbus, OH: Merrill.

Deutsch, K. (1963). *The Nerves of Government.* NY: The Free Press.

Dinerstein, H. (rev. ed., 1962). *War and the Soviet Union.* NY: Praeger.

Haas, M. (1969). "Communication Factors in Decision-Making." *Peace Research Society (International), Papers* 12 : 65–86.

Janis, I. (1958). *Psychological Stress.* NY: Wiley.

Jervis, R. (1968). "Hypotheses on Misperception." *World Politics* 20.

Kaufmann, W. W. (1956). "Limited Warfare." In W. W. Kaufmann, ed., *Military Policy and National Security.* Princeton: Princeton University Press.

——— (1958). "The Crisis in Military Affairs." *World Politics* 10.

Kennan, G. F. (1957). *Russia, the Atom and the West.* NY: Harper and Row.

——— (1960). *Russia and the West Under Lenin and Stalin.* Boston: Little, Brown.

Khrushchev, N. (1970). *Khrushchev Remembers* (trans. and ed., S. Talbott). Boston: Little, Brown.

Kolkowicz, R. (1967). *The Soviet Military and the Communist Party.* Princeton: Princeton University Press.

Korchin, S. J. (1964). "Anxiety and Cognition." In C. Sheerer, ed., *Cognition: Theory, Research, Promise.* NY: Harper and Row.

Korchin, S. J., et al. (1957). "Visual Discrimination and the Decision Process in Anxiety." *AMA Archive of Neurology and Psychiatry* 78 : 424–38.

Lanzetta, J. T. (1955). "Group Behavior Under Stress." *Human Relations* 8 : 47–48.

Luard, E. (1967). "Conciliation and Deterrence: A Comparison of Political Strategies in the Interwar and Postwar Periods." *World Politics* 19 : 185.

May, E. R. (1962). "The Nature of Foreign Policy: The Calculated Versus the Axiomatic." *Daedalus.* (pp. not available)

McClelland, D. (1961). *The Achieving Society.* Princeton: Van Nostrand.

McLellan, D. (1968). "Dean Acheson and the Korean War." *Political Science Quarterly* 83 : 16–39.

Mosely, L. (1969). *On Borrowed Time.* NY: Random House.

Neustadt, R. E. (1970). *Alliance Politics.* NY: Columbia University Press.

Postman, L., and Bruner, J. S. (1948). "Perception Under Stress." *Psychological Review* 551 : 1322.

Rusk, D. (1963). Interview of Secretary Rusk by David Schoenbrun of CBS News. In D. Larson, *The "Cuban Crisis" of 1962.* Boston: Houghton Mifflin.

Schelling, T. C. (1963). *The Strategy of Conflict.* Cambridge: Harvard University Press.

—— (1966). *Arms and Influence.* New Haven: Yale University Press.

Smock, C. D. (1955). "The Influence of Psychological Stress on the 'Intolerance of Ambiguity'." *Journal of Abnormal and Social Psychology* 50 : 177–82.

Taylor, A. J. P. (1964). *Origins of the Second World War.* Harmondsworth: Penguin.

Wohlstetter, A. (1959). "The Delicate Balance of Terror." *Foreign Affairs* 37 : 211–34.

Wohlstetter, A., and Wohlstetter, R. (1968). "Controlling the Risks in Cuba." In L. Miller ed., *Dynamics of World Politics.* Englewood Cliffs, NJ: Prentice-Hall.

Wohlstetter, R. (1962). *Pearl Harbor: Warning and Decision.* Stanford: Stanford University Press.

Yerkes, R. M. (1934). "Modes of Behavioral Adaptation in Chimpanzee to Multiple Choice Problems." *Comparative Psychological Monographs* 10 : 1–108.

PART FIVE

PREVENTION

.

INTRODUCTION

Ralph K. White

This part of the book (Part Five) is of course the payoff. Having clarified and perhaps modified some of the prevailing assumptions about the causes of war in general and nuclear war in particular, we are now in a better position to attack frontally the question of what can be done to prevent a nuclear holocaust.

Section XI

Negotiation, Bargaining, and Mediation

Section Editor: Jeffrey Z. Rubin

INTRODUCTION

Ralph K. White

Action to prevent war can occur on two levels: the level of government decision making and the level of citizen action. In a democracy the government's decisions can be continually evaluated by the citizenry and often, in the long run, modified, but not immediately. Action on the citizen level can be immediate.

This section, Section XI, deals primarily with the government level, focusing on the practice of diplomacy. Sections XII and XIII, on changing war-related attitudes and on peace education, deal with the citizen level.

Dean G. Pruitt in Chapter 28, and also Roger Fisher and William Ury in Chapter 29, talk about the art of negotiation, which of course goes on all the time on all levels, from a father negotiating with his son about whether the son should have a bicycle to an international crisis such as the Cuban missile crisis. Pruitt, a master of the experimental literature on negotiation and also a leading contributor to that literature, reflects the experimental findings but also makes skillful use of everyday examples such as the father and the bicycle.

Fisher, an international lawyer and Director of the Harvard Negotiation Project, is at home also on the governmental level and has had immense practical experience. William Ury, a linguist, anthropologist, and Associate Director of the Harvard Negotiation Project, has served as a third party in many kinds of disputes. Together they have written the very widely known book, *Getting to YES: Negotiating Agreement Without Giving In* (1981). Chapter 29 in this volume is the first chapter of that book. In it they come to a conclusion similar to Pruitt's: be firm on basic ends and interests, but be flexible and conciliatory on means to those ends.

Jeffrey Z. Rubin, in Chapter 30, deals intensively and systematically with a particular kind of negotiation: third-party mediation. He too considers it on all levels, from marriage counseling to Henry Kissinger's shuttle diplomacy, and shows a mastery of the experimental literature comparable to Pruitt's. Since the field of negotiation, bargaining, and mediation has seen an amount of good experimentation that can be compared with the experimentation on perception summarized by Philip E. Tetlock and Charles McGuire, Jr. (Chapter 17), and since both areas are very relevant to the causes and prevention of war, this section and Section VI on perception are two of the most important sections in this volume. It should also be noted that Chapter 10 by Herbert C. Kelman on the conflict-resolution workshop is closely allied to Rubin's chapter on mediation; both represent direct interaction between parties in conflict, but with relatively detached persons playing some role in setting the tone and guiding the interaction into constructive channels. Both represent in some degree what John Burton, a specialist on conflict resolution, calls "controlled communication" (1969), though "controlled" is perhaps too strong a word for what is usually most needed, and most possible.

28.

Achieving Integrative Agreements in Negotiation*

DEAN G. PRUITT

Integrative agreements in negotiations are those that reconcile (i.e., integrate) the parties' interests and hence yield high joint benefit. They can be contrasted with *compromises*, which are reached when the parties concede along an obvious dimension to some middle ground and which usually produce lower joint benefit (Follett, 1940). Consider, for example, the story of two sisters who quarreled over an orange (Fisher and Ury, 1981). A compromise agreement was reached to split the fruit in half, whereupon one sister squeezed her portion for juice while the other used the peel from her portion in a cake. For whatever reason, they overlooked the integrative agreement of giving the first sister all the juice and the second all the peel.

Integrative agreements sometimes make use of known alternatives, whose joint value becomes apparent during the controversy. But more often they involve the development of novel alternatives. Hence, it is proper to say that they usually emerge from creative problem solving. Integrative alternatives (those that form the basis for integrative agreements) can be devised by either party acting separately, by the two of them in joint session, or by a third party such as a mediator.

* Portions of this chapter were previously published in Dean G. Pruitt, "Achieving Integrative Agreements in Negotiation," pp. 35–50, in *Negotiating in Organizations,* edited by M. H. Bazerman and R. J. Lewicki. Copyright © 1983 by Sage Publications, Inc. Reprinted by permission of Sage Publications, Inc. The chapter was prepared with support from National Science Foundation Grant BN583-09167.

In the story of the sisters, the situation had unusually high *integrative potential* in the sense of allowing the development of an agreement that totally satisfied both parties' aspirations. Not all situations are so hopeful. For example, in negotiating the price of a car, both dealer and customer usually must reduce their aspirations in order to reach agreement.

However, most situations have more integrative potential than is commonly assumed. For example, car dealers can often sweeten the deal by throwing in a radio or other accessory that costs them little but benefits their customer a lot. Hence, problem solving is often richly rewarded.

There are four main reasons for bargainers (or the mediators assisting them) to seek integrative agreements rather than compromises (Pruitt, 1981):

1. If aspirations are high and both sides are resistant to conceding, it may be impossible to resolve the conflict unless a way can be found to join the two parties' interests.
2. Integrative agreements are likely to be more stable. Compromises are often unsatisfactory to one or both parties, causing the issue to come up again at a later time.
3. Because they are mutually rewarding, integrative agreements tend to strengthen the relationship between the parties. This has a number of benefits, including facilitating problem solving in later conflicts.
4. Integrative agreements ordinarily contribute to the welfare of the broader community of which the two parties are members. For example, a firm will usually reap benefit as a whole if its departments are able to reconcile their differences creatively.

Methods for Achieving Integrative Agreements

Five methods for achieving integrative agreements can be described. These are means by which the parties' initially opposing demands can be transformed into alternatives that reconcile their interests. They can be used by a single party, both parties working together, or a third party such as a mediator. Each method involves a different way of refocusing the issues under dispute. Hence, potentially useful refocusing questions will be provided under each heading. Information that is useful for implementing each method will also be mentioned, and the methods will be listed in order of increasing difficulty of getting this information.

The methods will be illustrated by a running example concerning a husband and wife who are trying to decide where to go on a two-week vacation. The husband wants to go to the mountains, his wife to the seashore. They have considered the compromise of spending one week in each location but are hoping for something better. What approach should they take?

EXPANDING THE PIE

Some conflicts hinge on a resource shortage. Time, money, land, automobiles, or what-have-you are in short supply but in long demand. In such circumstances, integrative agreements can be devised by increasing the available resources. This is called expanding the pie. For example, our married couple might solve their problem by persuading their employers to give them four weeks of vacation so that they can take two in the mountains and two at the seashore. Another example (cited by Follett, 1940) is that of two milk companies who were vying to be first to unload cans on a platform. The controversy was resolved when somebody thought of widening the platform.

Expanding the pie is a useful formula when the parties do not find each other's demands inherently aversive but reject them only because they seem to block the attainment of their own demands; for example, when the husband rejects the seashore because it keeps him away from the mountains and the wife rejects the mountains because they deny her the pleasures of the seashore. But it is by no means a universal remedy. Expanding the pie may yield strikingly poor benefits if there are inherent costs in the other's proposal (e.g., the husband cannot stand the seashore or the wife the mountains). Other methods are better in such cases.

Expanding the pie requires no analysis of the interests underlying the parties' demands. Hence, its information requirements are slim. However, this does not mean that a solution by this method is always easy to find. There may be no resource shortage, or the shortage may not be easy to see or to remedy.

Refocusing questions that can be useful in seeking a solution by pie expansion include: How can both parties get what they want? Does the conflict hinge on a resource shortage? How can the critical resource be expanded?

NONSPECIFIC COMPENSATION

In nonspecific compensation one party gets what he or she wants, and the other is repaid in some unrelated coin. Compensation is nonspecific if it does not deal with the precise costs incurred by the other party. For example, the wife in our example might agree to go to the mountains, even though she finds them boring, if her husband promises her a fur coat. Another example would be giving an employee a bonus for working during the Christmas holidays.

Compensation usually comes from the party whose demands are granted. But it can also originate with a third party or even with the party who is compensated. An example of the latter would be an employee who pampers himself or herself by finding a nice office to work in during the Christmas holidays.

Two kinds of information are useful for devising a solution by nonspecific compensation: (1) information about what is valuable to the other party (e.g., knowledge that he or she values love, attention, or money); and (2) information about how badly the other party is hurting by making concessions. This is useful for devising adequate compensation for these concessions. If such information is not available, it may be possible to conduct an "auction" for the other party's acquiescence, changing the sort of benefit offered or raising one's offer, in trial-and-error fashion, until an acceptable formula is found.

Refocusing questions that can help locate a means of compensation include: How much is the other party hurting in conceding to me? What does the other party value that I can supply? How valuable is this to the other party?

LOGROLLING

Logrolling is possible in complex agendas where several issues are under consideration and the parties have differing priorities among these issues. Each party concedes on low-priority issues in exchange for concessions on issues of higher priority to itself. Each gets that part of its demands that it finds most important. For example, suppose that in addition to disagreeing about where to go on vacation, the wife in our example wants to go to a first-class hotel while the husband prefers an inn. If accommodations are a high-priority issue for the wife and location for the husband, they can reach a fairly integrative solution by agreeing to go to a first-class hotel in the mountains. Logrolling can be viewed as a variant of nonspecific compensation in which both parties instead of one are compensated for making concessions desired by the other.

To develop solutions by logrolling, it is useful to have information about the two parties' priorities so that exchangeable concessions can be identified. But it is not necessary to have information about the interests (e.g., the aspirations, values) underlying these priorities. Solutions by logrolling can also be developed by a process of trial and error in which one party moves systematically through a series of possible packages, keeping his or her own outcomes as high as possible, until an alternative is found that is acceptable to the other party (Kelley and Schenitzki, 1972; Pruitt and Carnevale, 1982).

Refocusing questions that can be useful for developing solutions by logrolling include: Which issues are of higher and lower priority to myself? Which issues are of higher and lower priority to the other party? Are some of my high-priority issues of low priority to the other party and vice versa?

COST CUTTING

In solutions by cost cutting, one party gets what he or she wants and the other's costs are reduced or eliminated. The result is high joint benefit, not because the first party has changed his or her demands, but because the second party suffers less. For instance, suppose that the husband in our example dislikes the beach because of the hustle and bustle. He may be quite willing to go there on vacation if his costs are cut by renting a house with a quiet inner courtyard where he can read while his wife goes out among the crowds.

Cost cutting often takes the form of *specific compensation,* in which the party who concedes receives something in return that satisfies the precise values frustrated. For example, the employee who must work through the holidays can be specifically compensated by the award of a vacation immediately after New Year's Day. Specific compensation differs from nonspecific compensation in dealing with the precise costs incurred rather than providing repayment in an unrelated coin. The costs are actually canceled out rather than being overbalanced by benefits experienced in some other realm.

Information about the nature of one of the parties' costs is, of course, helpful for developing solutions by cost cutting. This is a deeper kind of information than knowledge of that party's priorities. It involves knowing something about the interests— the values, aspirations, and standards—underlying that party's overt position.

Refocusing questions for developing solutions by cost cutting include: What costs are posed for the other party by our proposal? How can these costs be mitigated or eliminated?

BRIDGING

In bridging, neither party achieves its initial demands, but a new option is devised that satisfies the most important interests underlying those demands. For example, suppose that the husband in our vacation example is mainly interested in fishing and hunting and the wife in swimming and sunbathing. Their interests might be bridged by finding an inland resort with a lake and a beach that is close to woods and streams. Follett (1940) gives another homely example of two women reading in a library room. One wanted to open the window for ventilation; the other wanted to keep it closed so as not to catch a cold. The ultimate solution involved opening a window in the next room, which satisfied both the need for fresh air and the need to avoid a draft. Bridging entails a creative synthesis of the parties' most important interests.

Bridging typically involves a reformulation of the issue(s), based on an analysis of the underlying interests on both sides. For example, a critical turning point in our vacation example is likely to come when the initial formulation, "Shall we go to the mountains or the seashore?" is replaced by, "Where can we find fishing, hunting, swimming, and sunbathing?" This new formulation becomes the basis for constructing a search model (Simon, 1957) that is designed to help locate a novel alternative. The process of reformulation can be done by either or both parties or by a third party who is trying to help.

People who seek to develop solutions by bridging need information about the nature of the two parties' interests and their priorities among these interests. Priority information is useful because it is rare to find a solution, like opening the window in the next room of the library, that bridges all the two parties' interests. In the final agreement, higher-priority interests are served and lower-priority interests are discarded. For example, the wife who agrees to go to an inland lake may have forgone the lesser value of smelling the sea air and the husband may have forgone his preference for spectacular mountain vistas.

In the initial phase of search for a solution by bridging, the search model can include all the interests on both sides. But if this does not generate a mutually acceptable alternative, some of the lower-priority interests must be discarded from the model and the search begun anew. The result will not be an ideal solution but hopefully one that is mutually acceptable. Dropping low-priority interests in the development of a solution by bridging is similar to dropping low-priority demands in the search for a solution by logrolling. But the latter is in the realm of concrete proposals, while the former is in the realm of the interests underlying these proposals.

Refocusing questions that can be raised in search of a solution by bridging include: What are the two parties' basic interests? What are their priorities among these interests? How can the two sets of high-priority interests be reconciled?

The Analysis of Interests

Two of the methods for achieving integrative agreements that were just described almost always necessitate an analysis of interests. These are cost cutting, which usually requires that somebody (one of the parties or a mediator) understand the interests of the party whose costs are cut, and bridging, which usually requires that somebody understand both parties' interests. Useful discussions of how to gain insight into interests can be found in Fisher and Ury (1981) and Pruitt (1971), and the points made in this section are supplementary to these discussions.

Interests are commonly organized into hierarchical trees, with more basic interests underpinning more superficial ones. Hence, it is often useful to go deeper than the interests immediately underlying a party's proposals to the interests underlying these interests, or even to the interests underlying the interests underlying the interests. If one goes far enough down the tree, an interest may be located that can be easily reconciled with the opposing party's interests.

An example of an interest tree can be seen on the left in Figure 28.1. It belongs to a hypothetical boy who is trying to persuade his father to let him buy a motorcycle. At the right are listed those of the father's interests that conflict with the son's. At the top of the tree is the boy's initial proposal (buy a motorcycle), which is hopelessly opposed to his father's proposal (no motorcycle). Analysis of the boy's proposal yields a first-level underlying interest, to make noise in the neighborhood. But this is opposed to his dad's interest of maintaining peace and quiet. Further analysis of the boy's position reveals a second-level interest underlying the first level, to gain attention from the neighbors. But again this conflicts with one of his father's basic interests, to live unobtrusively. The controversy is resolved only when someone (e.g., the father, the boy, the boy's mother) discovers an even more basic interest—the boy's desire to impress important people. This discovery is helpful because there are ways of impressing important people that do not contradict the father's interests (e.g., going out for the high school soccer team). At the bottom of the boy's tree is a fourth-level interest, self-esteem. But it is unnecessary to go down this far, because the controversy can be resolved at the third level.

Analysis of the interests underlying divergent positions often reveals that the initial area of disagreement had different meanings to the two parties. While there appeared to be disagreement, there was no fundamental opposition in what they were really asking. For example, one party may be more concerned with substance, while the other cares more for appearances; one may be seeking an immediate settlement, while the other is seeking a long-term solution; and so on. Fisher and Ury (1981, p. 77) list nine other dimensions of this kind.

Golan (1976) gives an example of a controversy that was resolved when a mediator discovered that one party was seeking substance while the other was seeking appearance. A cease-fire in the Yom Kippur War found the Egyptian Third Army surrounded by Israeli forces. A dispute arose about the control of the only road available for bringing food and medicine to this army, and the two parties appeared to be at loggerheads. After a careful analysis, the mediator, Henry Kissinger, concluded that Israel wanted actual control of the road while Egypt wanted only the appearance that Israel did not control it for the sake of public relations. A bridging solution was found that involved continued Israeli control but the stationing of United Nations soldiers at checkpoints on the road so that they seemed to control it.

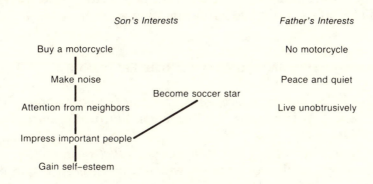

Figure 28.1
Son's interest tree in a controversy with father

The Nature of Problem Solving

Bargainers are sometimes able to "luck into" a highly integrative agreement, as for example when a good precedent has been set in a prior negotiation. But more often they must engage in problem solving, that is, seek a new option that better satisfies both parties' interests than those currently available. The more vigorous is this problem solving, the more integrative is the final agreement likely to be, up to the limits imposed by the integrative potential.

At its best, problem solving involves a joint effort to find a mutually acceptable solution. The parties or their representatives talk freely to one another. They exchange information about their interests and priorities, work together to identify the true issues dividing them, brainstorm in search of alternatives that bridge their opposing interests, and collectively evaluate these alternatives from the viewpoint of their mutual welfare.

However, a full problem-solving discussion of this kind is not always practical because of the realities of divergent interests. One or both parties may fear that such openness will deny them an opportunity for competitive gain, or give the other party such an opportunity. When these fears exist, individual problem solving is a practical alternative. A single person or small group on one side can perform all of the functions just described: seeking insight into the other party's interests, identifying the true issues, devising mutually beneficial alternatives, and evaluating these alternatives from a joint perspective. Alternatively, a third party can do the problem solving.

Steps in Creative Problem Solving

The following sequence of steps makes most sense for a bargainer who is seeking a creative solution to a controversy.

Step 1. Ask whether there really is a conflict of interest.
Perceived conflict of interest, which is what gets people into negotiation, may be *illusory*—based on a misunderstanding about the other's aspirations or a misconstrual of the meaning of the

alternatives that are readily available. If so, there is no point in continuing negotiation. Hence, the logical first step is to ask whether there really is a conflict of interest.

An example of illusory conflict can be seen in the case of a carpenter who came to look at a job in the home of the author and said that the estimate would cost fifty dollars. When asked why he expected a fee, he indicated that he feared that the author would file for an insurance payment on the basis of his estimate and then do home repairs. When assured that the homeowner was all thumbs with tools, he withdrew the request for a fee.

Step 2. Set reasonably high aspirations, based on one's basic interests, and be ready to stick to them.

Aspirations are the goals that underlie a party's demands. They are based on that party's interests, as he or she sees them; but they are not the same as interests, because they also reflect the party's assessment of the legitimacy and practicality of the various interests that might become involved in the controversy. By recommending high aspirations, we are urging bargainers to take their own interests very seriously. Bargainers who do not do so are likely to yield ground too rapidly. If one bargainer takes this approach, he or she will be exploited. If both bargainers do so, they are likely to reach agreement so fast that they overlook the integrative potential in the situation and achieve only a low-level compromise.

By urging bargainers to stick to their aspirations, we are saying that protracted conflict is often necessary for the development of truly integrative solutions (Filley, 1975). The party must maintain high aspirations even though they may at first seem incompatible with the other's aspirations. This seems paradoxical, but we hasten to add that we are not talking about heavily competitive conflict. Creative conflicts are in the category of vigorous discussions or mild arguments. Each party seeks to understand and foster its own basic interests while remaining flexible about the means for achieving these interests.

We are also not endorsing bull-headedness. Aspirations should start and remain high but not so high as to outrun any reasonable integrative potential. If they start or stay too high, time will be lost, and the other may withdraw because the conflict seems hopeless.

Step 3. Seek a way to reconcile both parties' aspirations.

Having set high aspirations, the party should seek a way to reconcile these aspirations with those held by the other. The various refocusing questions discussed earlier should be posed, and one or more search models developed in an effort to achieve the interests that both parties find most central. The success of Step 3 often depends on whether the party was in touch with his or her basic interests at Step 2, that is, whether the party's aspirations reflect the root interests that lie at the base of the interest tree underpinning his or her demands.

Step 4. Lower aspirations and search some more.

If agreement is not reached at Step 3, a choice should be made between two further options. Either party can reduce his or her own aspirations to some degree—that is, concede on or discard low-priority interests—and try again. Or, if the party's search model includes the other's aspirations as well as his or her own, the party can lower these aspirations and then, if a solution is found, try to persuade the other that such a reduction is desirable.

Step 4 should be repeated over and over again until an agreement is reached or a breakoff becomes inevitable.

BEING FIRM BUT CONCILIATORY

The strategy described in Steps 2 and 3 of the sequence just given can be described as *firm but conciliatory*. The party is advised to be firm about his or her own basic interests—yielding only when it is clear that they cannot be attained—but conciliatory toward the other in the sense of being also responsive to the other's basic interests. An important aspect of being conciliatory is to be flexible with regard to how one's own interests are achieved so as to be open to new ideas about how to reconcile them with the other's interests. Hence, this strategy can also be described as one of *firm flexibility*—the party should be firm with regard to ends but flexible with regard to the means to these ends. A quotation from Fisher and Ury (1981) captures the essence of firm flexibility: "It may not be wise to commit yourself to your position, but it is wise to commit yourself to your interests. This is the place . . . to spend your aggressive energies" (1981, p. 55).

An example of a firm but conciliatory strategy can be seen in actions taken by President John F. Kennedy in 1961 during the Second Berlin Crisis. The Russians, led by Premier Nikita Khrushchev, had been trying to end American occupation of West Berlin by threatening to sign a separate peace treaty with East Germany and buzzing planes in the Berlin Corridor. Recognizing that some concessions had to be made, Kennedy "decided to be firm on essentials but negotiate on non-essentials" (Snyder and Diesing, 1977, p. 566). In a speech on July 25, he announced three fundamental principles that ensured the integrity and continued American occupation of West Berlin. The firmness of these principles was underscored by a pledge to defend them by force and a concomitant military buildup (Pruitt and Holland, 1972). Yet Kennedy also indicated flexibility and a concern about Russian priorities by calling for negotiations to remove "actual irritants" to the Soviet Union and its allies. Two results were achieved: the building of the Berlin Wall, which can be viewed as a bridging solution that solved the problem of population loss from East Germany without disturbing American rights in or the independence of West Berlin, and eventual negotiations that put these principles in writing.

Searching for a Formula

When complex issues are under consideration, a two-step approach is often essential. The early stages of problem solving must be devoted to devising an overarching formula—a brief statement of common objectives that can serve as a roadmap to the eventual agreement. Only then is it possible to devise an efficient agenda for working out the details of the agreement (Zartman, 1977). If a formula is not developed, the proceedings are likely to get so mired down in detail that momentum will be lost and the parties will withdraw or turn to a contentious approach.

An example of a formula would be the basic agreement in the Camp David talks between Israel and Egypt. In essence, Israel agreed to withdraw from the Sinai and to begin talks about Palestinian autonomy in exchange for a peace treaty with Egypt. This formula, somewhat augmented in the Camp David accords, became the basis for many years of further negotiation to fill in the details.

The Role of Contentious Behavior

Contentious behavior consists of all those actions that are designed to elicit concessions from the other party. Examples include persuasive arguments, threats, and positional commitments.

Contentious behavior has traditionally been assumed to militate against the development of integrative agreements (Blake and Mouton, 1979; Deutsch, 1973; Walton and McKersie, 1965), and there is solid research evidence supporting this assumption (Pruitt, 1981). There are four reasons why this should be true:

(1) Contentious behavior ordinarily involves standing firm on a particular demand rather than standing firm on one's interests. Hence, it is incompatible with the flexibility about means that is an important element of successful problem solving.

(2) Contentious behavior encourages hostility toward the other by a principle of psychological consistency. This diminishes the party's willingness to contribute to the other's welfare and, hence, the party's willingness to devise or accept jointly beneficial alternatives.

(3) Contentious behavior encourages the other to feel hostile and engage in contentious behavior in return. A conflict spiral may ensue in which both parties become increasingly rigid and progressively more reluctant to take any actions that benefit the other.

(4) Contentious behavior signals to the other that the party has a win-lose orientation, calling into question the possibility

of achieving a jointly beneficial agreement. This reduces the likelihood that the other will engage in problem solving.

However, the indictment against contentious behavior has clearly been overdrawn. Under some circumstances, this behavior can actually make problem solving more likely or contribute to the effectiveness of problem solving. This can occur in two ways:

(1) It encourages the other to deal with the controversy. If present circumstances favor the other, it is often necessary for the party to employ threats to force the other to pay attention to the party's concerns. While such threats run the risk of eliciting contentious behavior in return and a conflict spiral, they are often successful at encouraging problem-solving behavior by the other party (Pruitt and Gleason, 1978), especially if presented tactfully and coupled with a promise of problem solving.

An example can be seen at the beginning of the Second Berlin Crisis, when Premier Khrushchev threatened to sign a separate peace treaty with East Germany if the status of West Berlin was not settled to his liking. At the same time, he proposed negotiation. Had he not made this threat, which was tantamount to a proposal to give East Germany control of the access routes to West Berlin, it is doubtful that the West would have accepted his offer of negotiation.

(2) It underlines the party's areas of firmness. Threats and other contentious actions are means of communication. They can be used to emphasize the rigidity of the party's high-priority interests, making it doubly clear that certain elements of the party's position are nonnegotiable. An example would be the Kennedy speech mentioned earlier in which he threatened to use force to defend the integrity of and American access to West Berlin. Concomitant troop movements added emphasis to his message. Such a message can contribute to the development of integrative solutions in two ways:

(a) It makes the other less hopeful of trying to dislodge the party from the party's areas of firmness. Instead, the party is motivated to try to devise a way to live within these constraints (i.e., to engage in problem solving).

(b) It provides information to the other about the party's interests, facilitating the other's problem-solving efforts.

In short, because of the risks associated with contentious behavior, there is a tendency to underrate its potential contribution to the development of integrative agreements. However, we must hasten to add that, in most cases, contentious behavior can make this contribution only if one is also ready to engage in problem solving. In addition to employing occasional hard tactics in an effort to underscore firmness about one's interests, one must also dramatize a concern about the other's welfare and one's flexibility about the means for achieving these interests. Otherwise, the other's response to contentious tactics will usually be limited to adoption of the same tactics for the purpose of defense or retaliation.

29.

Principled Negotiation*

ROGER FISHER and
WILLIAM URY

Whether a negotiation concerns a contract, a family quarrel, or a peace settlement among nations, people routinely engage in positional bargaining. Each side takes a position, argues for it, and makes concessions to reach a compromise. The classic example of this negotiating minuet is the haggling that takes place between a customer and the proprietor of a secondhand store (see Table 29.1)

Perhaps they will reach agreement; perhaps not.

Any method of negotiation may be fairly judged by three criteria: it should produce a wise agreement if agreement is possible; it should be efficient; and it should improve or at least not damage the relationship between the parties. (A wise agreement can be defined as one which meets the legitimate interests of each side to the extent possible, resolves conflicting interests fairly, is durable, and takes community interests into account.)

The most common form of negotiation, illustrated by the example, depends upon successively taking—and then giving up—a sequence of positions.

Taking positions, as the customer and the storekeeper do, serves some useful purposes in a negotiation. It tells the other side what you want; it provides an anchor in an uncertain and

* From *Getting to YES: How to Negotiate Agreement Without Giving In* (Boston: Houghton Mifflin, 1981).

Table 29.1.

Customer	Shopkeeper
How much do you want for this brass dish?	
	This is a beautiful antique, isn't it? I guess I could let it go for $75.
Oh come on, it's dented. I'll give you $15.	
	Really! I might consider a serious offer, but $15 certainly isn't serious.
Well, I could go to $20, but I would never pay anything like $75. Quote me a realistic price.	
	You drive a hard bargain, young lady. $60 cash, right now.
$25.	
	It cost me a great deal more than that. Make me a *serious* offer.
$37.50. That's the highest I will go.	
	Have you noticed the engraving on that dish? Next year pieces like that will be worth twice what you pay today.

pressured situation; and it can eventually produce the terms of an acceptable agreement. But those purposes can be served in other ways. And positional bargaining fails to meet the basic criteria of producing a wise agreement, efficiently and amicably.

Arguing Over Positions Produces Unwise Agreements

When negotiators bargain over positions, they tend to lock themselves into those positions. The more you clarify your position and defend it against attack, the more committed you become to it. The more you try to convince the other side of the impossibility of changing your opening position, the more difficult it becomes to do so. Your ego becomes identified with your position. You now have a new interest in "saving face"— in reconciling future action with past positions—making it less and less likely that any agreement will wisely reconcile the parties' original interests.

The danger that positional bargaining will impede a negotiation was well illustrated by the breakdown of the talks under President Kennedy for a comprehensive ban on nuclear testing. A critical question arose: How many on-site inspections per year should the Soviet Union and the United States be permitted to make within the other's territory to investigate suspicious seismic events? The Soviet Union finally agreed to three inspections. The United States insisted on no less than ten. And there the talks broke down—over positions—despite the fact that no one understood whether an "inspection" would involve one person looking around for one day, or 100 people prying indiscriminately for a month. The parties had made little attempt to design an inspection procedure that would reconcile the United States interest in verification with the desire of both countries for minimal intrusion.

As more attention is paid to positions, less attention is devoted to meeting the underlying concerns of the parties. Agreement becomes less likely. Any agreement reached may reflect a mechanical splitting of the difference between final positions rather than a solution carefully crafted to meet the legitimate interests of the parties. The result is frequently an agreement less satisfactory to each side than it could have been.

Arguing Over Positions Is Inefficient

The standard method of negotiation may produce either agreement, as with the price of a brass dish, or breakdown, as with the number of on-site inspections. In either event, the process takes a lot of time.

Bargaining over positions creates incentives that stall settlement. In positional bargaining you try to improve the chance that any settlement reached is favorable to you by starting with an extreme position, by stubbornly holding to it, by deceiving the other party as to your true views, and by making small concessions only as necessary to keep the negotiation going. The same is true for the other side. Each of those factors tends to interfere with reaching a settlement promptly. The more extreme the opening positions and the smaller the concessions, the more time and effort it will take to discover whether or not agreement is possible.

The standard minuet also requires a large number of individual decisions as each negotiator decides what to offer, what to reject, and how much of a concession to make. Decision making is difficult and time consuming at best. Where each decision not only involves yielding to the other side but will likely produce pressure to yield further, a negotiator has little incentive to move quickly. Dragging one's feet, threatening to walk out, stonewalling, and other such tactics become commonplace. They all increase the time and costs of reaching agreement as well as the risk that no agreement will be reached at all.

Arguing Over Positions Endangers an Ongoing Relationship

Positional bargaining becomes a contest of will. Each negotiator asserts what he will and won't do. The task of jointly devising an acceptable solution tends to become a battle. Each side tries through sheer willpower to force the other to change its position. "I'm not going to give in. If you want to go to the movies with me, its *The Maltese Falcon* or nothing." Anger and resentment often result as one side sees itself bending to the rigid will of the other while its own legitmate concerns go unaddressed. Positional bargaining thus strains and sometimes shatters the relationship between the parties. Commercial enterprises that have been doing buisiness together for years may part company. Neighbors may stop speaking to each other. Bitter feelings generated by one such encounter may last a lifetime.

When There Are Many Parties, Positional Bargaining Is Even Worse

Although it is convenient to discuss negotiation in terms of two persons, you and "the other side," in fact, almost every negotiation involves more than two persons. Several different parties may sit at the table, or each side may have constituents, higher-ups, boards of directors, or committees with whom they must deal. The more people involved in a negotiation, the more serious the drawbacks to positional bargaining.

If some 150 countries are negotiating, as in various United Nations conferences, positional bargaining is next to impossible. It may take all to say yes, but only one to say no. Reciprocal concessions are difficult: To whom do you make a concession? Yet even thousands of bilateral deals would still fall short of a multilateral agreement. In such situations, positional bargaining leads to the formation of coalitions among parties whose shared interests are often more symbolic than substantive. At the United Nations, such coalitions produce negotiations between "the" North and "the" South, or between "the" East and "the" West. Because there are many members in a group, it becomes more difficult to develop a common position. What is worse, once they have painfully developed and agreed upon a position, it becomes much harder to change it. Altering a position proves equally difficult when additional participants are higher authorities who, while absent from the table, must nevertheless give their approval.

Being Nice Is No Answer

Many people recognize the high costs of hard positional bargaining, particularly on the parties and their relationship. They hope to avoid them by following a more gentle style of negotiation. Instead of seeing the other side as adversaries, they prefer to see them as friends. Rather than emphasizing a goal of victory, they emphasize the necessity of reaching agreement. In a soft negotiating game the standard moves are to make offers and concessions, to trust the other side, to be friendly, and to yield as necessary to avoid confrontation.

Table 29.2 illustrates two styles of positional bargaining, soft and hard. Most people see their choice of negotiating strategies as between these two styles. Looking at the table as presenting

Table 29.2

Problem
Positional Bargaining: Which Game Should You Play?

Soft	*Hard*
Participants are friends.	Participants are adversaries.
The goal is agreement.	The goal is victory.
Make concessions to cultivate the relationship.	Demand concessions as a condition of the relationship.
Be soft on the people and the problem.	Be hard on the problem and the people.
Trust others.	Distrust others.
Change your position easily.	Dig in to your position.
Make offers.	Make threats.
Disclose your bottom line.	Mislead as to your bottom line.
Accept one-sided losses to reach agreement.	Demand one-sided gains as the price of agreement.
Search for the single answer: the one *they* will accept.	Search for the single answer: the one *you* will accept.
Insist on agreement.	Insist on your position.
Try to avoid a contest of will.	Try to win a contest of will.
Yield to pressure.	Apply pressure.

---

a choice, should you be a soft or a hard positional bargainer? Or should you perhaps follow a strategy somewhere in between?

The soft negotiating game emphasizes the importance of building and maintaining a relationship. Within families and among friends much negotiation takes place in this way. The process tends to be efficient, at least to the extent of producing results quickly. As each party competes with the other in being more generous and more forthcoming, an agreement becomes highly likely. But it may not be a wise one. The results may not be as tragic as in the O. Henry story about an impoverished couple in which the loving wife sells her hair in order to buy a handsome chain for her husband's watch, and the unknowing husband sells his watch in order to buy beautiful combs for his wife's hair. However, any negotiation primarily concerned with the relationship runs the risk of producing a sloppy agreement.

More seriously, pursuing a soft and friendly form of positional bargaining makes you vulnerable to someone who plays a hard game of positional bargaining. In positional bargaining, a hard game dominates a soft one. If the hard bargainer insists on concessions and makes threats while the soft bargainer yields in order to avoid confrontation and insists on agreement, the negotiating game is biased in favor of the hard player. The process will produce an agreement, although it may not be a wise one. It will certainly be more favorable to the hard positional bargainer than to the soft one. If your response to sustained, hard positional bargaining is soft positional bargaining, you will probably lose your shirt.

There Is an Alternative

If you do not like the choice between hard and soft positional bargaining, you can change the game.

The game of negotiation takes place at two levels. At one level, negotiation addresses the substance; at another, it focuses—usually implicitly—on the procedure for dealing with the substance. The first negotiation may concern your salary, the terms of a lease, or a price to be paid. The second negotiation concerns how you will negotiate the substantive question: by soft positional bargaining, by hard positional bargaining, or by some other method. This second negotiation is a game about a game—a "metagame." Each move you make within a negotiation is not only a move that deals with rent, salary, or other substantive questions; it also helps structure the rules of the game you are playing. Your move may serve to keep the negotiations within an ongoing mode, or it may constitute a game-changing move.

This second negotiation by and large escapes notice because it seems to occur without conscious decision. Only when dealing with someone from another country, particularly someone with a markedly different cultural background, are you likely to see the necessity of establishing some accepted process for the substantive negotiations. But whether consciously or not, you are negotiating procedural rules with every move you make, even if those moves appear exclusively concerned with substance.

The answer to the question of whether to use soft positional bargaining or hard is "neither." Change the game. At the Harvard Negotiation Project we have been developing an alternative to positional bargaining: a method of negotiation explicitly designed to produce wise outcomes efficiently and amicably. This method, called *principled negotiation* or *negotiation on the merits,* can be boiled down to four basic points.

These four points define a straightforward method of negotiation that can be used under almost any circumstance. Each point deals with a basic element of negotiation, and suggests what you should do about it.

People: Separate the people from the problem.
Interests: Focus on interests, not positions.
Options: Generate a variety of possibilities before deciding what to do.
Criteria: Insist that the result be based on some objective standard.

The first point responds to the fact that human beings are not computers. We are creatures of strong emotions who often have radically different perceptions and have difficulty communicating clearly. Emotions typically become entangled with the objective merits of the problem. Taking positions just makes this worse because people's egos become identified with their positions. Hence, before working on the substantive problem, the "people problem" should be disentangled from it and dealt with separately. Figuratively if not literally, the participants should come to see themselves as working side by side, attacking the problem, not each other. Hence the first proposition: *Separate the people from the problem.*

The second point is designed to overcome the drawback of focusing on people's stated positions when the object of a negotiation is to satisfy their underlying interests. A negotiating position often obscures what you really want. Compromising between positions is not likely to produce an agreement which will effectively take care of the human needs that led people to adopt those positions. The second basic element of the method is: *Focus on interests, not positions.*

The third point responds to the difficulty of designing optimal solutions while under pressure. Trying to decide in the presence of an adversary narrows your vision. Having a lot at stake inhibits creativity. So does searching for the one right solution.

You can offset these constraints by setting aside a designated time within which to think up a wide range of possible solutions that advance shared interests and creatively reconcile differing interests. Hence the third basic point: Before trying to reach agreement, *invent options for mutual gain.*

Where interests are directly opposed, a negotiator may be able to obtain a favorable result simply by being stubborn. That method tends to reward intransigence and produce arbitrary results. However, you can counter such a negotiator by insisting that his single say-so is not enough and that the agreement must reflect some fair standard independent of the naked will of either side. This does not mean insisting that the terms be based on the standard you select, but only that some fair standard such as market value, expert opinion, custom, or law determine the outcome. By discussing such criteria rather than what the parties are willing or unwilling to do, neither party need give in to the other; both can defer to a fair solution. Hence the fourth basic point: *Insist on objective criteria.*

The method of principled negotiation is contrasted with hard and soft positional bargaining in Table 29.3, which shows the four basic points of the method in boldface type.

The four basic propositions of principled negotiation are relevant from the time you begin to think about negotiating until the time either an agreement is reached or you decide to break off the effort. That period can be divided into three stages: analysis, planning, and discussion.

During the *analysis* stage you are simply trying to diagnose the situation—to gather information, organize it, and think about it. You will want to consider the people problems of partisan perceptions, hostile emotions, and unclear communication, as well as to identify your interests and those of the other side. You will want to note options already on the table and identify any criteria already suggested as a basis for agreement.

During the *planning* stage you deal with the same four elements a second time, both generating ideas and deciding what to do. How do you propose to handle the people problems? Of your interests, which are most important? And what are some

Table 29.3

Problem		Solution
Positional Bargaining: Which Game Should You Play?		Change the Game—Negotiate on the Merits

Soft	*Hard*	*Principled*
Participants are friends.	Participants are adversaries.	Participants are problem solvers.
The goal is agreement.	The goal is victory.	The goal is a wise outcome reached efficiently and amicably.
Make concessions to cultivate the relationship.	Demand concessions as a condition of the relationship.	**Separate the people from the problem.**
Be soft on the people and the problem.	Be hard on the problem and the people.	Be soft on the people, hard on the problem.
Trust others.	Distrust others.	Proceed independent of trust.
Change your position easily.	Dig in to your position.	**Focus on interests, not positions.**
Make offers.	Make threats.	Explore interests.
Disclose your bottom line.	Mislead as to your bottom line.	Avoid having a bottom line.
Accept one-sided losses to reach agreement.	Demand one-sided gains as the price of agreement.	**Invent options for mutual gain.**
Search for the single answer: the one *they* will accept.	Search for the single answer: the one *you* will accept.	Develop multiple options to choose from; decide later.
Insist on agreement.	Insist on your position.	**Insist on objective criteria.**
Try to avoid a contest of will.	Try to win a contest of will.	Try to reach a result based on standards independent of will.
Yield to pressure.	Apply pressure.	Reason and be open to reasons; yield to principle, not pressure.

realistic objectives? You will want to generate additional options and additional criteria for deciding among them.

Again during the *discussion* stage, when the parties communicate back and forth, looking toward agreement, the same four elements are the best subjects to discuss. Differences in perception, feelings of frustration and anger, and difficulties in communication can be acknowledged and addressed. Each side should come to understand the interests of the other. Both can then jointly generate options that are mutually advantageous and seek agreement on objective standards for resolving opposed interests.

To sum up, in contrast to positional bargaining, the principled negotiation method of focusing on basic interests, mutually satisfying options, and fair standards typically results in a *wise* agreement. The method permits you to reach a gradual consensus on a joint decision *efficiently* without all the transactional costs of digging in to positions only to have to dig yourself out of them. And separating the people from the problem allows you to deal directly and empathetically with the other negotiator as a human being, thus making possible an *amicable* agreement.

Each of the next four chapters expands on one of these four basic points. If at any point you become skeptical, you may want to skip ahead briefly and browse in the final three chapters, which respond to questions commonly raised about the method.

30.

Some Roles and Functions
of a Mediator*

JEFFREY Z. RUBIN

The Story of Wise King Solomon

One of the earliest and most dramatic illustrations of a third party's effectiveness comes from the pages of the Old Testament (1 Kings 3 : 16–28). King Solomon sat in judgment of two women, each claiming to be the mother of the same young child. As is often the case in protracted conflict, the issue in dispute was constant-sum in nature: only one of the women could be the child's true mother. Moreover, the only really acceptable outcome to the conflict was constant-sum as well; thus, apart from an awkward, and in those days untenable, shared custody arrangement or the physical division of the child at the expense of its life, there was no way to resolve the conflict other than by awarding the child to one woman rather than the other. Given that each woman claimed the proprietary right to the same child, how could the king render a wise decision?

King Solomon may well have realized that in order to resolve the issue of parentage he would have to move beyond the superficial proprietary implications of being a parent to the underlying implication of parental concern and love. Thus, although a bogus parent might claim ownership of a child as readily as the true parent, only the latter might be expected to

* Excerpts from Chapter 1 in J. Z. Rubin, ed., *Dynamics of Third Party Intervention: Kissinger in the Middle East* (New York: Praeger, 1981).

demonstrate genuine regard for the child's welfare. It was precisely by pitting parental proprietary rights against parental concern that King Solomon was able to determine the true parent. He called for a sword and commanded that the living child be divided in two, giving half to one woman and half to the other. The true mother then beseeched the king, rather than slay the child, to give it to the second woman—leading King Solomon to award the child to the first woman, its true parent.

Notice that the third party in this account, through the subtlety of his understanding of human motivation, was able to move an apparently intractable conflict to solution. By sorting out the underlying issue from its more superficial counterpart, by testing the disputants' commitment to particular positions and the basis for this commitment, and by transforming the size and scope of the issue in question, King Solomon was able to impose an arbitrated agreement that had the additional virtue of further enhancing his own reputation as a wise and just leader.

Bargaining

Once conflict has arisen between two or more parties, it is necessary that they develop integrative solutions to their dispute if they are to avoid the extreme alternatives of total domination or total withdrawal by one side. One of these alternatives, bargaining, functions at the interface of cooperative and competitive interests.

Because bargaining theory and research have been extensively reviewed elsewhere, nothing more need be said here about this important method for achieving conflict resolution. (See Chertkoff and Esser [1976], Druckman [1977], Nemeth [1972], Pruitt [1981], Pruitt and Kimmel [1977], Rubin and Brown [1975], Zartman [1977], and—in this volume—Fisher and Ury [1981].)

The second major alternative, and the focus of the present inquiry, is third-party intervention.

Some Third-Party Roles

ADVISORY VERSUS DIRECTIVE ROLES

Most third-party roles are advisory only, entailing a set of recommendations that may (but need not) be adhered to by the principals. A mediator has precisely this role, as does a conciliator provided by a court in order to intercede in a dispute between employers and employees, or a fact finder who has been selected to advise the principals about the issues in dispute. At the other end of the continuum are directive roles, in which the third party has the power to impose a particular binding agreement. An arbitrator—regardless of whether this person functions as a baseball umpire, a courtroom judge, or a conventional arbitrator in a labor-management problem—has precisely this sort of directive role in the intervention process. Lying somewhere between the extremes of mediation and arbitration are a number of other arrangements, including the procedure of "med arb," by which a third party first attempts to mediate a dispute and, if unsuccessful, goes on to impose a binding settlement.

Advisory roles clearly lack the "teeth" of enforcement; hence, one might expect such roles to be less effective than those that are more directive. To some extent this is precisely the case; directive third parties are indeed better able to elicit the concessions and impose the agreements they prefer. The issue is less clear-cut when one considers the effect of directive and advisory roles in the long run, when the heat of the dispute has passed and the third party is no longer on the scene. Here it may actually be those agreements that were reached under advisory, rather than more directive, intervention circumstances that are more likely to endure. Why? Because it may be that when disputants make concessions and reach agreement in the presence of a mediator or some other advisory third-party role, they tend to attribute their agreement, not to third-party coercion, but to their own willingness and motivation to settle the dispute. Since the disputants are likely to feel that they reached agreement not because they had to but because they chose to, they are likely to adhere to, and believe in, their agreement even when the third party no longer maintains surveillance over them. Ironically, then, although directive third-party roles may elicit speedier, more complete agreement between the principals in the short run, in the long run it may be the advisory roles that yield greater internalization of attitude change and greater endurance of any agreement reached. The most effective third-party role may thus be one in which the least necessary force and direction is applied in order to move the disputants to resolve the conflict.

CONTENT-ORIENTED VERSUS PROCESS-ORIENTED ROLES

Consider here the example of a conciliator such as a couple therapist. It is not typically the therapist's job, nor the therapist's objective, to preserve the relationship between the two people in question; indeed there may even be circumstances in which the couple is more likely to dissolve its relationship after having been in therapy than it was before. A more typical therapist role entails helping each member of a couple to understand better the way in which he or she talks and listens to the other, and how related communication skills can be improved; the degree to which the relationship is characterized by anger and mutual suspicion; some of the underlying reasons for the negative sentiment, and some techniques for managing and reducing it; and, most generally, some of the ways in which the members of the couple can learn to help themselves.

RELATIONSHIP-FACILITATING VERSUS RELATIONSHIP-INHIBITORY ROLES

Some third parties are in the business of bringing the disputants together, of reconciling differences between them, improving communication, and leaving the principals in a stronger, more durable working relationship than existed prior to the third party's intervention. Examples of such relationship-facilitating roles include those of conciliator, process-oriented mediator, and couple therapist. In general, third parties are typically presumed to occupy these sorts of facilitating roles.

On the other hand, there are also third parties whose very raison d'être is the separation of the principals, rendering unnecessary their direct interaction. By inhibiting or dampening the possibility of direct contact between the principals, these third parties have an effect similar to the conflict-preventive role described previously. A real estate broker or marriage broker, for example, by separating the principals until it has become time to conclude a contractual agreement, prevents the sort of conflict and misunderstanding that might arise were the parties to talk directly with each other. The realtor typically separates the seller from the prospective buyer, works closely with each person in an effort to convey a sense of understanding of each party's position and thereby engenders trust, bringing the parties together only after a contractual settlement (a deal) has been reached.

At another level entirely, relationship-dampening third-party roles may arise when the disputants are in the midst of an intense, protracted conflict that can only be managed by separating the parties and doing whatever is possible to terminate their direct relationship. An arbitrator in a chronic labor-management dispute, for example, accomplishes this end by removing (or accepting) control over the allocation of resources between the principals and unilaterally imposing a final settlement.

Some Third-Party Functions

MODIFICATION OF COMMUNICATION STRUCTURE

It is widely believed that if one can only get the principals in conflict to communicate with one another, thereby giving their mutual grievances a full airing, their conflict will surely resolve itself. Although it is true that communication between disputants expedites conflict resolution under many circumstances, such may not be the case in conflict-intensified relationships. Here the availability of communication channels may not only fail to generate pressures toward agreement but may actually escalate the conflict. An effectively functioning third party must know when to encourage communication between the principals and when such communication should be curtailed.

The effect of introducing communication into a deteriorating relationship was demonstrated some years ago in a classic series of laboratory studies by Morton Deutsch and Robert Krauss (Deutsch and Krauss, 1962; Krauss and Deutsch, 1966). Pairs of participants were asked to play a laboratory bargaining game known as the Acme-Bolt Trucking paradigm, the details of which need not concern us here. The ability to coerce one's bargaining adversary through the use of threat was made available to neither, to one, or to both members of a pair. The researchers discovered early in the experiment that the presence of bilateral threat potential led to the escalation of conflict, to the predominance of competitive motivation, and to poor bargaining outcomes.

Having succeeded in creating the conditions of intense conflict, Deutsch and Krauss set out to study the circumstances under which the resolution of such conflict could be facilitated through the introduction of communication channels. First, the researchers provided the bargainers with an intercom and allowed them to communicate at will about any topic they chose or, if they so wished, to say nothing at all. It was found that the introduction of such permissible communication had no effect on the bargainers' ability to reach agreement; they continued to achieve poor bargaining outcomes and failed to use the opportunity to communicate. In a subsequent experiment, Deutsch and Krauss therefore introduced compulsory communication, requiring the bargainers to say something to each other at the beginning of each turn in the game. As before, it was found that communication did little to reduce the conflict to more manageable proportions or to increase bargaining effectiveness. Interestingly, when required to communicate, the participants used the communication channel to heap abuse on each other, hurling insults, threats, and lies. Rather than facilitating the reduction of intense conflict, the introduction of compulsory communication exacerbated it.

In a third study, Krauss and Deutsch introduced an intervention that helped communication to work in the way that we would like to believe it is supposed to work. Bargainers were tutored by the experimenter in the effective use of communication; they were urged to put themselves in their adversary's shoes, to be fair, to make proposals that they believed were reasonable and acceptable for the other as well as for themselves. It was found that participants who were provided with this sort of intervention bargained more effectively and obtained higher outcomes than those who were not. So it was only when a third-party experimenter reminded the disputants how to communicate, and in effect explicitly urged them to cooperate, that they were able to use their communication channel effectively; the mere introduction of permissive or compulsory communication was not sufficient.

To summarize: A third party may be able to regulate the communication between the principals. In order for the introduction of communication to have a facilitating effect on dispute resolution, it must be paced in relation to the intensity of conflict. Whereas the introduction of full and open communication between the principals may help them to resolve a relatively low-level conflict—by allowing the parties to coordinate better the solution to a relatively easy problem—when conflict is intense or protracted, the third party may be best able to help by introducing a temporary cooling-off period. During this time the third party may choose to serve as a go-between, funneling (and occasionally filtering) information back and forth until the disputants are able and willing to address the issues in dispute through direct exchange.

SITE OPENNESS

Apart from influencing the process of communication between the disputants, a third party may be able to modify the exchange between the disputants and their respective constituencies, as well as a number of other audiences, by regulating the openness of the conflict site. Such variations in site openness are likely to affect the pressure experienced by the disputants to behave in particular ways. By selectively exposing or shielding the principals from various publics, the effective third party may be able to increase the chances of settlement.

Although they do not always have precisely this effect, constituencies typically apply pressure on their respective spokespersons to adopt a tough bargaining stance; indeed, this stance is often expected to be tougher than the spokespersons might adopt themselves were they left to their own devices. Given that disputants are in the midst of a conflict-intensified exchange, a third party may wish to isolate them from access to their respective constituencies, much as President Carter did to Prime Minister Begin and President Sadat during the 1978 meetings at the Camp David retreat. On the other hand, to the extent that the third party happens to regard the constituencies as a source of pressure toward agreement, it may be wise to selectively invite them to observe the proceedings in the conflictual arena and/or to communicate directly with the principals.

Although constituencies are apt to be the audience of greatest salience to the disputants, there are often other interested audiences whose presence and active involvement may be skillfully managed by a third party. These audiences include neutral figures, would-be allies or adversaries, and occasionally the media. As Rubin and Brown (1975) and others have documented, the effect of introducing such interested audiences is typically to increase the bargainers' need to appear competent or effective, and to avoid looking weak or foolish—in short, to save face by behaving in the "right" way.

Social psychologists have experimentally demonstrated that the presence of other people has the effect of strengthening an individual's "dominant response." Thus, if you are the sort of person who gets nervous when taking an exam, the presence of other people in the room should increase your test anxiety even further; conversely, if you are a person who likes to work under pressure, the presence of others should really get your adrenalin going and please you all the more. In like fashion, one might expect disputants' tendencies either toward intransigence or conciliation to be amplified in the presence of an interested audience.

RESOURCES

A third party may be able to modify the size of the pie over which the conflict is being waged. As Kerr (1954) has pointed out, third parties may be able to identify and promote the use of additional resources that are not immediately apparent to the principals. By soliciting additional money, land, or other tangible resources from parties that are external to the conflict, or by directly providing such resources themselves, third parties can attempt to transform a constant-sum dispute (characterized by outcomes that are acceptable to one party at the exclusion of the other) into a non-constant-sum exchange (in which mutually acceptable outcomes are possible). During Kissinger's step-by-step diplomacy in the Middle East, it was not uncommon for an apparently intractable conflict between Israel and Egypt, or Israel and Syria, to be resolved through the promised infusion of U.S. economic and military resources. More recently, Carter was able to "sweeten the kitty" during the Camp David talks by promising to build the Israelis a new airfield in the Negev Desert in return for the evacuation of the Sinai, and by promising enormous economic and military assistance to Egypt in exchange for its agreement with Israel. In some sense it can be argued that the 1978 Camp David agreement was made possible by the involuntary generosity of the American taxpayer.

IDENTIFICATION OF EXISTING ISSUES AND ALTERNATIVES

One of the most useful things a third party can do during conflict is to help the principals identify the issues in dispute. By directing their attention to the several points of agreement and disagreement, the third party can provide the disputants with accurate information about each other's preferences, expectations, and intentions with regard to the issues. Such information should help the disputants understand better which issues require considerable further work and which are close to resolution, which issues are particularly central to the conflict and which are more superficial and remote. By identifying the issues in dispute and developing an importance ordering among these issues, a third party can help the principals accurately evaluate the size and scope of their conflict.

Is it always helpful for a third party to encourage accurate evaluation of conflict intensity by the disputants? The answer, it appears, is no. Just as the introduction of communication between adversaries in a conflict-intensified relationship encourages the exchange of hostility—and may actually escalate the conflict even further than would have occurred in the absence of communication—the effectiveness of issue identification also tends to be integrally related to the amount of conflict in the disputants' relationship. Bonnie Erickson and her colleagues (1974) have found that issue identification by a third party results in more frequent settlement and in higher joint profit only when conflict is low. Under conditions of high conflict, the exact reverse is found: issue identification leads people to reach fewer agreements than they do in the absence of this procedure. When conflict is relatively small in intensity, issue identification helps the parties to zero in on the few problems that require their serious attention, while reminding them of the several points on which they are already in, or are close to, agreement. Under conditions of high conflict, issue identification by the third party serves to remind the disputants that they are in serious disagreement regarding most points, are able to see eye to eye on only a small number of issues, and that their chances of reaching a settlement are therefore negligible.

PACKAGING AND SEQUENCING OF ISSUES

It is occasionally the case that a dispute revolves around a single issue, as when two people are exclusively concerned with the division between them of a single tangible resource. Under such circumstances, there is little that a third party can do to structure the issue in new or interesting ways. More often than not, however, disputes involve multiple issues that can be packaged and ordered in ways that are likely to have a powerful impact on the number and kinds of issues that are addressed.

Given that multiple issues exist, a third party can affect the dispute resolution process by advising the principals to adopt either a holistic set (in which the multiple issues at stake are considered as an integrated unitary package) or a partitive set (in which the issues are addressed one at a time). All things considered, there is some reason to believe that a holistic approach is preferable. It has been found (Kelley, 1966) that negotiators who treat multiple issues as a package tend to have greater latitude to make concessions and trade-offs at a later time, and are less likely to make the sort of premature commitments and take the premature last stands that prolong the life of the conflict. Similarly, other laboratory research (Froman and Cohen, 1970), indicates that bargainers who are free to logroll multiple issues, by working on several at once, tend to reach more equitable agreements more rapidly than those who are required to settle the issues one at a time. The evidence from these studies and others suggests that a third party would be well advised to recommend the coupling of issues (Fisher, 1964).

Actually, as Erickson and her colleagues have demonstrated (1974), the situation turns out to be more complex. While they found that the participants in their laboratory experiment reached settlement more frequently when they were urged by a third party to adopt a holistic rather than a partitive set, these results held only when the parties negotiated under conditions of low conflict. When the conflict was high, the presence of a holistic or partitive set made no difference: subjects reached only half as many settlements as they did under conditions of low conflict, and their ability to do so was unaffected by the set they were given.

The sense of these findings is that a third party should take conflict size into account in making a recommendation for dealing with multiple issues; the integrative set that proves so effective under conditions of low conflict may be useless when conflict is high. In fact, given that a conflict is particularly intense, it may make sense for a third party to induce the disputants to address multiple issues in sequence. Assuming that these issues are of differential importance, as is likely to be the case, what order of address should the third party recommend? Should the third party advise the disputants to tackle the central problems first before moving on to more peripheral issues? Or should the reverse sequence be encouraged? Reasonable arguments can be advanced for and against either arrangement.

On the one hand, it may be argued that a third party should encourage the disputants to address the most important issue or issues near the outset of their exchange. After all, if the disputants can successfully resolve these central problems, they should have little trouble managing the more tangential issues that are considered later. Consider the example of a labor-management dispute consisting of four issues: employee wages, retirement benefits, hospitalization insurance, and vacation days. If a mediator can structure the issues in such a way that the most central issue (employee wages) is addressed first, and if this issue is resolved successfully, there is every reason to believe that solutions can be readily found for the three remaining issues. On the other hand, since it is often the case that the most important issues are also the most difficult to address, early efforts to resolve the major problems may well result in failure. Early failure, in turn, may create a climate of resistance that spills over to the more peripheral issues, making them more difficult to resolve than would have been the case had they been addressed first.

The argument in support of a third-party recommendation that less central issues be tackled first seems quite compelling. These lesser issues are more likely to be resolved successfully, and may help to establish the climate of goodwill, cooperativeness, and confidence that is necessary if more knotty problems are to be addressed effectively at a later time. Surely Carter was aware of this when he advised or encouraged the parties at Camp David to reach a bilateral agreement, and to defer the more central problems in the Middle East till later. Like Kissinger during the 1973–75 disengagement talks, Carter hoped to generate sufficient momentum at Camp David to keep a proliferating peace process in motion.

Unfortunately, the virtues of a third party addressing the easy issues first are offset by several potential difficulties. First, reaching agreement too early on tangential issues may reduce the possibility of later trade-offs on the more central and difficult problems. This is so because the less central issues tend to be easy to resolve, offering each side the possibility of making concessions at little cost to oneself, and making it possible to offer the other side the sweetener that may be necessary to reach a final, integrated settlement. Second, there is always the possibility that the disputants, for one reason or another, will fail to reach agreement on the peripheral issues, in which case there is very little hope for movement on the more central problems. Finally, and perhaps of greatest relevance to the Camp David illustration, it may be that, in addition to generating momentum, the disputants' successful management of easy issues also tends to generate an illusory sense of control over the conflict, thereby making subsequent setbacks all the more disappointing and infuriating and damaging the chances of an enduring settlement. The risk of Camp David is that the principals may have collectively generated the mirage of peace in the Middle East, only to discover that the really central issues—the fate of Jerusalem, the West Bank, and Gaza—not only failed to be addressed but actually seemed more difficult to tackle than ever before.

FRACTIONATION

A third party may attempt to break a conflictual impasse by dividing large, all-encompassing issues into smaller, more manageable pieces that were not previously apparent to the disputants. This technique, known as conflict fractionation, has been described in detail by Roger Fisher (1964), and serves the important function of encouraging concession making without loss of face. The concessions that each side was unwilling to make with respect to a monolithic issue may now be made more readily in relation to a series of smaller issues in which the disputants are likely to have far less investment. The history of United States mediation in the Middle East is dotted with instances of conflict fractionation, as efforts have been repeatedly made to gain a toehold on the peace process by developing issues over which the parties can agree.

Yet another example of the role of fractionation in the resolution of conflict is the 1962 Cuban missile crisis, in which the United States and the Soviet Union were engaged in an eyeball-to-eyeball confrontation with very little hope of escape. The solution that eventually evolved, allowing both superpowers to end the conflict without loss of face, did so because the monolithic issue of Soviet-American supremacy was successfully transformed by the principals into subissues that included United States assurances against the invasion of Cuba and Soviet assurances to destroy and withdraw all nuclear missiles and sites in Cuba, as well as an important bargaining issue: a United States promise to withdraw archaic and outmoded missiles in Turkey that it planned to withdraw even before the crisis arose.

SUPERORDINATE GOALS

A second important third-party technique involves the introduction of new goals and objectives that transcend the disputants' conflict, and are of shared concern to both sides. The effect of a third party's introduction of such superordinate goals is to transform, at least temporarily, a conflictual relationship into an exchange that requires cooperation if the shared objective is to be met. If only humanity were threatened by an invasion of aliens from another planet, it has been argued, the nations of the world would gather together to pool their resources in the face of this shared threat, and wars would presumably cease. The underlying principle, of course, is that disputants have both cooperative and competitive motives with regard to each other, and that the cooperative concern may be accentuated by introducing a transcendent objective that is impossible for either party to achieve alone (Sherif and Sherif, 1969). As a mediator in the Middle East for over a decade, the United States government has no doubt repeatedly reminded the regional protagonists that they are bonded together, not only by conflict, but also by a set of shared external concerns, including a harsh climate, economic woes, and a number of potentially hostile neighbors.

Superseding or Circumventing Commitments

Third, it is often true that conflictual impasses are accompanied by statements of overcommitment by the principals to a belligerent or intransigent course of action; such commitments are likely to seriously impede subsequent efforts to reach agreement. Pruitt (1981) has pointed out that under these circumstances a third party may be able to move the disputants out of the commitment trap in one of two major ways: (1) by proposing a decommitting formula, a new definition of a situation that changes it in ways that supersede the commitment; (2) by attempting to circumvent the commitment in one of several ways. One of the most important techniques for circumvention is the use of communication back channels, conduits for communication that exist behind the scenes, away from public view. Throughout the Cuban missile crisis, even during the moments of most heated public exchange and most vitriolic public commitment to conflict escalation, representatives for the United States and the Soviet Union continued to meet informally in the fine restaurants of Washington, D.C., in order to hammer out an acceptable agreement.

Concession Making Without Loss of Face

Numerous theorists have observed that people in conflict tend to have accentuated concerns with the image of strength, competence, honor and wisdom that they convey to their adversary and to various constituents, as well as with the image they have of themselves. Given the importance that disputants attach to saving face in the eyes of salient others and themselves, the presence or anticipated involvement of a third party provides a socially appropriate mechanism for managing such concerns. Thus, a concession that one was unwilling to make before lest it cast doubt on one's strength and resolve may now be made in the belief that it was done at the behest of a third party. The disputants can reason that they, as well as their adversary, have agreed to make a concession, not because they had to (i.e., because their adversary forced them to do so), but rather because they chose to (i.e., because the third party was seen as wanting or expecting such behavior). A concession that was taken as a sign of personal weakness before may now even be seen as a sign of personal strength, to the extent that it is viewed as the product of the moral determination to do the right thing, to bite the bullet, if necessary, and make a concession simply because the third party has asked one to do so. Moreover, if concession making subsequently leads to a mutually satisfactory agreement, the disputants can assume credit for their success; if it leads to exploitation at the hands of one's adversary, the disputants can blame the third party. In either case, concessions can now be made without loss of face.

It has been argued thus far that, almost by virtue of being a presence on the conflictual scene, a third party may reduce the disputants' concerns with loss of face and increase their motivation to work toward agreement. In addition, a third party may be able to deflect face-maintenance concerns onto his or her shoulders by taking a more active intervention role. Thus, by serving as a go-between who conveys offers back and forth between the principals—as President Carter's subordinates allegedly did at Camp David—a third party can prevent a face-to-face confrontation and all that it implies. Similarly, a third party may be able to encourage the disputants to make concessions that are labeled exploratory. The effect of such feelers, made at the third party's behest, is to encourage the disputants to test the waters for possibilities of compromise without committing them to a course of action that may invite exploitation.

TRUST

In order for the principals to be mutually motivated to reach agreement, they must be willing to trust both the third party and each other. The third party can engender trust by behaving in clearly trustworthy ways; that is, by personifying norms of fairness and impartiality and by never making commitments to the disputants unless they can be honored. Kenneth Kressel (1971) has reported that labor mediators list gaining the trust and confidence of the disputants as their single most important task.

The situation with respect to the disputants' trust of each other is considerably more complex. After all, the principals are in the midst of conflict, and the services of a third party have been deemed necessary at least partially because the parties are unable or unwilling to trust each other. A skilled third party must therefore be able to move the disputants away from a position of shared suspicion and hostility, in the direction of increased goodwill, tolerance, and understanding.

One of the things a third party can do in this regard is to teach the disputants to attend to those areas and issues for which their interests are convergent rather than divergent. For example, by requiring that any communication between the principals be prefaced with a statement regarding actual or potential areas of overlap, or insisting that points of disagreement be cast in as positive a light as possible, a third party may be able to encourage the disputants to focus on some of the desirable facets of their relationship.

IRRATIONALITY

The disputants will not be motivated to reach agreement so long as they harbor irrational feelings, particularly anger, toward each other. One of the things a third party can do to address this problem is to encourage the principals to vent their feelings, preferably not in the presence of the other person (Kerr, 1954). A second, related possibility is for the third party to volunteer to be the target for the disputants' angry displays, thereby deflecting this anger away from the adversary. Pruitt (1981) points out that a third party in such a role may have a function analogous to a psychotherapist dealing with negative transference; the therapist serves as a substitute target for the client's anger and emotion, allowing the client to experience catharsis and to adopt a more realistic outlook. Pruitt has pointed out that Kissinger performed this function in his dealings with the principals in the Middle East, particularly Israeli Prime Minister Golda Meir. A final technique for reducing irrationality, also used rather extensively and well by Kissinger, involves the timely injection of humor. A third party may be able to engender greater trust and greater distance from the negative climate of the dispute by poking gentle fun at the conflict, at the seriousness with which it is taken by all concerned, and at the third party's own role and input.

AUTONOMY

In order for the disputants to be genuinely motivated to reach agreement, a third party must acknowledge, and must help the principals to understand, the importance of their autonomy: it is their set of decisions to make and their dispute to resolve. All too often, scholars and researchers interested in the intervention process have made the assumption that disputants welcome outside intervention, that they view themselves as victims awaiting rescue by a white knight on a speeding charger. Perhaps they do not. Perhaps people in conflict very much want to find the solution to their shared problems without the intrusion of an outsider. If so, then it becomes increasingly important that an engaged third party be sensitive to the autonomy needs of the disputants and have sufficient insight to understand that the interests of the parties may best be served with the help of a catalyst rather than a messiah. To this end it is essential that a third party be able to judge when and for how long to intervene in a dispute, and when to withdraw. The best third party may be the one who is rendered obsolete and unnecessary by the quality of his or her intervention.

References

Blake, R. R., and Mouton, J. S. (1979). "Intergroup Problem Solving in Organizations: From Theory to Practice." In W. C. Austin and S. Worchel, eds., *The Social Psychology of Intergroup Relations.* Monterey, CA: Brooks/Cole.

Brown, B. R. (1968). "The Effects of Needs to Maintain Face on Interpersonal Bargaining." *Journal of Experimental Social Psychology* 4 : 107–22.

——— (1970). "Face-Saving Following Experimentally Induced Embarrassment." *Journal of Experimental Social Psychology* 6 : 225–71.

Burton, J. (1969). *Conflict and Communication: The Use of Controlled Communication in International Relations.* London: Macmillan, 1969.

Chertkoff, J., and Esser, J. (1976). "A Review of Experiments in Explicit Bargaining." *Journal of Experimental Social Psychology* 12 : 464–86.

Deutsch, M. (1973). *The Resolution of Conflict: Constructive and Destructive Processes.* New Haven: Yale University Press.

Deutsch, M., and Krauss, R. N. (1962). "Studies of Interpersonal Bargaining." *Journal of Conflict Resolution* 6 : 52–76.

Druckman, D. (1977). *Negotiations: Social-Psychological Perspectives.* Beverly Hills, CA: Sage.

Erickson, B.; Holmes, J. G.; Frey, R.; Walker, L.; and Thibaut, J. (1974). "Functions of a Third Party in the Resolution of Conflict: The Role of a Judge in Pretrial Conferences." *Journal of Personality and Social Psychology* 30 : 293–306.

Filley, A. C. (1975). *Interpersonal Conflict Resolution.* Glenview, IL: Scott, Foresman.

Fisher, R. (1964). "Fractionating Conflict." In R. Fisher, ed., *International Conflict and Behavioral Science: The Craigville Papers.* NY: Basic Books.

——— (1978). *International Mediation: A Working Guide.* NY: International Peace Academy.

Fisher, R., and Ury, W. (1981). *Getting to YES.* Boston: Houghton Mifflin.

Follett, M. P. (1940). "Constructive Conflict." In H. C. Metcalf and L. Urwick, eds., *Dynamic Administration: The Collected Papers of Mary Parker Follett.* NY: Harper and Row.

Froman, L. A., Jr., and Cohen, M. D. (1970). "Compromise and Logroll: Comparing the Efficiency of Two Bargaining Processes." *Behavioral Science* 15 : 180–83.

Golan, M. (1976). *The Secret Conversations of Henry Kissinger: Step-by-Step Diplomacy in the Middle East.* NY: Quadrangle.

Iklé, F. C. (1964). *How Nations Negotiate.* NY: Harper and Row.

Kelley, H. H. (1966). "A Classroom Study of the Dilemmas in Interpersonal Negotiations." In K. Archibald, ed., *Strategic Interaction and Conflict: Original Papers and Discussion.* Berkeley, CA: Institute of International Studies.

Kelley, H. H., and Schenitzki, D. P. (1972). "Bargaining." In C. G. McClintock, ed., *Experimental Social Psychology.* NY: Holt, Rinehart and Winston.

Kerr, C. (1954). "Industrial Conflict and Its Mediation." *American Journal of Sociology* 60 : 230–45.

Krauss, R. N., and Deutsch, M. (1966). "Communication in Interpersonal Bargaining." *Journal of Personality and Social Psychology* 4 : 572–77.

Kressel, K. (1971). "Labor Mediation: An Exploratory Survey." Unpublished manuscript. Teachers College, Columbia University.

Nemeth, C. (1972). "A Critical Analysis of Research Utilizing the Prisoner's Dilemma for the Study of Bargaining." In L. Berkowitz, ed., *Advances in Experimental Social Psychology,* Vol. 6. NY: Academic Press.

Pruitt, D. G. (1971). "Indirect Communication and the Search for Agreement in Negotiation." *Journal of Applied Social Psychology* 1 : 205–39.

——— (1981). *Negotiation Behavior.* NY: Academic Press.

Pruitt, D. G., and Carnevale, P. J. D. (1982). "The Development of Integrative Agreements." In V. J. Derlega and J. Grzelak, eds., *Cooperation and Helping Behavior.* NY: Academic Press.

Pruitt, D. G., and Gleason, J. M. (1978). "Threat Capacity and the Choice Between Independence and Interdependence." *Personality and Social Psychology Bulletin* 4 : 252–55.

Pruitt, D. G., and Holland, J. (1972). *Settlement in the Berlin Crisis, 1958–1962.* Special Study No. 18 of the Council on International Studies, State University of New York at Buffalo.

Pruitt, D. G., and Kimmel, M. J. (1977). "Twenty Years of Exper-
    imental Gaming: Critique, Synthesis, and Suggestions for the
    Future." *Annual Review of Psychology* 28 : 363–92.
Rubin, J. Z., and Brown, B. R. (1975). *The Social Psychology of
    Bargaining and Negotiation.* NY: Academic Press.
Schelling, T. C. (1960). *The Strategy of Conflict.* Cambridge: Harvard
    University Press.
Sherif, M., and Sherif, C. W. (1969). *Social Psychology.* NY: Harper
    and Row.
Simon, H. A. (1957). *Models of Man: Social and Rational.* NY:
    Wiley.
Snyder, G. H., and Diesing, P. (1977). *Conflict Among Nations.*
    Princeton: Princeton University Press.
Touval, S. (1975). "Biased Intermediaries: Theoretical and Historical
    Considerations." *Jerusalem Journal of International Relations*
    1 : 51–69.
Walton, R. E. (1969). *International Peacemaking: Confrontations and
    Third-Party Consultation.* Reading, MA: Addison-Wesley.
Walton, R. E., and McKersie, R. B. (1965). *A Behaviorial Theory
    of Labor Negotiations: An Analysis of A Social Interaction System.*
    NY: McGraw-Hill.
Young, O. R. (1967). *The Intermediaries: Third Parties in Interna-
    tional Crises.* Princeton: Princeton University Press.
Zartman, I. W. (1977). "Negotiations as a Joint Decision-Making
    Process." *Journal of Conflict Resolution* 21 : 619–38. Reprinted
    in I. W. Zartman, ed. (1978). *The Negotiation Process.* Beverly
    Hills, CA: Sage.

SECTION XII

Changing War-Related Attitudes

SECTION EDITOR: SEYMOUR FESHBACH

INTRODUCTION AND HIGHLIGHTS OF THE LITERATURE

Seymour Feshbach

The problem of attitude change has long been of interest to behavioral scientists, ranging from studies of "propaganda" in the World War II period (Lasswell and Casey, 1946), to experimental efforts to modify social prejudice (Smith, 1943), to programs designed to modify health-related attitudes (Leventhal and Watts, 1966), to basic research investigating the processes mediating attitude change (Hovland, Janis, and Kelley, 1953). There have been, perhaps surprisingly, rather few studies directly concerned with the modification of attitudes toward war or its causes. However, the research literature on attitude change even where the target of the attitude may be smoking or a particular social policy does address issues of relevance to the question of changing attitudes toward armament, disarmament, and other war-related actions.

Especially germane to the effort to engage the public in discussions of nuclear arms policies and to modify attitudes toward nuclear conflict has been a body of research bearing on the use of anxiety-arousing appeals. These appeals are communications that focus on the threatening consequences of persisting in some current behavior pattern (e.g., smoking) or of not adopting some recommended practice (e.g., receiving a complete medical examination once a year). They motivate the respondent through fright. They employ, as it were, a "scare" tactic (without any implication of distortion or misrepresentation). This research literature provides us with important guides as to how nuclear armament issues might be most effectively communicated.

The question arises about how effective efforts are to modify attitudes to nuclear armament policies that graphically depict and focus on the horrible consequences of a nuclear conflict: Do such kinds of appeals risk a backlash? Are people likely to become so frightened and upset that they are unable to take constructive action and prefer to avoid even thinking about the topic? Indeed, one does not have to use threatening appeals to elicit anxiety about nuclear warfare. Merely raising the topic of nuclear conflict can, in itself, be anxiety arousing, much as many individuals find it difficult to discuss cancer without feeling anxious and upset. Thus, it is helpful to consider the research literature on threat communications from the perspective of anxiety-eliciting topics as well as anxiety-eliciting appeals.

The research literature on threat appeals dates back some thirty years, to the study by Janis and Feshbach (1953). Later experimentation (e.g., Leventhal, Singer, and Jones, 1965; Rogers and Mewborn, 1976) expands and refines our understanding of the conditions determining when the arousal of fear is effective or ineffective in eliciting changes in beliefs, attitudes, and practices. The original Janis and Feshbach experiment was designed to investigate the possibility that the use of fear appeals in persuasive communications might have adverse effects resulting from the same kinds of defensive reactions that have been observed in clinical studies of clients' responses to threatening communications in psychotherapeutic situations. Such defensive reactions include disturbances in attention, manifestations of aggression, and motivated avoidance of the thematic content. These reactions, when elicited by a communication that is intended to change the attitudes and behavior of the respondent, are likely to interfere with the persuasive goal just as they interfere with therapeutic goals.

The particular area that Janis and Feshbach attempted to influence entailed dental hygiene beliefs, attitudes, and practices. A fifteen-minute illustrated lecture was prepared in three different forms, each of which contained the same essential information about causes of tooth decay and the same series of recommendations concerning oral hygiene prctices. The three forms differed only with respect to the amount of fear-arousing material presented. The *strong fear* appeal emphasized the painful consequences of tooth decay, diseased gums, and other dangers that can result from improper dental hygiene; the *moderate fear* appeal described the dangers in a milder and more factual manner; and the *minimal fear* appeal rarely alluded to the consequences of tooth neglect. High school freshmen were randomly exposed to one of these three appeals or to a control communication that dealt with a completely different topic.

Measures of the immediate effect of the communications indicated that the appeals elicited differing amounts of anxiety corresponding to the experimental intent. All three appeals were equally effective with regard to the amount of information imparted, and the strong appeal elicited ambivalence—students finding it the most interesting but also the most upsetting. Measures administered a week after the presentations assessed changes in dental hygiene practices. The greatest amount of conformity to recommended practices was produced by the communication that contained the least amount of fear-arousing material. The strong fear appeal group not only showed reliably less change than the minimal fear group but did not differ significantly from the control group. In addition, the respondents were asked to indicate their degree of agreement or disagreement with a countercommunication that contradicted a key persuasive recommendation that had been made the previous week. The minimal appeal proved to be the most effective in producing resistance to the counterpropaganda.

The ineffectiveness in this experiment of the strong fear communication suggested the hypothesis that "when fear is strongly aroused but is not fully relieved by the reassurances contained in a mass communication, the audience will become motivated to ignore or minimize the importance of the threat" (Janis and Feshbach, 1953, p. 90).

Subsequent research has yielded conflicting findings regarding the status of this hypothesis. While there have been some studies in which strong threat appeals have been found to be ineffective, there have been a number in which—in certain experimental conditions—strong threat communications proved to be significantly more persuasive than less threatening appeals. Extensive research in this area has been carried out by Howard Leventhal and his collaborators. One of their reports, by Leventhal, Singer, and Jones (1965), is briefly summarized below. An outstanding article by Rogers and Mewborn (1976) is presented in somewhat condensed form (as Chapter 34). Both offer alternative models to the defensive hypothesis proposed by Janis and Feshbach (1953).

Perhaps most germane to the question of communications designed to change attitudes toward nuclear armament policies, the subsequent research provides theory and data that delineate the conditions under which highly threatening persuasive efforts are likely to be counterproductive and the conditions under which they are likely to facilitate attitude and behavior change.

The experiment of Leventhal, Singer, and Jones, conducted with fifty-nine Yale undergraduate students, explored the effectiveness of a high-fear and a low-fear situation in getting them to take a tetanus shot. There was no significant difference in the amount of action resulting from those two conditions. However, there was a significant difference ($p < .01$) in favor of those who were given clear, specific instructions as to where to go and how to get the tetanus shot. Apparently in this case clear instructions were more important in inducing action than the amount of fear. It was also apparent, though, that *some* fear was necessary in order to get action, since in another group of thirty students, given only the clear suggestions for action but with no fear arousal at all, not one went to get a shot.

Another experiment with some direct relevance to nuclear war is "The Effects of Personal and Shared Threats upon Social Prejudice" (Feshbach and Singer, 1957). It provides clear evidence that threats to one's own *personal* welfare—marriage, mental health, fire, and accident—tend to increase expressions of social prejudice in the California E scale, along with some evidence that threats perceived as *shared* with others—flood, hurricane—may have the opposite effect. (An atomic war threat, though one might expect it to be viewed as a shared threat, did not have the same effect on social prejudice, but that finding was not statistically significant.)

31.

Fear Appeals and Attitude Change: Effects of a Threat's Noxiousness, Probability of Occurrence, and the Efficacy of Coping Responses*

**RONALD W. ROGERS and
C. RONALD MEWBORN**

In one of the earliest theoretical analyses of fear arousal and persuasion (Hovland, Janis, and Kelley, 1953), fear appeals were characterized as communications describing the unfavorable consequences that might result from failure to adopt the communicator's recommendations. This definition was sufficiently sweeping to allow fear-arousing communications to be operationalized in a variety of ways. For example, fear has been manipulated in some studies by presenting information on the amount of bodily injury *and* the likelihood of exposure at each level of the manipulation (e.g., Chu, 1966), by omitting the latter information at one level of the manipulation (e.g., Janis and Feshbach, 1953), and by omitting the latter information entirely (e.g., Rogers and Thistlethwaite, 1970).

If studies have varied different types of communication content, then it would be difficult to compare experiments and to

* Taken from the *Journal of Personality and Social Psychology* 34 : 54–67. Copyright 1976 by the American Psychological Association. Adapted by permission of the publisher and author.

determine the communication variables producing the theoretically relevant changes in attitudes. We believe that conceptualizations of fear appeals have been too global and that they now must be refined if more precise and unequivocal relations are to be generated. An important conceptual and empirical task is to identify the effective content variables and their associated mediational processes. Therefore, the major purpose of the present series of three experiments was to investigate some of the more important components of a fear appeal.

Rogers (1975) has proposed that an expectancy model, which includes all of the factors of concern to investigators on fear communication and to workers with the health belief model (e.g., Hochbaum, 1958), be applied to the fear communication problem in a more systematic manner. The three most crucial variables in a fear appeal are (a) the magnitude of noxiousness of a depicted event, (b) the conditional probability that the event will occur provided no adaptive activity is performed, and (c) the effectiveness of a coping response that might avert the noxious event.

Since the theory to be investigated, termed protection motivation, has been presented in detail elsewhere (see Rogers, 1975), only the most salient features are reviewed here. It is assumed that each of the three components of a fear appeal initiates a corresponding cognitive mediating process. Each of these processes appraises communication information about (a) noxiousness, (b) probability, or (c) efficacy by placing each stimulus on dimensions of (a) appraised severity of the depicted event, (b) expectancy of exposure to the event, or (c) belief in the efficacy of the recommended coping response, respectively. It will be taken as a working hypothesis that these cognitive processes are independent.

It should be noted that appraised severity is a cognitive mediator distinct from fear. This position is similar to Leventhal's (1970) important distinction between danger and fear control processes. Most important, as Leventhal noted, the fear appeal literature strongly suggests that cognitive processes are more important than emotional ones in mediating attitude change. Thus, protection motivation theory might be viewed as differentiating Leventhal's "danger control" process into three cognitive mediational constructs specifically linked to antecedent communication stimuli in a fear appeal.

The purpose of the present series of experiments was to test the utility of protection motivation theory by factorially manipulating the three communication variables and investigating their effects upon attitudes toward health dangers that produce incalculable, yet preventable, human suffering: lung cancer, automobile injuries, and venereal disease.

Method

DESIGN AND SUBJECTS

Separate experiments were performed on each of three health topics: cigarette smoking, safe driving, and venereal diseases (gonorrhea and syphilis). Each of the three experiments employed a $2 \times 2 \times 2$ factorial design with three between-subjects manipulations: high versus low magnitude of noxiousness of the depicted event, high versus low probability of that event's occurrence, and high versus low efficacy of recommended coping responses.

Subjects were 176 students enrolled in an elementary psychology course who participated to satisfy a course requirement. Of those, 64 served in the venereal disease study, 72 in the driving study, and 40 in the smoking study. Students could only participate in one study.

PROCEDURE

Subjects were run in groups ranging from four to eight members, and each group was randomly assigned to one of the magnitude of noxiousness conditions. Within each of these conditions, each student was randomly assigned to one of the probability of occurrence and efficacy of response conditions. Each experiment was presented as part of a project seeking college students' evaluations of public health programs.

STIMULUS MATERIALS

The low-noxiousness movie sequence for the smoking study depicts the case history of a man with lung cancer, portraying his discovery of his condition, an interview with his physician and a surgeon, and the surgical preparations for removing his lung. The high-noxiousness film condition consisted of the same film plus a five-minute presentation of the operation for removing his lung.

In the study on driving, the low-noxiousness film depicts controlled collisions using remotely operated cars with anthropometric dummies seated in them. The high-noxiousness film portrays the gory aftermath of fatal collisions.

The film on venereal disease selected for the low-noxiousness condition demonstrates the laboratory procedure for performing a serum test for venereal disease. No diseased tissue is shown. The high-noxiousness film depicts the surgical procedures used to remove diseased tissue from reproductive organs that had been destroyed by a venereal disease.

In each of the three experiments, the probability of occurrence and efficacy of response variables were manipulated by using written messages of approximately equal length. For example, in the smoking study, the high-probability essay would present a persuasive case, supported by logical arguments and descriptive statistics, that if one smokes cigarettes, there is a very high chance of contracting lung cancer. The low-probability essay would argue that although smoking can cause lung cancer, the chances of any given smoker actually developing cancer are very small. The high-efficacy essay would urge that the recommended preventative practices were extremely effective methods of avoiding the threatened event. The low-efficacy message provided little reassurance that the available coping response was efficacious. Within each experiment, both efficacy messages would mention the same recommendations.

DEPENDENT VARIABLES

A dependent measure of fear arousal, which was completed immediately after viewing the film and before reading the communications, consisted of six mood adjectives: *fright, tension, nervousness, anxiety, discomfort,* and *nausea.* In each experiment, as manipulation checks, there were three items assessing the perceived severity of the depicted event: three items measuring expectancy of exposure; and two items measuring the perceived efficacy of the recommended coping responses. Four items were used in each study to assess intentions to comply with the recommended practices. Examples of the intention items in the three experiments are as follows: "At the present time, I intend to stop smoking completely"; "When driving in the future, I shall always think ahead and plan ways I can avoid dangerous traffic situations"; and "I firmly intend to get pencillin treatments if I ever get a venereal disease." All items were rated on 10-point graphic rating scales.

Scores on all dependent measures are based upon the mean ratings for the items in each cluster.

Results

The three experiments were included as a replications factor in the analysis of variance design. Thus, all dependent variables were analyzed in a $2 \times 2 \times 2 \times 3$ design.

MANIPULATION CHECKS

The analysis of the six mood adjectives indicated that the high-noxiousness films produced higher levels of fear arousal than did the low-noxiousness films.

The films did not have a significant effect on the measure of appraised severity; the high-probability essay produced higher scores than the low-probability message.

The probability of occurrence communication was the only independent variable to affect expectancies of being exposed to the threatening events. The high-probability essay produced higher mean scores than did the low-probability message.

The groups exposed to the high-efficacy communication believed the recommended practices to be more highly effective preventives than the groups who read the low-efficacy messages. An Efficacy × Probability interaction effect indicated that the efficacy variable's impact was more pronounced in the high-probability-of-occurrence condition than in the low-probability-of-occurrence condition. Finally, there was a main effect associated with the noxiousness manipulation, with the high-noxiousness mean higher than the low-noxiousness mean.

Table 31.1
Mean Scores on the Measure of Intentions to Adopt the Recommended Responses

Experimental Condition	Probability	
	Low	High
Low noxiousness		
Low efficacy	5.9	5.5
High efficacy	6.1	6.8
High noxiousness		
Low efficacy	5.6	5.8
High efficacy	6.7	7.1

INTENT TO ADOPT RECOMMENDED RESPONSE

The obtained means are reported in Table 31.1. Compared with the low-efficacy condition, the high-efficacy condition produced stronger intentions to accept the preventive measures. This main effect must be interpreted in light of the Efficacy × Probability × Replications interaction effect. The Efficacy × Probability interaction effect was tested at each level of the Replications factor. These analyses revealed that the second-order interaction attained significance only in the smoking experiment. Figure 31.1 shows a plot of the obtained mean scores.

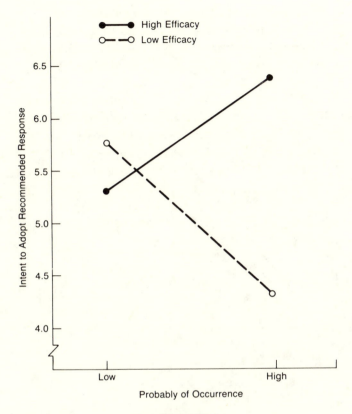

Figure 31.1
Interaction effect of probability of occurrence and efficacy of coping response
upon intent to adopt the recommended response in the cigarette
smoking experiment.

Examination of this interaction revealed that it arose from the increase in the high-efficacy condition and the decrease in the low-efficacy condition.

There was also a Noxiousness × Efficacy × Replications interaction effect. The Noxiousness × Efficacy interaction was tested at each level of the replications factor. These analyses indicated that the second-order interaction effect was significant only in the venereal disease experiment. These results are summarized graphically in Figure 31.2

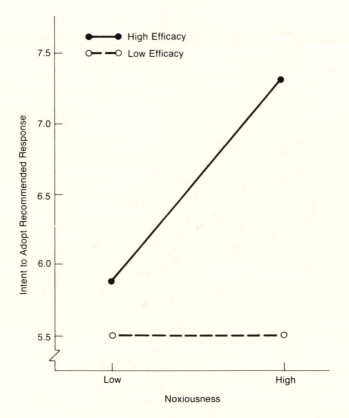

Figure 31.2
Interaction effect of magnitude of noxiousness and efficacy of coping reponse
upon intent to adopt the recommended response in the venereal
disease experiment.

REGRESSION ANALYSES

Since protection motivation theory assumes that the mediational processes are independent and directly affect intentions,
an ordinary multiple linear regression equation was computed
that entered the manipulation check items as predictors of the
criterion variable, intentions.

The obtained standardized partial regression coefficients were
as follows: for fear arousal, .13; for severity, .19 ($p < .05$); for
expectancy of exposure, .03; and for belief in efficacy, .32 ($p
< .01$). Thus, belief in the efficacy of coping responses explained

more of the variance than did any other predictor, and the appraised severity of the threatened event was the only other significant predictor.

Discussion

The results of the present series of experiments demonstrated that increments in the efficacy of recommended coping responses increased intentions to comply with the recommended practices. Regardless of what the threatened event was, or how noxious it was, or how likely it was to occur, the stronger the belief that a coping response could avert a danger, the more strongly people intended to adopt the communicator's recommendations. The main effect of the efficacy factor corroborates previous studies finding that this variable enhanced acceptance of medication (Chu, 1966), increased intentions to stop smoking (Rogers and Thistlethwaite, 1970), and reduced cigarette consumption (Rogers and Deckner, 1975). One practical implication is that mass media appeals should emphasize that their recommendations can effectively control an aversive event. The salutary effect of the efficacy of the recommendations extends the findings of Leventhal and his colleagues (see Leventhal, 1970) that specific action instructions facilitate behavioral compliance. The data indicated that the efficacy component acted upon intentions, not by making the threat seem less severe or less likely to occur, but by directly strengthening beliefs in the ability to cope with danger when it is confronted.

Increments in the magnitude of noxiousness in the venereal disease study facilitated attitude change only if the recommended coping response was highly effective (see Figure 34.2). If the response was relatively ineffective, it did not matter how severe the danger was. This interaction effect is consistent with Janis and Feshbach's (1953) defensive avoidance hypothesis. As elaborated by Rogers and Thistlethwaite (1970), this hypothesis suggests that "increments in fear-arousal should produce greater increments in acceptance of the recommended action when the audience is given high, rather than little or no, reassurance of the efficacy of the actions" (pp. 227–28).

The interactions in the smoking experiment showed that increments in the probability variable tended to increase acceptance of the recommendation only if the recommendation was a highly effective preventive practice. If the recommendation was ineffective, increments in probability of occurrence tended to have a boomerang effect. That is, if smokers were told that it was highly likely they could contract lung cancer and that stopping smoking would not improve their lot, they planned to *increase* their cigarette consumption. Leventhal (1970) reviewed evidence indicating that if an individual feels vulnerable to a threat, then resistances are aroused, and a boomerang effect is observed. The present findings suggest that this may occur only when individuals feel incapable of coping with the threat; if they can cope, increasing the probability of occurrence diminishes resistances and facilitates attitude change.

The interaction between the efficacy and probability variables suggests an extension of the defensive avoidance hypothesis: it need not be limited to an interaction involving fear or noxiousness. The key variable seems to be the inability to ward off a danger. Hence, regardless of the magnitude of noxiousness of a threat, when expectancy of exposure to a threat is strongly aroused but not fully relieved by belief in the efficacy of the recommended coping response, individuals may resist the communicator's recommendation.

32.

Implications for Changing War-Related Attitudes*

SEYMOUR FESHBACH

The peace advocate who is interested in stimulating community discussion and analysis of nuclear warfare and nuclear arms issues, and ultimately in increasing public support for nuclear disarmament efforts, is faced with a difficult challenge. In addition to the usual problems associated with the questioning of government policy, with conflicting expert opinions, and with addressing topics that seem to require highly specialized, if not arcane, knowledge, it is upsetting and anxiety provoking for many people to think about a nuclear war and its aftermath. The fear appeal literature tells us that if we attempt to persuade people to adopt a particular peace-oriented policy by stressing and detailing the horrible consequences of a nuclear war if such a policy is not pursued, we run the risk of provoking defensive reactions, including subsequent avoidance of the topic and of our policy recommendations. That literature also tells us that we might obtain some immediate desired effects—for example, volunteering or adoption of the favored position—but may find that changes stimulated by strong fear appeals are transient and very vulnerable to counterstatements. At the same time, the fear appeal literature indicates that threatening content engages the interest and emotion of the audience and that fear appeals are often an effective persuasive procedure. The critical factor

* Written for this volume.

mediating the effects of fear appeals appears to be the perceived effectiveness of the advocated action with regard to reduction of the threat—what Rogers and Mewborn refer to as "belief in the efficacy of coping responses."

Thus, the experimental literature indicates that what Leventhal refers to as the perceived danger of a threat (Leventhal, 1970) can stimulate effective coping responses. Leventhal postulates that a parallel process, evoked by the effect of fear as contrasted to the cognitive recognition of danger, can stimulate reactions that coincide with the individual's effort to cope with the danger or that disrupt that effort. The disruptive effects are particularly likely to occur when the person does not feel that the recommended action can avert the threat, cannot discern other ways of effectively coping with the danger, and feels helpless in the situation. Thus, persuasive efforts in regard to nuclear armament issues need to focus on providing credible recommendations with regard to the likelihood that the advocated actions and policies can successfully reduce the perceived danger of nuclear warfare.

In fact, in a recent survey by Feshbach, Kandel, and Haist (in press), it was found that individuals who were in favor of an armament buildup and who opposed a nuclear moratorium *did not materially differ* from those who supported nuclear disarmament and a moratorium *with regard to the perceived disastrous consequences of a nuclear conflict* and the amount of anxiety experienced in connection with the possibility of an outbreak of nuclear warfare. They *did differ in their perception of the malevolence and motives of the Soviet Union.*

This suggests that another decisive element in peace-oriented persuasion is cultivation of realistic empathy with the Soviet adversary (cf. White, 1984). While empathy is a complex cognitive and emotional process, it can be trained (Feshbach, Feshbach, Fauvre, and Campbell, 1983). Among the many challenges to psychologists concerned with the prevention of nuclear war is the extension to adult populations and further development of empathy-training programs that have helped children to resolve conflicts.

The perception of nuclear conflict as having disastrous consequences for both Russians and Americans would appear to be a relatively simple cognitive judgment that did not require much in the way of empathic demands. Yet, while people at one level may acknowledge that a nuclear conflict would be devastating for both the United States and the Soviet Union at another level they may feel that it would be more disastrous for one nation than for the other, that they and their families would survive, that one can effectively limit nuclear conflicts, and so on.

Two additional implications should be noted. There is research evidence that under many circumstances an argument that presents two sides of an issue is more effective than an argument that presents one side (Hovland, Lumsdaine, and Sheffield, 1949; Hovland, Janis, and Kelley, 1953). Second, in presenting both sides, one is less likely to take an extreme position that is too distant from that held by the individuals whose attitudes one is trying to change. And here also there is research evidence that positions that are too "distant" in this sense run the risk of being summarily rejected (Hovland and Pritzker, 1957). Both of these findings have obvious relevance to the strategy of the peace movement today. Finally, in acknowledging the diversity of arguments that exist on each side of an issue, one is assuming a role more consonant with that of a scholar than with that of a propagandist. As psychologists, we have to follow the canons of our discipline. And, in doing so, we will make a more substantial contribution to the cause of peace.

References

Chu, C. C. (1966). "Fear Arousal, Efficacy, and Imminency." *Journal of Personality and Social Psychology* 4 : 517–24.

Dabbs, J. M., Jr., and Leventhal, H. (1966). "Effects of Varying the Recommendations in Fear-Arousing Communications." *Journal of Personality and Social Psychology* 4 : 525–31.

Feshbach, S.; Feshbach, N.; Fauvre, M.; and Campbell, M. (1983). *Educating for Empathy: Classroom Activities for Social Development.* Santa Monica, CA: Scott, Foresman.

Feshbach, S.; Kandel, E.; and Haist, F. (in press). "Factors Influencing Attitudes Toward Nuclear Disarmament Policies: The Role of Information and Value Placed on Children." In Oskamp, S. ed., *Applied Social Psychology Annual.* Beverly Hills, CA: Sage.

Feshbach, S., and Singer, R. (1957). "The Effects of Personal and Shared Threats upon Social Prejudice." *Journal of Abnormal and Social Psychology* 54 : 411–16.

Freedman, J. L.; Carlsmith, J. M.; and Sears, D. O. (1970). *Social Psychology.* Englewood Cliffs, NJ: Prentice-Hall.

Hochbaum, G. (1958). *Public Participation in Medical Screening Programs: A Sociopsychological Study.* Bethesda, MD: U.S. Public Health Service.

Hovland, C.; Janis, I.; and Kelley, H. (1953). *Communication and Persuasion.* New Haven: Yale University Press.

Hovland, C.; Lumsdaine, A.; Sheffield, F. S. (1949). *Experiments on Mass Communication.* Princeton: Princeton University Press.

Hovland, C., and Pritzker, H. A. (1957). "Extent of Opinion Change as a Function of Amount of Change Advocated." *Journal of Abnormal and Social Psychology* 54 : 257–61.

Insko, C. A., and Schopler, J. (1972). *Experimental Social Pyschology.* NY: Academic Press.

Janis, I. L., and Feshbach, S. (1953). "Effects of Fear Arousing Communications." *Journal of Abnormal and Social Psychology* 48 : 78–92.

Janis, I. L., and King, B. L. (1954). "The Influence of Role-Playing on Opinion Change." *Journal of Abnormal and Social Psychology* 49 : 211–18.

Lasswell, H. D., and Casey, R. D. (1946). *Propaganda, Communication and Public Opinion.* Princeton: Princeton University Press.

Leventhal, H. (1970). "Findings and Theory in the Study of Fear Communications." In L. Berkowitz, ed., *Advances in Experimental Social Psychology.* Vol. 5 : 119–86. NY: Academic Press.

Leventhal, H.; Singer, R.; and Jones, S. (1965). "Effects of Fear and Specificity of Recommendation upon Attitudes and Behavior." *Journal of Personality and Social Psychology* 2 : 20–29.

Leventhal, H., and Watts, J. C. (1966). "Sources of Resistance to Fear-Arousing Communications in Smoking and Lung Cancer." *Journal of Personality* 34 : 155–75.

Leventhal, H.; Watts, J. C.; and Pagano, F. (1967). "Effects of Fear and Instructions on How to Cope with Danger." *Journal of Personality and Social Psychology* 6 : 313–21.

Rogers, R. W. (1975). "A Protection Motivation Theory of Fear Appeals and Attitude Change." *Journal of Psychology* 91 : 93–114.

Rogers, R. W., and Deckner, W. C. (1975). "Effects of Fear Appeals and Physiological Arousal upon Emotion, Attitudes, and Cigarette Smoking." *Journal of Personality and Social Psychology* 32 : 222–30.

Rogers, R. W., and Mewborn, C. R. (1976). "Fear Appeals and Attitude Change: Effects of a Threat's Noxiousness, Probability of Occurrence, and the Efficacy of Coping Responses." *Journal of Personality and Social Psychology* 34 : 54–61.

Rogers, R. W., and Thistlethwaite, D. L. (1970). "Effects of Fear Arousal and Reassurance upon Attitude Change." *Journal of Personality and Social Psychology* 15 : 227–33.

Smith, F. T. (1943). *An Experiment in Modifying Attitudes Toward the Negro.* NY: Teachers College, Columbia University.

Tedeschi, J. T., and Lindskold, S. (1976). *Social Psychology: Interdependence, Interaction and Influence.* NY: Wiley.

White, R. K. (1984). *Fearful Warriors: A Psychological Profile of U.S.-Soviet Relations.* NY: The Free Press.

SECTION XIII

Peace Education

SECTION EDITOR: PAUL R. KIMMEL

INTRODUCTION AND REVIEW OF THE MOVEMENT

Paul R. Kimmel

Since 1980 there has been a rapidly growing interest on the part of many educators and other professionals in the United States in the subject of nuclear war. These professionals have formed organizations to help educate themselves, their colleagues, and the general public about the consequences of nuclear war and how it can be prevented. Most of these groups follow the model of the United States medical doctors who founded Physicians for Social Responsibility in the early 1960s and helped to organize International Physicians for the Prevention of Nuclear War, Inc., in 1980. These two organizations gather and disseminate information about the medical consequences of nuclear war. Through medical school courses, lectures, adult education programs, articles and books, films and television programs, and speeches at legislative bodies from town meetings to the United Nations, these health-care professionals have reached a wide audience with the message that "prevention of nuclear war is the only cure." Similar groups in the United States include Nurses for Social Responsibility, Psychologists for Social Responsibility, the Lawyers' Alliance for Nuclear Arms Control, Social Workers for Peace and Nuclear Disarmament, and Educators for Social Responsibility (ESR).

ESR, a national organization of teachers, parents, and school administrators, has focused on helping United States public schools introduce courses on nuclear weapons, nuclear war, and conflict resolution. Most of its work has been with secondary schools, although it is involved with education at all levels. This section (Section XIII) includes a chapter (chapter 33) on some aspects of how to teach such courses, written by two ESR officials, Susan Alexander and Tony Wagner. It is entitled "New Ways of Teaching for the Nuclear Age."

Chapter 34, "Assumptions, Images and Skills," contains excerpts of an interview with Elise Boulding, a sociologist widely known for her peace-related activities. Among other peace education issues, she touches on innovative aspects of a National Peace Academy. Congress has now voted to establish a somewhat similar "United States Institute of Peace." That institute is discussed in a final chapter, Chapter 35, "A National Institute of Peace," by Paul R. Kimmel.

Educational programs about nuclear issues, and especially about the prevention of nuclear war, are not without controversy in the United States. There are those who believe that it is better not to discuss such issues or at least not to discuss them in the schools. Some feel that educational programs of this kind are likely to be biased, or unduly frightening to young people. Our writers believe, on the contrary, that bias can be minimized and that excessive fears can be diminished by an honest discussion of the nuclear situation.

Psychologists can help to facilitate the public discussion of nuclear education. Conflicts over this issue will continue and intensify, as the current controversy over a junior high school curriculum on conflict and nuclear war illustrates. In 1982 the National Education Association and the Union of Concerned Scientists developed and field-tested this curriculum with the help of forty-seven junior high school teachers in thirty-five states. Over 6,000 copies of the final, 1983, version of this curriculum guide (called *Choices*) have been sold, at least half of which are now being used in classrooms. The purpose of *Choices* is "to help students understand the power of nuclear weapons, the consequences of their use, and most importantly, the options available to resolve conflicts by means other than nuclear war" (Union of Concerned Scientists, Massachusetts Teachers Association, and National Education Association, 1983, p. 7). Critics of *Choices,* such as President Reagan, characterize this curriculum guide as "more aimed at frightening and brainwashing American schoolchildren than at fostering learning and stimulating balanced, intelligent debate" (*Washington Post,* July

6, 1983, p. A-3). On April 5, 1983, the *Washington Post* berated *Choices* for (among other things): the absence of information on Soviet expenditures for weapons, the contention that the United States is far ahead of the Russians in nuclear strength and spends more on military than on social programs, and the concentration on the devastation wrought by the bombing of Hiroshima (Lynn, 1983).

Of course, supporters of *Choices* disagree with most of these criticisms. They believe that students are worried about nuclear war and that the traditional courses are *not* adequate to deal with their concerns. They cite surveys by Schwebel (1982), Beardslee and Mack (1981), Escalona (1965), and others that have found that most children know about the threat of nuclear war before they enter junior high school. Studies by Wigutoff and Herscovici (1983) and Fleming (1983) conclude that the information about nuclear weapons and nuclear war in widely used history books is "inadequate, misleading and irresponsible." In addition, *Choices* advocates find little emphasis on the interests or world views of other nations in most high school courses (Jacobson, Reardon, and Sloan, 1983).

Psychologists with skills in group dynamics and conflict resolution can mediate conflicts such as this, moving them from win-lose confrontations toward dialogues that clarify issues and bring out concerns. Neither teachers, school administrators, parents, nor the government can act unilaterally in these conflicts and be successful. When a local consensus is reached on the value and goals of education for peace, psychologists can help to develop and evaluate the desired curricula. There are many areas of psychology that can provide ideas about the potential causes of, and strategies for, preventing nuclear war. The challenge is to translate our knowledge into educational programs and activities that students can understand and use (Kimmel, 1985).

33.

New Ways of Teaching
for the Nuclear Age*

SUSAN ALEXANDER and
TONY WAGNER

Schools of Education, like many other college or university departments, increasingly are coming to believe that they have a responsibility to educate for nuclear literacy. They are feeling that nuclear age education is necessary for two reasons. First, many young people express a lack of belief in the influence of individuals or groups on public policy (Goodman, Mack, Beardslee, and Snow, 1983). This view of government in a democratic society as indifferent to public opinion results in feelings of cynicism and apathy. As a remedy, many educators feel that education should provide opportunities for students, not only to inform themselves, but also to involve themselves in the critical issues of their time, especially nuclear issues. Second, recent studies indicate that many young people believe nuclear war is inevitable. Many feel helpless about a world they view as out of control (Snow and Goodman, 1984); they feel pervasive despair about the future of their nation and world (Beardslee and Mack, 1981). In light of these findings, educators are learning that nuclear education must do more than provide information about nuclear weapons; it must also enable young people to develop a realistic sense of hope and responsibility for the future.

* Reprinted by permission of the Bulletin of Atomic Scientists, a magazine of science and world affairs. Copyright © 1984 by the Educational Foundation for Nuclear Science, Chicago, IL 60637.

One of the first credit courses on teaching nuclear issues to be offered in a graduate school of education, "Education for Peace in a Nuclear Age," has been taught by Roberta Snow at Harvard. A common theme of her work and that of other pioneers in this field is that *what* is taught in this field is less important than *the teaching process itself.* In support of this belief, this course has involved experts in various relevant fields; videotapes; student journals to reflect on the course content, methodology, and impact; student-run class sessions; and student project presentations.

Snow and others have found that the traditional approach to controversal issues—the debate—is of limited value in classroom discussions of nuclear issues. Debate fosters adversarial positions, combativeness, and black-and-white thinking. Instead, materials chosen for the Harvard course have represented a variety of perspectives with the goal of discovering what may be right, not wrong, about each. As one teacher put it, "it's been enlightening to learn that teaching students to think critically means helping them to understand how [various] people view the world and why they think the way they do."

Through testing new high school curricula on nuclear issues, educators have found that a more collaborative approach to understanding the central problems of our time sparks students' belief in the possibility of creating change. One student wrote:

> The most embarassing part of this course was when you asked me to describe a time when I stood up for something that I believed in. I went home trying to remember and couldn't think of any time. . . . I hope by the end of the term I'll . . . have something to answer to that question.

Students are encouraged to develop action-oriented projects of their choice—for instance, to survey their classmates about problems of racism or to write a letter to the editor for or against the MX. These projects help students understand the importance of developing their own positions and of finding ways to effectively promote them.

In 1946 Albert Einstein observed that "the unleashed power of the atom has changed everything save our modes of thinking." (quoted by Nathan and Norden, 1960, p. 376). The emphasis of this movement in education is on creating new "ways of thinking."

34.

Assumptions, Images, and Skills*

ELISE BOULDING

Buckmaster: What is peace?

Boulding: It is a process. It's not an externalized condition. It's a way of being. But it's also a responsiveness to our own condition and the condition of others, a continual openness and listening and readiness for adaptation, for social inventions. Most of all it involves the capacity to image the future condition of a good society—a condition in which people are living together in peace . . . if you want peace you have to prepare for peace. I'm always amazed at the inability of people to visualize a functioning social order without weapons. This means human beings feel that human problems cannot be solved by human skill. Weapons become a security blanket, and this lack of faith in one's own skills, and the inability to visualize such a society, is astonishing, because people do, in fact, solve very difficult problems, peacefully, every day.

Buckmaster: Should we try to redefine security?

Boulding: Indeed we should! . . . In the broadest sense of the word, a certain level of insecurity is part of the human condition. To be able to function and live amid uncertainty— that's a clinical definition of sanity. We need to learn to accept uncertainty . . . and then intelligently to approach those un-

* Excerpts from an interview with Elise Boulding by Henrietta Buckmaster, editor of the *Christian Science Monitor*'s "Home Forum," published in the *Monitor,* December 29, 1980.

certainties by determining which need the greatest reassurance. . . . We all need nurturance. Human beings need some affirmation about themselves in order to risk taking on problem solving . . . we need to provide a lot of security for each other, confidence that we can explore. . . . We need to find ways to bring nurturance into the public sphere. . . . Gandhi did it and Martin Luther King. At their best, our political leaders have tried to do the same. But it's too low-keyed, not popular. We like to feel that we're being led by somebody strong and dominative.

Buckmaster: [You are suggesting] that we must restructure our societies in many ways, not be afraid of a new consciousness, challenge assumptions on a very broad basis.

Boulding: It's lack of courage which keeps us from that kind of exploration. I've given this a lot of study because I'm very concerned about beginning at the beginning—with children— helping them to become problem solvers rather than little fighters who battle their way through life. As I looked at different studies of violence and aggression in children's behavior, it became very clear that the more experience children have in different ways of doing things, the more they've been encouraged to think, the more answers they're able to pull out of their own minds when in a crisis. But a child who has very few ideas about what to do next sulks, strikes out, hits. The same is true of an adult. The more resources you develop, the more answers you find. It's the richness and compassion of the life experience in dealing with others that keeps you from hitting out.

Buckmaster: But so many of our assumptions about the other fellow are ideological. "There goes the devil," Russians say about Americans, and Americans about Russians. How do we deal with this?

Boulding: The study of history is a help; you get to know what the human race has come through, to learn what the Pax Romana was, to understand what the Pax Americana has meant to other parts of the world. The Pax Romana eventually hurt the Romans; the Pax Americana is hurting the Americans. Study of history is indispensable in coping with ideologies. . . . Societies generate images of the possible and then draw their behavior from those images. The fact that we cannot image a weaponless world means that we have nothing with which to organize our behavior in that direction because we say it's not possible. I've taken as my No. 1 task to try to develop a series of future imagings wherein people can ask: "What would it be like if fifty years from now we have no weapons? Just describe it. Don't say 'Could we do it?' Just say it's happened—a mental exercise—it's happened: no weapons. In a weaponless world how do people relate to one another? And then let's work back from that to see how we could achieve it." It's so elementary, basic and vital.

Buckmaster: You're at the center of much that is happening in the development of peace skills. What is happening?

Boulding: Here are three different things that are happening right now:

• The Costa Rica Peace University, proposed by Costa Rica, has been approved by the United Nations. Incidentally, Costa Rica disbanded its army thirty-five years ago.

• In 1974 the United Nations University, with headquarters in Tokyo, began operation. This university is not primarily a teaching university. It is a set of research institutes that deal with major world problems . . . of hunger, the use of natural resources, and human and social development from the perspective of world interest, not national interest. . . . This means exploring traditional folk knowledge . . . Indian and Chinese traditions in medicine, for example—along with the contemporary laboratory-based science and technology, the application of Marxist and capitalist views of development and the use of world resources, Buddhist and Hindu and Islamic conceptions of human development, all the approaches to end hunger and provide proper distribution. It's a university committed to the world's problems, using the best of the world's resources. . . .

• And finally there is hope of a Peace Academy in the United States. It's [been discussed] all around the country. . . . The stress is on . . . analyzing problems in such a way that alternatives to violence become evident. [For example,] special police training for dealing with domestic violence. When the police get the proper training the loss of life goes way down. To have a central academy which will both do the research and offer the training, the analysis, and make the body of knowledge

available [would mean] we've taken tremendous steps toward
a developed society. Such a society knowns and uses conflict
resolution and peacemaking skills.

When the Peace Academy Commission was holding hearings
around the country—to find what people felt about the need
for such a place—we were very struck by the extent to which
minority peoples, Chicanos and blacks, welfare mothers, were
making the connection between the incapacity of the United
States to deal with problems of violence and injustice in their
own communities and its attitude in dealing with the outside
word. They'd say, "If the United States can't handle violence
and injustice and poverty in Atlanta, how is it going to handle
it in the Soviet Union, Afghanistan, Iran, Iraq?" It was clear
to them that our own best ideals have to be cultivated first in
our own local institutions. . . .

The military academies themselves say our country draws far
too quickly on its armed forces—that armed forces should be
held in reserve for the absolutely unsolvable situations where
all human ingenuity has failed. But what happens, they say, is
that they are called in first instead of last. "When we are called
in," one officer said, "the United States has failed."

35.

A National Institute of Peace*

PAUL R. KIMMEL

The United States Congress has established a United States
Institute of Peace "to bring together and develop new and tested
techniques to promote peaceful economic, political, social, and
cultural relations in the world" (*Congressional Record,* 1984,
H10249). The passage of legislation to set up "the widest possible
range of education and training, basic and applied research
opportunities, and peace information services on the means to
promote international peace . . . without recourse to violence"
(*Congressional Record,* 1984, H10250) resulted from a recognition that: (1) national security requires more than military
defense; (2) recent efforts at dealing with international conflicts
have not been very effective; and (3) there are negotiation and
mediation techniques that could be more widely and effectively
used to manage international conflicts.

The United States Institute of Peace (USIP) is designed to
complement the United States government's defense and foreign
policy programs and to supplement research and training programs at educational institutions. Officials in the Departments
of Defense and State are aware that it is in our interest to
promote cooperation and accommodation among nations. However, their missions of deterring aggression and promoting national interest make it difficult for them to work on the processes

* Written for this volume.

of peacemaking as such. Their responsibilities make them participants in many international conflicts. As in sports or labor-
management disputes, it is very difficult for the participants to
be impartial about the contests in which they are involved. It
takes an outside, neutral party that has the appropriate training
to be an effective umpire, referee, or mediator. As an independent, nonprofit corporation that has no national policy responsibilities, the USIP will have the opportunity to become
such an outside party. Using the empirical methods of the social
sciences to explore alternatives to violence in international conflicts, the USIP can develop effective and credible research and
training programs in international peacemaking that will be of
interest to government policymakers in all nations. Through its
Jennings Randolph scholarships for leaders in peace, its mul-
tidisciplinary studies of past successes and failures in the quest
for peace and arms control, its educational programs to help
practitioners develop their skills in international conflict resolution, and its dissemination of information on its activities,
the USIP will promote cooperation and accommodation among
nations in ways that no private or governmental organization
can. The USIP will also play an important role in coordinating
and stimulating research and education on international peace
and conflict resolution at other institutions. At least one-fourth
of USIP's annual budget is designated for grants and contracts
to support such activities. Its own programs will generate, integrate, and make more relevant many projects both here and
abroad.

The opportunity to do real-world studies of international
conflict and negotiation, to work with and train professionals
who hold responsible positions in international affairs, and to
communicate with policymakers and the general public from a
position of knowledge and credibility is an exciting challenge
for psychologists and other social scientists. Access to primary
data and international actors will enable these scientists to apply
and adapt domestic models and techniques of conflict management to international events. They will be able to assess the
impact of different approaches to international conflicts and
ascertain which are most effective in managing such conflicts
without violence. They will build and refine programs to make

these approaches more available and useful to those who can apply them.

The real beneficiaries of the USIP are all of us. Through increasing our understanding of international conflicts, training more skilled negotiators, promoting techniques for finding common interests, and developing trust and improving communication among adversaries, the USIP will help us all learn how to manage conflicts without resorting to coercion or force. In these ways, we can achieve a more developed society and real international security.

References

Beardslee, W., and Mack, J. (December, 1981). "The Impact on Children and Adolescents of Nuclear Developments." *Psychosocial Aspects of Nuclear Development.* Washington, D.C.: American Psychological Association.

Congressional Record. House. Title XVII—United States Institute of Peace. Sept. 26, 1984, H10249 and H10250.

Decisionmaking in a Nuclear Age. Coordinated by Roberta Snow:

Dialogue: A Teaching Guide to Nuclear Issues and *Perspectives: A Teaching Guide to Concepts of Peace.* Developed by Shelley Berman, coordinator of the Boston chapter of Educators for Social Responsibility and members of the Boston chapter. All curricula are available from ESR, 23 Garden St., Cambridge, MA 02138.

Einstein, A. (1946). (Telegram to several hundred prominent Americans appealing for contributions, May 23 and 24, 1946.) Quoted in Nathan, O., and Norden, H., eds. (1960). *Einstein on Peace.* Avenel Books. P. 376.

Escalona, S. (1965). "Children and the Threat of Nuclear War." *Behavioral Sciences and Human Survival.* Science and Behavior Books.

Fleming, D. B. (November/December 1983). "Nuclear War: What Do High School History Books Tell Us?" *Social Education* 47 (7) : 480–84.

Goodman, L. A.; Mack, J. E.; Beardslee, W. R.; and Snow, R. (1983). "Threat of Nuclear War and the Nuclear Arms Race: Adolescent Experience and Perceptions." *Political Psychology* 4 (3) : 501–30.

Jacobson, W.; Reardon, B.; and Sloan, D. (November/December 1983). "A Conceptual Framework for Teaching About Nuclear Weapons." *Social Education* 47 (7) : 475–79.

Kimmel, P. R. (1985). "Learning About Peace: Choices and the U.S. Institute of Peace as Seen from Two Different Perspectives." *American Psychologist* 40 (5) : 536–41.

Lynn, B. W. (October 1983). "Polluting the National Security Debate." Washington, D.C.: The Fund for Peace and the Washington College of Law and American University.

Schwebel, M. (1982). "Effects of the Nuclear War Threat on Children and Teenagers: Implications for Professionals." *American Journal of Orthopsychiatry* 52 : 608–18.

Snow, R., and Goodman, L. (1984). "A Decisionmaking Approach to Nuclear Education." *Harvard Educational Review* 54 (3) : 321–28.

Union of Concerned Scientists, Massachusetts Teachers Association, and National Education Association (1983). *Choices: A Unit in Conflict and Nuclear War.* Washington, D.C.: National Education Association.

Wigutoff, S., and Herscovici, S. (1983). "Militarism in Textbooks: An Analysis." *Bulletin of the Council on Interracial Books for Children.*

Conclusion

RALPH K. WHITE

There are four conclusions that seem to stand out as more important than any others. In this final section I will explore the evidence that supports them, and will offer some guides to effective action. Each of the conclusions has two parts, a general psychological concept and a practical, action-oriented conclusion directly related to that concept. They are:

1. Realistic empathy and the need to recognize Soviet fear.
2. Healthy fear and the need for adequate armed deterrence.
3. The nearly universal recognition of overkill and the consequent psychological feasibility of minimal *nuclear* deterrence.
4. Psychic numbing and the need for clearness about preventive action.

1. *Realistic empathy and the need to recognize Soviet fear.*
   The word "realistic" is needed to remind the reader that the word "empathy," as used in this discussion, does not imply sympathy, compassion, goodwill, agreement, or approval. It means simply a realistic understanding of what is going on in other people's minds. It means seeing the worst as well as the best (and the merely human) in others. For example, it does not mean overlooking the element of expansionism in the minds of the tough, power-oriented men in the Kremlin, or the actions that may be needed to deter them from further forcible expansion. Yet it does imply, among other things, recognition of their more "human" side, which includes, above all, their intense desire—based mainly on their experience in World War II—to avoid another such war, and their realization that a nuclear war would be far worse.

The concept of empathy emerges in most of the chapters in this book. It is clearly present in the chapters by Shulman, Bronfenbrenner, and White, which deal directly with Soviet thinking. It appears in Jervis's stress on a realistic appraisal of an adversary's intentions, as a basis for determining whether the spiral model or the deterrence model is more appropriate in a given situation—and, specifically, for judging whether the Soviet decision makers' intentions are more like those of Hitler or more like those of both sides in the events leading to World War I. It appears in Deutsch's proposition that the malignant (spiral) process of hostile interaction, resembling the background of World War I, brings out the worst in both sides, so that there is usually a large element of realism in each side's expecting, and perhaps trying to deter, hostile, power-oriented behavior by the other. It appears in Deutsch's experimental evidence suggesting that threats of "punitive deterrence," which evoke excessive fear and anger on the other side, are likely to be counterproductive, while defensive, "nonpunitive deterrence" is much more likely (in his experimental situations) to have its intended effect. Empathy is important also in Kelman's description of how the right kind of conflict-resolution workshop or group experience, unlike the typical polemic interchange between outright opponents, can promote genuine mutual understanding. And, although there is no need to spell out here exactly how, the concept of realistic empathy appears in one way or another in several other chapters.

Does realistic empathy with the Soviet leaders necessarily include attributing to them an exaggerated, perhaps even "paranoid" (but genuine) fear of being attacked by us? *Are* they as afraid of aggression by us as we are afraid of aggression by them? Those who have read Osgood's vivid analogy of two men on a seesaw over an abyss may remember the crucial insight of one of those men: "Let us suppose that, during a quiet period in their strife, it occurs to one of these men that perhaps the other is really just as frightened as he himself is. If this were so, he would also welcome some way of escaping from this intolerable situation" (p. 195). There would have been no escape from destruction without that insight.

Naturally, the question of Soviet expansionism, including what is happening in Afghanistan, has to be addressed directly. Osgood's analogy of the men on the seesaw contains no recognition of that factor. Specialists on the subject tend to agree that there is a sizable element of expansion for its own sake as well as of expansion in order to be safe in Soviet motivation, at least in the minds of the leaders. They like power as such. We psychologists have no good reason to question the existence of such a desire for expansion. Frank's emphasis on pride and Schmookler's on power motivation are both relevant. As psychologists, we know that egoistic motives such as aggression and self-assertion are likely to be rationalized in terms of moral obligation or legitimate self-defense and are therefore likely to be unconscious or semiconscious rather than fully conscious. (That applies to us and our leaders as well as to the Soviet people and their government.)

Nevertheless, the power motive in Soviet minds needs to be kept in some kind of perspective. It may be outweighed by others. When anyone asserts that "the" Soviet goal (or the most important Soviet goal) is expansion, my own answer usually is to grant immediately that it is *a* goal but to add that in my judgment it is by no means the most important one. My tentative conception of the hierarchy of the Politburo's goals is this:

1. To stay in power in the USSR.
2. To hold on to power in the outlying territory that the USSR now controls, such as Eastern Europe and Afghanistan.
3. To avoid any big war, especially a nuclear war.
4. To build a stronger economy.
5. To expand the USSR's power abroad.

In its extreme form, a stress on Soviet power motivation includes asserting that the USSR's primary motive is to dominate the world. As Nitze puts it succinctly, "They don't want war; they want the world" (1980, p. 90). The question is: How much do they want the world? It is my impression that most of the best Western specialists on Soviet affairs would disagree with Nitze's emphasis. Robert Kaiser, for instance, says: "As Seweryn Bialer has put it so aptly, the Soviet leaders dream of world domination

but do not expect to achieve it. By discounting the likelihood
of success themselves, the Soviets can easily forgive the steps
they take (subjugating Afghanistan, for instance) that arouse in
Americans the fear that they are really bent on imminent world
domination" (1981, p. 517; italics Kaiser's).

If Soviet fear is in fact the main emotional source of the
Soviet arms buildup, Soviet hostility to us, and aggressive behavior by the men in the Kremlin (when they are clearly
aggressive), the implications for what we need to do are mo-
mentous. We would be wise to stress tension reduction more
than deterrence. Our own arms buildup, especially our present
focus on nuclear weapons capable of a first strike against the
Soviet homeland and the Soviet "deterrent" arsenal, is hardly
calculated to diminish the extent of Soviet arming or the "paranoid" fear that underlies it. The MX, the Pershing II, the
ground-launched cruise missile, and antisatellite weapons have
that first-strike character. While from our standpoint those weapons are intended only for deterrence, is it not inevitable, given
their preconceptions, that the Soviet leaders would interpret
such weapons the worst possible way, and that their unhealthy,
"paranoid" fear of us would be increased?

2. *Healthy fear and the need for adequate armed deterrence.*
While the words "healthy" and "adequate" cry out for definition, definitions of them will be temporarily postponed. It is
first necessary to note the striking fact that no chapter in this
book has challenged the desirability of a healthy fear of the
consequences of committing aggression or of some prudent
forms of strength and resolve as ways of discouraging aggression
by others. There is not a pacifist sentence in this volume, nor
is there a sentence recommending military weakness.

For instance, George and Smoke, whose book, *Deterrence in
American Foreign Policy* is often regarded as the classic work
in that field, propose here (chapter 22) that the concept of
deterrence should be broadened and that in many contexts the
broader term "influence" is preferable. In their book they discuss
the risks and frequent ineffectiveness of deterrence, especially
when it takes the form of explicit or implicit threats of military
action if an opponent does such-and-such, but they do not

challenge the need for some kinds of armed strength—a silent reminder to any aggressor nation that, if that nation commits clear aggression, it is likely to get into serious trouble. The same is true of Lebow's Chapter 23. He is right in his challenge of the term "deterrence," but criticizes only deterrence through demonstrating resolve by action in crises such as threats and mobilizations. He does not oppose deterrence through strength.

Now let us consider definitions. How should we define "healthy fear"? One possible definition, following the lead of Deutsch's distinction between punitive and nonpunitive deterrence, is that the healthy, peace-promoting type of fear is the fear in the minds of the leaders of a potentially aggressive nation that aggression by them will be strongly, effectively resisted by its victims and/or their allies, and that in the end the aggressors will fail in any attack on others. Most simply, it can be defined as fear of the *consequences* (but not necessarily catastrophic consequences) of *attacking* others. It is the kind of fear that defensive arms can create in a potential adversary if the defense is strong enough. Correspondingly, the unhealthy, war-promoting type of fear can be defined as an exaggerated, "paranoid" fear of *being* attacked, and a consequent undiscriminating, obsessive need to build up every sort of armed strength, including offensive strength—and perhaps, in a crisis, to act preemptively out of a panicky fear that the other side will do so if one's own side does not.

Obviously, powerful first-strike nuclear weapons that can reach the homeland of the adversary (such as the MX and the D–5) can create the unhealthy type of fear in the adversary, especially if they are perceived as going far beyond what is needed for defense, and therefore as proving hostile, aggressive intentions.

How should "adequate" armed deterrence be defined? In specific terms, there are perhaps as many definitions as there are definers. The one that comes most clearly from the chapters in this volume is Osgood's: the minimal type of deterrence is a relatively invulnerable second-strike capability (e.g., on a small number of submarines and a small number of bombers), plus an amount of strength in conventional arms, at least in Western Europe, that would be likely to deter the Soviet Union from an outright invasion even in a time of crisis. How great that amount of conventional strength should be in specific terms is a matter for experts on weaponry and experts on Soviet foreign policy to decide—not psychologists. On the question of an adequate nuclear capability, though, nonexperts have a right to an opinion, since it is generally known and accepted that a single nuclear-armed submarine could destroy the 100 largest cities in the opposing nation, and that our Western submarines, British and French as well as American, are relatively invulnerable. Although they may not continue to be invulnerable indefinitely, they will remain so for the next several years. Therefore, a comparatively small number of nuclear-armed submarines (let's say as many as five, to be conservative), plus a similarly small number of well-equipped bombers, should provide enough of a hedge against technological breakthroughs by the other side.

As the survey of opinion polls by Yankelovich and Doble has shown (Chapter 3) American public opinion, properly informed, should not be an insurmountable obstacle to that kind of redefinition of the type of nuclear arsenal we really need.

3. *The nearly universal recognition of overkill and the consequent psychological feasibility of minimal* nuclear *deterrence.*

Is there a necessary contradiction between tension reduction and armed deterrence? Or between empathy and maintaining a healthy fear of oneself in an opponent's mind? Is it impossible to make friends with a person while pointing a gun at him? Are the first two of our four conclusions incompatible with each other?

As a matter of emphasis, there certainly is a contradiction. It is impossible to go all out for armed deterrence (which is a fair description of President Reagan's defense policy, at least during his first term) and at the same time to go all out for reassuring the Soviet leaders that our intentions are peaceful. It is especially difficult if they believe, as they apparently do now, that in our nuclear arms buildup we are going well beyond equality and are aiming at maintaining an intimidating superiority.

Some of the chapters in this volume, especially those of Deutsch, Osgood and Pruitt, suggest that there is not simply a happy medium between all-out deterrence and all-out tension reduction. There is a discriminating creative synthesis that can give us the best of both.

The chief key to such an integrative solution of our most basic problem lies in the word "overkill." As the businessman Harold Willens (1984) has dramatically brought out in his visual comparison of 6,000 dots with 1 dot, George Kennan (1982) is completely right in calling the nuclear arsenal on each side "grotesquely redundant." Neither side needs more than a fraction of 6,000 times the firepower of World War II. And reduction to a fraction, by the intelligently planned stages that Osgood suggests—unilaterally if necessary, but challenging the other side at every step to match our steps in the march toward genuine stability—would in all probability not only stop the nuclear arms race but actually reverse its direction. The mushroom cloud that now hangs over us all might almost completely disappear. And we would not be "letting down our guard" in any important way.

What makes that last statement believable is not only the fantastic "redundancy" of the total number of nuclear weapons but the important distinction between first-strike and second-strike nuclear weapons. All our initiatives could be, for a long time, aimed at eliminating first-strike weapons. Each side now has both a much more than adequate second-strike capability (which in moderation makes for stability) and a *far* more than adequate first-strike capability (which in any amount makes for a perilous instability). Therefore, each side could, with enhanced rather than diminished security, cut back its first-strike capability, by stages, to a fraction of what it is now. Or, if a first-strike weapon is defined as a weapon that is both excessively vulnerable and capable of devastating the opponent's homeland (and therefore an invitation to preemption in a crisis), the cutback could eventually be to nothing—no land-based first-strike nuclear weapons. No MX, no MIRV'd Minutemen, no Pershing II, no GLCMs, no SS-18s, or SS-19s, or SS-20s. A few nuclear-armed, relatively invulnerable submarines and bombers would, in all probability, be adequate to deter the initiation of nuclear war by the other side, even in a crisis. Minimal deterrence, defined as adequate conventional strength plus that kind of ace-in-the-hole nuclear strength, should give us nuclear stability and nuclear peace. Wars could occur, but they would almost certainly not be nuclear.

A main reason for that prediction is psychological and involves the distinction between healthy and unhealthy fear. The unhealthy kind of fear is now rampant in the Soviet Union. The Soviet leaders apparently are more sure now than ever before that we are implacably Bad Guys, insisting on an intimidating superiority of the most unbelievably lethal weapons of all time. Because it predisposes them to take preemptive action in a crisis, that kind of unhealthy fear and intense anger is dangerous to us—to an extreme degree. It is probably by now so deeply ingrained that nothing less dramatic than Osgood's GRIT would change it substantially. But a policy resembling GRIT probably would. And since it would include maintaining the healthy kind of fear in Soviet minds, we can afford to adopt it.

Would it be psychologically and politically possible? The surprising answer is yes—probably. Not now but within the next few years, with intelligent leadership, it could be done.

The most persuasive evidence comes from public opinion polls and is summarized by Yankelovich and Doble in this volume. The "not now" part of the answer is abundantly verified by the consistent finding that Americans are deeply distrustful of the Soviet leaders and would not now tolerate any "losing of the arms race." But GRIT, as defined by Osgood, and unilateral initiatives, as defined by Etzioni, would *not* mean "losing the arms race" in the sense in which the public conceives of losing it. A redefinition of what "losing" means in this context, by intelligent leaders, could make a big difference. Leadership directed toward peace would be another way of describing it. A drastic shift of emphasis from nuclear to conventional defense would be another.

In any case, the premises on the basis of which the American public thinks have shifted in ways that few peace activists have fully realized. A careful rereading of what Yankelovich and Doble say in this volume could add much both to the self-confidence of the antinuclear activists and to their understanding of the nature of the psychological ground on which they now can build. For instance, and most important, "Americans have

. . . arrived at an astonishingly high level of agreement that we must adapt our future policies to these 'facts of life': . . . That both we and the Soviets now have an 'overkill' capability, more destructive capability than we could ever need, and the ability to blow each other up several times over (90 percent)" (p. 44). It is hardly a long step from this to the proposition that we have more than we need and could cut back without danger. There is also the truly astonishing fact that "More than eight out of ten Americans (81 percent) believe it is our *current* policy to use nuclear weapons 'if and only if' our adversaries use them against us first" (p. 52). In other words, the great majority of the American public assumes we already have a no-first-use policy. "Almost the same massive majority believes that this is what our national policy *should* be" (Yankelovich and Doble, pp. 52–53). In believing that, they are showing how little they accept the present official justification of our first-use policy, namely that we need a credible threat of first use in order to deter an attack on Western Europe. "Only 18 percent agree that we should use nuclear weapons against a conventional Soviet attack in Europe or Japan; and more than three out of four (76 percent) agree that we should use nuclear weapons if, and only if, the Soviets use them against our allies first" (p. 53). It is not a long step from there to clear thinking about the difference between first-strike and second-strike weapons and about the dangers inherent in deploying first-strike weapons at all.

4. *Psychic numbing and the need for clearness about preventive action.*

Five chapters, two at the beginning and three at the end, bring out this theme.

In Chapter 1, Lifton and Falk give striking examples of how "psychic numbing" works. They broaden out the concept by stating, "What I* am calling psychic numbing includes a number of classical psychoanalytic defense mechanisms: repression, suppression, isolation, denial, undoing, reaction formation, and projection, among others. [A follower of Harry Stack Sullivan

---

* Lifton is the chief author of the chapter excerpted here.

might add "selective inattention," a term about as broad as "psychic numbing" itself.] But the defense mechanisms overlap greatly around the issue of feeling and not feeling. With that issue so central to our time, we do well to devote to it a single overall category" (p. 12). Lifton describes also how his own anxiety and surprising reluctance to begin systematic study of the survivors of Hiroshima "seemed to recede as I found myself listening carefully during the interviews for psychological patterns in survivors' descriptions. In other words, I had begun to carry out my professional task, with the aid of the selective professional numbing I have mentioned in connection with surgeons" (p. 14). The cure, it seems, was involvement in a clear and meaningful course of action related to the source of anxiety.

Mack and Snow bring in the same theme when they describe the reactions of children and adolescents to the nuclear threat as more direct and honest than the reactions of most adults. The adults presumably have built up psychological defenses against candid recognition of the nuclear horror. The children, meanwhile, "having their whole lives to live and being less emotionally defended, penetrate with their words the barriers to feeling we have erected in relation to the nuclear threat" (p. 17). But action helps. "Some teenagers advocate specific actions, such as thinking actively about the nuclear threat, giving speeches, marching, and demonstrating. Those that recommend such actions seem to be more hopeful" (p. 25).

Section XII, "Changing War-Related Attitudes," addresses somewhat indirectly a very practical question: Should the antinuclear movement continue to emphasize fear appeals such as those in Jonathan Schell's *The Fate of the Earth* and in films such as *The Day After* (1984)? Or, for those whose reaction to them is some form of psychic numbing, have they become counterproductive?

The classic, path breaking experiment of Janis and Feshbach (1953) first raised doubts about the effectiveness of strong fear appeals. In keeping with much clinical evidence of resistance to painful thoughts, it had the surprising result that strong fear appeals seemed to change behavior less than weaker fear appeals did. In this volume Feshbach briefly reviews some later studies.

The majority of them, such as that of Ronald Rogers and C. Ronald Mewborn (Chapter 31) have not shown that strong fear appeals are counterproductive; and some of them, in some experimental conditions, have indicated that strong fear appeals are a good deal more effective than are weak ones.

My inference from these findings, and more directly from the experiment of Cohen (1957), is that the antinuclear movement would be wise to continue *occasional* strong fear appeals, as a reminder and a revitalizer of motivation, with one essential proviso: that *each strong fear appeal should be followed by discussion of preventive actions and of reasons why some preventive actions are likely to be effective.*

As we have seen, the chapter by Yankelovich and Doble provides strong factual backing for hope that intelligent remedial actions, which take into account the new characteristics of American public opinion, *are* likely to be effective, most notably on the no-first-use issue. Chapter 31, by Rogers and Mewborn, gives strong support to our proposed proviso. It and other evidence shows that the clearness of paths of escape from danger is unquestionably more important in determining the effectiveness of a fear appeal than is the strength or weakness of that appeal.

Chapter 33, "New Ways of Teaching for the Nuclear Age," by Alexander and Wagner, brings out a similar theme. It stresses the need for hope, and for confidence in one's own ability to take constructive action, as major goals of peace education in the schools. "Educators are learning that nuclear education must do more than provide information about nuclear weapons; it must also enable young people to develop a realistic sense of hope and responsibility for the future" (p. 538). "A more collaborative approach to understanding the central problems of our time sparks students' belief in the possibility of creating change. . . . Students are encouraged to develop action-oriented projects of their choice—for instance, to survey their classmates about problems of racism or to write a letter to the editor for or against the MX" (p. 539).

Similarly, though more briefly, Kimmel, in his introduction to Section XIII, "Peace Education," ends with this sentence: "The challenge is to translate our knowledge into educational programs and activities that students can understand *and use*" (p. 537; italics added). And, in Chapter 34, Boulding stresses the need for children to develop resourcefulness and confidence in knowing or discovering what to do. "As I looked at different studies of violence and aggression in children's behavior, it became very clear that the more experience children have in different ways of doing things, the more they've been encouraged to think, the more answers they're able to pull out of their own minds in a crisis. But the child who has very few ideas about what to do next sulks, strikes out, hits. The same is true of an adult. The more resources you develop, the more answers you find. It's the richness and compassion of the life experience in dealing with others that keeps you from hitting out" (p. 542).

Psychological Guides to Effective Action

In other parts of the book, especially Part Two, "Major Alternatives," there are many ideas on "what to do" on the national level. (For a summary see the introduction to Section IV). In light of our fourth major conclusion—the importance of clearness about preventive action as a way of overcoming psychic numbing—those ideas take on additional importance. They are important, not only for the long run as ways of preventing war, but also for the short run as ways of promoting hope and mental health for the individual who feels confused or hopeless about the world's nuclear predicament.

In addition to what to do on the national level, there is the question of what to do on the individual level. What can you and I do, effectively, to prevent war?

It is a complex question, and unfortunately this book has not had much to say about it. It is a question ripe for research, especially action research and participant observation. Some general types of action are obvious: informing ourselves and others on the actions of various congressmen and members of the executive branch; writing or telephoning congressmen; writing letters to the editor of a newspaper; contributing money to intelligently managed political action groups; joining and becoming active in profession-centered action groups; talking and giving talks about the questions handled in this volume; promoting and improving peace education in the schools; talking with the unconverted in non-peace-centered groups such as churches; studying typical responses of people different from ourselves; talking with children and young people; and as has just been said, dramatizing the seriousness of the danger (not too often), along with thoughtful discussion of action alternatives. What is not so obvious is the relative effectiveness of those broad types of action (and more important, since all of them seem clearly desirable) the art of doing each of them in ways that are likely to be most effective.

In that connection, however, there is one broad principle, supported by everyday observation as well as by much psychological experimentation, that urgently calls for some discussion in these final pages. It can be called the *Principle of Optimum Disagreement*. It is that in a given situation effective persuasion calls for *an optimum amount of disagreement between the message communicated and what is already believed or felt by the recipient—neither too little disagreement nor too much.*

Each of its two parts, "not too little" and "not too much," is well supported by experimentation. For instance, Hovland and Pritzker (1957); Weiss (1958); and Hovland, Harvey, and Sherif (1957) have confirmed the "not-too-little" principle; and Hovland, Harvey, and Sherif, in the same investigation, have also confirmed the "not-too-much" principle. Apparently, when a message is seen as only slightly different from what was previously believed, the recipients assimilate it into their previous belief pattern and see no reason to change or to think in new ways. The message is accepted fully but does not move or challenge them. It may even bore them. Yet, when the discrepancy is too great, and especially when the initial beliefs are deeply held (Freedman, 1964), there is a tendency to exaggerate the contrast and to reject the message as ridiculous, irresponsible, beyond the limits of serious consideration. Minds are turned off at that point. Some intermediate degree of disagreement can catch real attention and not overburden it.

This suggestion may sound like an invitation to pussyfoot. It is not. The likelihood of disagreeing too little for real effectiveness is ever-present. It is present, for instance, when a meeting or

discussion group is organized that turns out to be little more than "talking to the converted." Talking with five of the unconverted may be more productive than talking with twenty of the "converted." Of course, confronting disagreement often takes some courage. Talking with the like-minded is like the safe, seductive cosiness of what Janis calls groupthink. That is not the way to bring around the great middle majority of the American people who, as Yankelovich has shown, are acutely anxious about the nuclear threat but are also deeply distrustful of the Soviet Union and are not yet ready to endorse any antinuclear proposals that are much more drastic than a bilateral nuclear freeze or a no-first-use policy.

The very minimum of boldness that the principle of "not too little disagreement" calls for is to call attention to Yankelovich's finding that the great majority already favor a no-first-use policy and even assume that the United States already has that policy. In fact, to do so calls for no boldness at all. Merely giving the information that we do not yet have such a policy should do the main job, and a strong argument that we should immediately change our policy is likely to evoke immediate agreement from most of any reasonably representative group of Americans.

A good deal more willingness to confront disagreement is called for from those who strongly favor, as I do, deep cuts in first-strike nuclear weapons, by stages in roughly the way that is advocated by Osgood and Etzioni in this volume, and by mutual agreement where possible but unilaterally if necessary. Advocating any such unilateral initiative is not pussyfooting. It takes some courage, since it is almost sure to evoke occasional ad hominem accusations that those who favor it are "unilateral disarmers" (a devastating epithet, in the eyes of many); naive dupes of the communists; or even, most devastating of all, "soft on communism." It is necessary to have the toughness to face such accusations and take them in stride—to explain, patiently and with good humor, how and why they are not justified.

It may be necessary for the accused individual to repeat that what he advocates is by no means total disarmament, since both conventional forces and an ace-in-the-hole nuclear second-strike capability would remain; that what has been called unilateral can also be called simply taking intelligent initiatives toward genuine security; that drastic unilateral reduction of first-strike weapons has important security advantages, since, far from increasing security, such weapons increase the dangers of an uncontrolled arms race and of Soviet preemption in a crisis; that deep cuts would have major economic as well as security advantages; that overkill has reached grotesque proportions—a proposition that even the hardest hard-liner is likely to agree with; and that communism as a system is not the issue. The arguer for deep cuts may also want to add, as I do, that he finds some of the behavior of the men in the Kremlin positively revolting, including their incarceration of dissidents in mental hospitals and their ruthless destruction of villages in Afghanistan, but that they do have enough elementary common sense to see their mutual interest, with us, in avoiding nuclear annihilation. For those middle-majority people who may never have thought along some of these lines and whose initial total rejection was a kind of knee-jerk reaction against everything that seemed to resemble dangerous weakness or lack of patriotism—a rejection that puts all such thoughts beyond the pale of responsible thinking—such discussion may serve to bring at least this kind of antinuclear thinking within the pale. None of this would have occurred if there had not been bold disagreement in the first place.

The possibility that a middle-majority individual might close his mind before even listening to such explanations is the other danger to be kept in mind. Too much disagreement with an audience can also be counterproductive. There is such a deeply ingrained condemnation of total pacifism as naive and cowardly, in at least the great bulk of the male members of the middle majority, that an initial rejection of a speaker, even if based on misunderstanding, may continue. If it continues it is likely to prevent genuine listening and preclude all attitude change. Therefore any advocacy of total pacifism or of unilateral and total nuclear disarmament seems likely to have this effect. A peace activist who is also a total pacifist would be wise to keep that aspect of his thinking to himself, unless directly asked.

Another corollary of the Principle of Optimum Disagreement is that antinuclear persuaders would probably be wise not to focus their persuasive efforts mainly on either end of the distribution—neither on the already converted nor on the harder hard-liners—but on the more receptive members of the unconverted; in other words, on the middle majority.

A closely related outcome of much experimentation is, as Feshback puts it on p. 529, that "under many circumstances an argument that presents two sides of an issue is more effective than an argument that presents one side." He cites the work of Hovland, Lumsdaine, and Sheffield (1949) and of Hovland, Janis, and Kelley (1953). It is sometimes called the "yes-but" technique and consists, not of giving equal stress to an opponent's argument and one's own, but of granting whatever can be honestly granted in an opponent's case and then going on to present one's own case with greater emphasis, plus (some of us would add) a genuine attempt to reach a discriminating, integrative combination of the two. This "two-sided presentation of an argument" is in a way a corollary of the "not-too-much" part of the Principle of Optimum Disagreement. To show understanding of the strong points of an opponent's argument, and even accept some of them, is often to put oneself within the range of reasonable, responsible discussion in the mind of that opponent, especially if the opponent's mind is at all open.

The yes-but technique is applicable to a number of situations that the antinuclear persuader may deal with. It applies, for instance, to evaluations of the USSR. "Yes, I agree that communism is a terrible system, but the self-interest of the communist leaders can lead them to do what is in our interest too." And it applies to ways in which the crucial concept of deterrence is handled. "Yes, we need armed deterrence. We need at least two kinds, a relatively invulnerable second-strike nuclear capability and an adequate conventional force. But our first-strike weapons are a net liability even to us." These are only some possible ways of handling the issues, but they may serve to illustrate the technique as well as how closely related it is to the Principle of Optimum Disagreement. Both tend to put the communicator somewhere within what the recipient regards as the range of responsible opinion.

In closing, it is appropriate to return to the Introduction and quote again the magnificent words of Jonathan Schell:

> If we reject our doom, and bend our efforts toward survival— if we arouse ourselves to the peril and act to forestall it, making ourselves the allies of life—then the anesthetic fog will lift; our vision, no longer straining not to see the obvious, will sharpen; our will, finding secure ground to build on, will be restored; and we will take full and clear possession of life again. One day—and it is hard to believe that it will not be soon—we will make our choice. Either we will sink into the final coma and end it all or, as I trust and believe, we will awaken to the truth of our peril, a truth as great as life itself, and, like a person who has swallowed a lethal poison but shakes off his stupor at the last moment and vomits the poison up, we will break through the layers of our denials, put aside our faint-hearted excuses, and rise up to cleanse the earth of nuclear weapons.

Both the Principle of Optimum Disagreement and the nature of the Soviet Union suggest that we in the West should think twice before advocating total unilateral nuclear disarmament. But, if Schell's clarion call is interpreted as a call to thought as well as action, not only is it wholly acceptable, but it is what our imperiled planet needs most.

References

Cohen, A. R. (1957). "Need for Cognition and Order of Communication as Determinants of Attitude Change." In C. I. Hovland, ed., *The Order of Presentation in Persuasion*. New Haven: Yale University Press.

Freedman, J. L. (1964). "Involvement, Discrepancy and Change." *Journal of Abnormal and Social Psychology* 69 : 290–95.

Hovland, C. I.; Harvey, O. J.; and Sherif, M. (1957). "Assimilation and Contrast Effects in Reactions to Communication and Attitude Change." *Journal of Abnormal and Social Psychology* 55 : 242–52.

Hovland, C. I.; Janis, I. L.; and Kelley, H. (1953). *Communication and Persuasion*. New Haven: Yale University Press.

Hovland, C. I.; Lumsdaine, A.; and Sheffield, F. D. (1949). *Experiments on Mass Communication*. Princeton: Princeton University Press.

Hovland, C. I., and Pritzker, H. A. (1957). "Extent of Opinion Change as a Function of Amount of Change Advocated." *Journal of Abnormal and Social Psychology* 54 : 257–61.

Janis, I. L., and Feshbach, S. (1953). "Effects of Fear Arousing Communications." *Journal of Abnormal and Social Psychology* 48 : 78–92.

Kaiser, R. G. (1981). "U.S.–Soviet Relations: Goodbye to Détente." *Foreign Affairs*. Special issue, "America and the World, 1980." 59 (3) : 500–521.

Kennan, G. F. (1982). *The Nuclear Delusion: Soviet-American Relations in the Nuclear Age*. NY: Pantheon.

Nitze, P. (1980). "Strategy in the Decade of the 1980s." *Foreign Affairs* 59 (1) : 82–101.

Weiss, W. (1958). "The Relationship Between Judgments of a Communicator's Position and Extent of Opinion Change." *Journal of Abnormal and Social Psychology* 56 : 380–84.

Willens, H. (1984). *The Trimtab Factor: How Business Executives Can Help Solve the Nuclear Weapons Crisis*. NY: William Morrow.

Selected Bibliography

(Grouped by subject matter. Asterisks indicate books designed for the general reader as well as for social science professionals.)

1. General Treatments
   * Frank, Jerome (1982). *Sanity and Survival: Psychological Aspects of War and Peace.* NY: Vintage Books.
     Kelman, Herbert C., ed. (1965). *International Behavior: A Social-Psychological Analysis.* NY: Holt, Rinehart and Winston. See especially chapters by Alger; Janis and Smith; Kelman, Pool, Pruitt, Rosenberg; Sawyer and Guetzkow; White.

2. Psychological Effects of the Nuclear Threat
   * Schell, Jonathan (1982). *The Fate of the Earth.* NY: Knopf.
   * Lifton, Robert Jay, and Falk, Richard (1982). *Indefensible Weapons: The Political and Psychological Case Against Nuclearism.* NY: Basic Books.

3. Psychology of the Soviet Decision Makers
   * Cox, Arthur M. (1982). *Russian Roulette: The Superpower Game.* NY: Times Books.
   * Gottlieb, Sanford (1982). *What About the Russians?* Northfield, MA: Student/Teacher Organization to Prevent War.
   * Kennan, George F. (1982). *The Nuclear Delusion: Soviet-American Relations in the Nuclear Age.* NY: Pantheon.
   * Khrushchev, Nikita (1970). *Khrushchev Remembers.* Trans. and ed., Strobe Talbott. Boston: Little, Brown.
     Nitze, Paul (1980). "Strategy in the Decade of the 1980s." *Foreign Affairs* 59 (1) (Fall 1980).
     Tucker, Robert C. (1971). *The Soviet Political Mind.* NY: Praeger.

4. Nonviolent Paths to Security

   Deutsch, Morton (1973). *The Resolution of Conflict: Constructive and Destructive Processes.* New Haven: Yale University Press.

   * Osgood, Charles E. (1962). *An Alternative to War or Surrender.* Urbana: University of Illinois Press.

   * Sharp, Gene (1980). *Making the Abolition of War a Realistic Goal.* NY: World Policy Institute. (Pamphlet.)

5. War-Related Motives

   * Fromm, Erich (1973). *The Anatomy of Human Destructiveness.* NY: Holt, Rinehart and Winston.

6. Perception and Misperception in International Conflict

   Jervis, Robert (1976). *Perception and Misperception in International Politics.* Princeton: Princeton University Press.

   * White, Ralph K. (1984). *Fearful Warriors: A Psychological Profile of U.S.-Soviet Relations.* NY: The Free Press.

7. Deterrence

   George, Alexander, and Smoke, Richard (1974). *Deterrence in American Foreign Policy.* NY: Columbia University Press.

   Reichart, John F., and Sturm, Steven R. (1974). *American Defense Policy.* Baltimore: Johns Hopkins University Press. See especially chapters by Burt, Ermarth, Howard, Jervis, Robert Osgood, and Richard Smoke's historical study, "The Evolution of American Defense Policy."

8. Government Decision Making and Crisis Management

   Allison, Graham T. (1971). *Essence of Decision: Explaining the Cuban Missile Crisis.* Boston: Little, Brown.

   * Janis, Irving L. (1973). *Victims of Groupthink.* Boston: Houghton Mifflin.

   Lebow, Richard Ned (1981). *Between Peace and War: The Nature of International Crisis.* Baltimore: Johns Hopkins University Press.

   Snyder, Glenn, and Diesing, Paul (1977). *Conflict Among Nations.* Princeton: Princeton University Press. (A thorough study of 16 crises).

9. Escalation

   Holsti, Ole R. (1972). *Crisis Escalation War.* Montreal: McGill-Queens University Press.

Smoke, Richard (1977). *War: Controlling Escalation.* Cambridge: Harvard University Press.

10. Negotiation and Mediation
    * Fisher, Roger, and Ury, William (1981). *Getting to YES: Negotiating Agreement Without Giving In.* Boston: Houghton Mifflin.
    Pruitt, Dean G. (1981). *Negotiating Behavior.* NY: Academic Press.
    Rubin, Jeffrey Z., ed. (1980). *Dynamics of Third-Party Intervention: Kissinger in the Middle East.* NY: Praeger.

11. Changing War-Related Attitudes
    Hovland, Carl; Janis, Irving; and Kelley, Harold (1953). *Communication and Persuasion.* New Haven: Yale University Press.

12. Arms Control
    Adelman, Kenneth L. (1984–85). "Arms Control with and Without Agreements." *Foreign Affairs* 63 (2). (A cogent plea for seeking stability even without agreements, by President Reagan's chief of the Arms Control and Disarmament Agency, ACDA).
    Bundy, McGeorge; Kennan, George; McNamara, Robert; and Smith, Gerard (1982). "Nuclear Weapons and the Atlantic Alliance." *Foreign Affairs* 60 (4) (Considers the case for no first use).
    ——— (1984–85). "The President's Choice: Star Wars or Arms Control." *Foreign Affairs* 63 (2).
    Einhorn, Robert (Winter 1981–82). "Treaty Compliance." *Foreign Policy* 45. (A well-documented answer to those who say "The Russians don't live up to their agreements.")
    McNamara, Robert S. (1983). "The Military Role of Nuclear Weapons." *Foreign Affairs* 62 (1). (The military case against nuclear weapons for any purpose except to deter their use by opponents.)

13. Peace Education
    Wien, B. J., ed. (1984) *Peace and World Order Studies.* NY: World Policy Institute. (Consists mainly of syllabi of peace-related courses at many colleges and universities.)

Name Index

Subject Index

Italicized numbers indicate chapters in their entirety.